The Russian Image of
GOETHE

VOLUME ONE

The Russian Image of
GOETHE

Goethe in Russian Literature of the
First Half of the Nineteenth Century

ANDRÉ VON GRONICKA

upp

University of Pennsylvania Press
PHILADELPHIA

*This work was published with the
support of the Haney Foundation.*

Copyright © 1968 by the Trustees of the
University of Pennsylvania

Library of Congress Cataloging in Publication Data

Von Gronicka, André, 1912–
  The Russian image of Goethe.

  Includes bibliographies and indexes.
  Contents: v. 1. Goethe in Russian literature of the
first half of the nineteenth century—v. 2. Goethe in
Russian literature of the second half of the nineteenth
century.
    1. Goethe, Johann Wolfgang von, 1749–1832—Appreciation
—Soviet Union. 2. Goethe, Johann Wolfgang von, 1749–
1832—Influence. 3. Goethe, Johann Wolfgang von, 1749–
1832—Translations, Russian. 4. Russian literature—19th
century—History and criticism. I. Title.
PT2173.R8V66   1985   831'.6   84–28060

ISBN 0–8122–7985–9 (v. 1)
ISBN 0–8122–7986–7 (v. 2)

PRINTED IN THE UNITED STATES OF AMERICA

For

My Mother

and

Hilde

CONTENTS

---

* This is the spelling used by Herzen when signing his name in Latin script.

Acknowledgments

It is a great satisfaction to express once again my abiding sense of indebtedness to the late Professor Robert Herndon Fife and to Dr. Arthur Luther, who first set me on the course of investigations into Russo-German literary relations, as well as to Professors Ernest Simmons and Emil Staiger, who sustained with their advice and encouragement my early efforts on this book. A full measure of gratitude goes out to Dr. Johannes Urzidil for the challenge and guidance he offered me with his splendid scholarship in a related field, and to Professor Heinz Politzer for his faith in my undertaking and for his sympathetic prodding at times of crisis and discouragement. It is impossible to acknowledge all the help I have received from willing and able librarians in this country and abroad, from faithful friends and colleagues on both continents. May they all feel certain of my lasting appreciation of their share in the growth of this study. Last but by no means least, my thanks to Hilde von Gronicka who kept up my courage in the often trying labors, offered helpful counsel from the ample store of precious common sense and the ever-willing help of a conscientious proofreader and untiring typist.

The work could not have been carried out without the generous assistance by the Guggenheim Foundation, the American Council of Learned Societies, the Social Science Research Council, and a Fulbright grant. The research leave granted me by the University of Pennsylvania in the spring of 1963 has contributed significantly to the completion of the present volume and will be always gratefully remembered. Those chapters of this work which had previously appeared in article form are reprinted, partially revised, by permission of the *Germanic Review, Comparative Literature,* the *Revue de littérature comparée,* and the *Publications of the Modern Language Association.* A German version of the Tiutchev section has appeared as a contribution to the *Festschrift* in honor of Professor Heinz Otto Burger under the auspices of Professor Conrad Wiedemann in the Erich Schmidt-Verlag, Berlin.

The Russian Image of

GOETHE

Introduction

One of the striking developments in Western scholarship during the last quarter-century is the phenomenal growth of interest in the Slavic world. Especially in the United States the departments of Slavic and East European studies have rapidly multiplied, harboring ever-increasing numbers of competent scholars and eager students of the subject. The scholarly contributions, always respectable in quantity and quality, have recently threatened to swell into a veritable flood. Nevertheless, the broad and fertile area of Russo-German literary relations continues to attract relatively few Western scholars, especially when compared with the flourishing fields of Franco-German and German-American research. To be sure, some substantial contributions have recently been made as, for example, Edmund Kostka's investigations of Schiller in Russia,[1] or Charles Passage's studies of the impact of E.T.A. Hoffmann on Russian literature[2] and, specifically, on Dostoevski.[3] The equally important theme of Goethe's influence on and reception in Russia, however, has not received its due share of attention by Western scholars. Some articles on special phases of that problem—many of them centering on Aleksander Pushkin's relations to Goethe[4]—have appeared, primarily in 1932, the anniversary year of Goethe's death.[5] Yet, we still lack a systematic effort on a large scale which would carry this important theme beyond the promising beginnings made by such Western scholars as Otto Harnack,[6] Joseph Matl,[7] Arthur Luther,[8] and most successfully by M. Gorlin,[9] among some others.[10] Soviet scholarship, on the other hand, has produced very substantial contributions, the outstanding among these being the works of S. Durylin[11] and V. Zhirmunski.[12] These scholars have accumulated a great amount of relevant materials which were buried in archives and scattered in sundry Russian journals difficult if not impossible of access. Without their labors the present work could not have been carried out. We are deeply indebted to their pioneer efforts.

These works, however, have not been translated and thus have remained unknown and inaccessible to the great majority of Western

Goethe scholars. Moreover, while the collection of materials is impressively extensive and accurate, the interpretations, especially those of Durylin, generally follow officially sanctioned lines and are not always free from ideological bias.

The aim of the present work is to furnish a readily available comprehensive survey of the Russian reaction to Goethe's works from their appearance on the Russian literary scene to the present day. Mindful of the formidable language barrier which still keeps a majority of Western Goethe scholars from easy access to the Russian originals, we decided to quote more liberally and to translate more literally than we would otherwise have done. In fact, one of the more important purposes of this book is to serve as a verbatim record *in extenso* of Russian authors' acclaim and critique of Goethe, the man and the poet.

Much of my work, being of a pioneering nature, had to be carried out along the lines of the positivistic tradition. An ever-growing number of cross-references to relevant sources, primary and secondary, biographical, epistolary, essayistic and belletristic, had to be followed up and these materials collated. My main effort then was centered on the interpretation of these rich materials in the general framework of Russia's intellectual history as one of its significant and highly revealing facets. As my investigations progressed, I grew increasingly conscious of the truth of M. Gorlin's observation that "in Russia's attitude toward Goethe is mirrored its entire cultural development,—at least in its main facets,"[13] an observation corroborated by the foremost authority on Goethe in Russian literature, V. Zhirmunski: "The history of the creative reception and theoretical interpretation of Goethe's work in Russian literature illuminates with varying degrees of intensity the entire history of that literature."[14] Finally I also carried out a comparative thematic and formal study of Goethe's works in their influence on Russian belles lettres wherever such influence could be clearly established.

Delving into the problem of Goethe's reception in Russia, I soon came to realize that recording the full chorus of Russian voices, all imitations and translations of Goethe's works, would prove an impossible task. Being forced to set limits, I decided to concentrate on the foremost Russian authors and, among the second- and third-rate figures, on those who had made the most significant contributions to the Russian image of Goethe. I excluded discussion and evaluation of the long series of Russian renderings by professional translators as well as of ephemeral journalistic contributions to Russian Goetheana. Nor did I consider in my context the numerous contacts Goethe had with Russian official circles when these proved to be of a purely social or political nature. I am conscious of the fact that with this effort I am but laying the foundation, furnishing the materials, providing some guidelines and, it is hoped, posing a challenge for future investigations of the complex problem of Russia's reactions to the personality and the works of Goethe, reactions which shed such a revealing light on the turbulent course of Russia's intellectual life.

A word must be said about my method of translation and transliteration. I translate all Russian and provide English prose versions of Russian and German verse. German titles are given in the original. For my method of transliteration I have adopted the "Library of Congress System" (System II) as the one best suited to my purpose. It is acceptable to most specialists and most helpful to the non-Russian reader. I have settled on this choice although I am fully aware that the so-called "International Scholarly System" (System III) is recommended for "publications directed primarily or exclusively to linguists or literary scholars."[15] The confusion which this system causes the nonspecialist and the non-Russian reader—and these my book would include among its audience—is neatly defined by the following quotation from a recent review in the *London Times Literary Supplement:*

> "Not that even Mr. Karlinsky's greatest admirers will necessarily fall for the transliteration system [System III] he advocates; there is something to be said for a "č" for "ts," "š" for "sh," "šč" for "shch," and so on; but "x" for "kh" would surely be confusing if one saw, for instance, a play called *The Cherry Orchard* by someone called Čexov—"[16]

I agree, and for that reason use "System II," deviating from it only in the transliteration of personal names ending in -ii, in which cases I use the simplified "System I," writing Dostoevsk*i* instead of Dostoevsk*ii*, Belinsk*i*, Zhirmunsk*i*, etc. It is my hope that the present multiplicity of systems will soon be set aside in favor of an efficient generally accepted code of transliteration.

CHAPTER ONE

Early Russian Reaction to Goethe and His Work

A novel cultural experience is always a challenge and often a shock. It is fortunate indeed if the shock does not prove too great, does not produce feelings of resistance and resentment so violent as to cause total rejection of the alien cultural phenomenon. Even under favorable conditions, the process of its assimilation by the recipient can rarely be carried forward without misinterpretation and distortion, which grow more pronounced the more startling, complex and subtle, the more demanding the cultural experience proves to be. Such a startling, subtle and complex experience for the world was Goethe's work, his "storm and stress" lyrics, his dramas, the much-maligned and much-praised *Sufferings of Young Werther*. The appearance of Goethe on the German scene left not only the average reader but many a critic nonplussed, even resentfully hostile. So perceptive and welltrained a mind as that of Frederick the Great remained totally unreceptive to the new art, and even the most progressive critics, as Lessing, for instance, could only divine but not really comprehend the "new dawn" of German literature.

Small wonder that the Russian public, across a language barrier, could at first catch no more than an indistinct and often distorted glimpse of the rising German genius. It was only natural that the early Russian reaction to Goethe's personality and work was even less informed, less just and penetrating than had been Germany's, that it more often than not went wildly and ludicrously astray. Many of these documents of Russia's initial confrontation with Goethe's personality and work will startle our readers with their lack of insight, amuse them with their naïvete and outright obtuseness. They cannot, of course, compare in importance with the rich and meaningful materials we were able to gather from later decades of the nineteenth century. Nevertheless, as the earliest available records, they have at least a historical value; they are, moreover, an integral part of our study of the Russian image of Goethe and deserve inclusion as its proper introduction.

Among these early records we have discovered an interesting account by a certain Filip Filipovich Figel of the first impact on the Russian cultural élite of Germany's new literature, specifically of its "storm and stress" dramas. In his *Memoirs*[1] Figel describes the first performances of some of these plays on the stage of the German Theater in St. Petersburg and vividly characterizes the shocked and hostile reaction of the Russian audience. With bitter invective and cruel ridicule they rejected them out of hand, would have none of these "grotesque oddities" imported from Germany, strove to drive them off the stage with "bursts of derisive laughter." And Figel gives his reasons for this typical behavior of an audience quite unprepared for a novel cultural experience: "Slavishly following the French example, we dared not break with Aristotle's law of the three unities. . . . The French, our esteemed guardians and guides, had taught us to recognize in the Germans nothing but ridiculous figures." He continues his vivid account with a detailed enumeration of the salient elements of content and form of these "grotesque" plays that met with the Russians' disapproval and derision: the excessive number of the *dramatis personae* and the "low station" of all-too-many of their "heroes and heroines," the rapid shift of scenes, the "base language," the "homely" settings. "Bursts of derisive laughter," Figel recalls with unfeigned exasperation, "would greet the hero upon his entrance." And why? Merely because the author had not cast his hero in the classical mold, had not observed the sacred rule of the unity of time, instead had his hero pass through a whole lifetime right on stage before our very eyes. These heroes "would enter as youths in the first act to grope, in the last, their way upon the stage, men suddenly grown aged." No, such a break with the classical canon could not and would not be tolerated by an audience reared in the French tradition! "The very names of these German plays," Figel assures us, "aroused mirth and consternation: *Minna von Barnhelm, Goetz von Berlichingen, Doktor*

Faustus. What grotesque oddities! And who ever heard of a Mephisto, the Devil incarnate, loosed upon the stage? One could just as well have ushered a drunken shoemaker into the drawing room of a nobleman." "All this," according to our witness, "appeared to the St. Petersburg society in the worst possible taste, an unpardonable, revolting breach of etiquette!"

If such was the Russians' attitude toward Germany's most recent dramatic output, toward Goethe's *Götz,* could other works by the rebellious German genius expect a more favorable, more perceptive reception? Surprisingly enough, at least one of Goethe's creations did receive a most cordial welcome, was acclaimed and "universally admired" upon its very first appearance in Russia. It was of course his *Werther.* In fact, such a sensation was this novella that for a time it quite overshadowed all other creations of Goethe that soon were crossing the geographical and linguistic barriers into Russia. It also obscured the interesting fact that it was not *Werther* which was to have the distinction of being the first to be rendered into Russian; rather, this distinction went to another one of Goethe's works, one with much less claim to fame and immortality. Soviet research has now definitely established O. P. Kozodavlev's translation of Goethe's *Clavigo* of 1780 as that "first." It antedates F. Galchenkov's rendering of *Werther* in 1781 by at least a year.

Kozodavlev (1754–1819), who studied at Leipzig in 1769, just after Goethe had left the university, seems to have been well acquainted with Goethe's early works. In the introduction to his translation, he tells us that the choice for a Russian rendering among Goethe's extant dramatic masterpieces was difficult in the extreme, and that he settled on *Clavigo* only after he was forced to discard *Egmont* for political reasons, *Stella* because of its theme of polygamy, and *Götz* because of that play's complex Shakespearean form and historical content, which he considered to be too demanding both for the technical capacities of the contemporary Russian stage and for the Russian public's taste of the time.[2]

In the preface to the second edition of his translation, Kozodavlev praises Goethe for "having imitated nature exclusively in every

one of his works" and for having "never followed rules which tended
to distance nature from the writer's eye," praise which was to recur
in many subsequent Russian appreciations of Goethe. Kozodavlev,
like his contemporaries generally, singles out *Werther* as the work
upon which rests Goethe's fame. Having identified Goethe as the
author of this famous novel, he considers it "unnecessary to give a
detailed account of the writer of the drama [*Clavigo*] and of his
merits, since they are already known to all lovers of literature. *The
Sufferings of Young Werther,* that wonderful creation of his
[Goethe's] pen, has earned for him great fame and has placed him
on a par with Germany's greatest writers, just as this dramatic creation, his *Clavigo,* has received from all initiated readers the highest
possible praise."[3]

Goethe's *Werther* had indeed attracted wide attention and admiration in Russia. As early as 1787, N. I. Novikov had included Goethe's name in his *Dramaturgical Lexicon (Dramaticheskii
Slovar')* and had singled out the novel as a "remarkable work which
is everywhere being praised."[4] Galchenkov's pioneer translation was
followed within five years by another attempt by I. Vinogradov.
This translator relies heavily on his predecessor and thus perpetuates
most of his grievous errors, among them Galchenkov's howler of
mistaking Klopstock's name for a technical term from the game of
billiards, "Klopfstoß." On second thought, Galchenkov must have
realized the complete inappropriateness of the term under the cir-
cumstances and especially on the lips of Lotte, billiards not being
exactly a lady's game. He lets Lotte forget "Klopfstoß" and billiards and instead has her invite poor Werther to a "hand of cards,"
thus only compounding the absurdity of his rendering. Five years
later, when Vinogradov attempted his translation, the name of Klopstock was obviously still unknown to him, for he follows blithely in
Galchenkov's footsteps with the following, less-than-inspired rendering: "Charlotte leaned on her elbow, glanced aside, then gazed to
heavens, then looked at me and placing her hand upon mine, spoke
in a tear-choked voice: 'Let us go, play cards."[5]

It is hardly believable that, despite such ludicrous infelicities
and distortions of Goethe's work, these early Russian versions of

Werther were "universally praised." But one can readily understand how they would contribute to the general misunderstanding of Goethe's work, even by the best-informed and most sensitive Russian readers. They mistook it for a typical example of the "sentimental" school of literature and missed altogether its "storm and stress" themes and quality of style. Now there are, of course, far more basic reasons for this typical misunderstanding than the blatant inaccuracies of the Russian translations. These misinterpretations are the product of prevailing literary tastes. For it was the fate of Goethe's *Werther* to appear in Russia just after Rousseau's and Richardson's novels had enjoyed an enthusiastic reception in Russia and had established the esthetic canon of the day.[6] Reading Goethe's novel with sensibilities conditioned by Richardson's *Clarissa* and Rousseau's *Nouvelle Héloise,* Russian readers quite naturally recognized and welcomed in Werther the sentimental hero grown so dear to their hearts in the works of the English and French writers. They can hardly be expected to have had the independence of judgment and keenness of insight to detect at once the subtle difference between the familiar French and English characters and Goethe's Werther, to appreciate in Goethe's protagonist not merely a hapless victim of unrequited love but, beyond that, the representative of the "storm and stress" *Geniekult.* Even rebellious spirits among the Russian readers failed to appreciate the theme of social protest in Goethe's work and insisted on reading it merely as a "sentimental novel." Such a reader was the radical Radishchev. He too remained insensitive to the sociopolitical message of the work. Like Kozodavlev, A. N. Radishchev (1749–1802) was a student at the University of Leipzig during the years 1766 to 1771. He had more than a nodding acquaintance with the early works of Goethe. His is one of the earliest references to *Werther.* In the "Klin" chapter of his famous *Voyage from Petersburg to Moscow,* he describes his reaction to the singing of a blind beggar and fool-in-Christ Aleksei, using the following revealing comparison: ". . . . and my tears were as sweet to me as those wrung from my heart by Werther."[7] Radishchev, despite his iconoclastic view of Russian society and culture, is here indulging in the Russian cult of Werther as the "tender friend," whose darkling fate "wrings sweet tears" from the "sensitive heart." This much-quoted passage from his widely read book added considerable impetus to the "sentimental" interpretation of Goethe's work.

Nikolai M. Karamzin (1766–1826), the eminent Russian historian and author of the short story *Poor Lisa,* provides a more revealing record of early Russian reaction to *Werther* as well as the first report of a visit by a Russian to Goethe's Weimar (July 1789). Karamzin does not mention Goethe among the prominent Weimar residents to whom he intended to pay his respects.[8] At the city's gates, Karamzin inquires of the sentry the whereabouts of the residences of Wieland and Herder, not about that of Goethe. Again, in his interview with Herder, when asked whom he considered to be Germany's greatest poet, it was not Goethe whom he singled out. "I answered falteringly," Karamzin recalls, "that I considered Klopstock to be the *loftiest* of the German poets." Herder accepted this judgment as "eminently fair" but pointed out that Klopstock was being read much less at the time than many another author, adding: "There are many readers who have hopelessly bogged down in the tenth canto of the *Messias,* never again to return to this lovely poem." Herder then praised Wieland, and especially Goethe. He had his young son fetch "a new edition of Goethe's poems, and read to me with great verve several of Goethe's minor lyrics. Herder liked especially the little poem 'Meine Göttin,' " praising it for being "altogether Grecian" and rapturously exclaiming about its language: "What purity! What grace!"

Karamzin's own reaction to Goethe's poems is hardly indicative of intimate knowledge or independence of judgment. He offers little more than a verbose paraphrase of the cue furnished him by Herder. Indiscriminately, he lumps together in his evaluation "Herder, Goethe, and other such poets[!]." He then proceeds to laud these "and their like" for "having recaptured the very spirit of the ancients, approximating their language to that of the Greeks, thus making it the richest and poetically the most serviceable." He concludes his generalization with a sweeping judgment and grandiloquent flourish: "That is why neither the French nor the English are able to match those translations from the Greek with which the Germans have recently so greatly enriched their literature. Homer is truly Homer in their renderings; there is that selfsame natural, noble simplicity in their language which was the very soul of ancient times, when queens fetched water at the well and kings knew the exact count of their sheep."

After his visit with Herder, Karamzin sought out Wieland. Twice he failed to find him at home, but he persisted and finally met the much-admired author. Karamzin's detailed report of this meeting corroborates our impression that it was Wieland, not Goethe who, in the year 1789, was being acclaimed by a Russian traveler as the foremost German poet. The recorded conversation makes no mention of Goethe, though it contains many references to the great of literature and philosophy, especially to Voltaire and Kant. As could be expected, the discussion centered on Wieland's works. Karamzin attempted a well-turned compliment by ranging Wieland's *Agathon* and *Oberon* far above the "dry philosophy" of Kant or Voltaire; it failed to produce the intended effect. "But pray," Wieland exclaimed, "is not my *Agathon* a philosophical book? In it are resolved the most important questions of philosophy!" Karamzin hastened to agree. When he finally left, he carried away an unforgettable impression of the admired poet "Never, oh, never shall I forget Wieland!"—and sent a page-long eulogy of this "famous German author" to his friends in Russia. Not once does Goethe's name appear in the lengthy letter.

Karamzin's indifference toward Goethe is striking indeed when compared with his eagerness to meet Wieland and Herder, though it is by no means atypical. For some years to come Weimar was to be Wieland's city to Russian visitors, not Goethe's; their attention continued to center on Wieland's works. Thus Zhukovski, in a letter of 1806 to his young friend and pupil A. I. Turgeniev, still singled out Wieland's *Agathon* as a "holy book" and planned as late as 1814 a work in the spirit of Wieland's *Oberon*.

Karamzin's slowness in contacting Goethe actually cost the Russian a meeting with the German poet. He had to content himself with a brief glimpse of him which he happened to catch while strolling one evening past Goethe's house. "Last night, passing the house in which Goethe lives, I saw him gazing out the window. I stopped and for a minute examined him: a dignified Grecian face!" By the time Karamzin finally made up his mind to pay a formal call, Goethe had left for Jena. He seems never to have regretted the lost opportunity of a personal meeting with Germany's greatest poet.

As we turn to Karamzin's appreciation of *Werther,* we find it to be typical of the times. He emphasizes *Werther's* total dependence on Rousseau's *Nouvelle Héloise.* The basic theme of Goethe's novel, he claims, "is the same, and many of the situations," according to him, "are taken straight from the *Héloise* novel." Without the great French model "there never would have been a German Werther!" He relents sufficiently in his appraisal of Goethe's masterpiece as a totally derivative fabrication to admit that "there is more nature description"[9] in the German work, but he fails to recognize the basically different character of this description, arising as it does from Goethe's pantheistic experience of nature. In fact, all the elements which transcend Rousseau's rationalistic sentimentalism and place *Werther* in the literary current of German "storm and stress" remain either unnoticed by or unacceptable to the Russian critic.

Karamzin is insensitive to Werther's passionate individualism, unreceptive to his revolutionary views on art, and highly critical of the genius' revolt against society and the confining limitations of life. He criticizes Werther's suicide on grounds of artistic and logical inconsistency. According to Karamzin, Werther's suicide does not logically grow out of the plot, nor is it in keeping with the generally "Romantic" situation of the *Nouvelle.* He also condemns the suicide on grounds of immorality. As a gesture of protest he will not deign even to glance at Werther's grave:

> The ill-starred Werther is not a law:
> There is his grave; my eyes I cover with my hand.[10]

This attitude toward Werther's suicide is all the more striking since in Karamzin's own novel, *Poor Lisa,* the heroine commits the same "immoral" act. She dies by her own hand. In fact, this turn of plot is virtually the only possible instance of influence by Goethe on the Russian author's work, which otherwise keeps strictly in the mood and follows consistently the typical plot patterns of the French and English novels.

Karamzin's "sentimental" and moralizing reading of *Werther* proved tenacious not only among the Russian public at large but even with literary figures of considerable prominence and wide cultural horizons. Thus, Constantin N. Batiushkov (1787–1855), an outstanding representative of Russia's "golden age of poetry" and well versed in French and Italian literature, echoes this view in his description of Weimar, where he spent several weeks as an officer of the Russian army of liberation. This visit took place in 1813, some thirty-three years after the first publication of *Werther* in Russian and twenty-four years after Karamzin's journey to Germany. And yet Goethe was still regarded by Batiushkov as the "sentimental author" of *Werther*. In a letter to his friend N. I. Gnedich, Batiushkov compares the one-time glories of Weimar with its present-day atmosphere: "Under these elms and cypress trees the great creative geniuses of Germany were fond of resting from their labors; under these very same elms our officers now chase after girls. . . . Here Goethe dreamed of his Werther, of the tender Lotte; here Wieland pondered the plan of his *Oberon,* his thoughts soaring in the realms of pure imagination." Batiushkov must surely have known that Goethe was all done with "dreaming about Werther and tender Lotte" by the time he came to Weimar. Yet for Batiushkov Goethe remained the sentimental author of that early work and still was overshadowed by Schiller and Wieland. In his letters Batiushkov mentioned Goethe only as the author of *Werther*. He spoke of Schiller, with whose work he came to terms primarily under the impact of the magnificent performance of his tragedies on the Weimar stage: "In it [Weimar theater] are being performed comedies, dramas, operas, and tragedies, the latter—not at all badly, to my great surprise. *Don Carlos* I liked very much indeed, and have become reconciled with Schiller. The characters of Don Carlos and of the queen are splendid." He spoke of Wieland and raved about Voss' *Luise*: "You know of my new passion for German literature. I am losing my mind over Voss' *Luise;* one has to read her in the original and here in Germany."[11] Yet we find not a word about Goethe save the cited anachronistic reference to Werther and "tender" Lotte and a passing remark that he had caught a glimpse of him in the theater. That this was not a quickly passing phase in the Russian poet's estimate and characterization of Goethe is proved in a letter to his parents written almost a month later: "Do you know my newest passion? It is the German language. Recently, living in Germany, I have learned to speak German and am reading all German books; do not be surprised at this. Weimar is the native city of Goethe, the author of *Werther,* of famous Schiller and Wieland; here is a wonderful library, theater and an English garden, in which I frequently take walks."[12] Batiushkov had been reading in Weimar's "excellent library" where he must have come upon many a work by Goethe other than his novel. He probably saw Goethe's plays performed on the Weimar stage. And yet he could not free himself of the "sentimental" view of Goethe as the "author of *Werther.*" There is no mention of Goethe's achievements in his "Classical" period, no appreciation of his stature as a lyric poet, and this by a writer who himself was predominantly a lyricist! Surely, we must take this for further evidence of the staying power of the association of Goethe solely with his *Werther.*

Among the many Russian officers passing at this time through Weimar was Theodor N. Glinka (1786–1880), whose *Letters of a Russian Officer in the Years 1812 and 1813* became a best-seller of the day. Glinka sent a copy of his work to Goethe with a most revealing dedication: "To famous Goethe," so it runs in a prose rendering of its original Russian verse, "the author of *Werther,* of *Hermann and Dorothea,* etc. etc. . . . The unknown singer flowering far from the vales of Germany, dwelling in a modest hut of the cold North has read your works, O Goethe, *tender friend of sentimental hearts!* Has read them and in *sweet rapture* has paid to you, O nursling of the Muses, the tribute of his veneration."[13] Glinka's mood of "sweet rapture" as he reads Goethe, his appellation of Goethe as the "tender friend of sentimental hearts"—all this again is quite in the tradition of the Radishchev-Karamzin "sentimental" view of Goethe. The passage of three decades and the publication of *"Hermann und Dorothea,* etc. etc." could not essentially change this persistent image of Goethe.

One final figure may attest to the spread and longevity of this image. N. I. Grech (1787–1867), a popular author and editor of the periodical *Son of the Fatherland,* visited Weimar in 1817, twenty-six years after Karamzin. In sharp contrast to Karamzin's indifference and procrastination in obtaining an appointment with Goethe, Grech showed himself very eager and persistent, and after several disappointing efforts was finally ushered into the presence of the "venerable old man." Thus Grech became one of the first Russians to give us an eyewitness impression of the aging Goethe. He was received by Johanna Schopenhauer, who had been, Grech felt, sent to stall for time and whose conversation "in a strange dialect" greatly annoyed him. He was growing thoroughly uneasy when finally Goethe appeared. "He was clad in a simple light-grey frock coat," Grech recalls. "His head, gently swaying with old age, was covered with silvery grey hair . . . his face was expressive, one might actually call it—beautiful!" Grech assured Goethe that he had read his biography "with sincere pleasure and not merely once: first in St. Petersburg and again in Frankfurt, where I actually visited the places you describe. I have diligently searched for Gretchen!"[14] Without commenting on these personal references, Goethe changed the conversation to "his trips in France and Switzerland and led us into his study where there was a wonderfully worked small-scale model of the Swiss Alps, a gift of the Duke of Weimar. With another sudden shift of conversation, he came to speak of Russia and wanted to know all about his Petersburg acquaintances, N. M. Karamzin, S. S. Uvarov[15] and the friend of his youth, Maximilian Klinger."[16]

Having conversed with Goethe for almost an hour, Grech finally took leave, deeply impressed with Goethe's appearance: "The features of the great poet shall never be erased from my memory." As to Goethe's works, they impressed the Russian far less. He confesses that he has not joined "the inner circle of Goethe's ardent readers," that he does not "see in *Faust* what others see in it," and that he quite fails to "appreciate the greatness of *Wilhelm Meister.*" Yet he has to admit that "he knows of nothing more lofty than his

Werther." There it is again, the persistent, limited view of Goethe! Grech has just come away, deeply impressed, from the presence of the "venerable old man," he has read Goethe's masterworks, his *Hermann und Dorothea,* his *Wilhelm Meister* and the incomparable *Faust.* Nevertheless *Werther* remains for him the "loftiest" product of Goethe's pen.

At this point it could be objected that these readers of Goethe were, after all, persons who remained distant from him and took no particular interest in his development as an author. The fact remains, however, that even among his "ardent admirers" the same "image" persisted with surprising stubbornness, despite a slowly growing awareness of Goethe's various other achievements. Thus, the first "Goethe-nest," the fervently Germano- and Goethephile circle formed by the Turgeniev brothers, Andrei (1781–1803) and Aleksander (1784–1845), together with their German tutor Georg Christian Tobler (1757–1812), a relative of Lavater and an acquaintance of Goethe, could not escape the *Werther* fever altogether, even though they strove, with some success, to broaden their appreciation of the German genius.

The membership, literary tastes, and activity of this group, organized in the 1790's under the name of the Friendly Literary Society (Druzheskoe Literaturnoe Obshchestvo) have been described by Aleksander Turgeniev: "Several young people," he writes, "mostly university students, set about to obtain virtually everything in the way of belles lettres that made its appearance in Germany; they translated tales and the flowers of dramatic literature from among the works of Wieland, Schiller and Goethe; in fact, almost the entire contemporary German dramatic output was rendered by them into Russian."[17] Unfortunately, next to nothing of this prodigious output has been preserved. We have only a fragmentary translation of *Werther* by Andrei Turgeniev and his friends Vasili A. Zhukovski (1783–1852) and Aleksei Fedorovich Merzliakov (1778–1830).[18] This translation had been undertaken despite the fact that *Werther* had been rendered before into Russian[19] and was extant in three editions: 1781, 1794, and 1796. Moreover, the friends had heard of still another translation just completed in St.

Petersburg. "I have started to translate *Werther* with Werther's
letter of June 6th, on May 24, 1799, at the University, in my room
at 10:00 o'clock in the evening," Turgeniev entered in his diary.
"Having translated one letter I have stopped, and so has Merzliakov,
for we have just heard that in St. Petersburg another rendering was
ready."[20] Nevertheless, after some hesitation, he and Merzliakov
finally "decide, on August 19, 1799, to translate the whole of
Werther and are beginning with the first part."[21] This decision to proceed with the translation, despite the lively competition, was obviously motivated by a profound admiration for the German poet. Andrei,
moreover, recognized in Werther a kindred spirit. To his friend
Zhukovski he confides: "My condition much resembles the one
described in *Werther* in the letter you have translated."[22] In Goethe
Turgeniev worshiped the "free genius of nature" and composed the
first Russian characterization of the German author in dithyrambic
verse, which was destined to re-echo in the annals of the Russian interpretation of Goethe and which is herewith rendered into prose:
"Inspired by the free genius of nature, he set it [nature] forth in
fiery lines; subject to no other law, he took for his sole guide
his heart's emotions."[23]

In reading Goethe's *Egmont,* Turgeniev was impressed by
Goethe's realism, by the lifelike portrayal of the hero: "This
character is so vividly portrayed, with such truth and naturalness,
so close to human nature, that it seems to me I knew him personally, enjoyed his company, lived with him." Under the impact of
Goethe's work, Turgeniev's view on drama shifts from an admiration of French classical models to those of the German "storm
and stress": "The reading of Goethe's *Egmont* has caused me to
look at the heroes of other dramas, for example on Schiller's
Don Carlos, in the same light, and in this illumination the German
drama proves superior to the French, in which kings, etc., hold the
stage, characters, that is, to whom we cannot possibly feel close."[24]
The novel, "subjective" measure of the greatness of an author in
this appreciation, is certainly most striking. No longer did Turgeniev
hold that a writer's ability to create in close conformity to the
artistic canon of French pseudo-Classicism determines his stature

as an artist; it is the intensity of the writer's empathy, the heart-felt vitality and immediacy of his message that had become Turgeniev's standards of evaluation. It is young Goethe's directness, his immense warmth, his unfeigned sympathy with his fellow men, the intensity of sentiment, "his heart's emotions," that captured the Russian's admiration and love.

Thus, despite the growing scope and depth of Turgeniev's appreciation of the German poet, it basically remains akin to Glinka's praise of Goethe as the "tender friend of sentimental hearts." Characteristically, Goethe the Classicist left Turgeniev cold, even repelled him. "Having read Goethe's poems in Schiller's *Musen-almanach,* I have turned again to his *Werther,*" he wrote. Since these lines are dated November 26, 1799, it is safe to assume that he is referring to the Almanach of 1796–99, containing some of the most perfect lyrics, ballads, and elegies of the mature, the "Classical" Goethe; "Die Braut von Korinth," "Amyntas," "Euphrosyne," to mention but a few major titles. And yet, Turgeniev returns from this reading to his favorite *Werther* as to a native country from barren foreign lands. "What an experience," he exclaims, "just as if I had returned from unpleasant, cold and empty foreign lands to my beloved native country. Here I find Goethe once again, a Goethe before whom one is forced to kneel in admiration. Again that mighty, kindly, dignified Goethe—in brief, Goethe again as he should be. What fire, what power, what a feeling for nature! . . . How nourishing, how interesting! What a wonderful sensation to have turned to *Werther* once again, after all that other reading and to find once again all that Goethe represents. I cannot express this feeling: it somehow warms and consoles me."[25]

A premature death cut short any potential development in Andrei Turgeniev's view of Goethe. His younger brother, Aleksander Ivanovich, however, lived to change from an ardent Goethe enthusiast to a genuine *Goethe-Kenner* of startlingly wide scope, and finally to a critic of the German author. Aleksander Ivanovich was truly a man of the world with numerous personal contacts among the European élite of birth and brain. To enumerate his friends and acquaintants is to call the roll of Europe's great in the decades of the flowering of European culture, from the early twenties to Turgeniev's death in 1845. His friends called him "godfather of all Europe" and characterized him as a "walking encyclopedia." It is safe to say that he was one of the few among the Russian Goethe enthusiasts who had a thorough, first-hand knowledge of Goethe's life and works. He knew the German language well, and, what is more, he was capable of sustained, systematic, penetrating reading. He kept his interest for Goethe alive throughout his long and active life.

Aleksander Ivanovich's first introduction to the world of Goethe dates back to his boyhood days under the tutelage of George Christian Tobler, that enthusiastic admirer of Goethe. Small wonder that the Turgeniev brothers were brought up in an atmosphere of Goethe worship. In 1802 we find Aleksander Ivanovich in Göttingen studying history with the great A. L. von Schlözer. "From Göttingen," he writes, "we shall go to Weimar, where now are living Schiller, Goethe, Wieland, Herder."[26] Nothing, however, was to come of this project; Turgeniev had to wait almost twenty-four years before he finally met Goethe on March 16, 1826. He has surprisingly little to report of this visit: "Was at Goethe's. At the threshold—'Salve.' He is publishing his collected works. Told me of his preoccupation with natural science: 'It [natural science] has discovered me, I did not seek it out.'"[27] That is all. Shedding far more light on Turgeniev's reverence for Goethe's genius is his report of a literary meeting held at the Salon of Theresa Emilia Winkel, which he attended not quite a year after his Weimar visit in January 1827. At this meeting, Johann Friedrich Kind, the well-known librettist of the *Freischütz,* had launched a sharp attack on Goethe, claiming that Goethe had lifted the plot for his *Hermann und Dorothea* from an article in the *Rheinische Journal.* Turgeniev spiritedly rejected Kind's claim as absurdly irrelevant: "As if a Goethe had need of hiding his borrowings of fact! Has not his genius transformed this material altogether, elevated it, ennobled it in his incomparable poem? Phidias could be accused with equal justice of having stolen the marble for his Venus. . . . It's not the block of marble but the form, the expression of the ideal divineness that matter here! Just as Correggio is not indebted to his pigments for the creation of his Madonna, just so Goethe's Dorothea, though existing in nature, is altogether Goethe's own; *he* created her, *he* idealized her. Correggio would have more readily found inspiration for his Madonna in the church music of his time than Goethe for his Hermann in contemporary journalism." Turgeniev thinks he has detected the spread of a "spirit of animosity toward Goethe." "Yet," he continues, "these enemies of Goethe are so insignificant as to be hardly visible as they attack the giant. These pigmies continue to fret and fluster, oblivious of the debt Germany owes Goethe, forgetting that *he* is the true representative not only of German letters but of the entire German culture." According to Turgeniev, Goethe "is the living expression of the German national intellect." In this respect Goethe surpasses Shakespeare and Voltaire, who do not express their national cultures in the same comprehensive manner. "For Goethe is not merely Germany's poet laureate, he represents the Germans in all the phases of their national life, in science as well as in philosophy influencing them and through them the whole of Europe." To Turgeniev, Goethe is "the most faithful mirror of German emotions and of their intellect, the very product of these." Here again Turgeniev sees a fundamental difference between Goethe on the one hand and Shakespeare and Voltaire on the other. He is ready to admit that "Shakespeare and Voltaire have, respectively, created the English taste and French culture of the day," yet, he argues, "they are not themselves the products of these"[28] to quite the same degree and in the same manner that Goethe is of German cultural life.

When we analyze Turgeniev's eulogy of Goethe, focusing on its essential message, we are struck by two salient facts. First, it represents a spirited defense of a product not of the young "sentimental" but of the "Classical" Goethe, a defense not of *Werther* but of *Hermann und Dorothea*. This is a clear indication that Aleksander Turgeniev had moved well beyond the limited view of Goethe held by his brother Andrei. The second, even more significant fact is that Goethe the natural scientist and thinker had become clearly visible to Turgeniev and had impressed him greatly.

With this we have entered upon a new phase of Russia's appreciation of Goethe. Goethe's genius was beginning to be recognized in its imposing range as the loftiest manifestation of German culture, at once its creator and its creature.

Turgeniev's attitude toward Goethe did not long remain at this high pitch of enthusiasm. Soon a note of distrust crept in, a warning against Mephisto-in-Goethe was sounded. By 1836, in a description of a visit to Tiefurt, Turgeniev recognized in Goethe's genius "the spirit of Mephistophele" with its "cold doubts." Though Goethe had "encompassed everything" he had failed to "achieve everything."[29] Turgeniev is quoting here from famous eulogies of Goethe by Zhukovski and Baratynski who had credited Goethe with both an "all-encompassing" and an "all-achieving" spirit, seeking to convey with the term "all-achieving" Goethe's gift of participation in and interpenetration of all that is human, in contrast to a mere "coldly admiring visit" (kaltstaunenden Besuch). This gift of empathy and sympathy Turgeniev now denied Goethe, accusing him of "cold doubt," nonparticipation in human affairs, a lack of faith in man and God. He recognized in him a streak of cynicism and a sarcastic sharpness bordering on nihilism which were thoroughly repugnant to Turgeniev.

This change in the attitude of Turgeniev toward Goethe may well have been brought about, in some measure at least, by an image of Goethe which had been drawn in a much-publicized, widely read speech[30] by the Russian Minister of Culture, Sergei Semënovich Uvarov, whose acquaintance Turgeniev had made in 1810. Their relations had remained close ever since, offering many an occasion for an exchange of views on Goethe. This acquaintance of long standing, the undeniable similarity of certain aspects of Turgeniev's view of Goethe to Uvarov's, Turgeniev's interpretation of Goethe's *Faust* as a poem imbued with the "Mephistophelean spirit" of "terrifying sarcasm," which clearly echoes Uvarov's crassly slanted interpretation of Goethe's masterpiece in his anniversary address—all these facts would seem to support our theory of influence, even though this theory must remain hypothetical in the absence of explicit autobiographical evidence.

S. S. Uvarov (1785–1855) was a brilliant man with high-flying ambitions, an accomplished diplomat whose winning ways and quick, retentive, resilient and conveniently pragmatic—not to say unscrupulous—intelligence, propelled him headlong into an astounding academic and political career as court favorite of the liberal Aleksander I as well as of the arch-reactionary Nicholas I. He quickly rose to the dizzying heights of "Minister of Public Enlightenment" and the presidency of the Russian Academy of Sciences. He can serve well as a representative of the "official" Russia in our study of the Russian attitude toward Goethe, for it is he who formulated and disseminated most effectively the "administration's" view of the German poet and Privy Councilor of the Grand Duchy of Weimar.

As a young man, Uvarov had been sent to Germany to study at Göttingen, then to Vienna, there to join the Russian consulate. Having mastered the German language to glib perfection, uncannily aware of seats of eminence and power, he eagerly sought and soon achieved contact with the "Patriarch" of Weimar by way of a lively correspondence in which he cleverly played his connections with Russia's court and academic circles to impress the Privy Councilor. In turn, he cultivated assiduously the image of a "friend of Goethe" to impress—if anything with even more success—his Russian colleagues and superiors. In these letters,[31] all in German, he unabashedly employs over and over again the familiar and adulatory forms of greeting: "Verehrter Freund!" "Edler, herrlicher Freund!" to receive in at least one reply from the Olympian, "Verehrter Freund!"—oh triumph!—in return. These letters are filled to excess with fulsome eulogies, of which the following may serve as a fair sample: "In ihren unsterblichen Werken herrscht überall die Fülle des hohen Geistes, der gern in dem weiten Felde des besseren Alterthums verweilet, um sich dann als Schöpfer zu dem Gipfel der höchsten Poesie emporzuschwingen."*[32]

In 1814, Uvarov wrote a brief essay on *Wilhelm Meister,* the

---

* In your immortal works there are everywhere the riches of a lofty spirit, you love to linger in the ample sphere of grand antiquity, in order then to soar as a creator to the summit of highest poesy.

first by a Russian, and sent it to Goethe with the modest words of an admiring disciple: "Whether I have found in it a just point of view on *Wilhelm Meister* I do not know, but certain it is that I have written it with love and enthusiasm."[33]

Inspired by Goethe's lyrics, young Uvarov even tried his hand at German verse "dans le genre de Goethe," as he disarmingly put it, producing derivative lines in quasi-Goethean free rhythms such as the following:

> Sehnsucht
>
> Träume der Jugend,
> Farben des Frühlings,
> Töne der Lyra,
> Seyd ihr verschwunden,
> Auf immer verstummt?
> Ernst ist das Leben,
> Dunkel die Zukunft,
> Der Mensch, er muß streiten
> Mit feindlichen Mächten,
> Mit der ewigschaffenden
> Alles zerstörenden
> Mutter Natur.* [34]

The lines indicate a facile command of the language, an assimilative reading of Schiller as well as of Goethe, but certainly no originality or profound empathy into the world of Goethe's poetry.

It is all but impossible to discern in the diplomatic cant of Uvarov's letters his true attitude toward Goethe, the depth and quality of his appreciation of Goethe's works. There can be no doubt, however, that Uvarov made every effort to equip himself impressively in order to gain the friendship and esteem of Goethe by immersing himself in German life and letters. When Turgeniev first met Uvarov, he was greatly impressed with the Russian's grasp of German literature and history. "He knows his German literature so well that he puts me quite to shame with it—as he does with his

---

* Longing
Dreams of youth, colors of spring, tones of the lyre, have you departed, have you forever fallen silent? Life is serious, the future dark, man must do battle with hostile powers, with the eternally creative, all-destroying Mother Nature.

knowledge of German history."[35] Moreover, it is an established fact
that among his Russian contemporaries Uvarov was the first to
recognize Goethe's greatness as a natural scientist.[36] To be sure, he
had a distinct advantage over his countrymen which greatly facili-
tated this "discovery": he could approach Goethe not merely as a
private Russian citizen, as a humble man of letters, but in the impressive official capacity of the right-hand man to the Russian Minister of Culture, Count Razumovski, his influential father-in-law.
As his representative, Uvarov sent Goethe a plan for an "Asiatic
Academy of Oriental Studies," which he had developed not without
the competent assistance of specialists in the Ministry. This project
could not but arouse the lively interest of Goethe, who at the very
time (1810) was deep in his own studies of Oriental cultures.
Goethe's response was immediate and personal. He confided to his
"young friend" his preoccupations with "Orientalistic" and, by
natural association in the course of a developing correspondence,
many another of his scientific thoughts, especially on his *Farbenlehre*.[37] Small wonder that Uvarov could steal a march on his compatriots as an informed admirer of Goethe.

Still, what impresses us most forcibly in Uvarov's relation with
Goethe is not the amount of information he was able to gather or
the insights he could gain into Goethe's activities and achievements
but rather his unabashed opportunism, his adroit use of Goethe's
name and fame to support his elaborate maneuvers in furtherance
of his highly successful academic and political career. Under the
liberal regime of Aleksander I, Uvarov sought and actually ob-
tained Goethe's support and approval of his "liberal" ideas on a
universal culture which would break down all national barriers,
especially that of language. With this in mind, he dedicated to
Goethe a learned treatise written in German on the "last ancient
Greek poet," Nonnos of Panopolis[38]. Uvarov's dedicatory lines serve
a complex purpose: they advertise for the home audience Goethe's
past benevolent attitude toward the "young friend"; they curry new
favors from the mighty Privy Councilor in Weimar; and incidentally
they show off to best advantage Uvarov's erudition and cosmopoli-
tanism to impress both Goethe and his influential Russian au-

dience, above all the Czar. "The kind interest and friendly appreciation with which you [Goethe] have always received my past efforts" give Uvarov courage "to express herewith publicly my profound respect and gratitude to you. . . . The glorious fruits of your genius, which in the past, on German soil [during Uvarov's *Bildungsreise*], had been so greedily devoured by the youth whose spirit and imagination had become fully attuned to yours, now sustain the mature man in the chaotic surroundings of the world of business. It was your encouragement that influenced me profoundly in my decision to step forward today as an author in a language foreign to me. I enjoy your protection, and who would dare censure me if, in the future, I were to receive from your hands the right to citizenship in the world of German letters?" Having thus paid his compliments to the mighty one in Weimar and made his none-too-subtle hint, Uvarov develops his cosmopolitan ideas: "It is devoutly to be hoped," he writes, "that we have left behind once and for all the politically motivated notion that any particular language could claim superiority in the realm of science. Surely, the time has come when every scientist . . . should have the right to choose that language which most effectively expresses the ideas he wishes to present."[39] It is not surprising that Goethe was quick to give his blessing to these plans and convictions of his cosmopolitan friend.[40]

Alas, the sincerity of these convictions is suspect. For with the turn of Russia from liberalism under Aleksander to reaction under Nicholas, Uvarov's "convictions" turned too. As Minister of Public Enlightenment he provided the regime with its reactionary master plan and its famous slogan: "Orthodoxy—Autocracy—Nationality" (Pravoslavie—Samoderzhavie—Narodnost').[41] As he had previously sought Goethe's support for his "liberal" ideas, so he now enlisted for his reactionary plans and projects the help of Goethe, the illustrious "autocrat and dictator in the realm of the spirit." Goethe could by that time no longer object. He had died just one year before the hundredth anniversary of the Russian Academy of Sciences, celebrated in 1833. On that solemn occasion Uvarov, as President of the Academy, paid his final tribute to his "edler, herrlicher Freund," placing him side by side and hand in hand with that other illustrious "autocrat and dictator," this one in the realm of "Realpolitik," Nicholas I, Uvarov's new benefactor. Like Nicholas—thus runs Uvarov's argument—Goethe had been steadfast in his support of long-established values amid the onslaught of revolutionary forces: "When all was overturned in the storm of revolutionary upheaval, when even the most perceptive German minds were overcome by its acrid fumes, Goethe was not swept along in the general current, maintained an aloof silence. He remained the steadfast aristocrat in his self-imposed rules of conduct, in his desires, in his tastes and sensibilities; he openly showed his proud disdain for the opinions of the rabble now raised triumphant. Stern, adamant in his greatness, he remained unassailable by the ephemeral passions and fancies. In sharp contrast to Voltaire, Goethe declared without equivocation that all the genuflection before the mob was to him so much saccharine sentimentality, that it had left him absolutely cold. He knew the mob for what it was— utterly incapable of governing itself in the realm of the spirit as in the sphere of politics." And Uvarov concludes his grandiloquent speech by expressing his sympathies with the German nation, which had lost in Goethe "her last and only ruler in the realm of the spirit, a ruler raised above the heads of all upon the shield of the established rights of genius as well as the unanimous vote of his compatriots, and yet a ruler definitely *not* 'constitutional,' one who did *not* like to hear of 'literary charters' . . . and stood superior to 'popular rule' in the arts as in the sciences."[42]

There are other characteristic facets of the image of Goethe that Uvarov develops in this speech. He emphasizes the "universality" of Goethe. Zhirmunski argues plausibly that Uvarov had adopted this view of Goethe with his usual adroitness for his own purposes from Wolfgang Menzel's *Die deutsche Literatur,* which became available to him in the German original shortly upon its publication in 1827.[43] In keeping with his sharply critical view of Goethe, Menzel had accused the poet of eclecticism in art and had dubbed him a "chameleon" in politics. What was in Menzel's eyes a weakness, even a vice, reappears in Uvarov's view of Goethe as a virtue. Mengel's "chameleon," Goethe, experiences in Uvarov's interpretation an Ovidian metamorphosis into a "Proteus." Goethe's all-embracing genius is shown to be capable of giving canonical expression in his artistic creations to the multifaceted spirit of the Germans: to their sentimentalism in his *Werther,* to their penchant for times medieval in his *Götz,* to their enthusiasm for Italy in his *Torquato Tasso,* to their "Griechenlandsehnsucht" in his *Iphigenie auf Tauris,* and so forth through the everchanging kaleidoscope of his major works. Not limited to the sentiments and sensibilities of his countrymen, "this true Proteus" was capable of entering at will the spirit of all the lands and all the epochs. "He placed upon the German stage his *Götz von Berlichingen,* that true and forceful expression of medieval days, the very flower of its native soil. . . . And having achieved this inimitable creation, the poet never returned to a work of this type. . . . He moved on to write his *Iphigenie,* beauteous, radiant like a Greek statue, melodious as Sappho's songs, pristine as the ancient scrolls unearthed at Herculaneum. . . . In his *Torquato Tasso* we hear the musical voice of the Mediterranean lands, here resounds their mellifluous, melodious language. To this day no imitator has so much as approached this enchanting play of the poet's imagination."[44]

As has been suggested above, there is reason to believe that this flamboyant picture of Goethe as the Protean genius had some effect on Aleksander Ivanovich Turgeniev.[45] More important, however, for Turgeniev in the final phase of his Goethe appreciation or, rather, his Goethe critique, was Uvarov's elaboration in his anniversary speech on the theme of Goethe's penchant for irony, satire, and sarcasm. It is this theme that Uvarov stressed in a clearly reactionary interpretation of *Faust* which sought to portray Goethe as a bitter foe of all progressive stirrings and especially of the French Revolution. Uvarov claimed that Goethe "had never, before his *Faust,* mounted such a fierce attack on the spirit of the times [i.e., the French Revolution]; never had he blasted the works of his contemporaries with *such bitter and devastating sarcasm.*" In *Faust* Uvarov recognized "a *powerful satire* on the Germans' penchant for burrowing in the depths and chasms of the ineffable to uncover its mysteries. Here Goethe castigates his compatriots' empty chatter and inquisitiveness [i.e. their quest for truth] with his *terrifying sarcasm*."[46]

This theme, cleverly used by Uvarov to buttress political reaction with Goethe's authority, is echoed—in a different spirit to be sure—by Turgeniev in his critical view of Goethe. We remember that Turgeniev in his later years had discovered in Goethe's personality the "spirit of Mephistopheles," a streak of cynicism, of "terrifying sarcasm," qualities which he, just like Uvarov, now found most clearly expressed in Goethe's *Faust*. He sharply rejected this greatest of Goethe's works as a dangerous voice of beguiling power, speaking the language of Mephistopheles, spreading abroad the spirit of "cold doubt," of soul-destroying cynicism and destructive nihilism. In a letter written from Berlin to his friend P. A. Viazemski, Turgeniev wrote of the "oppressive feeling" with which he had left a performance of Goethe's drama. "No," he continued, "I would never have written it, not even if I had the genius of Goethe. I am rooted in the fear of God and in a spirit of love for the good people for whom one must preserve the Christian God and whom one should protect from the devil and all his deeds, and that includes a genius such as is Goethe's in his *Faust*."[47] Uvarov, the Minister of Public Enlightenment, in the style of Nicholas I, could have been well satisfied with this pronouncement of Turgeniev, made in the true spirit of "orthodoxy and nationality," of a proper paternalistic concern for the spiritual welfare of the "good people," though, of course, the suave diplomat would never have directed so open an attack on the name and fame of the departed friend and favorite of the Czar. With his rejection of "Goethe's genius in his *Faust*" as a "deed of the devil," Turgeniev arrived at a position not unlike that of the most conservative Slavophiles in their denunciation of the dangerously corrosive spirit of the godless West. Turgeniev seems to have maintained this attitude toward Goethe up to his death in 1845.

With this discussion of Uvarov's and Turgeniev's view of Goethe and his works we have moved well beyond the "early Russian reactions to Goethe." The close-range survey of these reactions

has made it strikingly evident that they were, in large measure, determined by the "sentimental" appreciation of literature prevalent
in Russia at the turn of the century, largely conditioned by Rousseau's and Richardson's dominant influence on Russian tastes in
literary matters. In these early years we found a growing interest in
Goethe that culminated in the ardent Goethe cult of the Friendly
Literary Society. At the same time, we saw little if any development in the Russian appreciation of Goethe's works beyond the
Karamzin-Radishchev school of interpretation with its emphasis on
Werther as Goethe's incomparable *chef d'oeuvre.* To be sure, by
the end of the first decade of the new century a more comprehensive view of Goethe was being ushered in, most effectively by the
intimate friend of the Turgeniev brothers, Vasili A. Zhukovski.
Vissarion Belinski, the great Russian critic, reminisced about the
decisive impact this poet had upon the cultural life of his generation by way of his translations from German and English. "Already
as children having no clear idea as yet of what was a translation,
what an original, we learned his renderings by heart as the *works of
Zhukovski.* Thus was established in us a kinship to German and
English poetry which allowed us later to enter their sanctum not as
profanes but as if born initiates. . . . Thus was developed in us the
ability to assimilate the Germans' view of art, their criticism, the
German mode of thought. And all that was accomplished, single-
handedly, by Zhukovski, solely by the impact of his translations."[48]
On the basis of such evidence we consider it appropriate to continue our exposition of the Russian image of Goethe with a study
of Zhukovski as a foremost mediator between the Russian and
German cultural spheres and, specifically, as the outstanding translator and interpreter of Goethe.

CHAPTER TWO

Vasili A. Zhukovski: Goethe's Translator and Interpreter[1]

Vasili A. Zhukovski (1783–1852) is generally considered the father of Russian Romanticism.[2] Belinski extolled him as "the Russian Columbus who has discovered the American continent of Romanticism"[3] and went on to define Zhukovski's translations from German and English as his "true, great and immortal service to Russian literature." "Only with the advent of Zhukovski did Russian literature begin to free itself from the domination of French literature." M. Bakunin, another informed observer of the literary scene, praises Zhukovski for his "noble efforts to acquaint us with the German world."[4] Zhirmunski considers Zhukovski to have been the "very first Russian poet who proceeded in his translations of Goethe's poetry from a comprehensive knowledge of Goethe's personality and work" and sees in him "the true progenitor of the 'German' school of Russian poets (Venevitinov, Tiutchev, Fet, A. Tolstoi, *et al.*) who were most firmly rooted in the literary tradition of Goethe."[5]

Zhukovski had first been introduced to German literature in the broadest sense by his friend Andrei Turgeniev.[6] Throughout his mature life, Zhukovski felt deeply indebted to the German world of letters for his development as a poet.[7] To Aleksander Turgeniev, the brother of Andrei, he confessed that "Goethe and Schiller . . . had educated him." We know from Andrei Turgeniev that Zhukovski at nineteen had already translated a letter from Goethe's *Werther* (*ca.* 1802), though it must be stressed that at that early stage in his development, Zhukovski's main interest and effort as translator were still centered on English and French authors, on Gray, Thomson, and LaFontaine rather than on Goethe and Schiller. As late as 1805 he frankly admitted that "German literature is little known to me," and not before 1806 did he begin to "imitate [!] Schiller, Bürger, and Goethe" and to "respect German authors and German philosophy, because," as he put it, "they elevate the soul, causing it to be more active, and awaken our faculty of enthusiasm."[8]

The year 1808 ushered in a decisive reorientation. That year Zhukovski translated his first poem by Goethe: "Meine Göttin"; in the same year he became chief editor of the influential journal *Messenger of Europe* and proceeded to dedicate its pages to a veritable cult of Goethe. There followed a decade of his greatest activity as cultural mediator between Germany and Russia. Not all of Zhukovski's ambitious plans materialized.[9] He did, however, translate in this fertile period (*ca.* 1808–20) ten poems of Goethe: "An den Mond," "Erlkönig," "Der Fischer," "Mignon," as well as "Zueignung" from Goethe's *Faust;* "Wer nie sein Brot mit Tränen aß," "Trost in Tränen," "Neue Liebe, neues Leben," "Schäfers Klagelied," and "Der Wanderer." Zhukovski never again reached such a peak of productivity as translator of Goethe. This is all the more startling since it was only *after* this period that he actually met the revered poet.

On October 3, 1820, Zhukovski's dreams of a visit to Germany at long last became a reality. "I shall see Schiller's and Goethe's tragedies," he rejoiced. He set out for Dresden and proceeded "by way of Weimar to Kassel, from Kassel to Frankfurt."[10] Berlin welcomed him with open arms. Here he met a number of German Romanticists, among them E. T. A. Hoffmann, Jean Paul, de la Motte-Fouqué, and Bettina von Arnim, whom he found to be "a very affected person." On May 5, 1821, Zhukovski noted in his diary: "A dinner at the home of (Anton Heinrich) Radziwill," the well-known composer of music to Goethe's *Faust*. At this dinner he also met, "among many other notables and admirers of Goethe, Wilhelm von Humboldt" and on a later occasion "Alexander Wolf, the talented actor and protégé of Goethe," as well as Goethe's old friend, the composer Karl Friedrich Zelter.[11] But his most enthusiastic "introduction to Goethe" Zhukovski received from Sulpiz Boisserée, who was much taken with the Russian's love for and knowledge of German art and literature. Boisserée's letter of recommendation to Goethe is eloquent in praise of the Russian poet and, it would seem, not altogether indifferent to the protégé of the Grandduchess Aleksandra of Russia:

> Stuttgart, 6. October 1821. . . . Before I close, I must sing the praises of a Mr. von Zhukovski from the suite of Grand Duchess Aleksandra, née Princess of Prussia. This brilliant man has the liveliest appreciation of art and poetry and especially of all that the Germans have achieved in these fields. Not only does he know your works and those of Schiller, but he has translated many of them into Russian. Before returning to Petersburg, he plans to take the Rhine trip, and would reach you in about five weeks. On arrival he very much hopes to enjoy your personal conversation. I have come to value his company so much that I cannot refrain from drawing your attention to this man to assure a friendly welcome for him. Once you have made his acquaintance, you will most certainly like him.[12]

Zhukovski arrived in Weimar on October 29. His diary provides us with little more than key words. To be sure, he had planned to expand his notes at leisure into a full-scale report, but he never realized his good intentions. Nevertheless, these jottings furnish a surprisingly direct and vivid reflection of Zhukovski's impression of Goethe and Weimar. His very first entry attests to this keen sense for the important and unique: "October 29, Weimar. Struve,[13] . . . Goethe's house: the staircase; busts and plaster casts; Salve,[14] a long antechamber; the Olympian Jupiter and Achilles; museum; busts of Schiller, Herder, Goethe, of moderns and ancients. The garden. Goethe's grandson. A long reception room; drawings, sofa, above it a drape-covered picture 'Les noces d'Aldobrandini';[15] Madonna. The room containing portfolios and antiques." We can follow the Russian poet in his progress through Goethe's house, the museum, through Goethe's garden, meeting Goethe's grandson, Wolfgang, then back to the house again.

Goethe was at the time at Jena. Grandduchess Maria Pavlovna provided Zhukovski with a carriage to take him there, and he was received by Goethe that very day "with kindness." His diary traces his progress toward Jena by way of Schneckenburg and Mühltal, marks "the picturesque location" of the city and offers some jottings on the meeting itself: "Goethe; French language; table; a map of Rome; bust; on the topic of Märchen; Alles ist Wahrheit; Wahrheit und Dichtung. An unfortunate impediment." Again the remarks are tantalizingly cryptic. Fortunately collateral sources shed important light. In a letter to the Grandduchess Aleksandra Fedorovna, his Imperial Russian patroness, Zhukovski speaks of his "fog-shrouded trip on the Rhine" and his "gracious reception" by the Grandduchess Maria Pavlovna, who—as we already know—made his meeting with Goethe possible. "But," he continues, "my meeting with him resembled the Rhine trip; it was shrouded in mists though he received me with kindness."[16] The real key, however, is furnished by an unexpected source, a volume edited by Julius Wilhelm Eckardt, a personal acquaintance of Zhukovski: *Neue Bilder aus der Petersburger Gesellschaft*. Eckardt speaks of Zhukovski's enthusiastic reception in Dresden, Weimar, and Switzerland, mentions his friendship with Justinus Kerner and finally comes to speak of Zhukovski's visit with Goethe. It had been far from a success. "Zhukovski had introduced himself to the 'greatest lyric poet of the West' in French but noticed at once Goethe's difficulty in expressing himself in that language and, being a sensitive and polished person, felt that he would be but carrying out the unspoken wish of his highly revered acquaintance when, after a while, he changed into German. But Goethe evidently took it as an insult and henceforth was so tense and laconic that his Russian guest left him somewhat disenchanted."[17] The meaning of the diary jottings: "French language . . . an unfortunate impediment" now becomes evident. Goethe must have felt the awkwardness of the meeting. To Boisserée he wrote in explanation almost apologetically: "He [Zhukovski] arrived here with the Russian chargé d'affaires, Mr. von Struve, unannounced, just as I was preoccupied with very different matters. I did compose myself quickly, mindful of your recommendation. Still, it does take some time to collect oneself and I must confess his departure saddened me. After an hour they continued on their journey and only after the farewells did it occur to me what I should have asked and said. I intend to write him a friendly word and send him something, also to make arrangements so that we would hear occasionally from one another, which should be an easy matter, considering our connections."[18]

Goethe carried out his intention on November 16.[19] Zhukovski's answer to Goethe's letter was delayed by his belated return to St. Petersburg, where he arrived on February 16, 1822, and found Goethe's letter waiting for him. His reply was couched in the conventional French of polite society; he assured Goethe of the indelible impression he had carried away from their meeting and thanked him for the "undeserved presents" and the letter which he had at once placed in safekeeping as a most cherished memento "from a dear hand."[20]

In the spring of 1826, Zhukovski started out on his second European trip. He revisited Frankfurt on August 31, 1827. His diary records: "Goethe's house; three lyres on the coat of arms; courtyard; the well; mansard roofs; Gretchen. Surroundings of Frankfurt." Obviously, Zhukovski's mind was on Goethe as he was strolling through the streets and environs of the poet's birthplace. On his way to Weimar Zhukovski read "Helena," which —as he tells us—"had just appeared as the Classico-Romantic phantasmagoria, an *intermedia*[21] to *Faust*."

On September 3, Zhukovski arrived in Weimar. "To Goethe. Porch with a turn. Dog. In the entrance hall: *Jupiter du Capitole, Pallas de Velletri*. In the drawing room Aldobrandini, paintings. A table with portfolios. The head of Juno is colossal. Baron [Christian Wilhelm] Schweizer; grandson Wolfgang. With the prince. With Madame Sylvester.[22] Evening at home." On the fifth of the month he was again with Goethe in the company of his painter friend, Gerhardt von Reutern. Chancellor Friedrich von Müller supplies some interesting details of the meeting:

Wednesday, 5. September. Zhukovski's and von Reutern's visit this morning put Goethe into such a friendly mood that I have hardly ever seen him more affable, milder and more communicative. Whatever he could give to these friends of pleasantries, intimacy, of helpful judgment, hint, acclaim and love, he brought forward and expressed. We had already examined Reutern's drawings. He [Goethe] admired particularly the incisiveness of his conceptions and contours. He seemed to be moving in a new, long-yearned-for, fresh ambience [Lebens-atmosphäre] while he was talking with Reutern about art- and nature-representation [Kunst- und Natur-Darstellung]. Happy with my having talked the friends into a longer stay, he made the statement: "My time is so arranged that there is always enough of it for my friends."[23]

A more vivid account of the occasion is furnished by von Reutern as he gives us a rapturous description of the poet in a most benign mood: "The magnificent sage was completely sincere, attentive, sociable and inexpressibly obliging, but all this in such a way that we were seized with trembling, not knowing was it a dream, was it reality or had a higher being descended from on high to lift us up to his luminous sphere!? And joyous at once and awestruck we strove with indescribable ardor to seize upon and to hold all that we were witnessing." Goethe was paying high praise to von Reutern's work.

Von Reutern quotes Goethe as saying: "In all your drawings . . . there is clearly perceived nature . . . a grasp of the characteristic and of the beautiful. Everywhere there is a fine sensitivity for composition and where you use colors, I observe rich tones and it is wonderful that you are not afraid to take them as brilliant as nature itself presents them. You always see nature as a painting [als Bild]; I find this in all of your work."

There is much in Goethe's praise that is typical of his view on art. He singles out von Reutern's ability to grasp "the characteristic and the beautiful"; by way of praise he urges him to remain ever-faithful to his medium, to stay close to nature, to seize upon it in its character of a painting, to see it always "als Bild." One is reminded of Goethe's famous essay, "Einfache Nachahmung der Natur, Manier, Stil," some of the tenets of which he is applying here to von Reutern's art, projecting his own way of seeing and reproducing nature into the rather commonplace works of the Russian painter. Von Reutern concludes his account with a glimpse of Zhukovski, who—he tells us not without a touch of pride— "was deeply stirred by the acclaim my work received from Goethe, and together we experienced the profoundest joy at having found such a judge and such a patron."[24]

The next day, September 6, began, according to Zhukovski's

diary, with a visit to Madame Sylvester, whence he proceeded to the home of Chancellor von Müller, who showed him "personal papers of Herder, Schiller, Goethe, and Jacobi." Upon leaving the Chancellor, Zhukovski visited Julie von Egloffstein and admired a portrait of Goethe which she had just finished. Finally, he was received once more by Goethe himself. It is at this point that the laconisms of the Russian's diary become particularly intriguing, for they no more than hint at what must have indeed been an interesting conversation. We read: "To Goethe. Conversation about Helena, about Byron. Goethe places him alongside Homer and Shakespeare. 'The sun, the stars, they nevertheless remain genuine; they are no copies.' " That is all. Goethe makes mention of this meeting in his *Tagebuch* just as laconically: "6th of September, 1827: Mr. von Reutern and Zhukovski, conversation with comments and explanations on Helena. . . . Messrs von Reutern and Zhukovski, again. Both presented beautiful drawings. Received medals in return."[25] Fortunately, Chancellor von Müller's report is more complete:

> Thursday, 6th of September. When Zhukovski, Reutern, and I visited Goethe toward evening, we found him weary, exhausted, and ailing. We therefore did not stay long. Nevertheless, when the conversation turned to the mania of certain would-be experts to declare all pictures for copies, he made a witty comment: "That is how they have brushed aside many an old parchment. I for one would rather take a copy for an original than vice versa. After all, in that faith I can edify myself as I contemplate the picture. But let them have their way; sun, moon and stars they must leave us, they cannot turn them into copies. And that may suffice in an emergency. Just don't let yourself be confused, exercise your judgment ever more vigorously and let it grow ever more sure of itself."[26]

Zhukovski's diary then mentions "a walk in Goethe's garden. The house where Goethe wrote and composed *Iphigenie*. The little house of the duke [evidently his small castle at Tiefurt]. The place where he [Goethe], Schiller, Wieland, Jacobi, Herder were wont to sit. The river Ilm." The day, according to Zhukovski's jottings, was then concluded with another, the final, brief call on Goethe.

On November 7, 1827, Zhukovski departed for Russia. As a parting gift he presented Goethe with a painting by Carl Gustav Carus showing a Gothic-style balcony with a harp leaning against a vacant chair, draped with a cloak, suggesting that someone had just departed. The moon is shining through the strings of the harp and in the misty background rise the spires of a Gothic cathedral.[27] Goethe said of this picture: "ein merkwürdiges Bild von Carus drückt die ganze Romantik dem bewundernden Blicke aus. . . ."[28] On it Zhukovski had inscribed the following lines in Russian and French:

> A çelui, dont la Lyre a crée un monde de prodiges,
> Qui a levé le voile mystérieux de la création
> Qui anime le passé
> Et prophetise l'avenir.[29]

These were not the only parting words Zhukovski wrote. "In the morning hour of departure" he composed a eulogy in Russian and German, the German version being, if anything, the more forceful of the two. He handed it "offen" to his friend, Chancellor von Müller, who transmitted it to Goethe and reproduced it in his *Unterhaltungen*. The German version, addressed "to the kind, great man," runs as follows:

> Du Schöpfer großer Offenbarungen! Treu werde ich in meiner Seele bewahren den Zauber dieser Augenblicke, die so glücklich in Deiner Nähe dahinschwanden.
> Nicht vom Untergange spricht Deine herrlich flammende Abendsonne! Du bist ein Jüngling auf der Gottes-Erde und Dein Geist schaffet noch, wie er schaffte.
> Ich trage in meinem Herzen die Hoffnung, Dir noch einmal hier zu begegnen! Noch lange wird Dein Genius sein der Erde bekanntes Gewand nicht ablegen.
> In dem entfernten Norden verschönerte Deine Muse mir die Erde! Und mein Genius Goethe gab Leben meinem Leben!
> O warum vergönnte mir nicht mein Schicksal, Dir in meinem Frühling zu begegnen? Dann hätte meine Seele ihre Flamme auf der Deinigen entzündet!
> Dann hätte eine ganz andere wunderherrliche Welt sich um mich gestaltet; und dann vielleicht auch von mir wäre eine

Kunde zu der Nachwelt gelangt: *er war ein Dichter.*

Schukoffsky, den 7. September, 1827*[30]

This effort of the Russian poet to express his admiration and debt to the German genius, though certainly not great poetry, has a personal note that rings true. It is highly characteristic of Zhukovski to view Goethe as the great prophet, the "creator of great revelations," and to apply to him a religious term signifying transcendence. Zhukovski's lament, moreover, of belated contact with Goethe's genius goes well beyond the polite cliché. It indicates Zhukovski's awareness that Goethe's influence, had it come in his formative years, might well have given his talent a more positive direction toward the concrete, objective, phenomenal world, a world which was the "altogether different wondrous world"[31] to him, now that he was irrevocably rooted in a predominantly mystical, sentimental, romantic sphere. Zhukovski knew that "the flame of his soul" had not been lit at Goethe's flame, that his poetic spirit was not kindred to Goethe's.

Goethe in his rather cold reaction to the poem agreed essentially with this characterization by Zhukovski. He detects with interest, even with a measure of admiration, "something oriental, profound, priestly" in the poem, yet at the same time remarks to his friend, Chancellor von Müller: "Zhukovski should have been far more insistently directed toward the objective." Goethe's reception of the poem left the kindly Müller quite chagrined: "Much too coldly did Goethe receive Zhukovski's wonderful poem of parting, even though he did acknowledge something oriental, profound, priestly in its tone."[32] It may have been a consolation to him that

---

* You creator of great revelations! Faithfully I shall safekeep in my soul the magic of those moments, which passed so happily in your presence. Your gorgeously flaming evening sun does not speak of decline! You are a youth upon God's earth and your spirit continues to create as it has created. I harbor in my heart the hope, to meet with you here again! For a long time to come your genius will not take off its familiar earthly raiment. In the distant North your muse has beautified the earth for me! And my genius Goethe gave life to my life! O why did not fate grant me to meet with you in my springtime? Then my soul would have kindled its flame at yours! Then an altogether different wondrous world would have taken shape around me; and then perhaps tidings of me too would have come down to posterity: *he was a poet.* Zhukovski, September 7, 1827.

Zhukovski did not depart without a memorable gift from Goethe, a copy of the "Marienbader Elegie" in which the poet had inscribed in personal dedication the lines from *Tasso:*

> Und wenn der Mensch in seiner Qual verstummt,
>
> Gab mir ein Gott, zu sagen, wie ich leide.[†][33]

Zhukovski's second visit failed, as had the first, to stimulate him as a translator and interpreter of Goethe's work. It probably made him more keenly aware of the difficulties posed by Goethe's art for his predominantly elegiac, Romantic, subjective muse and thus discouraged him from further efforts. At any rate we find in this final period only four additional translations of Goethe: two *Zahme Xenien:* "Wär' nicht das Auge sonnenhaft" und "Liegt dir gestern klar und offen" (1829); three lines from *Tasso:* "Die Stätte, die ein guter Mensch betrat" (I, 1), and "Adler und Taube" (1833). Finally, in 1848, he attempted an interpretation of two scenes from *Faust,* Faust's Bible translation and "Nacht. Offen Feld." Surely, this was not a rich harvest for a period of over two decades.

Although these were the last fruits of Zhukovski's activity as Goethe's translator and interpreter, his interest in Goethe remained intense. Under the impact of the news of Goethe's death, he turned with renewed eagerness to the admired author's work. His diary has numerous references to Goethe. Among them we find a singularly apt characterization of Goethe's style, and unreserved praise of the originality of Goethe's thinking. The very terseness of the comments makes them all the more striking: "Lucidity and verve. There is nothing superfluous. On everything, original ideas. Eigentümlichkeit, Faßlichkeit und Bild—that is the character of Goethe's style. Brevity and unforced orderliness in his presentation; unobtrusive, yet perceptible thought."

At the time Zhukovski made these diary entries, he was back in Germany. The memory of Goethe accompanied him everywhere. On September 3, 1832, in Frankfurt, he noted "a conversation about Goethe with a bookdealer by the name of Karl

---

† And when man falls silent in his torment, God gave me [the power] to say how I am suffering.

Jügel"; on the eighth of the month he inspected "an edition of Goethe's *Faust* with engravings by Peter Cornelius"; on the tenth, in Heidelberg, his attention was attracted "by an old building with a quaint staircase described," as he remembered, "in *Götz von Berlichingen*." On a visit to the Heidelberg castle, admiring the "sparkling Rhine, the candlelit windows in the valley below, and the moon rising from behind the mountain," Zhukovski's thoughts turned inevitably to Goethe and inspired him "to contemplations on the destiny of the soul." Zhukovski was drawing Goethe, the *dedizierte Nichtchrist,* into his own deeply religious, mystico-sentimental world; he would make Goethe a partner in his "quest after the secrets of life hereafter."

Weimar's attraction proved as usual irresistible, and on August 24, 1833, Zhukovski returned again to that city. With Chancellor von Müller he went to a performance of Schiller's *Jeanne d'Arc* (*sic*), enjoyed "anecdotes about Goethe," and quoted verbatim in his diary Goethean maxims which someone, probably von Müller, recalled upon the occasion: "Never let yourself be bored by bad theater, never offer compliments without having meant them sincerely—of such matters I speak only with God." Next day, Friedrich Theodor Kräuter, Goethe's personal secretary and archivist, led Zhukovski on a tour of the Weimar library, pointed out to him "Goethe's bust by David," talked of "Goethe's attachment to Schiller," and spread before him "Wieland's letter about Goethe to Jacobi as well as letters of Goethe's parents." Then Kräuter took him to "Goethe's house" where Zhukovski inspected "a room with medals from the Middle Ages; bronzes, a plaster cast of Schiller's skull" and was told by the secretary the story of its discovery which, in turn, led to the topic of "Schiller's death in 1804 [*sic*], his burial in 1815; the reconstruction of his skeleton; of his skull." They viewed "Dannecker's bust of Schiller" and several "portraits." At this point in the diary we read: ". . . entrance upon showing tickets," which leads us to suspect that Zhukovski and Kräuter had left Goethe's house, had entered Schiller's "upon showing the tickets," and had there viewed "Schiller's bust" and his "portraits." There they also met "Schiller's personal servant," who reverently showed them "two teeth" of his beloved master.

The following morning was spent with Chancellor von Müller in conversation "about Goethe's *Faust*." Later that day Zhukovski departed for Berlin and thence to Russia, not to return until 1838.[34] On May 31 of that year he was back in Berlin and heard "in the Singakademie" Anton Heinrich Radziwill's music to Goethe's *Faust* and discussed "the acts in Goethe's *Faust*" with Ludwig Tieck, who at the time was busy trying to arrange *Faust Part I* into regular acts. In Weimar, where he arrived on September 6, he repeatedly visited Goethe's house (September 8, 9, 13) and singled out with loving care every detail. "In Goethe's house . . . conversation with Eckermann and Kräuter. Description of Goethe's death. The diminutive size of his [bed]room [which Zhukovski evidently saw for the first time]. The stuffiness in the long-unventilated chambers. The bedpan. The pretty calendar in its case. March 22. [The calendar had been left turned to the date of Goethe's death.] Bust of the [Russian?] Empress. A pyramid made of cardboard: *Sensuality* in green color, *intellect* [Vernunft] in yellow, *imagination* in red. Poems and diary. Inkspots. Goethe's drawings." On September 14, Zhukovski visited "Goethe's tomb," and on the following day "drew in Goethe's study." Despite its brevity, the last jotting seems to transmit some of the sweet delight and pride our sentimental poet must have experienced at his seclusion "in the study," in the ambience of the worshiped master.

Zhukovski's last visit to Weimar took place in 1846. In Goethe's house he admired "the drawings of [Asmus] Carstens; inspected [the replicas of ?] Schiller's, Wieland's and Herder's rooms as well as the death masks of Schiller, Goethe, Napoleon, Charles XII, Cromwell, the Duke [Carl August?] of Weimar, Friedrich II, Joseph II, and [Johann Nepomuk] Hummel. A head of the Madonna." The last diary entry referring to Goethe's world is the ever-recurring leitmotif: "To Goethe's house."

As we have seen in the foregoing, Zhukovski's diary does little to clarify his appreciation of and attitude toward the work of Goethe, as it is largely descriptive of his contacts with the poet, his home and the cities of Frankfurt and Weimar. Other direct statements by Zhukovski on his view of Goethe as a man and writer are strikingly few. Besides the two poems eulogizing the German genius, there is another four-line verse, "To Goethe's Portrait," written in 1819; it echoes Andrei Turgeniev's dedicatory poem which, as we remember, he had inscribed in a copy of Goethe's *Werther* and sent to Zhukovski in token of their friendship and mutual admiration for the German poet. In a prose rendering, Zhukovski's lines run as follows: "Having accepted bold freedom as his only law, he soared above the world on wings of all-perceiving thought. He conquered everything on earth and nothing forced subjection upon him."[35]

There exists, in addition, an apocryphal record of conversations of Zhukovski on Goethe, set down "verbatim" by an illustrious gossip monger, A. O. Smirnova, and published in her *Notes*. Smirnova, had all the flair and faults of a Hollywood society columnist. She certainly knew how to dramatize her characters and situations and, in the process, to secure for herself a spot in the limelight. As an eye- and earwitness she set the stage and let us in on the intimate thoughts of her "stars":

> Last evening at the Karamzins Orest and Pylades, Zhukovski and Pushkin were off by themselves in a corner talking, and I was being educated, while writing down every word they uttered. They spoke of Lessing, of Goethe, of Schiller and of Kleist. . . . Zhukovski, true champion of Goethe that he is, recited the "Bride of Corinth." He argued that Goethe was not an egoist, nor indifferent to the heavy lot of mankind but that he simply could not bear sentimentality. Goethe is to Zhukovski least like a German of all Germans, he always *thinks,* never merely *enthuses,* his mind must have always been calm as we can see from the expression on his face.

With obvious relish Smirnova passes on some choice bits of gossip snatched from the lips of Zhukovski:

> Rumor has it that Lotte loved Goethe but did not wish to refuse Kestner, since she knew him before her acquaintance with Goethe. He, Zhukovski, had had a conversation with Schlegel [August Wilhelm?] in which Schlegel had assured him that Goethe would never have married her [Lotte], having had

at the time no intention whatever of marrying. And on his own authority Zhukovski had added: Goethe loved his sister sincerely. Her death had been one of the most terrible blows of his life. With this Zhukovski wanted to stress that at such a tragic time thoughts of marriage could hardly have been in Goethe's mind. Zhukovski concluded the conversation with an observation from personal experience: But Goethe's nature was not at all expansive and he rarely spoke of what he felt.

Goethe's reticence must have greatly impressed the expansive Russian. Zhukovski then turned to a comparison of Goethe with Schiller. Smirnova registers surprise at Zhukovski's "claim" that "there had been times when Schiller was more ardently Greek than Goethe, that, as a matter of fact, in his youth Goethe had not been such a fervent Grecophile at all." Comparing Schiller's and Goethe's achievements as dramatists, Zhukovski gave the edge to Schiller for the greater scenic effectiveness of his plays. Both authors he considered to be "tendentious" in their plays: *"Die Räuber* and *Kabale und Liebe* are tendentious, as are *Egmont* and *Don Carlos."* Zhukovski then launched into a spirited defense of *Werther* as being less "dangerous" than the *Wahlverwandtschaften* which "had turned the heads of a far greater number of women than the number of suicides traceable to *Werther."* Surely, Zhukovski must have made this drastic observation in rebuttal to the anti-Werther sentiment particularly deeply entrenched in the Karamzinian circle and going back to the early negative criticism of the work by Karamzin himself.

Smirnova's "record" of Zhukovski's statements on Goethe concludes with some excerpts from a conversation of Zhukovski, Gogol and Pushkin on *Faust.* Zhukovski had opened this exchange of views by asking Gogol what he thought of Goethe's *Faust* and had drawn from him an evasive generalization: "I am completely overwhelmed by the genius of Goethe. Schiller, with whose works I am rather well acquainted, now appears in an entirely different light," to which Zhukovski replied: "Yes, Schiller is a great poet, but Goethe is, in addition, a great thinker." Then he had brought the conversation back to *Faust,* claiming for this work "marvelous scenic effectiveness." Pushkin, warming to the discussion, extolled the work as an inimitable creation: "*Faust* stands altogether by it-self. It is the ultimate expression of German literature, a unique world, as incomparable as the *Divine Comedy, . . .* as much of a cosmos as are the works of Shakespeare."

To all this, Smirnova assures us, Zhukovski had eagerly nodded agreement: "Quite true," he exclaimed, "*Faust* has the same marvelous effect as have *Hamlet, Othello, Macbeth, Richard III.*" Pushkin would not be outdone. He claimed for Goethe's mas-terpiece "more thought, more original ideas, more philosophy than in all of the German philosophers put together, not excluding Leib-niz, Kant, Lessing, Herder and others," surely no small claim, which again was enthusiasticly supported by Zhukovski: "That is truly the philosophy of life, *die Philosophie des lebendigen Le-bens!*" This much from Smirnova's *Notes*.[36]

Finally, there are the two commentaries from Zhukovski's pen on Goethe's *Faust*. They are of late date, 1848, belonging to a period in Zhukovski's Goethe interpretation when the Russian poet's views had congealed into a rigid pietism, far removed from Goethe's unorthodox spirit. The Russian literary critic Veselovski de-fines the character of these commentaries aptly with the summary statement: "The pietistic nature of the commentaries does not speak for a deeper understanding of the text. . . . In all this there is not a trace of the 'lebendige Idee.' Goethe would have found such explication at the very least 'herzlich fromm.' "[37]

Zhukovski began his interpretation with an examination of the famous scene in which Faust strives to recast the gospel's phrase, "Im Anfang war das Wort," into a more adequate statement of his life's philosophy. Zhukovski concluded that Goethe had intro-duced this scene "merely to prove the all-embracing nature" of that passage from the Bible and to demonstrate the futility of all ef-forts to improve upon it. Certainly this is a prejudiced reading of Goethe's meaning and message.

In his second comment, Zhukovski takes to task two illustra-tors of Goethe's work, Friedrich Retzsch and Peter von Cornelius, both of whom, he argues, had totally misconstrued the deeper mean-ing of Goethe's scene "Nacht, offen Feld," when they populated the eerie spot with ghosts, skeletons, and demons. "Was that Goethe's true intention?" asked Zhukovski, and answered with an emphatic "No." "Not ghosts and demons of darkness but angels of light" had been assembled by Goethe upon the hallowed spot which soon was to witness pure, innocent Gretchen's execution. Mephisto recognizes the apparitions for what they are and trembles. He strives to mask his faint-heartedness with a show of crude invective against them." Had Goethe assembled spirits of the netherworld, he would merely have duplicated his efforts in the *Walpurgisnacht*. Having assembled the heavenly hosts, he has succeeded admirably in giving symbolic expression to the central theme of his work: "the triumph of humility and repentance over the powers of hell and godless pride of man. The pure hands of angels hallow the place where blind human law will satisfy *earthly* justice by punishing a criminal, while an all-seeing God achieves *heavenly* justice, receiving into His mercy a repentant soul." And what of the effect of this angelic assembly upon Faust himself? According to Zhukovski, "the angels seek to protect Faust at the very brink of destruction, yet Faust, ensnared as he is by the powers of evil, gallops past, grasps the meaning of the angelic vision only when—forcibly torn from Margarete in the dungeon—he hears fading behind him the vainly pleading voice of Gretchen."[38]

It is, of course, easy to agree with Veselovski that in these "interpretations" there is hardly a breath of the "lebendige Idee" of Goethe's work, yet they do show us in a starkly revealing light an aging Zhukovski, striving to carry off a rehabilitation of his admired master in the spirit of orthodoxy.

By far the most revealing evidence for Zhukovski's characteristic approach to Goethe and his work is in his numerous renderings into Russian of Goethe's lyrical masterpieces. It is these translations that have helped form the Russian view of Goethe more fundamentally and lastingly than any other single contribution by any other Russian interpreter or translator of the German poet. Certain elements which Zhukovski lent this image, such as the strong sentimental-Romantic overtones, proved to be most persistent among the broader circles of the Russian reading public, if not among the more prominent Goethe admirers and experts. Zhukovski's translations of Goethe developed as much staying power in Russia as the Tieck-Schlegel translations of Shakespeare continue to have among the English bard's German readers.

In an essay, "About Fables Generally and the Fables of Krylov," Zhukovski gives us a clear definition of what he considers the proper attitude of a translator of lyric poetry toward the original. "A translator of *prose*" must, of necessity, be "a slave to the original author; a translator of *verse,* his competitor." A prose translation must render faithfully every detail of the original text; a translation of verse "must, above all, be faithful in the rendering of the over-all harmony of the original poem," which obviously here means harmony of *mood*. To this harmony "may be sacrificed exactness and force of the original." "Poetry is like a musical instrument in which fidelity of tone must yield to pleasantness of effect."[39] Obviously from a translator holding such views on his art, we cannot expect a literal rendering. Rather we must expect to find Goethe's lyrics reflected in and refracted by the Russian poets' personality, his basic mood.

For his first translation of a Goethe lyric in 1808, Zhukovski chose the famous poem "Meine Göttin."[40] He expressly designated this first rendering as "an imitation of Goethe," and for good reasons. It is a greatly expanded and altered version. The first nine lines of the German original are turned by Zhukovski into fourteen; in these he specifies, with utmost explicitness, place, persons and plot. Here are Zhukovski's lines in a verbatim translation back to German, placed for comparison alongside Goethe's text:

Goethe:	Zhukovski:
Welcher Unsterblichen	Welche Unsterbliche
Soll der höchste Preis sein?	Soll man bekränzen
Mit niemand streit' ich,	Vor allen Göttinnen
Aber ich geb' ihn	Des Olymps über den Sternen?
Der ewig beweglichen,	Ich streit nicht mit den Pfleglingen
Immer neuen,	Der prüfenden Weisheit,
Seltsamen Tochter Jovis,	Mit den gestrengen Gelehrten;
Seinem Schoßkinde,	Doch mit frischer Girlande
Der Phantasie.	Bekränz ich die fröhliche,

> Beflügelte, liebe,
> stets andersgeartete,
> immer belebende
> Lieblingstochter des Zeus,
> Die Göttin Phantasie.*

In his lines Zhukovski explicitly elevates "Phantasie" above all the other Olympians, shows us the prize, a "wreath of flowers," and bestows upon Jove's daughter five adjectives to Goethe's three, suppressing, however, Goethe's most striking appellative, "Schoßkind." To be sure, clarity of a sort is thus gained but at what cost to the limpidity and charm of Goethe's lines!

But even more than these introductory lines, it is Goethe's two descriptive strophes beginning, respectively, with the lines "Sie mag rosenbekränzt . . ." and "Oder sie mag / Mit fliegendem Haar . . ." which inspire Zhukovski's muse to its boldest variations on the theme. Goethe's seventeen lines are expanded to sixty-six. Jove's "Schoßkind" assumes the most varied guises, flutters as a robin redbreast through fragrant dale and over grass-clad hill; as a "little bee" it settles on a great variety of "sweet little flowers" to suck with its "lips the honey-sweet dew." All is sweetness, all is daintiness, a riot of color and aromatic scents! Then, with a change of mood in Goethe's next strophe, Zhukovski's goddess "Phantasie" undergoes a drastic metamorphosis into a pensive, melancholy figure and all about her is transformed into an elaborate Ossianic setting. In a prose translation, Zhukovski's lines convey the following scene: " 'Phantasie' is seated upon a steep cliff; her wild locks are fluttering in the wind, her eyes express melancholy sadness, her head is bending low. Lost in thought she looks out upon a desolate sea, harkens to the wild waves beating against a rock-ribbed shore."

The "Mondesblicke" of Goethe's original—"Immer wechselnd

---

* Goethe: To which of the immortals shall be given the highest prize? I shall not quarrel with anyone, but as for myself, I shall give it to the eternally agile, ever new, strange daughter of Jove, to his lap-child, imagination.

Zhukovski: Which of the immortals deserves the wreath before all the Gods of Olympus above the stars? I shall not quarrel with the acolytes of scrutinizing wisdom, with the austere savants; yet with a fresh garland I wreathe the gay, winged, beloved, ever-changing, ever-animating favorite daughter of Zeus, the goddess imagination.

/ wie Mondesblicke . . ."—release in the Russian poet another surge of imagination. He now creates an Anacreontic scene with all ethereal trappings. Jove's daughter now cavorts merrily "on a moonlit glade" or again "with the Naiads on the glistening waters of a forest stream" or "with Zephyr over dreaming lilies" and other assorted flowers.

After these flights of Anacreontic fancy, Zhukovski approaches the original more closely with an almost verbatim translation of Goethe's lines: "Laßt uns all / Den Vater preisen." However, Zhukovski again disrupts the stylistic unity of the German poem by transforming Zeus' command to his daughter, couched by Goethe in indirect discourse and with a great lightness of touch, into a ponderously dramatic speech: " 'May you, O foolish one,' said he to her, 'be his [man's] faithful companion in good as well as bad fortune, his consolation and refuge.' " This ponderousness, moreover, is emphasized by the regular dactylic meter,[41] which replaces Goethe's irregular measure, slowing its tempo and creating a pensive mood not unlike that characteristic of the Russian "bylinas."

Obviously, Zhukovski did not strive for an authentic rendering. He must have been aware that he was giving Goethe's poem a prettiness and daintiness quite foreign to it, by injecting a saccharine Romanticism which does not stem from Jena or Heidelberg but rather is reminiscent of Meissen's porcelainware. The crisp, sure lines of Goethe's poem, its charm, wit, and urbanity are all but lost under a heavy overlay of pseudo-Ossianic and Anacreontic motives. And yet, Zhukovski must have felt that he was doing no violence to the essential "harmony" of the German poem, that he was but emphasizing and elaborating elements present in the original.

The same reinterpretation of Goethe, the same "view" is evident in Zhukovski's next translation, a free rendering of "Die Freuden" under the telltale title, "The Butterfly."[42] Again Goethe's original fifteen lines are expanded into a poem of six strophes. Goethe's unique blend of imagery and thought, of thought in imagery, is translated into an overly explicit, elaborate, sentimental descriptive piece with a moralizing ending. Goethe's deft, didactic thrust in the last line—"So geht es dir, Zergliedrer deiner Freuden!"—Zhukovski expands into an eightline strophe of heavily sentimento-elegiac tone. Tearfully he laments the evanescence of beauty and joy, their sudden vanishing at the very moment when they seem to be within our grasp.[43] In the Russian rendering we do not find the typically Goethean thought which centers in the word, "Zergliedrer," the thought that living form and emotions, mechanically analyzed by grasping inquisitiveness, are destroyed, and we are left with dead and dull *disiecta membra;* Zhukovski misses Goethe's insight that only the process of dynamic comprehension and vital experience, the "lebendige Anschauung," yield the secrets of organic life and bestow the blessings and joys of intimate contact with it.

The next group of eight translations, made in the productive years 1816 to 1818 and first published in an anthology entitled *For the Few,*[44] represents some of the most faithful renderings of Goethe. Nevertheless, even here the Romantic point of view predominates. Zhukovski's typical "bias" remains in force. The very choice of pieces makes this clear. It is the Goethe of the popular ballad and of the elegiac or sentimental piece that attracts Zhukovski's special attention. One wonders whether Zhukovski was even fully aware of the other facets of Goethe's art. Of all the available ballads—and those of the Classical period were already extant—Zhukovski chose only "Erlkönig" and "Der Fischer"; three other pieces must have endeared themselves to him by their very titles: "Trost in Tränen," "Schäfers Klagelied," "Wer nie sein Brot mit Tränen aß." "An den Mond," "Mignon," and "Neue Liebe, neues Leben," which are also included might, at first glance, be considered exceptions. Yet their treatment by the Russian poet transposes them into the same Romantic-sentimental key.

It must be stressed that, by and large, in this group of poems Zhukovski does render the meter and the rhythm, imagery and ideas of the originals with amazing skill and fine empathy; yet some minor deviations suddenly flash sharp lights upon Zhukovski's typical tendency to prettify and to sentimentalize. For instance, in "Der

Fischer" Goethe's angler sits at the river's edge "peacefully" (ruhevoll). Zhukovski's sits there "steeped in thought," his soul filled with "cool calm"; from Goethe's river rises "a moist woman" (ein feuchtes Weib), from Zhukovski's "a beauty" raises "her moist head." In Goethe's "Schäfers Klagelied" the shepherd simply "follows the grazing herd." Zhukovski has him follow "with heavy sigh and with slow step."[45]

The great fidelity of Zhukovski's Russian version of the "Erlkönig,"[46] obviously a most congenial poem to the translator, is nevertheless disrupted at certain critical points. Thus the epic opening lines of the original are changed, probably under the influence of Bürger's much-admired "Lenore,"[47] to a dramatic staccato introduction: "Who gallops, who dashes . . .," and the fairy-tale-like atmosphere of Goethe's description of the elf-king's realm is much exaggerated in Zhukovski's typical manner: "Much joyousness is in my realm, Turquoise flowers and streams of pearls. / My palaces are fashioned of molten gold." Zhukovski completely fails to bring off the tense realism of Goethe's dialogue between father and son. For the persuasive calm of Goethe's: "Sei ruhig, bleibe ruhig, mein Kind," he manages only the rather insipid line: "Oh no, my baby, you must have heard wrong." Goethe's powerful concluding image of the terrified father racing with death, the groaning child in his arms, is badly blurred by inappropriate verbiage: "The rider, overwhelmed with fear, does not gallop, he flies; / The child grieves, the child shouts." A strange lapse of taste, this, which would seem to indicate Zhukovski's insensitiveness to the stark realism and severity of mood which lend such force to Goethe's conclusion. Though these lapses do mar the total impression, though Zhukovski fails to convey the structural and stylistic unity of Goethe's composition, he does succeed in transmitting the plot and some of the poetic substance of the German original.

"Trost in Tränen"[48] is as if made to order for the recreative talents of the Russian poet. Its meter, its mood, almost every detail of the original coincide perfectly with his sentimental, elegiac spirit. Zhukovski dwells with relish on the central theme: consolation in tears. He brings out most effectively the contrast between the light-hearted company of friends and the lonely *melancholicus* who has gained wisdom in "sweet sorrow," a favorite concept, a much-used and -abused term in Russian sentimental pieces. This rendering must be judged among the most successful of Zhukovski's faithful interpretations of Goethe. Another little masterpiece is his version of "Wer nie sein Brot mit Tränen aß."[49] The reproduction of the rather complex rhythm is faultless. The meaning and mood of the original are fully conveyed. It is obvious that Zhukovski feels thoroughly at home in this facet of Goethe's lyrical genius.

"Mignon," under the conventionalized title, "Mina,"[50] is again an "imitation" and scarcely that. Deviations are numerous, though by no means all significant. Worthy of special mention is the change of the refrain which underscores the theme of longing and nostalgia of the original and adds a note of gloomy hopelessness which the original lacks: "Thither, thither / Longing is calling . . . yet will one ever be there?" Moreover, some of the color and deeper meaning of the poem is lost by the reduction of the variety of appellations in the refrain—Geliebter, Beschützer, Vater—to the monotonous "friend" of Zhukovski's version, a change evidently designed to help place the Russian rendering more definitely into the sentimental genre of "friendship" poetry so popular in Russia at the time.

Goethe's "An den Mond"[51] presented a challenge to which Zhukovski was not equal. He fails to reproduce the emotional range of the original. Zhukovski stabilizes the poem, as it were, on one emotional plane, tunes its music to the soft chords of a "lonely lyre," that favorite instrument of the Russian sentimental poet, by dropping outright the passionately dramatic strophe beginning: "Wenn du in der Winternacht / Wütend überschwillst" and by transposing the preceding strophe which prepares this burst of passionate feeling into a minor key. "Flow, oh flow, my little brook / And attune the murmurings of your waters to the sound of my lonely lyre." Goethe's last two strophes escape Zhukovski completely. In his translation there is no reference to the nether-depth of human nature, that "Labyrinth der Brust" through which mystery courses in the dark of night. Typically, he sings of those joys that come from sharing with a kindred soul, in seclusion, that which is disdained by the vulgar crowd: "Happy he who shares with a kindred soul hidden from the people that which is disdained by the crowd or is alien to it." Again we have the characteristic transformation: Goethe's incomparable poem is changed into a set Romantic piece. Goethe shows us nature in all its moods, lets us experience the mystery that is man. Zhukovski stylizes nature into a sweetly idyllic setting and, in the manner of the Romantic esthete, extolls the bliss enjoyed by the happy few, endowed with noble sentiments and refined sensibilities, safely sheltered from the common crowd.

Turning to Zhukovski's rendering of "Neue Liebe, neues Leben"[52] and with it to the last poem by Goethe in the anthology, we encounter an extremely complex system of changes, all designed to make of Goethe's gay, witty, boyish, even roguish poem an elegiac plaint of sweet torments, of consuming passions, closing on a note of languor and resignation. It is virtually impossible to register and define every subtle change, yet their sum total produces a marked shift both in content and in form. It is startling to see what has become of Goethe's opening lines: Herz mein Herz, was soll das geben? / Was bedränget dich so sehr?" Instead of restricting himself to Goethe's questions, Zhukovski piles them up: "What is paining you? Why are you boiling up again? What has set you aflame again?" Goethe's "heart" had known sadness before being overwhelmed by love; Zhukovski adds the inevitable touch of "sweetness" to the "sadness" and has his heart "grieve sweetly." Zhukovski's young love does not have, like Goethe's "Jugendblüte," a glance "voll Treu und Güte." Such bourgeois qualities Zhukovski willfully replaces with a "flaming sweetness of glance." While Goethe's youth strives to escape the enfeebling toils of love and to take courage again— "mich ermannen"—Zhukovski's hero would have none of the "ermannen" and longs instead to cast at his beloved "a languishing glance" and is "glad of the sadness" which love is causing him. He is more than ready to surrender to his passion, he wants to love. "I want to love," he exclaims, "evidently, my dear heart, it must be thus!" These are the concluding lines of the Zhukovski version. It is difficult to imagine a sharper contrast in attitude and mood to Goethe's ending: "Die Veränderung, ach wie groß! / Liebe! Liebe! laß mich los!" With Zhukovski a languorous resignation, with Goethe spirited resistance; with Zhukovski an atmosphere surcharged with an artificially nurtured emotionalism, with Goethe youthful buoyancy of spirit and a wholesome realism. No better example could be found of Zhukovski's tendency to recast Goethe's work to approximate his own prevalently sentimental mood in the Karamzin tradition which extolled the sweet sorrows of a heart in hopeless love.

To this group of poems may be added, on grounds of chronology as well as characteristic recasting, Zhukovski's "imitation" of Goethe's "Zueignung," first published in 1817 in the journal, *Son of the Fatherland,* under the title, "Longing; an Imitation of Goethe," and later used as an introduction to his ballad, "The Twelve Sleeping Maidens."[53] Zhukovski retains most faithfully the *ottava rima* measure of the original, carefully avoiding any expansions or alterations which would endanger the purity of form. Nevertheless, such seemingly minor changes as are introduced do add up to a significant reorientation of the total mood and message of the poem.

Goethe's original, born of the concrete situation of the poet's rededication of his creative energies to a long-dormant task, the prosecution of the "Hauptgeschäft" of *Faust,* carries along with pensive retrospect the prospect of renewed activity. Zhukovski slants his imitation to conform to the popular genre of elegiac poetry. He freely introduces the inevitable trappings of this genre: the "pensive lyre," "sweet memories," the "languid heart" throbbing with yearnings "for that other mysterious world," a heart filled with "sad longing for the blessings of bygone times." Moreover, most revealing of his transformation of Goethe's mood and outlook is a change in the first line of the third stanza. Here Goethe speaks of "folgende Gesänge," of *future* songs; Zhukovski characteristically substitutes the "*last* song," which will no longer reach the ear of his departed friends. The very act of retrospection inspires Goethe to renewed creative activity, while Zhukovski totally surrenders to the enervating sweetness of sad retrospect and reverie, with no thought whatever of new creative enterprise.

Two years were to elapse before Zhukovski would come forward with another Goethe rendering, his famous poem "Der Wanderer." This translation, like that of the "Zueignung," first appeared in the *Son of the Fatherland* under the title; "The Traveler and the Peasant Woman," in 1819.[54]

In a perceptive interpretation of Goethe's poem, Walter Silz characterizes it as "both 'naive' and 'sentimental,' both 'Classical' and 'Romantic.' " With fine insight Silz adds: "It [the poem] conveys the mood of the young Goethe's Sturm und Drang and it foreshadows the older Goethe's classicism at its best, that is, where it represents a blending of the cultural heritage from antiquity with the persistent naturalness of Goethe's mind, his native 'Naturhaftigkeit.' "[55] At its first appearance in 1774 in the *Göttinger Musenalmanach,* the full originality of Goethe's complex achievement was by no means grasped. The poem was generally read as a pastoral idyll in the spirit of Rousseau extolling the bliss and beauty of patriarchal life at nature's breast and casting a sentimental glance at the evanescence of the works of man. This reading of the work Zhukovski must have shared. Yet in his Russian version he does manage to convey something of Goethe's laconic, stern simplicity, of his "Classical" spirit. Somehow he managed to stop just short of sentimentality in rendering the poem, which readily invites a sentimental reading. Moreover, he was even able to preserve much of the poetic force of Goethe's irregular verse, which could have easily deteriorated to wingless prose in less skillful hands. True, Zhukovski cannot always equal Goethe's inimitable imagery and turn of phrase. For Goethe's neologistic "weggewandelt" he finds nothing better than the commonplace "departed"; for the ingeniously concise "Und hohes Gras wankt drüber hin" of the original, the well-worn and overly explicit phrase: ". . . and the wind stirs the grass above them [the ruins]." Zhukovski conventionalizes the spontaneously natural behavior and the speech of Goethe's "young woman," changing, for instance, her "Du Schelm!" "you rogue!", with which she addresses the baby in her arms, to the saccharine "Oh, my beloved one!" The passages in which Goethe's "storm and stress" spirit bursts forth in all its vigor leave Zhukovski rather helpless. Thus, the lines, "Glühend webst du / über deinem Grabe, / Genius!" Zhukovski renders with a phrase dangerously close to a cliché: "Undying, you soar above your grave."

And yet, all these examples of deviation, and such few as could be added, leave the basic excellence of this translation unimpaired, in fact, they serve to heighten our awareness of the immense difficulties overcome by the Russian translator in bringing to his audience one of Goethe's greatest poems.

As has already been pointed out, Zhukovski failed to produce anything of importance after his personal acquaintance with the German poet in the twenties. The translations of the six-line poem, "Ländliches Glück," under the title, "Vows," and of excerpts from the "Maximen" and from *Tasso*[56] cannot be said to have contributed anything new to Zhukovski's view of Goethe. Finally, his rendering of Goethe's verse fable, "Adler und Taube,"[57] which appeared after a long pause in 1833, clearly indicates that in this translation of the German poet Zhukovski moved farther away from rather than closer to the center of the Goethean world. From out of the abundance of poetic treasures that Goethe had spread before him in his completed life's work, Zhukovski saw fit to choose this relatively minor item. He was probably attracted to it by its apparent message and general mood, its idyllic setting with its cooing doves, the pathos of the wounded eagle, and, especially, its preachment—as Zhukovski understood it—of "contentment as the only form of true happiness," all of which the Russian poet must have found thoroughly congenial. Unable or unwilling to recognize the ironic accents of the original, he seems to have accepted at face value the message of bliss in dovelike contentment, this being consonant with the Christian gospel of humility of which by now he had become a dedicated apostle. It was, as we remember, in this spirit of the devout pietist that Zhukovski wrote his last Goethe item, the two essays on *Faust* (1848) in which he sought to prove Goethe's orthodox Christianity.

We have come to the end of our exposition of Zhukovski's

life and work insofar as it touched upon and dealt with the German poet. From the detailed materials before us it is not difficult to deduce, in summary fashion, Zhukovski's view of Goethe.

It was, undeniably, a one-sided, highly subjective appreciation that emphasized those elements in Goethe's personality and work which were kindred to Zhukovski's own and eschewed or else distorted those facets which the Russian poet felt uncongenial to his temperament, interests and predilections. Thus Goethe the scientist received no attention whatever, nor were the impressive efforts of the man of state affairs in the Duchy of Weimar so much as mentioned. Goethe the dramatist and writer of imperishable prose failed to enlist the efforts of Zhukovski the translator or interpreter. It was Goethe the lyricist who attracted Zhukovski's admiration and recreative energies, and here again it was not the poet in all his many-sidedness but exclusively the creator of the popular Romantic ballad and of the sentimental and elegiac verse. The emotional force and uncompromising realism of the youthful Goethe in the period of "storm and stress," the Classical "coldness" of the mature poet were consistently passed over.

In his translations, Zhukovski did not hesitate to subject the original to considerable stylization, even when he strove to produce a faithful rendering, and was not satisfied with a mere "imitation." In his effort to bring Goethe close to his Russian readers, he freely expanded and elaborated in order to gain a greater explicitness of statement and a more obvious and conventional imagery. Zhukovski liked to prettify, relished the amassing of colorful or sentimental detail for its own sake, and showed no great understanding for conciseness of expression and consistent unity of style. He tended to soften the most radical stylistic innovations in Goethe's language, to substitute for Goethe's concrete, earthy imagery one that was far more airy, vaguely emotional or fanciful. Goethe's active, forward-looking spirit he often deliberately changed into the passive attitude of reverie and retrospection. Consistently he shied away from or toned down Goethe's progressive, unorthodox thoughts and strove in every way to keep his benevolent father image of Goethe as the "kindly grand old man," the "dobryi, veliki chelovek," unsullied by contact with the strife and turmoil of the terrestrial sphere.

It cannot be denied: Zhukovski placed before his Russian audience an image of Goethe, reflected and refracted in the medium of his own predominantly sentimental, Romantic, mystical nature, his own elegiac, nostalgically retrospective mood and, in the end, devoutly pietistic faith.[58] Much had to be added to Zhukovski's portrait, much had to be revised and rectified, before Goethe's true self became visible to the Russian public. Nevertheless, a notable beginning had been made by Zhukovski in opening up to his compatriots a rich and novel world of poetry. His place in Russian literary history as the greatest of the early champions, interpreters, and translators of Goethe is secure.

CHAPTER THREE

A. S. Pushkin and M. Y. Lermontov

One might justifiably assume that Russia's greatest lyricists would have fallen under the spell of the greatest German poet, whose fame was spreading among the Russian intelligentsia at the time Pushkin appeared on the literary scene and had reached its height when Lermontov was establishing himself as Pushkin's un-challenged successor upon that poet's tragic death. We do, in fact, find numerous and often significant instances of influence by Goethe on the content as well as the form of the work of both Russian poets. Pushkin is much more articulate in his characterization and evaluation of Goethe, if only because his autobiographical materials are so much richer, his essayistic efforts more numerous than Lermontov's, from whom we have only some fifty letters and an insignificant number of diary jottings.[1] Neither poet contributed significantly as a translator of Goethe. The only noteworthy effort we have is a free rendering by Lermontov of Goethe's "Wanderers Nachtlied: Ein Gleiches."[2] Pushkin's *Scene from Faust* cannot be properly considered a translation.[3] Nevertheless, there is ample evidence that both poets knew Goethe's work, admired it, and adopted certain of its motifs and figures for their own use, each in his characteristic manner.

1. Aleksander S. Pushkin (1799–1837)

The problem of Pushkin's approach to Goethe, and the degree and nature of his dependence on his work for themes and inspiration, has been and continues to be debated by Russian literary scholars, and has not been altogether neglected by scholars in the West.[4] Non-Russian contributors, however, tend to slight the rich biographical materials which Russian research on Pushkin has made available and do not pay sufficient attention to the general cultural background against which Pushkin's attitude toward the German poet must be viewed for proper perspective.

As a boy and impressionable youth, Pushkin moved in a cultural environment that was, by and large, indifferent if not actually hostile to German art and letters and, in particular, to literary products from the pens of the "storm and stress" authors which were just then beginning to reach the Russian public. A vivid picture of this prevailing attitude in the circles in which Pushkin's family played a prominent role is provided in the memoirs of Figel, that rich source of cultural and biographical information which we have had occasion to draw upon.[5] Figel was an ardent Germanophile among a predominantly pro-French St. Petersburg society. He was a member of the Arzamas, a literary group with pro-German leanings. He was also an energetic supporter of the German Theater in the Russian capital and a voracious reader of German literature, especially of his favorite, Schiller, earning for himself among his fellow Arzamasians the nickname, "Crane of Ibicus."

We will recall, how severely critical Figel was of his contemporaries in their ignorance of and indifference to the recent flowering of German literature, especially the drama, how he took them to task for failing to avail themselves of the rich offerings provided by the German Theater of St. Petersburg. He accused his fellow citizens of cowardly subservience to ruling taste: "Who would have dared," he asks, "in 'good society' to step forward as the champion of German literature, of the German drama? Not one! Who would have cared to acquaint himself with the works of Lessing, Schiller, Goethe?" His special ire was aroused by the German immigrants who had adopted with such dispatch and emphasis the pro-French tastes of their host country: "Why, those young Germans, they—one and all—the Palens, the Benckendorffs, the Schöppings, these darlings of Russian high society, they all suddenly developed sympathies and tastes more strongly pro-French than our own." Yet, the native Russians were hardly less emphatic in their espousal of the French models and in their repudiation of those German literary products of "a barbaric taste." Among these

Russian critics, one of the most prominent and vehement was young Pushkin's father. Continuing his account, Figel assures us that he will "never, in all my life, forget Sergei Pushkin, Aleksander Pushkin's venerable sire, the great Count Pushkin, as he rose to announce categorically his unshakable determination to continue to prefer Molière to Goethe, and Racine to Schiller, unafraid of the wrath of those newfangled Romanticists and into the teeth of Schlegel [A. W.?]."[6]

Such was the prevailing literary taste that surrounded Pushkin at home and in the social circles in which he moved as an impressionable boy. An outstanding Pushkin expert, Arthur Luther, categorically states: "Only French was spoken in Pushkin's family. Small wonder that the first poetic efforts of the eight-year-old Pushkin were written in that language."[7] Such German fragments as are scattered through Pushkin's writings tend to confirm the generally held theory that Pushkin never mastered that language. It is revealing of Pushkin's insecure hold on it to compare the stilted German phrases of Rosen, a German in Pushkin's *Boris Godunov,* with the idiomatic French spoken by Marzheret in the same scene of that play.[8] Pushkin's efforts at translation from German originals furnish no definite clue to his mastery of the language. His translation of "Werther's letter to Lotte," a standard piece of Russian Wertheriana, is so free that it could well have been based on a French or Russian model which were then available. His collaboration with E. I. Huber on a translation of *Faust* again fails to furnish positive proof of a thorough knowledge of German, since the extant marginal notes affixed by Pushkin to Huber's translation deal exclusively with a more idiomatic rephrasing of the Russian text furnished by the translator.[9]

Thus, it would seem sound to assume that the German originals of Goethe remained largely *terra incognita* for Pushkin. The records of his library contain none of Goethe's works in German, and indicate that his reading of Goethe must have been largely, if not exclusively, in the few Russian translations then available and in the more numerous French versions. Information on Goethe's personality and life and on the enormous range of his interests and achievements Pushkin seems to have derived from sources popular at the time, Mme de Staël's world-famous *De l'Allemagne* and Russian periodicals which echoed French opinions on German life and letters.[10]

Not until 1825, when Pushkin came under the influence of the Russian Romanticists, those ardent Goethe enthusiasts,[11] did his attitude toward the German poet take on discernible form. Even then it remained singularly ambivalent. Pushkin found words of praise for the "German patriarch," that "giant of Romantic poetry," yet he refused to follow Zhukovski, Dmitri Venevitinov, Stepan P. Shevyrëv and others of his friends in a thorough study of Goethe's works; he would not plunge with them into "that vast German ocean."[12] On the other hand, it cannot be said that Pushkin remained altogether indifferent toward the efforts of the Romanticists to bring to the Russian public a deeper understanding of the works of the German author. Thus we find him joining the group in the jubilations occasioned by Goethe's high praise of Shevyrëv's perceptive study of the "Helena" scene from *Faust,* Part II, published in the *Moscow Messenger*.[13] "Honor and fame to our Shevyrëv!" Pushkin writes to M. P. Pogodin, the editor of the journal, "You did well in publishing the letter of our patriarch in Germany." [14] Having voiced his enthusiastic approval, Pushkin fell silent on Goethe in the pages of the *Messenger,* even though he continued to be an active contributor to the journal. Nor did he join his Russian compatriots in the all-but-obligatory pilgrimage to Weimar. The foremost Russian poet never made the personal acquaintance of the greatest German.[15]

Against this biographical background, which is so clearly lacking in first-hand contacts with German culture, it is rather surprising to find as many references to Goethe as we have actually been able to locate in the now-available Pushkin materials.[16] Though these references fail to indicate an extensive or intensive knowledge of the poet's work, they do present clear evidence of Pushkin's gradually increasing interest and admiration. The comments grow in frequency and perceptiveness after the year 1826, and center chiefly on *Faust* and *Götz von Berlichingen.* They tend to disprove

J. Matl's claim that "around 1828 there began an estrangement and liberation [of Pushkin] from the Goethean-Faustian ideal."[17]

Pushkin approached Goethe's *Faust,* significantly, by way of a comparison with Byron's *Manfred* and *Childe Harold.* His youthful enthusiasm for Byron was tempered by his contact with Goethe's genius—which raises the intriguing question of what Pushkin's attitude might have become, had not his untimely death cut short this trend in his reorientation. In an article on P. A. Katenin, he compared Byron's imitation of Goethe's *Faust* with Zhukovski's imitation of Bürger's *Lenore* and concluded that both imitators "devitalized the spirit and the form of the originals."[18] And again, in his *Notes from the Years 1834–35,* Pushkin emphasized Byron's inability to cope with Goethe's genius: "Goethe had a great influence on Byron," he wrote. "*Faust* continued to trouble the imagination of Childe Harold. Twice Byron wrestled with this titan of Romantic literature—and both times came away lame like Jacob."[19]

Pushkin "stands in awe before Goethe's masterpiece, his *Faust.*"[20] To him this work is "the mightiest creation of the eighteenth century [!]." "It serves as a beacon for modern times precisely as the *Iliad* towers eternally as the most splendid monument of antiquity."[21] In creating this monumental work, Goethe was inspired by "the highest form of audacity of inventiveness, of creativity; here a truly bold, creative spirit has encompassed a vast design and brought it to fruition." "Such audacity," Pushkin exclaimed, "is Shakespeare's, is Dante's, is Goethe's in his *Faust* and Molière's in his *Tartuffe.*"[22] He even dared to compare Goethe with the Holy Ghost to the distinct advantage of the poet. He admits that, as he reads the venerable Book of Books, the Holy Ghost is, at times, after his own heart, but—and we can sense the consternation of the faithful—"I really do prefer in general my Goethe and my Shakespeare,"[23] an apostasy which is known to have contributed not a little to Pushkin's exile from St. Petersburg to his mother's estate, Michailovskoe.

Goethe's *Götz* receives somewhat briefer and less enthusiastic mention, mainly in connection with Pushkin's discussion of the nature of historical drama and, of course, specifically of his own *Boris Godunov*. *Götz von Berlichingen,* and by implication Goethe's *Egmont,* earn for the German poet the singular honor of being coupled with Shakespeare as the "creator of the historical drama."[24] In a letter to his friend, N. Raevski, Pushkin credits Shakespeare with having seized upon the passions of historical figures, while Goethe excelled in recapturing the general atmosphere, the "costume" of bygone epochs: "Shakespeare a saisi les passions, Goethe le costume."[25]

It is as the great realist, the "objective" genius, that Goethe gradually displaced Byron as an inspiration and guide for Pushkin. With growing maturity Pushkin came to appreciate ever more fully Goethe's all-encompassing view of life, to admire his sharp eye for the "details of reality." He praised Goethe's bold break with "servile predilection for kings and nobles," typical of French pseudo-Classical drama, and his introduction of lowly and humble lives on a level with the heroic and grand. "Schiller, Goethe and Walter Scott do not share [with the French school] that servile predilection for kings and nobles. They [i.e., the characters of these three writers] do not resemble the serfs aping la dignité et la noblesse," and, continuing in French, Pushkin added: "Ils [the writers] sont familièrs [*sic*] dans les circonstances ordinaires de la vie, leur parole n'a rien d'affecté, de théâtre même dans les circonstances sollennelles—car les grandes circonstances leur son familièrs."[26]

These biographical links between Pushkin and Goethe have sent scholars in search of Goethean themes in Pushkin's works. But most instances of "borrowing" they track down prove, upon close scrutiny, far-fetched and insufficiently incisive to shed much light on our central problem, Pushkin's view of Goethe. To choose but two:

How substantial is Berkov's claim[27] that Tatiana's rejection of Onegin[28] is patterned after Lotte's rejection of Werther? To be sure, there is a brief and distant echo in Tatiana's words to Onegin of Lotte's to Werther[29] yet such superficial similarity as may be detected only underscores the totally different situation in which they are spoken. Tatiana had loved Onegin and her love had been

rejected coldly, almost cynically, by the "lover"; she had then married another man and now rejects Onegin in turn, not without a
wistful glance at a happiness that had been "so possible, so near!",
and now is lost forever. "My fate is sealed," she says to the
stunned, unbelieving Onegin, who had been so supremely confident
of victory over Tatiana's tender heart. The distance between this
scene and that in Goethe's *Werther* is obvious. Granted that there
is similarity in the words spoken by Tatiana and by Lotte, granted,
too, that among Tatiana's favorite heroes we find Werther "the
rebellious martyr," granted finally that Lenski's soul is all aflame
with the "poetic fire" of Schiller and of Goethe, these scattered
references prove only Pushkin's undoubted acquaintance with the
German poet's famous work. But they do not shed any light on the
nature of Goethe's influence on the Russian poet and even less on
Pushkin's "view" of Goethe.

Or again, how tenable is Bem's claim that Hermann, the hero
of *Queen of Spades* is the "first Russian Faust" and that "Lisaveta's
love affair is the Russian staging of Gretchen's tragedy"?[30] Tomski,
Hermann's boon companion, does ascribe to Hermann "the profile of Napoleon and the soul of Mephisto"[31] and Lisaveta is struck
by Hermann's likeness to a "portrait of Napoleon"[32] that is, of the
man in whom Goethe recognized the very personification of the
demonic. Does this make of Hermann the "first Russian Faust?"
Are we to see in this demonic trait a link with Goethe's hero? How
can Hermann's obsessive greed for money be justifiably identified or even compared with Fausts's heaven-storming quest for the
ultimate encompassed in that "supreme moment," the "höchste
Augenblick"? Though in the grip of a "demonic" obsession with
the acquisition of wealth, Hermann's nature is that of a calculating, penny-pinching German "Bürger," not to say *"Spießbürger"*
(Babbitt), whose three cardinal virtues and most "reliable cards"
are "calculation, moderation, and assiduity." Are we not dealing
here rather with a parody of Goethe's hero—if a relationship between the two has to be established? Consider also Hermann's
"love" for Lizaveta, that pitifully harassed and humiliated lady-
in-waiting to a splenetic old countess. This affair has not a touch

of kinship with Faust's tragic love for Gretchen. To Hermann, Lizaveta is merely a means to acquire the fortune of the old dowager. Far from being Goethe's "übersinnlicher, sinnlicher Freier," that "sublimely sensuous suitor," Hermann is a coldly calculating, conscienceless intriguer. And Lizaveta, though thrilled in her lonely, loveless life by the sudden attentions of the mysterious youth, is quickly disenchanted and, far from suffering a tragic end, promptly forgets the impostor to enter upon a bourgeois marriage and, by obvious implication, to live happily ever after—a lot far removed from Gretchen's derangement and violent death. Again, this is, if anything, a parody of Goethe's immortal creation.

One could claim with far greater justification a parallel in Goethe's dungeon scene from *Faust,* Part I, and the closing scene of Pushkin's epic poem *Poltava.* Here Mazepa, having abducted Maria, the daughter of Kochubei, his one-time friend, and having treacherously caused Kochubei's execution, is fleeing the wrath of Peter the Great. Not far from Kochubei's homestead, Mazepa, utterly exhausted, is sinking into troubled sleep when he is suddenly startled awake by the voice of Maria. The shock of her father's violent death and of Mazepa's treachery have deranged the girl's mind. Like Gretchen, she is reeling helplessly between past and present; she pleads with her lover to flee with her, and then recognizing in him her father's bloodstained murderer, recoils in horror before his "derisive and terrifying gaze,"[33] his "blood-encrusted beard." Here, indeed, we find more than a semblance of Goethe's famous scene, hear the clear echo of Gretchen's distraught voice. And yet, even this case, like so many others, is probably no more than a case of fortuitous parallelism and coincidence.[34]

Investigations of this type are unlikely to result in an incisive grasp of Pushkin's relationship to Goethe. A different approach is called for and is happily suggested by Pushkin himself. In a momentous passage of his diary he confides a central experience in his life, a true *Urerlebnis:* "In the best years of our life, when we are not yet chilled by life's contradictions, our heart is receptive to the beautiful. It is credulous, tender. Gradually the eternal contradictions of existence give birth to doubts, a tormenting experience yet one of short duration. Soon the mood passes, but not before it has corroded the very best and most creative stirrings in our soul."[35] This autobiographical passage, read in the context of Pushkin's life and work, reveals itself as an effective "key" to the Russian poet's approach to Goethe's work. It explains why, upon contact with Goethe's *Faust*, Pushkin could at once recognize in the figure of Mephisto the very incarnation of his *Urerlebnis,* of those "eternal contradictions of existence" of which the passage speaks, of those "contradictions which corrode the very best and most creative stirrings in our soul." Small wonder that our poet seized upon this figure as a fertile source of inspiration. We have shown the Mephistophelean trait woven into the character of Hermann; the "corrosive" spirit of Mephisto is also easily recognizable in Onegin. But it is in Pushkin's poem, "The Demon," that Mephisto makes his most striking reappearance. Pushkin states explicitly that in this poem he sought to give artistic expression to his profound, personal experience of "the life-killing skepticism . . . which corrodes the very best and most creative stirrings in our soul . . . and is the evil demon of our age." Do we note the parallel phrasing in this and the autobiographical passage quoted above? Moreover, paraphrasing Goethe, Pushkin supplies convincing evidence of a significant thematic interplay between his Demon and Goethe's "Geist, der stets verneint." "For the very best of reasons," he writes, "did the great Goethe call the *spirit of negation* the eternal enemy of mankind." And Pushkin continues with the rhetorical question: "Did not Pushkin (*sic*) seek to personify in his 'Demon' that very spirit of negation and of doubt and to render a vivid representation of his destructive influence upon the spiritual climate of our age?"[36]

Here then, we are justified, by the poet's own testimony, to claim significant influence by Goethe on Pushkin. Here we have indeed a clear case of "borrowing," illustrative of Pushkin's manner of appropriating from Goethe's work elements which would assist him in bodying forth certain central experiences, in realizing his poetic visions.

This type of creative borrowing is exemplified on an ampler scale and in a more complex manner in Pushkin's *Scene from Faust,* which he wrote while in close contact with the Romanticists.[37] Venevitinov had just translated part of the "Wald und Höhle" scene. The fragment undoubtedly impressed Pushkin and may well have inspired him to compose his *Scene.* There is, in fact, a certain resemblance in the plot. Closely following Goethe's model, Pushkin has his Mephisto and his Faust discuss Gretchen's fate. Like Goethe's Faust, Pushkin's reminisces on the raptures of love, only to be answered with cynical sarcasm by Mephisto. However, here the parallel ends. Pushkin's locale, the seashore, sharply differs from Goethe's "Wald und Höhle." Far more significant than this difference in setting is the contrast in the "inner" situation in which Pushkin's Faust finds himself. His Faust has already wrought the ruin of Gretchen;[38] he is looking back to a happiness forever lost and forward to a life of utter boredom, devoid of all hope and ideals.[39] For in the soul of Pushkin's Faust the "spirit of negation and of doubt" has totally "corroded" the "best and most creative stirrings," has ended all idealistic striving. In the sharpest possible contrast to Goethe's hero, Pushkin's lacks completely the questing spirit, that capacity of self-rejuvenation in mystic contact with nature's revitalizing forces possessed to such a remarkable degree by his German prototype. Undeniably this Russian Faust is far more Mephisto's *Doppelgänger* than his idealistic antagonist. He is the victim of an all-pervasive boredom, a mood which finds its drastic expression in the very first words of the *Scene*: "Devil, I am bored."[40]

It is the development of this trait in Faust that represents Pushkin's most original achievement.[41] It may be argued that Goethe's Faust is also "ennuyiert" and that Pushkin's merely apes his model. Yet Goethe's Faust is bored only with those shallow pleasures which Mephisto serves up to him. The boredom of Pushkin's Faust is all-encompassing. It springs from utter satiety and a hyperintellectualism that sicklies over every emotion and nips in the bud every stirring to creative action. This boredom seems to emanate from that hellish sphere of which Mephisto is the ruler and to enslave this Faust beyond redemption.

In focusing so sharply on this facet of the complex nature of Goethe's hero and developing it in depth to the exclusion of all others, Pushkin was surely influenced to some extent by Mme. de Staël's interpretation of Faust in her *De l'Allemagne;*[42] moreover, Pushkin may still have felt the influence of the Byronic spleen which held such fascination for him. The primary, determining impulse for his Faust portrayal must, nonetheless, be sought in deeper layers of his nature, rooted in that personal experience of his own best self being attacked by the spirit of negation, sinking into boredom and destructive nihilism. With this portrayal Pushkin places his Faust at the head of a long line of typically Russian heroes—his own Onegin, Lermontov's Pechorin, Turgeniev's Rudin, Goncharov's Oblomov, all those "superfluous people" whose incurable malaise is that very boredom, that ennui experienced so poignantly by Pushkin's Faust.

And more, by giving artistic expression to "boredom as a metaphysical problem,"[43] Pushkin anticipates by several decades a line of thought that leads by way of Kierkegaard and Schopenhauer to Heidegger and Sartre's *La Nausée.* Heidegger in his *Was ist Metaphysik?* has given us a very apt definition of Faust's boredom: "The profound boredom in the depths of being, moving hither and thither like a hovering mist, fuses all objects and persons, including oneself, into a strange indifference."[44] Romano Guardini, in his profound study, *Vom Sinne der Schwermut,* uncovers the deep-rooted causes of this state of boredom, of this ennui. He speaks of:

> a certain type of boredom, such as is experienced by particular individuals. . . . This boredom arises from a search in objects for something they do not possess. This search is characterized by a painful sensitivity and the inability to accept that which one could call, in the most positive sense, the bourgeois attitude ["das Bürgerliche"], namely, the willingness to compromise with the possible and to appreciate comfort ["Behagen"]. Rather, such a sensibility strives to lay hold of things in the form and shape it expects them to be; it seeks to find in them that yearned-for import ["Gewicht"] that earnestness, that glow of passion, that power of fulfillment—only to be frustrated. And this defect in

life's essence means disenchantment for the heart which yearns
for the unconditional ["Unbedingtheit"]. This disenchantment spreads and turns into a sensation of emptiness. . . .
Now nothing exists that is worthy of existence. And nothing
is of sufficient importance to merit attention.[45]

In Pushkin's Faust this profound disillusionment with things
terrestrial and finite, this "strange indifference" and "sensation of
emptiness" which are so characteristic of him at the beginning of
the *Scene,* becomes sharpened toward its end into a hate-charged
disgust with life that culminates in the abrupt command to Mephisto
to sink a ship with its grotesque cargo of three hundred scoun-
drels, two monkeys, barrels of gold and chocolate, and venereal
disease. "Drown all of it!"[46] are Faust's last words, resembling
the command of Goethe's Faust to Mephisto and his minions to do
away with Baucis and Philemon: "So geht und schafft sie mir
zur Seite!"[47] There is a profound difference, however, in the motivation for these two ruthless commands. Goethe's Faust orders
the "removal" of the pair, being stirred by a complex set of drives,
at once destructive and dynamically constructive: He seeks to free
himself once and for all of that small warning voice of conscience
sounding from on high as the bell from Baucis' chapel on the hill;
he is obsessed with the desire to round out his power and possessions
into an all-embracing dominion; he is determined to remove the last
obstacle—be it symbolic rather than material—balking his plans of
"colonization," conceived in a constructive spirit of idealism and
pushed foreward with unflagging energy to his dying moment. In
sharp contrast, Pushkin's Faust utters his command in a mood of
total *Lebensekel,* of utter disgust with life that has been recognized for what it is, a "ship of fools," with a motley crew, devoid
of reason, perverted, debauched, ripe for its destruction—clearly a
crucial difference in motivation, characteristic of Pushkin's basic
transformation of Goethe's prototype.

Pushkin's Faust, his Demon, his Hermann and Onegin all bear
witness to the Russian poet's creative use of archetypes furnished
him by Goethe. Yet, such was the many-sidedness of Pushkin's
genius that, while writing his *Scene from Faust,* he was also able

to complete his historical drama, *Boris Godunov* (1825), for which an entirely different Goethe furnished the model and the inspiration—Goethe the realist of "storm and stress," the masterly recreator of the atmosphere and the "costume" of past ages.

It will never be possible to establish with complete precision the nature and extent of Goethe's influence on this play, since, in writing it, Pushkin reached beyond Goethe to a common source: Shakespeare.[48] Thus almost every Goethean aspect of the play has, at the same time, an unmistakable Shakespearean quality about it. Shakespeare certainly influenced the sombre monumentality of Godunov and furnished the pattern for dying Godunov's last counsel to his son Fiodor.[49] The blank verse of the play also suggests the English model. And yet, despite its being cast in verse, the dialog of the common people in Pushkin's drama[50] has a completely unstylized, naturalistic quality characteristic not so much of Shakespeare as of Goethe's *Götz*.

The extreme brevity of the great majority of the scenes, with their rapid, drastic shifts in locale and theme, also point to Goethe's play as a model—the Russian author carried the implications of the loose, typically "storm and stress" construction to a logical conclusion by dropping all division into acts. Another striking correspondence in dramatic device can be noted in the scene of "The Castle of the Voivod Mnishek in Sambor." In this scene a sequence of pairs of *personae* move across the stage, speak a few salient words, and are quickly replaced by the next pair, a device strongly reminiscent of the garden scene of *Faust*, Part I, with its alternating pairs: Mephisto and Marthe, Faust and Gretchen. To be sure all these features of Pushkin's play: realistic dialog, rapid shift of scenes, quick alternation of pairs of *dramatis personae,* as well as other more general dramatic devices, can also be found in Shakespeare.

All these specific instances corroborate the general impression that Pushkin, in writing his historical drama, kept to a middle course between his English and German models, drawing inspiration from both Shakespeare and Goethe for the new type of historical drama which he himself, characteristically, called "Romantic."[51]

In a recapitulation of our findings on Pushkin's attitude toward Goethe it should be recalled that his approach to the German poet was blocked, at the outset, by formidable obstacles, by the Germanophobic atmosphere in his family and in the social circles in which he moved as a young man, by his evident preference for French culture and literature rather than the German, by his lack of a thorough knowledge of the German language. Even after Pushkin had come under the influence of the Russian Romanticists, those ardent Goethe worshipers, his acquaintance with Goethe remained limited to a few of his masterpieces by way of French and Russian translations and to some accounts of his life and work, primarily that by Mme de Staël in her famous but by no means unbiased *De l'Allemagne*. The barrier of language continued to cut him off from Goethe's lyrics, nor did Pushkin ever develop an interest in Goethe's work as a natural scientist. Glebov makes an important point in his comparative study of the two authors when he stresses the fact that, while for Goethe human life appeared rooted in and was an integral part of the life of nature, for Pushkin it was mainly an historical phenomenon. "And if for both poets, generally speaking, the central concern was with the fullness of life here and now, their basic attitudes toward life were diametrically opposite. . . . Pushkin shows no interest whatsoever in a scientific exploration of life in the Goethean sense, nor does he make any attempt to develop a philosophy of nature."[52]

Surely, everything seemed to conspire to keep Pushkin at a distance from Goethe's world. All the more noteworthy is the extent to which the German poet did, nonetheless, impress and influence the Russian poet. This influence, to be sure, never equaled that of Byron or Shakespeare or even that of Walter Scott. Nevertheless, it was definitely developing at Pushkin's untimely death. It is interesting to speculate what his attitude toward and evaluation of Goethe might ultimately have become, had his development not been cut short so ruthlessly, so senselessly. Pushkin had recognized the greatness of Goethe's *Werther,* had drawn inspiration from his *Götz* and *Faust.* Especially the figure of Goethe's Mephisto had assumed a central importance for the Russian poet, as we have been able to demonstrate on the basis of autobiographical and textual evidence. In sum, while remaining a distant and but vaguely perceived figure, Goethe did increasingly attract Pushkin's attention, provided a growing measure of inspiration, and gained the Russian poet's respect and admiration.

2. Michael Y. Lermontov (1814–1841)

Essentially the same can be said of Lermontov's attitude toward Goethe as was said of Pushkin. Unfortunately, the claim that Lermontov had bypassed Goethe altogether has become deeply entrenched in Russo-German literary scholarship. Harnack, Strich, Durylin and Zhirmunski, in their studies of Goethe's influence on Russian literature, either make no mention whatever of Lermontov or devote a few paragraphs to him with the customary reference to his "translation" of Goethe's "Über allen Gipfeln ist Ruh." Zhirmunski sums up this prevalent opinion when he writes: "Lermontov bypassed the infatuation with philosophy characteristic of the 'German School' of the thirties. . . . Therefore it is understandable that for the poetic development of Lermontov, Goethe could not have been of great importance. . . . Traces of an acquaintance with Goethe in the works of Lermontov are insignificant."[53]

While it is true that other foreign authors, foremost among them Byron and Schiller,[54] had a greater and, above all, a more obvious influence on Lermontov than did Goethe, the above theory is not borne out by a closer study of the problem. B. Eichenbaum, that eminent Lermontov authority, has effectively pointed to the multiplicity and significance of foreign influences in Lermontov's work. Calling an impressive roll of the models and idols in the Russian poet's tragically brief career, Eichenbaum comes to the conclusion that in Lermontov's work "we are confronted not with just a simple case of influence, but rather with a general indebtedness to the great of foreign literatures for their support and help."[55] There is, in fact, considerable evidence that Goethe too had offered a significant measure of such "support and help" to the Russian poet.

In his appreciation of German literature and of Goethe's works in particular, Lermontov enjoyed a distinct advantage over many another outstanding Russian author, over Pushkin, for instance, by having been raised in a Germanophilic home. His father admired German culture and was particularly impressed with Germany's flowering universities. He was determined to send his gifted son on the obligatory *Bildungsreise* to Germany, but was crossed in this plan by the boy's rich grandmother, Elizaveta Alekseievna, who held the purse strings, and who was just as determined to send the young man off to France. In compromise, Lermontov entered the University of Moscow without a *Bildungsreise,* and never made the personal acquaintance of Germany or its greatest poet.[56]

Lermontov had not yet turned three when his mother died and the boy was placed in the care of a German nurse, Christine Ossipova Römer, who became, in his own words, a second mother to him. Her great passion consisted of "German novels of the sentimental-Romantic kind." She regaled the impressionable youngster in her native German with tales of knights and robbers replete with ravishing maidens, with castles, caves and moonlit clouds, deeply stirring his excitable imagination.[57] Much later, Lermontov was to recall how, as a child, he had "loved to look up at the many-shaped clouds thronging about the moon," which for him would turn into "medieval knights in full armor, torn with jealousy and emotional turmoil, escorting their damsel Armida to her castle."[58] This nurse seems to have also read to the boy the poetry of "the poets of the patriotic war," most likely that of Arndt and Körner, as well as Uhland's verses. She well remembered the stormy days of the French invasion of Germany and would conjure up for the boy the figure of Napoleon in all its diabolical greatness, as seen through German eyes.[59] Thus, Lermontov came into early contact with German literature, was made aware of some of the great historical events that took place on German soil, and grew up with the German language as his second mother tongue.

Later, his wealthy grandmother, eager to give the gifted boy the best possible education, drew to her house as private tutors some of the outstanding members of the faculty of Moscow University, among them A. Zinov'ev, who was quite an expert in English and

German literature. "He skillfully guided his [Lermontov's] interests, recommending the best in European literature—Shakespeare,
Goethe, Schiller."[60]

Thus soundly instructed, Lermontov entered the celebrated
preparatory school, "The Noble Pension of Moscow University"
(Blagorodnyi Pansion Moskovskogo Universiteta), and found German language and literature well represented in its program. "The
history of German literature from the Middle Ages to the present
day, with special emphasis on the *explication de text* of works by
the best German authors, especially Schiller," was among the required subjects.[61] Moreover, this course was being taught in the
senior year by none other than Aleksei Fedorovich Merzliakov,
whom we have met in these pages as an intimate friend of Andrei
Turgeniev and Zhukovski, as collaborator in their pioneering translations of Goethe's *Werther,* and as a member of the Germanophilic "Friendly Literary Society".[62] He had risen over the years
to the eminence of an Ordinarius in Aesthetics and Literature at
Moscow University and was honored and admired by the university
students as well as by those of the Pension, including even the pre-
cociously critical Lermontov. Merzliakov was superbly equipped
by his artistic temperament, thorough training, and long-standing
personal contacts with German literature, to lead the eager students
to the beauties and subtleties of the "German poets, of Lessing,
Klinger, and, quite especially, of Goethe and of Schiller."[63]

Another teacher of the institute who had great influence among
its pupils was S. E. Raich. He introduced them to the newest
literary criticism and current literary periodicals. Thus it is certain
that Lermontov read in the leading journals of the day, among them
the *Moscow Messenger,* the organ of the Russian Romanticists. In
its pages he must have come upon many a translation of Goethe's
poems and prose as well as the famous interpretation by Shevyrëv
of Goethe's "Helena" scene.[64]

There seems to have flourished among the students a veritable cult of Pushkin, Byron, and Schiller, and, to a lesser degree, of
Goethe, too. At the March convocation (1828) of the institute,
a classmate of Lermontov's, P. Vistenhof, delivered a speech in

German on "The History of the German Drama" in which "he presented an evaluation of the works of Lessing, Schiller, and, Goethe."[65] Another student, Nikolai Kolachevski, busily translated Goethe's lyrics and had the signal success of having two of them, "Der Fischer" and "Meeresstille und glückliche Fahrt" (*sic.*) accepted for publication in the leading periodical, *Moscow Telegraph.*[66] Of Lermontov we know that he was reading Goethe at this time both at the Pension and during his vacations on his grandmother's country estate Srednikovo, which had a very fine library, collected by his cultivated and bibliophilic maternal granduncle.[67] Here it was that Lermontov translated from Goethe's *Werther.* Unfortunately, this translation has been lost.

Still, it was not Goethe but Schiller whom young Lermontov was holding in highest esteem, whom he vied with and freely imitated in his youthful dramas, *Menschen und Leidenschaften*—note the German title!—and *A Strange Person.*[68] This predilection can be partly explained by the immense success Schiller's plays enjoyed at the time on the stage of the Moscow Malyi Theater, where the incomparable Mochalov appeared in the roles of Karl Moor and Don Carlos. The students, one and all, were "enthusiastic to the point of rapture." One of them writes, in retrospect, about the Moscow première of the *Robbers:* "To this day I cannot forget the overwhelming acting [of Mochalov] in the scene of Karl Moor's reunion with his old father. When his robber-companions carry the emaciated old man out to him from the dungeon, and Karl, turning to his companions and pointing to the all-but-lifeless figure, intones, *'this is my father'*—at that moment there rose in the dead silence of the theater the irrepressible moan of the whole auditorium. My hair stood on end, my breath was choked off. Never again has an actor made such an impression on me!" Lermontov, under the immediate impression of these performances, writes to his aunt, Maria Akimovna Shan-Girei: "Do you remember, dear Aunt, you used to say that our [Moscow] actors were inferior to those of Petersburg? Too bad you could not see the performance here of the *Robbers.* You would have changed your mind."[69]

Yet there is a far more basic explanation for Lermontov's

preference for Schiller over Goethe. He shared it with a large group of high-spirited, idealistic youths who were impatient with Nicholas I's reactionary regime, eager for reform, prepared to resort to revolution. He and his fellow rebels saw themselves as champions of the star-crossed Decembrists who had so nobly fought for constitutional government in Russia, only to end on the gallows, in prison, or in Siberian exile. A. I. Herzen, a fellow student in the preparatory school, has characterized their mood—with special reference to Lermontov—in his famous reminiscences: "We all of us had been too young to participate in the deeds of the fourteenth of December [in the revolt of the Decembrists on Dec. 14, 1825]. Forced to silence, pressing back the tears, drawn back upon ourselves, we learned to carry our thoughts hidden within us. And what thoughts! These were no longer those of enlightened liberalism, thoughts merely of progress—these were deep doubts and negation, these were thoughts charged with rage and indignation. Lermontov had made these thoughts his own, they were part of him, and thus he could no longer find solace and salvation in lyricism, as Pushkin had still done."[70] And it was this "lyricism" that Lermontov recognized as Goethe's special province. No, it could not satisfy the ardent youth's rebellious spirit. He fervently greeted in Schiller's "storm and stress" dramas the call "in tyrannos," kindred emotions and thoughts, the temperament and language of a born dramatist. They became the chief source of inspiration and support for his daring, youthful attacks on the sham and hypocrisy of contemporary society.

And yet, Goethe, too, influenced the complex nature of this Russian genius. Among his meager autobiographical jottings that have come down to us, we find a revealing reference to Goethe, which dates from this early period in his development as a poet. Lermontov here compares Rousseau's *Nouvelle Héloise* with Goethe's *Werther* and finds the German poet's work superior. "I am reading *Nouvelle Héloise*. I must confess I expected more genius, a profounder knowledge of nature, of truth. It is too cerebral; ideals, yes—but what is in them? They are beautiful, heavenly, still they are at bottom miserable sophisms, clothed in sparkling rhetoric which cannot hide what they are, mere—'ideals.' *Werther* is better; there the human being is more of a human being."[71] Lermontov defines here precisely the importance of Goethe for him as the great creator of "human beings."

But the inimitable tone and imagery of Goethe's lyrics also made a profound impression on the Russian poet, to be echoed, ever so subtly, in his poetry. Often it is but a word or familiar line adroitly chosen from a famous poem by Goethe that makes us aware, with a start, of a "borrowing" by the Russian poet. A good example is the opening verse of Lermontov's poem, "The Turk's Laments," which runs, in a rhythmic German rendering, "Kennst du das wilde Land . . ." instantly calling up in our mind Goethe's "Kennst du das Land . . .," even though Lermontov's poem continues on an independent course in its imagery and mood, characteristically transposing Goethe's nostalgic longing for the Classical south into a sharp attack on the foreign oppressors of the Turks, Goethe's Italian landscape into the "wild" land where man "groans in the chains of slavery".[72]

Or again, it can be a particularly striking image or even a group of images that Lermontov lifts from Goethe's poems to imbed by way of imaginative combination and variation in his own quite independent poetic creations. His epic poem *Mtsyri* (Georgian for "Novice") furnishes a particularly striking example of this "montage" technique. Lermontov is describing his hero's escape from the hated monastery. Mtsyri has lost his way in a boundless forest. Lermontov's verses paint the horrifying night amidst the impenetrable wilderness, when we are suddenly struck by a startlingly familiar line: "And with a million black eyes the darkness of night looked out of the branches of every bush."[73] One is forcefully reminded by these verses of Goethe's inimitable lines in his famous poem "Willkommen und Abschied": "Wo Finsternis aus dem Gesträuche / mit hundert schwarzen Augen sah."[74] Lermontov's lines are but an exaggerated rendering of the German original, changing hyperbolicly Goethe's "hundred black eyes" into a "million."

Our attention having thus been alerted, we soon spot another more extensive "loan" from Goethe. Mtsyri, totally exhausted, falls into delirium. In his feverish fantasies he finds himself "on the moist (vlazhnom: feuchten) bottom of a deep river" and feels "so sweet and lovely there"—"so wohlig auf dem Grund." A school of goldfish plays round about him and the fairest of them all addresses him: "Her silver voice / whispered strange words to me / it sang to me . . ." ("Sie sang zu ihm / Sie sprach zu ihm . . ."). Surely, by now we recognize the "borrowings"; as we continue with the goldfish's "song" we become convinced that we have indeed come upon a most effective and ingenious amalgam, upon an adroit montage of images and motifs from Goethe's ballads "Der Fischer" and his "Erlkönig."

Lermontov had grasped the basic similarity in the situation and action of the two poems: in both a human being is lured by personified elemental forces through enticing blandishment into a strangely alluring yet fatal world, the realm of death. He skillfully adopted this central theme, with its unforgettable images, to his own purpose. In his poem, in the delirium of *his* hero, Goethe's two tempters, the "feuchtes Weib" from "Der Fischer" and Goethe's elf-king coalesce into one personification of the alluring element, the goldfish. Speaking entreatingly with the voice of the King of the Elves, Lermontov's goldfish begs the "dear child," the "dear one"—surely a strange appellation for the grown youth, Mtsyri—to stay with her: "My child, my darling, do stay with me," she entreats in words that are a clear echo of the elf-king's: "Du liebes Kind komm, geh mit mir." She confesses her intense love for him just as rapturously as had the elf-king: "Ich liebe dich, mich reizt deine schöne Gestalt," and seeks to hold him in her "free, cool, and peaceful element" (Goethe's "wohliger Grund" once more) where he would find eternal health and peace, the very element into which Goethe's "feuchtes Weib" entices her half-willing, half-resisting victim: "Ach wüßtest du, wie's Fischlein ist / so wohlig auf dem Grund, / Du stiegst herunter, wie du bist, / Und würdest erst gesund." In words clearly reminiscent of those spoken by the elf-king to the delirious boy, Lermontov's goldfish promises the delirious Mtsyri revivifying joys of song and dance among her beauteous

sisters, the dance, moreover, being specifically the "pliaska kruga-
vaia,"[75] the "Reihn," the "Reigen" of Goethe's ballad: "Meine
Töchter führen den nächtlichen Reihn, / Und wiegen und tanzen
und singen dich ein. . . ." What a striking instance, this, of the
Russian poet's creative "borrowing" from Goethe's poems, down to
specific verbal correspondence which surely could never be the product of mere accident or coincidence.

There are instances of Lermontov's explicit reference to Goethe
as to his source and model. Perhaps the best known is the title
to his translation of Goethe's "Wanderers Nachtlied. Ein Gleiches"[76]
which clearly points to Goethe's work for its source: "Iz Gete"—
"from Goethe." Another such instance is the poem simply entitled,
"Zaveshchanie: Iz Gete"—"Testament: from Goethe".[77] Despite
the explicit reference to Goethe, the source for Lermontov's "Testament" remains enigmatic. There is no poem by Goethe of this
title with an even remotely similar context. It has been ingeniously
but inconclusively traced to Werther's last letter to Lotte where we
do have the same "last will and testament" in a kindred sentimental elegiac mood.[78] The resemblance of Lermontov's verse to
Goethe's prose is, however, so tenuous in the details of plot and
local as to obviate comparison.

Lermontov's variation on Goethe's "Wanderers Nachtlied. Ein
Gleiches,"[79] on the other hand, illustrates most brilliantly his method
of fashioning under Goethe's powerful inspiration a poem quite his
own which yet is strongly reminiscent of Goethe's original—at least
on a first, uncritical reading. Once we focus on the imagery and the
rhythmic patterns, Lermontov's departures from Goethe become
strikingly evident. His metrical pattern is far more regular. The only
freedom that Lermontov permits himself is changing the trochees of
the first four lines to the iambs of the last four. The imagery defin-
ing the locale is changed from Goethe's native Thuringian Forest to
Lermontov's beloved Caucasian mountainscape. The very first lines
effect this transformation:

The mighty mountaintops	Gornye vershiny
Sleep in the dark of night . . .	Spiat vo t'me nochnoi . . .

Our gaze is drawn precipitously upward to the majestic peaks of the

Caucasian giants and thence into the mist-shrouded valley far below. Thus, the impression of height and depth is grandly emphasized; we experience a mighty mountain vista. At the bottom of the valley a road is winding. Not a breath of air raises its dust or stirs the foliage of the trees alongside. Characteristically, in Lermontov's poem the "birds in the forest" are not only "silent" as they are in Goethe's but are altogether absent. Obviously, Lermontov does not hesitate to depart freely in his imagery from the German original. Even such an apparently "faithful translation" as the "mountaintops" proves in reality to be a subtle variation. The Russian "gornye vershiny" makes us aware of the majesty and might of the Caucasian peaks far more forcefully than the German "Gipfel" of the hilltops in Goethe's setting.

Unavoidably, much of Goethe's inimitable onomatopoeia is lost in the Russian rendering. So are some other important elements, the effective rhyme, for instance, of "Gipfeln" with "Wipfeln" or that meaningful reference back to the "du" of the beholder in the "spürest du" emphasized by its poignant consonance with "Ruh". The "kaum einen Hauch" we experience in Lermontov's version by inference only. Perhaps the most significant loss suffered in the Russian translation is that inimitable effect of the "Über" in Goethe's opening line "Über allen Gipfeln ist Ruh." Read with proper stress on the "Über" and "allen," this line conveys a peace that reigns *above all* terrestrial heights. We are transported into a realm beyond time and space and seem to experience that ultimate peace that awaits us all beyond the bounds of our earthly existence. Lermontov's poem does not "transcend" in this manner; its imagery does not direct the gaze into a realm beyond. The awesome peaks stand as the dominant feature, the *non plus ultra* in Lermontov's mountainscape. And yet, within its terrestrial scope, the pervasive mood of Goethe's poem is magically preserved, that pensive, motionless stillness of nature at the moment of evening twilight is exquisitely recaptured. With unsurpassable simplicity and economy of expression the promise of release from life's suffering and turmoil in the peace of death closes Lermontov's lyrical masterpiece with the inevitability of the original. We venture to suggest that it was this promise of release in death, this pervasive mood of evening quiet and repose so longed for by the Russian poet's tortured soul that spoke as a kindred voice to him and inspired him to surmount the barriers of language in a supreme act of empathy, thus to recreate for Russia Goethe's inimitable poem.[80]

Lermontov's friend, P. Strugovchikov, himself a talented translator of Goethe, supplies some revealing biographical evidence of the special affinity Goethe's poem held for the Russian poet. Strugovchikov reports that he had met Lermontov "at the end of November 1840 at the home of their mutual friend," Count Sollogub. "On that occasion Lermontov asked me whether I had ever translated Goethe's 'Wanderers Nachtlied.' I answered him that I had indeed been rather successful in rendering the first half of the poem ("Der du von dem Himmel bist . . ."), but that the graceful euphony and the inimitable rhythm of the second had eluded me. 'I, on the other hand, could translate only the second half of the poem,' replied Lermontov and, in response to my request, at once wrote down his poem, 'Gornye vershiny.' "[81]

Thus, Goethe the lyric poet offered Lermontov, as Eichenbaum has put it, "support and help." And so did Goethe the *creator of lifelike, complex characters,* typical of their times and for all time. The "human" figures in the pages of *Werther* were not the only ones that Lermontov admired, preferring them in their richer "humanity" to the heroes of Rousseau's *Nouvelle Héloïse.* There were other *personae* in Goethe's work that attracted his special attention. The instances are numerous in Lermontov's poetry and prose, some obvious, some elusive though no less significant. When, in a sharply satirical poem,[82] Lermontov has three protagonists, the journalist, the reader, and the writer, face one another in debate on the state and function of contemporary literature, it is not difficult to recognize the Goethean model. It is, of course, the "Vorspiel auf dem Theater," introducing Goethe's *Faust.* Lermontov sharpens Goethe's conciliatory tone to bitter irony and sarcasm. Goethe in his "Vorspiel" identifies to a degree with all three speakers, Lermontov only with the poet, whose espousal of a literature of lofty thoughts and profound realism, whose terrible suffering in an indifferent, derisive world, are all his very own. The message has been changed to fit Lermontov's time and country, and with it the tone and attitude of the figures. And yet, one remains aware of the Goethean prototypes that have inspired the Russian poet.

In another satirical narrative poem, having for its title, fittingly enough, the hero's nickname, *Sashka,* a Mephisto figure appears in comic disguise in keeping with the burlesque tone of the work. His name is Zafir. He is an ebony-black Negro, whose darting, sparkling eyes, flashing grin, and throaty voice "strike fear into one's heart." "He lived with Sashka as his servant-spirit. Like a Mephisto, agile and obedient, he worked in silence, with complete equanimity, good and evil. His only law was his master's every desire."[83] We have here a thumbnail sketch of the exotic servants actually found in Russian high society of the day, wittily stylized into a demonic figure ("worked . . . with complete equanimity, good and evil"), endowed by Lermontov with some traits that may well have been suggested by the "servant-spirit" of Goethe's Faust. Many similar examples of influence could be supplied.[84] There is one striking instance of Lermontov's explicit acknowledgment of his indebtedness to Goethe. In creating the heroine of his prose masterpiece *Taman',* an enigmatic figure intentionally left nameless, more nature-spirit than human being, a "Rusalka," an "Undine," hovering between fable and reality, Lermontov wove into his portrayal certain characteristic traits of Goethe's Mignon. We recognize her before we read the Russian author's slyly ironical, slightly condescending reference to that "most eccentric creation of his [Goethe's] German imagination."[85] The appearance of Lermontov's "Undine" is ushered in by a "strange melody, now slow and sad, now fast and lively." Suddenly she skips past our hero, "humming to herself another tune, snapping her fingers like castanets." "A strange creature!" exclaims Pechorin. Yet, he cannot detect any signs of madness in her face. "On the contrary, her eyes fastened upon me with lively perceptiveness, eyes that seemed to be endowed with some sort of magnetic power; her every glance seemed to expect a question. And yet, as soon as I began to speak, she would run off, smiling craftily. . . . My songstress seemed to be no older than eighteen. The unusual suppleness of her body, the way she would incline her head, her long auburn hair, some kind of golden sheen upon the slightly sun-tanned skin of neck and shoulders, and particularly the flawlessly straight nose—all that bewitched me." In her sidewise glances Pechorin recognizes a wildness and suspiciousness, in her smile something elusive, indefinable. Her behavior was completely unpredictable: "She suddenly leapt up, burst into song and was gone, like a bird flushed from the bushes." Our hero imagines he has "discovered Goethe's Mignon." "Truly," he assures us, "there was much similarity: the same lightning-quick transitions from the most intense restlessness to rigid immobility, the same enigmatic words, the same capers, the same strange songs."

Had Lermontov really "discovered" Mignon and transferred her to his own work? Had he really striven to establish "much similarity," to draw a close likeness of Mignon in his smuggler girl? At most, he adopted and adapted those facets of Mignon's complex personality that could strengthen the lineaments of the enigmatical "serpent-like nature" of his "Rusalka," his "Undine": Mignon's sudden, apparently quite unmotivated changes of mood, the agility and litheness of her movements, the mercurial quality of her temperament. These we do recognize in Lermontov's creation. On the other hand, Mignon's melancholy, her nostalgic longing for the far-off land of her dreams, that peculiar aura of soulful suffering, Mignon's transcendence, these all are lost in a transformation which may be felt most intensely in a juxtaposition of Mignon's famous *Lied* to the song of Lermontov's smuggler girl. The emotional depth and subtle complexity of Goethe's *Lied* yield in Lermontov's song to straightforward mood and imagery in the folk tradition. Lermontov's figure does not long for a world of her dreams but stands at the shore of "the green sea," braced against the storm, and boisterously challenges "the bad sea" not to touch "her little boat," her "two-oared boat." She is supremely confident that her smuggler lover Janko, that "bold daredevil" of a man, will guide his boat safely back to shore.

This "Rusalka," despite such mystery as does admittedly surround her, is a creature far more realistically drawn, more active, willful, earthbound than the ethereal Mignon, that "most eccentric creation of Goethe's German imagination." Once again, as in his rendering of Goethe's "Über allen Gipfeln," the Russian poet proves himself to be a thoroughgoing realist despite his fondness for certain Romantic or, more precisely, Byronic trappings. Examining in detail Lermontov's appropriation of Goethe's figure of Mignon, we recognize in it a case not of sensitive empathy, not of a faithful borrowing, but rather one of adroit, all-but-playful montage with an eye to enhancing the effectiveness of the quite independent, sharply contrasting portrayal of his heroine.

More subtle, and at the same time more pervasive, is the influence on Lermontov of Goethe's figure of Mephisto. We can detect it in his central characters, in the Demon of his greatest epic poem, *The Demon,* and in Pechorin, the hero of his prose masterpiece, *A Hero of Our Time.*

We will recall that Pushkin in his *Demon* has sought to personify Goethe's "Geist, der stets verneint," that Mephistophelean "spirit of negation and of doubt in its corrosive influence upon the spiritual climate of our age."[86] There is no doubt that Lermontov too, in his *Demon,* had this for his purpose. The dependence in theme and imagery of Lermontov's poem on Pushkin's has been demonstrated and is beyond denial. Though Byron's is the predominant, perhaps decisive, influence on Lermontov's "mournful spirit, spirit of banishment," there can be little doubt that Goethe's "Geist des Widerspruchs" stood also as an archetype behind Lermontov's figure. Brodski's authoritative biography of Lermontov specifically lists Goethe's Mephisto as among the foremost influences.[87] Most importantly, the text of the poem itself offers decisive evidence. There is an obvious parallel between the central theme of Goethe's *Faust* and that of Lermontov's poem. In both works the force of evil strives to gain possession of a human soul, in Goethe's it is the agonized and questing soul of Faust, in Lermontov's it is the pristine soul of Tamara, an innocent young girl, a novice in a convent. Both intended victims are ultimately saved by the uplifting power of the "eternally feminine" and of a selfless love, though in the case of Faust it is his eternal striving that is the crucial force in his salvation.

Even more important for our thesis of influence is the pervasive kinship in the characters of Lermontov's Demon and Goethe's Mephistopheles. Lermontov's "fallen angel" banished from paradise, a "restless, depraved, corrupted spirit" harbors in his "cold, loveless and haughty heart" disdain and hatred for man and nature.[88] "Hating all creation he lived without faith in anything,"[89] "everything noble he besmirched / And everything of beauty he despoiled,"[90] "he hated or disdained / All that he saw before him."[91] These traits of nihilistic doubt, cynicism and hatred are typical of Lermontov's Demon; they are quite as typical of Goethe's Mephisto and underscore effectively the fact that, in creating his demonic figure, Lermontov did indeed find "support and help" in Goethe's demonic prototype.

The other central figure in Lermontov's total work, Pechorin, is essentially a "demon"-figure too, transplanted from the realm of myth and Romantic fantasy into a modern social milieu, into "the spiritual climate of our age" as "a hero of our time." He too has had his "fall," his "banishment," conveyed here not in the imagery of a Romantic imagination, but in the soberly analytical language of a searching psychological statement: "I was shy," so runs Pechorin's revealing self-analysis, "and one accused me of deception: I grew secretive. I had a lively feeling for good and evil; nobody caressed me, everybody injured me: I became rancorous. I was gloomy—other children were gay and talkative. I felt superior to them—everyone considered me inferior: I became envious. I was prepared to love the whole world—nobody understood me, and I learned to hate; . . . fearing ridicule I hid my noblest feelings deep in my heart: and there they died."[92] Here, as in Pushkin's description of his profound existential experience, his *Urerlebnis,* "the eternal contradictions of existence . . . had corroded the very best and most creative stirrings" of a soul. Here is the "banishment" from innocence, the "fall from grace" drawn in starkly realistic terms, an idealist turned cynic, destined to share salient character traits with Goethe's archcynic Mephistopheles.

We need not stress or even mention the obvious fact that Lermontov's novel, having for its centerpiece Pechorin's diary jottings, stands in the tradition of the biographical and epistolary novel and has for one of its important immediate models in form Goethe's *Werther,* and that it is moreover removed in style and structure as far as possible from Goethe's lyric-dramatic *Faust.* Yet, let the focus be shifted from the formal aspects of the two works to the figures of their respective heroes and we shall at once perceive how far removed Pechorin is in character from Werther. Werther was all heart, all sensibility and emotion. He "fondled his heart." Pechorin has lost his. He "has become incapable of noble impulses." Werther was weak-willed, Pechorin has emerged from life's crucible as "hard and cold as steel,"[93] with an indomitable will and demonic powers over his fellow men. Werther's misanthropy, his shrinking withdrawal from a sophistic and callous high society into the unspoiled world of children, of simple people (Bauernbursch, verlassenes Mädchen) and of nature, has become sharpened in Pechorin into an aggressive cynicism of diabolical destructiveness that reminds us not at all of "the sweet friend of tender hearts" as a sentimental age was fond of calling Werther, yet very forcible of that "spirit of doubt and of negation" as Pushkin called Goethe's Mephisto.

Lermontov underscored Pechorin's kinship to the "Geist der stets verneint" in many suble ways. Taking great care not to disrupt the realism of his novel by identifying his hero explicitly with the figure of Mephisto, he yet achieved identification by indirect suggestion. One of Pechorin's most intimate companions is Doctor Werner. As Pechorin says of him: "We quickly came to understand each other and could read each other's soul."[94] To this Doctor Werner Lermontov lends quite a few Mephistophelean characteristics, enough to have his young companions dub him "Mephisto." He is "a skeptic and materialist," "has a caustic tongue"; "his small black eyes, always restless, sought to penetrate into your innermost thoughts, . . . his fleshless, bony, vein-marked smallish hands were resplendent in bright yellow gloves.

His coat, tie and waistcoat were always black: The young set dubbed him Mephistopheles."[95] Having this man for his soul-companion, Pechorin, too, is drawn by intimate association into the Mephistophelean sphere.

Lermontov is indeed ingenious in establishing and fortifying the interconnection between his hero and Mephisto as his prototype. He emphasizes Pechorin's similarity to Mephisto by his description of Princess Mary's reaction to him, deliberately phrased in such a way as to remind the initiated reader of Gretchen's reaction to Mephisto.

Mary is struck by Pechorin's "unpleasant, aggressive gaze"[96] and notes his "haughty, insolent glance. He must have an exalted opinion of himself."[97] We recall Gretchen's words: "Sieht er immer so spöttisch drein." Pechorin is "on Mary's black list." She calls him to his face "a dangerous man." She would rather fall victim to a murderer's knife than to his evil tongue. And when Pechorin asks: "Do I look like a murderer?" she bursts out: "You are far worse than that."[98] Like Goethe's Gretchen, Lermontov's Mary recognizes instinctively "the insolence," the "evil tongue and evil eye," the "threat to life itself,"[99] in the diabolical make-up of Pechorin, this next of kin to Goethe's Mephisto.

This kinship of Pechorin to the figure of Mephisto was deliberately emphasized and deepened. Lermontov gave his hero typically Mephistophelean traits: Mephisto's cynicism, his nihilism, his diabolical compulsion of casting an icy chill of sardonic laughter over genuine emotions, over the enthusiasms of friendship and love. "I laugh at everything in this world; especially I laugh at feelings."[100] He delights, Mephisto-like, in goading with contradiction, in wounding with biting irony and bruising sarcasm. "I am born," he confesses of himself, "with a passion for contradiction." "Contradiction is with me an innate passion; my entire life has been an endless chain of sad and frustrating contradictions to heart and reason."[101] Pechorin is indeed the "Geist des Widerspruchs."

Moreover, there are traits in Pechorin that are compounded of Mephistophelean and Faustian elements. Such are Pechorin's ennui, his *Lebensekel*. "I have entered this life," Pechorin writes in his diary, "having lived it through mentally, and was seized with boredom and disgust as one who reads a miserable imitation of a book familiar to him from way back when."[102] "I am like a guest, yawning at a ball, who does not depart merely because his coach has not yet arrived."[103] Pechorin shares this ennui not only with Pushkin's Faust but also with Goethe's Mephisto, who has nothing but hate and derision for the "alte Sauerteig" of life, and would destroy it if he could. Nor is this emotion alien to Goethe's Faust in his depressions. With him, however, the spirit of eternal striving, the drive to action gains, ever and again, the upper hand. And it is here that Lermontov's hero proves closer to the Goethean Faust than to Pushkin's hero in the *Scene from Faust,* who had fallen victim to unrelieved boredom and disgust with life. In Pechorin there is still alive more than a memory of that idealism, that yearning for the lofty, the sublime, that had been his before the "fall." He knows that his life "must have had a purpose," that "his destination must have been a noble one," for even now he felt a "boundless strength in his soul."[104] Yet, in Pechorin, this "strength of soul," the Faustian restlessness, the surge to renewed activity, have lost their purpose and direction, are nipped at their first stirrings by skepticism, by that "spirit of doubt and of negation," his Mephistophelean heritage.

Faust's egocentricity, ameliorated if not overcome by the social impulse of the "colonizer," has become exaggerated in Pechorin and remains altogether unrelieved in him to his dying day. He suffers throughout his life the torments of the egocentric craving for emotional gratification which is totally self-centered and thus doomed to remain forever unfulfilled, precisely because of the victim's inability to surrender in self-forgetfulness to a fellow human being. The anguish that Faust pours out in the lofty verses of self-castigation in the "Wald und Höhle" scene, Pechorin entrusts in the sober prose of self-analysis to his diary: "My love has not brought happiness to anyone, because I made no sacrifice for those I loved; I loved only for self-gratification, only to satisfy that bizarre need of my heart to devour greedily their feelings, their tenderness, their joys and torments, and never could I satisfy my hunger."[105] He was always left "with redoubled hunger and despair." This is an experience very much like that to which Goethe's Faust gives voice in the famous lines:

> So tauml' ich von Begierde zu Genuß
> Und im Genuß verschmacht ich nach Begierde.*

In Pechorin's path lie strewn the ruins of the lives of those who had been drawn to him by his demonic—or is it Faustian?—magnetism, the lives of Bela, Princess Mary, and Vera, all of them sisters in suffering to Gretchen. In despair Faust had exclaimed:

> Und ich, der Gottverhaßte,
>
> . . . .
>
> Sie, ihren Frieden mußt ich untergraben!
> Du, Hölle, mußtest dieses Opfer haben!†

and Pechorin, at a lower emotional pitch but in the same intrapunitive mood, sees himself in the "miserable role of the executioner or traitor." "Is it possible that my only function on earth is to destroy the hopes of others? Ever since I have lived and acted, fate somehow has always put me in charge of the denouement of tragedies, just as if without my presence no one could die or despair! I have always been the indispensable *persona* in the fifth act; inescapably I have been destined to play the miserable role of the executioner or traitor."[106]

Like Faust, Pechorin has in his breast "two souls." He knows: "There are two persons in me. One of them *lives* in the full meaning of that word, the other analyzes and judges his every action."[107] To be sure, the two souls in Faust are those of the sensualist and the idealist, of the "sinnlich, übersinnlicher Freier." The two "persons" in Pechorin are those of the activist and of the skeptic. Yet the striking fact remains that Pechorin and Faust have in common this inner dualism, this pull and tug of antithetical drives, and, what is more, both are painfully conscious, as of a curse, of this loss of unity and harmony within.

It is perhaps this schizoid state of Pechorin's personality that

---

* Thus I reel from craving to enjoyment, and in enjoyment I perish for craving.

† And I, hated by God, I had to destroy her, undermine her peace. You hell, had to have this sacrifice!

makes of him, more than any other character trait, "the hero of our times" of Lermontov's Russia, whose intellectual climate was inextricably compounded of a Mephistophelean cynical analysis of life and of self and a Faustian restlessness and yearning after high ideals, doomed to remain unsatisfied. It was but natural that Lermontov, in creating his hero, would turn for inspiration and motifs to Goethe's masterpiece in which the German poet had embodied that very "spirit of our times" in the archetypal figures of his Mephisto and his Faust.

With our interpretation we hope to have indicated Lermontov's manner of creative borrowing and adaptation and to have dispelled the impression that Lermontov "by-passed Goethe."[108] We have sought to show that, in fact, Lermontov knew Goethe's work, especially his lyrics, *Wilhelm Meister,* and *Faust,* certainly more intimately than did Pushkin. To be sure, like Pushkin, he too, was ignorant of or indifferent to Goethe's scientific work. Goethe remained to Lermontov above all the lyric poet able to create a striking image, a poignant mood, an unforgettable rhythmic pattern. Goethe was to him the master of character delineation, who fashioned lifelike figures in whom mankind could find itself mirrored with its timeless and its timebound aspirations, trials and tribulations.

In his informed and thoughtful study of Lermontov's debt to Schiller, Edmund Kostka has established that "Schiller's influence on Lermontov is . . . ended . . . after the completion of the drama *The Two Brothers,*" when the poet "was ready to move to the novel."[109] Our study indicates that Goethe's influence, on the other hand, while never reaching the high tide that Schiller's did, persisted into the mature period of Lermontov's work on his masterpiece, *The Hero of Our Time.* Thus, it was Goethe rather than Schiller, the idol of his youth, who was to give Lermontov a measure of "support and help" until the very end, until that fateful day when a bullet in a senseless duel cut down the poet in the very prime of his productive life.

CHAPTER FOUR

The Pushkin Pleiade and the Decembrists

1. The Pushkin Pleiade

Most of the friends and associates of Aleksander Pushkin had been reared, just as he had been, in French culture. English and Italian literature was more familiar to them than was German literature. Goethe remained for them the distantly revered "German patriarch" of letters, aloof, unreal. In the writing of such central figures of the group as Peter A. Viazemski (1792–1878), Vladimir Benediktov (1807–73), Nikolai M. Iazykov (1803–46) and Anton A. Delvig (1798–1831) there is little evidence of a real understanding of Goethe as a person and author. To be sure, one comes across references to the "poet-philosopher Goethe." He is addressed as the "poet-seer" who has "encompassed all human knowledge," who "has plumbed the depths of human emotion," has "penetrated into the deepest secrets of nature," and has "transcended the limitations of mere mortals." Yet these phrases fail to ring true; they sound like echoes of the only noteworthy statement on Goethe to come from the Pushkin Pleiade, of Evgeni Baratynski's (1800–44) much-admired and much-quoted poem, "Upon the Death of Goethe."

Peter Viazemski seems to have had almost no knowledge of German literature, being preoccupied with French and Italian writers. Both as a poet and as a critic, he by-passed Goethe; as a translator, the only rendering of a Goethe lyric which he deemed worthy of publication was his "Sizilianisches Lied," to which can be added a free paraphrase of Goethe's eighth "Venezianische Epigramm," "The Gondola, an imitation of Goethe."[1] The only other time Viazemski turned to Goethe's works was to fashion a verbose and awkward rephrasing of the song of Mignon, probably intended as a tongue-in-cheek twitting of the Germanophilic Romanticists. He gave it for its impossible motto the line: "Kennst du das Land, wo blüht Oranienbaum?"[2]

It has been claimed that Anton Delvig had been influenced in his lyrics by Goethe.[3] To his doubtful credit, Delvig made, in fact, a rather sentimentalized rendering of Goethe's "Nähe des Geliebten" and did introduce the first collection of his writings with lines from Goethe's "Der Sänger": "Ich singe wie der Vogel singt." It is an all but obligatory nod by a Russian poet to the German and certainly no proof of Delvig's intimate acquaintance with Goethe's lyrics.[4] In fact, our examination of Delvig's poetry revealed it to be closer in spirit to that of Friedrich Matthisson or, at its best, that of Hölty than to Goethe's. Goethe's forthright realism, his "pagan" spirit, the erotic element of Goethe's "Römische Elegien," are altogether lacking in the "Classical" pastoral poems of Delvig, which, in their less sentimental parts, seem to echo the general spirit and tone of the idylls of Johann Heinrich Voss, which were quite widely known in Russia at the time. Biographical data corroborate Delvig's distance from Goethe. According to Pushkin, Delvig read "Klopstock, Schiller, and Hölty under the inspiring guidance of his friend Wilhelm Küchelbecker."[5] Significantly, Pushkin makes no mention of Goethe.

Nikolai Iazykov, who had lived for some time in Dorpat and there acquired an adequate command of German, was one of the few members of the group who could read Goethe in the original. He held him in high esteem, characterized his *Faust,* Part I, as "shockingly beautiful"[6] and censured his compatriots for lack of a thorough knowledge of the works of such "truly great poets as Shakespeare and Goethe." This lamentable lack, he argued, led the Russian writers all too frequently to measure their own work with "an inadequate yardstick." "We kneel before these giants and yet we think ourselves their equals either because we do not really know *them* or because we fail to know *ourselves* and what constitutes true poetry."[7] If only Iazykov had actually shown how he would have had Goethe supply his fellow writers with the proper yardsticks for self-evaluation and with a proper appreciation of "true poetry"! But extant materials fail to furnish any further clues of Iazykov's views on Goethe as a poet or as a man.

It is indicative of the distance of this group from Goethe that their "laureate," Vladimir Grigorievich Benediktov, seems to have remained in his work completely uninfluenced by the German poet, first cultivating a *precieux* style of labored metaphor and simile, later developing into a smooth versifier, the "idol of all the romantically inclined officials of every rank throughout Russia,"[8] hardly the type of writer to develop a compelling taste for Goethe's poetry or prose.

Among these writers, Evgeni A. Baratynski is the only one who developed a more positive attitude toward German culture and specifically toward Goethe. Though reared in French esthetics and philosophy, much like the other members of the Pushkin Pleiade, he gradually moved to a position rather close to the Russian Romanticists and came to share their view of Goethe as the incomparable sage, the all-embracing genius, the "prophet" and "ideal poet." He recognized in Goethe the unique synthesis of nature and intellect, spontaneity and erudition, of the Romantic and the Classical spirit, which he strove to encompass in his own personality and work. Goethe became to him the very incarnation of his own yearnings and aspirations. With his profound constitutional melancholy, his "sympathy with death" that sought and found lyrical expression—poems on passing and death abound in his work and are among his finest achievements—Baratynski was predestined to step forward as Russia's outstanding panegyrist of Goethe. According to Mirsky, Baratynski's threnody "displays an almost Spinozan power of reasoning."[9] This Russian *In Memoriam* of the German poet is a splendidly rhetorical and withal poignant statement of Baratynski's view of Goethe. It was to live in Russian Goetheana as the definitive poetic statement of the highly influential view of Goethe developed and championed by the Russian Romanticists.

In Baratynski's poem Goethe appears as a well-nigh mythical figure, omniscient, omnipotent, who has encompassed with his genius the whole terrestrial sphere:

Hat alles vollbracht, was im irdischen Kreis
Dem edelsten Mühn ist beschieden.*[10]

Goethe's thoughts have winged afar, knowing no limit save infinity itself:

Es flog sein Gedanke weit und breit
Seine Schranke war die Unendlichkeit.†

In these lines we can detect the echo of Zhukovski's quatrain, "To Goethe's Portrait," (1819) in which he had, in turn, echoed a dedicatory poem by his friend, Andrei Turgeniev sent him as a token of their friendship and mutual admiration for the German poet. Rendered into prose Zhukovski's lines run as follows:

> Having accepted bold freedom as his only law, he [Goethe] soared above the world on wings of all-perceiving thought. He conquered everything on earth and nothing forced subjection upon him.

And Turgeniev's:

> Inspired by the free genius of nature, he [Goethe] set nature forth in fiery lines; subject to no other law, he took for his sole guide his heart's emotions.[11]

Thus, the thematic thread stretches from Baratynski's poem back to one of the earliest statements of the Russian reaction to Goethe's genius.

Baratynski continues his eulogy of Goethe by extolling his lofty spirit, which had been nurtured by the philosophy and art of all the ages. His imagination was able to enter at will the humble hut and the royal palace. His "eagle's eye" had penetrated to the innermost being of man:

Ergründet war und zutiefst durchschaut
Von ihm des Menschen Wesen.‡

Nor could nature hold any secrets from him; his identification with the cosmos was total:

Sein Atem war eins mit dem atmenden All,

---

* Has accomplished all that is granted to the noblest efforts within the terrestrial scope.

† His thought winged its way far and wide, its limit was infinity.

‡ Man's being was sounded in its depths and most profoundly perceived by him.

Er verstand das Gemurmel der Quellen,
Des Laubes Geflüster, des Schauers Schall,
Und hörte die Knospen schwellen.
Er sah in der Bibel der Sterne hell;
Ihm vertraut' ihr Sehnen die Meereswell.*

It is this strophe in which the Romanticists recognized their conception of Goethe as the Romantic poet par-excellence, the seer, the intuitive genius, forever in mystical rapport with the cosmos.

Baratynski closes his poem with a veritable apotheosis of Goethe. The poet

Entschwebt als Lichtgeist zum ewigen Licht
Und das Irdische trübt ihn im Himmel nicht.†

These lines, too, the Romanticists were to adopt as a perfect poetic expression of their view of Goethe as the "divine poet-seer," as the lofty Olympian, unsullied by earthly imperfections.

M. Gorlin, in his study of Goethe's reception in Russia, has the highest possible praise for Baratynski's poem. He considers it to be "probably the most profound and apt statement that has ever been written about Goethe in Russia. . . . The universality of Goethe receives full expression. . . . The humanistic quality of his thought is fully preserved."[12] Together with Tiutchev's famous eulogy, "On Goethe's Death,"[13] Baratynski's poem has remained to this day the best-known, best-loved, and most frequently quoted encomium to Goethe in the Russian language.

2. The Decembrists

A view of Goethe that stands in sharp contrast to the one expressed in Baratynski's eulogy was held by another group of writers closely associated with Pushkin, the Decembrists.[14] With the significant exception of Wilhelm Küchelbecker‡ (1797–1846), the

---

* His breath was one with the breath of the Universe. He understood the murmuring of the spring, the whispering of the foliage, the sound of rain, and he could hear the swelling of buds. He clearly saw [he could read] in the Bible of the stars; the sea wave confided to him its longing.

† He took wing as a spirit of light to the eternal light, and terrestrial [imperfection] does not tarnish him in heaven.

‡ The original German spelling of Küchelbecker's name is used.

outstanding members of this group, K. F. Ryleev (1795–1826), Aleksander I. Odoevski (1802–39)[15] and A. A. Bestuzhev (pseudonym: Marlinski, 1797–1837) were either indifferent or hostile toward Goethe; their admiration was reserved for that passionate champion of downtrodden humanity, Lord Byron.[16] Ryleev, the generally acknowledged leader of the group, seemed to have had no contact with Goethe's work. Odoevski makes no noteworthy mention of him. Bestuzhev is the only one to have made an explicit statement of his view of Goethe.

Bestuzhev's preoccupation with German literature and with Goethe's works falls into the years of his Siberian exile, 1827 to 1829. In a letter from Irkutsk he informs his relatives that he has had time and energy to master the German language and to "immerse himself in Germanism [!]." This immersion, the letter continues, has left him quite unconvinced of the greatness of German Romanticism. He is wary of Goethe's and Schiller's "fièvre de Schwärmerei," though he must admit that the "Schwärmerei" of these two is imbued with a grace at once naïve and captivating.[17] Reading Goethe, especially his *Faust,* Bestuzhev finds to be quite a chore. "Goethe causes me much difficulty," he bitterly complains in a letter to his brothers. "My efforts to get to the bottom of his incomprehensible profundities often tire me. I throw the book aside and send the author to the devil."[18] In this same letter he characterizes the scene in "Auerbachs Keller" as "superfluous." Mephisto's sleight of hand, so his argument runs, is lost on the drunks, is boring to Faust. What sense could it have, lest it be an ineffectual demonstration of the paltriness of all mundane entertainment? Surprisingly, Bestuzhev's negative attitude toward the work leads him nevertheless remarkably close to an acceptable interpretation of the true significance of the scene.

Though obviously beyond his grasp, the work nevertheless continues to challenge him. "Lately, I have taken hold in earnest of Germanism [!], have recently finished *Wallenstein* and now am racking my brains over *Faust*."[19] For consolation and release from the rigors of Goethe's "philosophic, esthetic idealism" he turns to the warm and human, sound and practical Benjamin Franklin: "Of

late I have been consoled by Franklin. What a warm love of mankind! What convincing clarity of explication! Now there is a man
for you!"[20] In the sharpest possible contrast to this praise of Franklin stands Bestuzhev's disapproval of Goethe's "pessimism," his
"total disenchantment with the world" which Bestuzhev finally discovered to his amazement and dismay to be the all-pervasive mood,
the central theme of *Faust*.

It is supreme poetic justice that Bestuzhev, this implacable detractor of Goethe's fame, should have been the one to elicit from
his fellow poet, the great Aleksander S. Griboedov (1795–1829),
one of the most fulsome accolades to Goethe's genius on record in
Russian Goetheana. Moreover, it is Bestuzhev who furnishes us
with the only extant statement on Goethe by this outstanding Russian dramatist. This singular service Bestuzhev rendered by drawing Griboedov into an argument on the comparative greatness of
Shakespeare, Byron, and Goethe, then having the good sense to
record the discussion.[21]

Bestuzhev had claimed "equal greatness" for Byron and
Goethe. Griboedov, accepting "greatness" for both, significantly
continued his argument: "As between the two, preeminence in
greatness must go, in every respect, to Goethe: Goethe, through
the power of his intellect, explains all mankind; Byron—with all
the richness of his thought—illumines for us only the individual."
This is a rare instance of unequivocal elevation of Goethe above
Byron, not excluding the evaluations of the two poets by the Romanticist Goethe worshipers.

Even more startling is Griboedov's comparison of Goethe and
Shakespeare. In radical contrast to accepted valuation, Griboedov
did not see in the English poet the incomparable genius; he would
not even recognize in him the peer of Goethe. Rather, he called
him a mere precursor of the German poet. He admitted that the
"enlightened times" favored Goethe's development but hastened to
stress that he was not speaking of Goethe the *man* but was comparing the *works* of the two writers. "And, surely," he concluded,
"the works of Shakespeare can bear no comparison with those of
Goethe!" With this astounding estimate of Goethe's stature Gri-

boedov stands absolutely alone among the members of the Pushkin
Pleiade and the Decembrists with whom he is usually associated.

It is all the more startling to note the all-but-total absence of
Goethe's influence on Griboedov's work. To be sure, at least one
Russian critic claims *Faust* as an inspiration for Griboedov in his
"philosophical plans" from which was developed his dramatic masterpiece, *Woe from Wit (Gore ot Uma)* but he fails to make a
convincing case.[22] The only concrete evidence of Griboedov's adaptation of Goethe's work to his own purpose is a rather free paraphrase of the "Vorspiel auf dem Theater" which must have had
a special appeal to Griboedov's strong satirical bent. In his treatment of the "Vorspiel", Griboedov lays hold of the Director's lines
beginning with "Bedenkt, ihr habet weiches Holz zu spalten" and
ending with "Zu solchem Zweck die holden Musen," expands
these eighteen lines into twenty-four, changing in the process the
good-natured twitting by Goethe's director of the theater-goers into
a hard-hitting attack on the most vicious elements in Russian society: the caviling, slanderous critic, the scheming, callous prosti-
tute, the crafty cardshark, the lurking police spy—a completely
different crew from the innocuous bores, the pleasure-seeking tipplers
and gluttons, and the vain, flirtatious damsels that people Goethe's
stage. The ironic, patronizing, yet tolerant tone of Goethe's director has turned into the shrill, sharply aggressive voice of Chatski,
the bitterly sarcastic hero of Griboedov's social comedy. The Russian dramatist adapts Goethe's "Vorspiel" to strike a far more
radical note.[23]

But let us return to Bestuzhev. Four years after he had
grappled so unsuccessfully with the unfathomable *Faust,* in 1833,
he was ready to draw up his final balance sheet on Germany and,
with it, on Goethe, in whom he recognized the "focal point of the
German spirit." "Just as his *Faust* stands at the core of Goethe's
genius, just so Goethe himself stands at the center and focal point
of the German spirit."[24] In that position he shares fully in that nation's virtues and achievements as well as in its grave shortcomings.
Among these shortcomings, according to Bestuzhev, the gravest is
the failure to recognize political reality for what it is and take prompt

and effective action. When Napoleon sought to enslave humanity, Russia and England—for different reasons, to be sure—had none-theless taken an unequivocal stand against that archenemy of the rights of men. Only Germany and its representative genius, Goethe, had failed to recognize the enemy and to offer effective resistance. "Soaring high above the mundane world, steeped in speculative subtleties, the ear attuned to the harmonies of the celestial spheres, they failed to hear . . . the enemy even then storming the sacred citadels." And again by force of well-established association, Bestuzhev leveled his criticism against Goethe quite as much as against Germany when he accused that nation of inability to plant its feet squarely upon this earth and strike out energetically along the road of progress toward a nobler future for humanity. "Half-buried in the dust of feudalism, half-soaring in the clouds of abstraction, at once laughably naïve and learned to the point of tears," the German nation continued to vacillate "between the potatoes and the stars." Bestuzhev was quite ready to recognize the lofty achieve-ments of the German spirit and saw them mirrored most resplend-ently in the personality and works of Goethe. Yet, over against these he had to register a central failing that all but cancels them out —the lack of patriotism in both the nation and the poet. "All that the German genius has created for posterity in the realm of the mind and the imagination has found its summation in the genius of Goethe. All that is brilliant in our world is mirrored in his works, everything—except the noble feelings of patriotism!" And he con-tinues with a broad, bold generalization: "It is by this absence of patriotism that he [Goethe] personifies most perfectly the German mind which has extracted the soul from the human being to examine it outside the context of national life, which has disected and iso-lated nature's laws oblivious of their relationship to the human being." Obviously, this judgment of Germany and Goethe is as unjust as it is superficial and utterly distorted. Yet, the fact re-mains that it is typical of Bestuzhev's attitude toward the German poet and, essentially, that of his fellow Decembrists. The reasons for this attitude are not hard to find. These ardent champions of social and political reform, who had been ready to lay down their lives for their ideals and were now paying for them with their liberty, naturally expected to find in their literary great the same devotion to a cause, the same faith in social reform, their own "warm love of mankind," their own ideological pathos. On all these counts they found Goethe signally wanting when viewed from where they stood. Their ethics and esthetics were bound to clash with Goethe's; they could not possibly come to terms with Goethe's views on life and art. One of them, Wilhelm Küchelbecker made a sincere, sustained effort, but in the end he too failed and turned his back on his one-time idol, Goethe.

According to his own and his friends' testimony, "Teuton-Küchel"—as he had been affectionately and significantly nicknamed—had been introduced to German culture and literature by none other than Vasili Zhukovski, that eminent interpreter and translator of Goethe. It had been a signal event in the young man's intellectual development, the full importance of which he was quick to realize. In Zhukovski he recognized at once the revolutionary spirit who was to influence so fundamentally the future course of Russian intellectual life and, specifically, of its literature. In one of his earliest critical efforts, while still a student at Tsarskoe Selo, Küchelbecker acclaimed with remarkable foresight Zhukovski's achievement: "Zhukovski," he predicted at the time, "is not only on the point of changing the external form of our literature, he is actually transforming its basic character. Taking for his models the great geniuses who have recently spread abroad the fame of German letters, he is instilling into the Russian language a harmonious quality which is an apt expression of our national spirit, reflecting its freedom and independence."[25] Many years later, in his Siberian exile, Küchelbecker looked back with undiminished enthusiasm to that central event in his intellectual life and reaffirmed his gratitude to Zhukovski for "having opened the door to us inexperienced youths of those far-off days . . . to the sanctum sanctorum of all that is truly wonderful. It was you who forced us to study the great foreign writers as the incomparable models. None of your successors has achieved your perfection in rendering the works of Schiller, of Goethe, of Byron."[26]

No doubt it was Zhukovski who guided Küchelbecker to the works of Goethe. In 1819, Küchelbecker's diary records as an important event the acquisition of a copy of Goethe's *West-östlicher Divan*. Not only did he immediately set about memorizing many of the poems, he even prepared an outline of Goethe's annotations: "Noten und Abhandlungen zu besserem Verständnis des West-östlichen Divans."[27]

The next year, 1820, brought an even more important development: the realization of his long-cherished dream of a visit to Germany and Goethe's Weimar. As secretary to the Russian envoy, A. L. Naryshkin, Küchelbecker traveled first to Dresden, where he met Ludwig Tieck, and thence to Weimar, where, on November 22, 1820, he stood in the presence of the revered poet. Goethe has recorded the visit: "Young von Küchelbecker from Petersburg in the suite of Prince Naryshkin."[28] To his mother, Küchelbecker writes with obvious elation and pride of his friendly reception by the venerated master: "In Weimar I have made the personal acquaintance of the great Goethe; he was very gracious toward me and, seemingly, was much interested in Russian literature. He well remembers Papa Breitkopf, inquired about him with much sympathy. He made me a gift of his latest work."

The "Papa Breitkopf" in Küchelbecker's letter is none other than Goethe's close friend of the Leipzig days, Gottlob Breitkopf, the second son of Gottlieb Breitkopf, the famous inventor of movable type for musical notation and founder of the Breitkopf publishing house. Gottlob was an adventurous spirit, went off to Russia and there married a Küchelbecker. The "latest work" mentioned by Küchelbecker was Goethe's "Maskenzug" in honor of Maria Fedorovna, a copy of which Goethe had presented to the Russian visitor with the signed dedicatory inscription: "Herrn Küchelbecker zu freundlichem Andenken, Weimar. d. 23. Nov., 1820. Goethe."[29]

Küchelbecker's next report on the great event, this one to his poet friend Delvig, is marked by a more sober tone; even a note of disappointment can be detected in its closing lines. To be sure, the opening words of the letter exult in having a cherished dream come true: "I have seen the immortal one." Küchelbecker is im-

pressed with Goethe's "lively, fiery eyes charged with inspiration."
But then he is quick to check his enthusiasm. He "had envisioned
Goethe as a giant even in his physical appearance. As a matter
of fact, I find myself quite mistaken." Soberly he notes: "Goethe
is of medium height. He is slow in his speech: his voice calm and
pleasant. For a long time I could not believe that I was in the
presence of Goethe, the giant." Speaking of his works, I even addressed him in the third person, actually using his name. Goethe
knows the works of our Tolstoi and admires in him a truly great
artist.[30] He seemed pleased with our Zhukovski for having acquainted us Russians with some of his lyrics. About our conversation there is really little to report, dear friends. The visit was
brief. I hope that tomorrow he will be somewhat more accessible
and I, for my part, more bold."[31]

Shortly before his departure, Küchelbecker fervently requested
a farewell visit with "the teacher . . . to whom I owe so much in
the education of my soul." He is aware of the inconvenience
caused Goethe by the many requests for meetings by those who
would merely flatter their vanity in being able to say: "I too have
seen the immortal!" He, Küchelbecker, however, acts not from
such vanity: "Surely, when I seek to imprint on my heart the
features of my teacher, of the one I owe so much in the education
of my soul, then, surely, I have a pure, a noble purpose!"[32] With
this letter he sent a literal interlinear retranslation into German of
Zhukovski's Russian rendering of Goethe's "Harfner" as well as of
his own dedicatory poem entitled "Prometheus." This eulogy of
Goethe by the young Küchelbecker is a unique document in the
development of the Russian image of Goethe. The German poet
had been compared to numerous *personae* of his works, to Werther,
to Wilhelm Meister, even to Mephistopheles. He had been apotheosized as the Olympian, the aloof, awe-inspiring, omnipotent Zeus.
Nobody, however, before Küchelbecker or, for that matter, after
him, seems to have eulogized him as a second Prometheus, the rebel
and bold challenger of established, supreme power. This unique
eulogy deserves to be quoted in full. We give it in its German version supplied by Küchelbecker himself:

O Prometheus, unter Sängern des Landes von Tuiskon!
  Erschaffer
Leichter mächtiger Geister, in denen unsterbliches Leben!
Du ihnen erzähltest alle Seiten der Herzen; erzähltest das
  Weltall.
Ich sehe: Sie aus deiner ewig blühender Seele
Im Schwarme auffliegen und plötzlich ein heiliger
  triumphierender Chor
Alle umringen mich. Starker, Göttlicher, du,
Dein Pyritheus, dein Schiller und Herder, der Weise, der Sänger,
Mit Zauber süßen Lyra Seele meine ihr entbranntet.
Der liederliebende Stamm der Slaven wird hören mit Liebe
Die Harfe, welche du in klar-heiligen Stunden
Du mir gabst und ich durch dich werde unsterblich.
O nehme an denn, Prometheus, alles mein Bestes zur Gabe
Nicht Bewunderung bloß sondern Liebe und Töne einfache
Furchtsamer noch, aber durch dich kühn gestimmter Saiten!*[33]

It is evident that Küchelbecker does not attempt to adhere to
the German syntax but offers a word-for-word, often ungrammatical
rendering of the Russian original which is a most striking document in the clash of its imagery and the inconsistency of tone. In
an introductory line, the author assures us that his poem is done
in the "elegiac measure": "Das Versmaß ist elegisch." Yet time
and again this measure is disrupted by an impetuous, dynamic
rhythm attesting to the writer's temperament and mood which are
obviously the very opposite of "elegisch." Its imagery, too, lacks
homogeneity. It is characterized by an unresolved clash between
the Promethean Goethe, the rebellious titan, the "strong, divine

---

* O Prometheus, among the singers in the Tuiscon land! Creator of ethereal
powerful spirits, in whom there is eternal life! You told them of all the facets
of the heart; told them of the universe. I see: They swarm up out of your
blossoming soul and suddenly surround me, a holy, triumphant choir. O
strong one, divine one, you, your Pyritheus, your Schiller and Herder, the
wise, the singer, with the sweet magic of the lyre you inflamed my soul. The
song-loving race of the Slavs will hear with love the harp which you have
given me in clear-holy hours and I shall become immortal through you. O
then accept, Prometheus, all my best as a gift, not only admiration but love
and the simple tones from the still timid strings which have been boldly tuned
through you.

spirit" with all its "storm and stress" associations, and a Goethe
conceived in typically Romantic terms as the "Sänger," the "creator
of limpid spirits" which rise as a "holy, triumphant choir" from his
"ever-flowering soul." This Prometheus does not bring the gift of
fire; he bestows upon his poet the "sweet lyre," the "harp which
will make him immortal." It was a striking montage of altogether
novel elements upon traits well established by Zhukovski in his
portrayal of Goethe—certainly not a unified poetic creation!

Goethe must have received this enthusiastic homage with an
indulgent smile, recalling perhaps those distant days when he too
had expressed with youthful enthusiasm his admiration and gratitude to *his* great teacher—to Shakespeare. Whatever Goethe's
reaction to the Russian's eulogy, he did grant his request and invited him to dinner on November 27.[34] In a brief comment in his
Tag- und Jahreshefte Goethe indicates his interest in the conversation of the young Russian: "Dr. Küchelbecker from Petersburg,
von Quandt and spouse, von Arnim and painter Ruhl imparted to
our sociable days a great diversity through their most interesting
conversations."[35] This was to be Goethe's last mention of Küchelbecker.

From Weimar, Küchelbecker went by way of Paris to Nice
where he witnessed the Piedmontese rebellion and its cruel sup-
pression by Austrian troops in March and April of 1821. The
impressions of his visits with Goethe found a curious fusion with
this stirring experience in his poem, "Nizza." While the political
events provided the immediate impetus for its composition as well
as its central theme, it was Goethe who furnished much of its
mood and imagery. Küchelbecker introduces his poem with the
much-quoted line in the original German: "Kennst du das Land wo
die Zitronen blühn," then proceeds to make embarrassingly ama-
teurish use of the theme of longing and of a number of descriptive
lines from Goethe's poem. In a literal translation, the first stanza
of Küchelbecker's less-than-successful effort runs as follows:

> I too have been in that wonderful land,
> There, whither thoughts of longing fly
> Where under a blue sky,

Insatiably our eye does roam,
Where only the mule can find its way
Amidst wild cliffs and rapids to the mountaintop,
Where in the green darkness of the forest
Glows red the succulent orange.[36]

These heavily derivative lines are followed by strident verses filled with the din of battle and with lament for the cruel fate of the brave fighters in their "native land of the splendid muses, of battles and of freedom." So obvious was Küchelbecker's borrowing from Goethe that N. A. Polevoi, who published the poem in the *Moscow Telegraph,*[37] changed the original title, "Nizza," into the dedicatory one, "To Goethe," a change which also served admirably to camouflage for the censor the revolutionary message of the poem.

Küchelbecker's transformation of the "Mignon" song into a vehicle for a revolutionary theme, a "politisch Lied," is symptomatic of the young poet's basic inclinations, of his rebellious temperament which was soon to involve him in the abortive Decembrist uprising and send him to prison and thence to a lifelong Siberian exile. It is this basically political spirit of the Russian revolutionary which must be singled out as the underlying cause for the gradual but inexorable change in his attitude toward Goethe, and, for that matter, toward German culture in general. In fact, his criticism was, at first, not directed specifically toward the admired German poet. As early as 1824, Küchelbecker developed a clearly negative attitude toward German literature, especially toward the "immature" Schiller, while still upholding the greatness of Goethe. At this time he even attacks his teacher Zhukovski for his Germanophilism for which, only a few years earlier, he had so enthusiastically praised him: "Zhukovski had been the first among us to imitate the *newest* German writers, especially Schiller. . . . Let us be grateful to Zhukovski for having freed us from the yoke of French literature . . . but let us not permit him, nor anyone else . . . to place upon us the fetters of German or English domination."[38] Certainly a striking transformation in Küchelbecker's views on the desirability of "foreign models"! He now is ready to claim that Russia's "vice" of indiscriminately bowing to foreign influences

has deprived Russian literature of much of its vitality, originality
and native greatness. "If imitate we must, then at least let us be
sure we know whom to imitate! Instead, our living catalogues [the
critics and literary historians] blithely place all [models] on the
same level: the Greek and Latin, the English and the German
literatures, the great Goethe and the immature Schiller." Goethe,
"the great," fared surprisingly well in this critical reappraisal. This
high esteem for Goethe persisted in an essay entitled "A conversation with F. V. Bulgarin,"[39] in which Küchelbecker set up a list of
virtues which raise Goethe far above the run of contemporary authors and, quite specifically, above hapless Schiller: "In the first
place, Goethe does not have Schiller's prejudices." Goethe was
willing and able to deal with the French, to penetrate into their very
being and mode of thought—and this despite the fact that Goethe
must have felt them to be his "sworn enemies." "Secondly, Goethe
has the gift of freeing himself from his ego, to live and breathe in
his heroes, in his Götz, his Tasso, his Faust, his Werther. Thirdly,
Goethe always knows what he is about, what he is searching and
striving for."

Finally, Küchelbecker grew enthusiastic over Goethe's truly
Protean nature, his magic ability to re-create the very essence of
far-off lands and bygone days. With this Küchelbecker struck a
theme we met in Uvarov's appreciation of Goethe, which was typical of the Russian Romanticists. Küchelbecker becomes rhapsodic
as he marvels at the ease with which Goethe's creative mind moves
from land to land, from age to age:

> In *Faust* and *Götz* he resurrects with a touch of his magic
> wand the fifteenth century, the Germany of emperors Sigis-
> mund and Maximilian; in *Hermann und Dorothea,* in
> *Wilhelm Meister* we meet our contemporaries, our fore-
> bears, the Germans of the eighteenth and nineteenth cen-
> turies, of all age groups, of all occupations, and from all the
> various socioeconomic strata; in the 'Römische Elegien,' in the
> 'Venezianische Epigramme,' in his travel notes on Italy [!]
> we meet, in turn, the contemporaries of Tibullus, the com-
> panions of Raphael and of Benvenuto Cellini, the wise
> German scholar and the keen observer [i.e. all the various
> facets of Goethe's many-sided personality]; in his *Iphigenie*

Goethe is a Greek, an ancient Teuton in his *Walpurgisnacht;* in his poem 'Die Bajadere' [!] he is a worshiper of Brahma, and, finally, in his *Divan* he is a Persian in the manner and to the extent attainable to a European who had never set foot in Asia.

This many-sidedness of Goethe's genius is effectively emphasized by a comparison with Schiller, whose work is criticized for monotony of theme and lack of consistency. In Küchelbecker's extraordinarily one-sided comparison of the two poets, all light falls on the "mature" Goethe towering over the "juvenile" Schiller, who is denied "originality and poetic tact."[40]

Surely, all this is impressive evidence of Küchelbecker's continued admiration for Goethe. Nonetheless, as we examine his pronouncements on literature in the succeeding issues of *Mnemozina,* all published within the year 1824, we cannot escape the impression that his admiration for the German poet gradually began to ring hollow and academic. Küchelbecker's sympathies turn toward a new hero: Byron. Most revealing of Küchelbecker's temperament and orientation are those qualities of Byron's personality and work which he singles out for special praise: Byron's indomitable revolutionary spirit, his constant struggles with pen and sword in the cause of freedom and social justice. To Byron he predicts immortality "in the company of those other noble fighters for liberty and justice, Tyrtaeus, Themistocles, Leonidas."[41] Byron's death, on April 19, 1824 he commemorates with a grandiloquent ode, "The Death of Byron,"[42] while he seems not to have had a word to say on Goethe's death.

Despite Küchelbecker's silence on that occasion, his diary indicates that in the gloomy, solitary years of imprisonment in the dungeons of fortress Dinaburg and in his exile, his thoughts frequently turned to Goethe. He drew solace from the growing conviction that as a fellow poet he was, in fact, related in spirit to his erstwhile idol, even if only distantly, that he did share with him certain experiences. "Today I had an experience which Goethe also tells of: explaining to my good pastor here the plan of my 'Ivan, the Merchant's Son,' its central idea grew suddenly far more profound and clear. The oral, lively communication of my thoughts had served me for inspiration, just as it had, on occasions, Goethe in *his* work."[43]

Another time he recalls his boyhood love for fairy tales and relishes the thought of having this taste in common with "young Goethe."[44] Goethe even appears to him in his dreams, together with two of his closest friends, Pushkin and Delvig. "Today I had extremely vivid and, may I say, clever dreams: I discussed the most intriguing problems and guess with whom? With Goethe, Pushkin, Delvig. Oh, why could this not have been reality!"[45]

The twenty-seventh of May, 1834, was a red-letter day for Küchelbecker. On that day he received a packet of Goethe's works in his fortress solitude.[46] Several months later that same year he was elated at the news of the publication of new works of Goethe. "The news of the posthumous publication of works of Goethe is thrilling, especially the installments [!] from the final volume of *Dichtung und Wahrheit*. I can identify myself in spirit with Goethe's ideas. My best works too, my *Izhorski,* are creations of nature, like Goethe's, rather than being the products of calculating artistic design."[47] Küchelbecker wondered whether the hero of his *magnum opus (Izhorski)* "could not be transmuted into another *Faust*." Such a Russian *Faust* had been Küchelbecker's lifelong ambition; he obviously strove to realize it in his *Izhorski*. In fact, the work, a heavily philosophical and symbolic "mysterium" abounding in heavenly and hellish spirits, apparitions and voices, does recall at moments Goethe's play. Its hero has for his companions not one but two Mephistolike figures and in his life a noble lady, Lidia, plays a part not unlike that of Gretchen in Faust's. Yet Küchelbecker's Izhorski, steeped in unrelieved gloom, ennui and Weltschmerz reminds one of Pushkin's Faust, and of Byron's Manfred and Cain, rather than of Goethe's ever-questing hero. Moreover, it has been plausibly suggested that the Polish writer Adam Mickiewicz might well have been another, perhaps the chief, influence and inspiration.[48]

Küchelbecker continued his readings in Goethe's works. On September 9 of that year he turned again to *Werther* and while reading it with a critical eye could not help falling under the spell of that great work of Goethe's youth: "I am reading *Werther*. Though it contains many flaws, I cannot but confess that I do prefer that work to certain others of Goethe's latest products; there is in *Werther* an unfeigned warmth, to be sure, also that something which the Germans call "exzentrisch" but, at any rate, none of that chilling stand-offishness, that fake simplicity, that shameless egotism which one meets with in his notes, in his *Wilhelm Meisters Wanderjahre,* etc."[49]

Next day Küchelbecker amplifies this revealing evaluation not only of *Werther* but, in its light, of Goethe's later work: "There is a vast amount of poetic life in *Werther* but, alas, from Goethe, the author of *Werther,* to Goethe, the writer of—let us say—*Epimenides [Erwachen],* there is a distance no less vast than that between Werther and his oh-so-prudent friends. I shall not ask which of them is the better; yet, without doubt, *Werther* and its author are more attractive than is the decorous author of *Epimenides,* together with those people who are in life what the author of *Epimenides* is in literature. The only pity is that Werther whines so much."[50]

It is not difficult to derive from these lines a distinct picture of Küchelbecker's attitude toward Goethe the man and his work. To begin with, Küchelbecker had rid himself of the attraction which "Werther of the lacerated heart" and of the tearful eye held for the sentimental generation. He was impressed with the "warmth" of Werther, which we are safe in interpreting to mean his warm-hearted sympathy with the lot of the simple folk. We are fortified in this interpretation by Küchelbecker's appreciation of the lack in this work of "shameless egotism" and "chilling stand-offishness" which, we can be certain, Küchelbecker found and was repelled by not only in "certain later works" of Goethe's but in the aloof, Olympian Privy Councilor himself. It is striking, how basically consistent Küchelbecker's appreciation of Goethe remains. As in his youth, so now, some fifteen years later, it is not the Olympian Goethe but the Promethean Goethe, the warm-hearted champion of man, who still holds his admiration and brings him solace in his solitude and amid the hardships of imprisonment and exile.

It would not be merely coincidence if Küchelbecker's criticism of Goethe's "shameless egotism" and "chilling stand-offishness" should sound familiar to readers versed in the history of German literary criticism; this criticism echoes the sharp attack on Goethe that Wolfgang Menzel, that implacable enemy of the "immoral" Goethe, had launched in the late 1820's. Menzel's views on Goethe had been presented to Russian readers serialized in leading periodicals as early as 1834. On June 13 of that year, Küchelbecker had read in the *Son of the Fatherland* "Wolfgang Menzel's discussion of Schiller and Goethe."[51] By 1839 Menzel's, *Die deutsche Literaturgeschichte*[52] had finally reached Küchelbecker in his Siberian exile. He confesses that he had been at once enamored with certain of Menzel's views: "I came to love him with all my heart." But he hastens to add, "even though I could not agree with him completely, or—to put it more precisely—with his judgment of various writers."[53] Unfortunately, we do not know which writers Küchelbecker was referring to. As for Goethe, Küchelbecker does subscribe in part to Menzel's sharp censure, at least as far as Goethe the man is concerned. "I know, too, and possibly have voiced this view well in advance of Menzel, that Goethe's vanity, his sultan-like mannerisms, his coquetry, his eternal genuflection before his own great self are quite *ridiculous*. Yet these weaknesses and foibles are of the *man,* not of the *poet*."[54] Küchelbecker makes much of this distinction between the artist and the man. Moreover, even the *man* Goethe, with all his shortcomings, is, in his estimate, morally far superior to Voltaire, for instance, or to Rousseau. "There is in Goethe none of Voltaire's blasphemousness nor is there in him the shamelessness of Rousseau, who had the temerity of confessing to kleptomania, to the dastardly blackmail of an innocent girl and to God only knows what other crimes—and in the same breath could declare: 'je suis intimement persuadé qu'il n'y a pas de meilleur homme que moi.' "[55]

In his defense of Goethe the *artist,* Küchelbecker is far more emphatic. He rejects Menzel's application of moral standards to a writer as an artist. A poet's influence, he argues, is of a quality that cannot possibly be measured by the yardstick of accepted morality. Such criticism, he holds, is simply irrelevant.

> I do not consider Goethe to have been a moral poet, but
> neither do I see in him an immoral one. The poet's business
> is to surrender himself to life's impressions, then to transmit
> these to his readers; it can never be his duty to moralize, to
> preach! Fortunate indeed the artist who is at once a man of
> moral principles, as were, for instance, Schiller and our own
> Zhukovski. But these are rare! Yet every poet, every *true*
> poet—and that Goethe was such a one there can be no doubt
> whatever!—is valuable to mankind, for he inspires love for
> the refined delights. I realize, of course, that a person develop-
> ing an appreciation of Goethe and of Shakespeare would not
> thereby be turned into a kindly family man, a faithful son of
> his fatherland or an orthodox Christian. Yet I refuse to be-
> lieve that such a man, so influenced, could ever lose all love
> for the beautiful, could turn into an odious niggard or into a
> crude boor with women.[56]

At this point Küchelbecker's letter breaks off abruptly. This
much is evident: Küchelbecker was still unwilling to abandon
Goethe the artist to criticism he considered to be unfair; he was
even prepared to rise in defense of Goethe's character. Yet this
struggle in behalf of his one-time idol proved to be a rearguard
action. Goethe's narcissism and his Olympian aloofness and antisocial attitudes became unbearable to Küchelbecker, in whom imprisonment and exile further intensified his strong social consciousness and sharp political awareness and inflamed his hatred of the
status quo. He was no longer prepared to condone in an artist
indifference toward the burning questions of the day. Küchelbecker's
denunciation of his one-time "God," Goethe-Prometheus, became
unequivocal, as evidenced by the following diary entry of March
27, 1840: "Disillusionment with a person makes it most difficult
to remain just to him. Goethe's reign over my soul has come to a
definite end, and no matter what Hazlitt [William Hazlitt in the
Revue Britanique] might say in his support, I, for my part, shall
never again kneel before my former idol, as I did in that year of
1824, forcing all Russia to do likewise. I gave them a golden calf
and to this day they continue to bow down before it and to chant
hymns of praise, each more stupid than the other. Only I can no

longer see a God in the golden calf."[57]

A year later, almost to the day, Küchelbecker wrote in his diary the last reference to Goethe. It is a pledge not to touch on the painfully complex subject again. The remark is made in connection with an article by Belinski on Menzel and Goethe which Küchelbecker had read in the periodical *Patriotic Notes:* "The author [Belinski] is both right and wrong [in his appraisal of Menzel]. He must be young for he knows not patience; he is one-sided. As to Goethe—not a word, il serait trop long de disputer sur çela."[58] Too long and too painful! Küchelbecker seems to have kept his pledge. He never mentioned Goethe again.

In his revealing characterization of his changing attitude toward Goethe, Küchelbecker was guilty of two striking inaccuracies. One of these, his belief that in the forties Goethe was still held in highest esteem, must have been due to the isolation of his exile, which put him out of touch with the rapidly changing Russian attitude toward Goethe. As a matter of fact, Goethe's prestige had gone into sharp decline and very few "hymns" were being sung to Goethe by the year 1841. For by that year the "critical realists" had gained ascendancy under the leadership of the highly influential critic Belinski, the very one whom Küchelbecker, from the distance of his Siberian exile, quite correctly suspected of "being one-sided and lacking in patience." The other inaccuracy must be attributed to Küchelbecker's wishful thinking. Surely, he must have known that it had not been he who had "forced all Russia to kneel" before Goethe, that, at the very most, he had but assisted the Russian Romanticists, Venevitinov, Odoevski, Shevyrëv and others in their efforts to spread Goethe's fame throughout Russia. In our next chapter we will record, analyze and evaluate these efforts, tracing the image of Goethe as it was developed by the Russian Romanticists, by the Liubomudry, or "Lovers of Wisdom," as they called themselves.

CHAPTER FIVE

The Russian Romanticists

1. The Liubomudry

In the year 1823 a group of young men under the leadership of Dmitri Vladimirovich Venevitinov (1805–27) formed a society for the cultivation of German philosophy and art. Its membership included such prominent figures as Prince Vladimir F. Odoevski (1803–69), M. P. Pogodin (1800–75), S. P. Shevyrëv (1806–64), N. M. Rozhalin (1805–34), and A. I. Koshelëv (1806–83), among others. Their venerated mentor was Vasili Zhukovski. They chose for themselves the name Liubomudry, "Lovers of Wisdom," a term they found in the Masonic and mystical writings of the eighteenth century. This name was to differentiate them from the philosophers of the French school, whom they scorned. As Odoevski bitingly put it: "People up to this moment cannot imagine a 'philosopher' except in the guise of the French prattler [govoruna] of the eighteenth century. Therefore, in clear-cut distinction from such prattlers, we shall call the true philosophers "Lovers of Wisdom.' "[1] It goes without saying that they considered themselves such "true philosophers." They were enthusiastic admirers of Schelling, the sworn enemies of French rationalism and materialism. They shared Goethe's high esteem for Spinoza's pantheism. "We valued especially highly Spinoza's thoughts and considered his works far superior to the gospel and any other religious writings," recalls Koshelëv in his *Notes,* which are a rich source of reminiscences from the brief but productive years of the society's existence. They met, he recalls, "in the two tiny studies of young Faust [Venevitinov!]. Here German philosophy reigned supreme, Kant, Fichte, Schelling, Oken, among others. Here we sometimes read our own philosophical productions, but most frequently we discussed the works of the German lovers of wisdom."[2]

115

In their scornful disregard of the mundane and commonplace aspects of existence, especially of politics, in their celebration of art for art's sake, in their pantheistic worship of nature, the Liubomudry gave the most faithful and forceful expression to the Romanticist temper of their generation.[3] They saw a new dawn of imperishable philosophy and poetry arising in Germany, the "land of ancient Teutons." Prince Odoevski greets it rapturously: "O land of ancient Teutons! O land of glorious thoughts! To you I turn my awestruck gaze."[4] Among them flourished a veritable cult of Goethe as the ideal poet, a brother-in-spirit of the great of all ages. He fulfilled their loftiest demand that a true poet be at the same time a great thinker. Goethe to them was a poet-sage, whose wisdom was all-embracing, whose poetry soared on the wings of inspiration high above the dross of life. His genius nourished the "two souls" in the breast of these young enthusiasts, their poetic aspirations and their quest after the most profound philosophical insights.

2. D. V. Venevitinov and V. F. Odoevski

The acknowledged leader of the group, Dmitri Venevitinov, was a man of rare talents and, for his years, of astounding erudition. The Russian literary historian Mirsky speaks of his "truly Faustian thirst for knowledge," and compares him with Goethe in "the essential sanity and balance" of his nature. "He was a man with a dazzling' abundance of gifts—a strong brain, a born metaphysician, a mature and lofty poet. . . . There was in him an essential sanity and balance of all the functions of soul and body that remind one of Goethe."[5] His contemporary, S. E. Raich, admired in Venevitinov the supremely gifted poet, who could have brought "to our northern land the flower of German poetry, *Faust,* judging by the glorious fragments he has left us."[6] But it was not to be! A tragic death at twenty-one—ironically of a cold he caught driving home from a ball on a winter's night—cut short Venevitinov's literary career, one of the many cruel blows dealt to Russia's cultural life.

Throughout Venevitinov's work the influence of Goethe is

clearly evident. He was to him his guide and "mentor," as he called him in a poem, "To Pushkin": "Our mentor, your mentor, . . . whose heart, despite old age, has not grown cold, . . . who wings his majestic flight—a swan—to celestial heights, singing, as he soars, his inspired song,"[7] a rather strained metaphor, but one expressive of Venevitinov's image of Goethe as the "swan" unsullied by mortal imperfections, an ethereal poet yearning for the loftiest ideals.

Venevitinov centers considerable gifts as a translator on Goethe's poems and his *Faust*. His selections are revelations of his view of Goethe. He searches for and finds in Goethe's lyrics his own ideals of poet and of poetry. Thus he selects for his first translations Goethe's lyrical dramolets "Künstlers Erdenwallen," and "Künstlers Apotheose."[8] Reading these poems as an expression of his own high hopes and joys, his own striving and tribulations as a poet, he lends to Goethe's slightly ironic doggerel lines rather too much ponderous regularity of measure, an elegiac note, a freight of metaphor that seems to hark back to the Russian Classical tradition. To give but one example: Goethe's "Da sie noch ruhen all meine lieben Sorgen! Gutes Weib! Kostbare Kleinen!"[9] Venevitinov rendered as: "While you enjoy repose in the embrace of sleep, you dear objects of my labors and my care, little ones, good wife": (Poka vy nezhites' v obiatiakh sna, / Predmety milye trudov i popecheni, maliutki, dobraia zhena.)[10]

From Goethe's *Faust* Venevitinov selects those famous passages which draw most vividly the sublime and suffering soul of genius. They are Faust's dialog with Wagner in "Vor dem Tor": "O glücklich wer noch hoffen kann . . ." to "und lispeln englisch, wenn sie lügen," and Faust's soul-searching monolog in "Wald und Höhle."[11] Here Venevitinov found the "two souls" in Faust's tortured breast, so kindred to his own emotions. Here was his own Romanticist longing to soar with the sun into the infinite:

Ihr ewges Licht zu trinken,
Vor mir den Tag, und hinter mir die Nacht,
Den Himmel über mir, und unter mir die Wellen.*

---

* To drink its eternal light before me the day, and behind me the night, heavens above me and below me the waves.

Faust's monolog attracts Venevitinov as a powerful expression of pantheistic worship of nature so dear to the heart of this devoted Russian disciple of Schelling and admirer of Goethe's youthful pantheistic "storm and stress" poetry. His best translation by far, it became also the most influential among the group of the Liubomudry, fixing for them Goethe's image as the divinely inspired poet of all-embracing creative powers. The lines: "Erhabner Geist, du gabst mir, gabst mir alles . . ." became a key passage of the Russian Romanticists' interpretation of Goethe as the all-embracing, all-perceiving genius.

Venevitinov was less successful with another of his renderings from *Faust,* Gretchen's spinning song.[12] Here his language—the Russian language before Pushkin—fails to transmit the heartfelt simplicity, the naive tenderness of the "Lied." There is in the Russian version a certain artiness, not to say artificiality, a certain theatricality. Let the last stanza, as the least successful, stand as an example. In literal translation, without regard to the rhyme pattern, which is not maintained by Venevitinov, it runs as follows: "To embrace him, to hold him / to kiss him, to kiss / And, dying, from his lips / Another kiss to tear" (Obniat' evo, derzhat' evo, / Lobzat' evo, lobzat' / I, umiraia, s ust evo / Eshchë lobzaniia rvat').[13] The choice from the elevated "Classical" Russian vocabulary of the key verb, "lobzat' ": "to kiss," in place of the more colloquial "tselovat,' " is most unfortunate. Even more serious is the distortion of Gretchen's character into a veritable dying Maenad, bent on "tearing still more kisses from his lips," Goethe's tender Gretchen, who "an seinen Küssen vergehen sollt"!

Together with these excerpts from *Faust,* Venevitinov left us a considerable fragment from Goethe's *Egmont,* Scenes 2 and 3 of Act I.[14] The translation shows Venevitinov's great sensitivity to the characteristic rhythm and tone of Goethe's prose, his ability to render them all-but-unimpaired into his native tongue. Perhaps its most successful part is the charming *Soldatenlied* which Klärchen sings, "Die Trommeln gerührt / Das Pfeifchen gespielt . . ." Though rather free, it captures ingeniously the verve, the buoyancy of the original, effectively conveying by image and rhythm its central message: Klärchen's desire to be a "Mannsbild," and to ride into battle side by side with her beloved Egmont.

In the meager critical materials by Venevitinov that have come down to us, we find only one reference to Goethe's work of some importance. In a brief essay, "Answer to Mr. Polevoi," he is able to correct that critic's mistaken notion that "Pushkin's *Onegin* belongs to the genre of Byron's and Goethe's epic poems" by pointing out with assurance and a touch of irony "that Goethe wrote only two such poems: *Hermann und Dorothea* and *Reineke Fuchs;* the first of these, in the manner of Voss' *Luise* [!], is also in some degree an idyll and describes family life in a small German town; in the second, animals act, not people; thus, neither develops the character of an educated person in the setting of 'grande monde.' "[15] The very fact that Venevitinov knew of the existence of *Reineke Fuchs* is indicative of a wider acquaintance with Goethe's work than that enjoyed by most of his Russian contemporaries.

Venevitinov himself considered his knowledge of Goethe's work as being sketchy, fragmentary; he felt that he was far from grasping the full depth and scope of Goethe's genius. As he wrote in his "Poem to Pushkin," Goethe had remained for him a mysterious, awe-inspiring figure, "hidden in his native land, that distant land of our dreams." And yet, Venevitinov's "Faustian search for knowledge," his intuitive empathy, his poetic nature subtly attuned to Goethe's, had offered his Russian countrymen more than a glimpse of the German poet's personality and work. Despite the tragicly brief span of his productive life, he had, nonetheless, been able to make a contribution to the Russian appreciation of Goethe which was destined to be richly developed by his fellow Liubomudry in the years immediately following his untimely death.

The other central figure of the Liubomudry group, Prince Vladimir F. Odoevski, lacked Venevitinov's lyric gifts; he had little appreciation of Goethe as a lyric poet. His interest centered on Goethe's prose writings. He made an important contribution to the Liubomudry's image of Goethe as the unequaled artist-philosopher.

It is no exaggeration to say that Odoevski was destined by

his very nature to make this particular contribution. For in him
there was that unusual blend of a highly analytical mind and
artistic sensibility. Instinctively he sought the same combination
of qualities in the great figures he would admire and set up for his
models. Every truly great poet, Odoevski argued, seized intuitively
upon the great truths at which philosophers arrived laboriously by
the circuitous route of logic. In Goethe he recognized and worshiped a genius who had anticipated the philosophy of Schelling.
"In Homer you find Plato anticipated; in Dante, Giordano Bruno;
in Goethe, Schelling. The famous reorientation in German philosophy had been prepared by Herder and by Goethe."[16]

Among those writers whose influence on Odoevski can be
readily established, Goethe occupies a singular place as his "sole
guide and inspiration." Neither E. T. A. Hoffmann, whose influence
is prodigious, nor Jean Paul, to whom Odoevski is obviously indebted, are ever given that distinction.[17] Odoevski places Goethe
in the company of Shakespeare, among the geniuses of foremost
rank.[18] Goethe is assigned a place as a "central personality in
human history" among the few "elect."[19] None of the Romantic
poets can be compared with Goethe. He towers above them as Pushkin rises above all Russian poets. Only in Goethe and in Pushkin
Odoevski finds that "unique synthesis of a powerful poetic imagination and a vigorous grasp of life's realities," that "genuine artistic
creativity."[20]

Direct references to Goethe are not numerous in Odoevski's
writings, yet among them we have some curious bits of evidence
of his special interest in and high esteem for the German writer.
One of these we find in his fragmentary utopian novel, *The Year
4338.*[21] Here Odoevski offers a most disquieting preview of the cultural and political situation in that far-off year. Global rule will
have passed by that time to Russia and China, Russia having become the universally acknowledged leader in the cultural realm, "the
center of world-wide enlightenment." German culture, on the other
hand, will have suffered an all-but-total eclipse. The only evidence
of German genius which Odoevski permits to survive this general
obliteration are, significantly, "a few fragments" of Goethe's writ-

ings: "Of the Germans . . . there will be preserved nothing but a few fragments from the pen of their supreme poet—Goethe."²²

Another indication of Odoevski's orientation toward Goethe may be seen in the fact that he gives to the hero of his major work, *Russian Nights*, the name of the hero of Goethe's masterpiece, *Faust*. To be sure, the kinship between Odoevski's protagonist and his Goethean namesake is slight. We find it in the spirit of skepticism toward their environment and in their striving "to rise above the earth without losing contact with it."²³ Yet, the very fact of the adoption of Faust's name for this central figure who expresses Odoevski's own idealistic philosophy and who is generally regarded as his alter ego²⁴ would seem to indicate the Russian writer's desire to establish a not-too-veiled identification with Goethe's questing hero. A formal influence of Goethe on *Russian Nights* has also been suggested. Sakulin supports the theory that the composition of *Russian Nights* in the form of a "chain of narratives" may well have been carried out by Odoevski in imitation of Goethe's *Unterhaltungen deutscher Ausgewanderten,* though his primary model was, admittedly, Hoffmann's *Serapionsbrüder*.²⁵ That Odoevski did have his mind very much on Goethe's work while composing his own, is also borne out by his use of lines from *Wilhelm Meisters Wanderjahre* for its motto: "Lassen Sie mich nun zuvörderst gleichnisweise reden," as well as by an effective reference to the famous Flea Song from Goethe's *Faust*. We find it in a tale of the *Russian Nights* entitled "Beethoven's Last Quartet." Here Odoevski has a musician of the type of Hoffmann's Kreisler sing "with a hoarse but true voice the melody of the well-known song of Mephisto: Es war einmal ein König, / Der hatt' einen großen Floh, but his song would glide now and again, against his will, into that mysterious melody with which Beethoven had interpreted Goethe's Mignon."²⁶

Odoevski places Goethe's works, specifically his *Werther,* among those "central creations, the knowledge of which was imperative for anyone striving to educate himself."²⁷ At the top of his list stands Goethe's "incomparable" *Wilhelm Meister*. Odoevski cautions the uninitiated not to expect easy access to this work.

He knows from bitter experience that Goethe's novel will not yield its treasure to the impatient reader in search of a thrilling plot. Goethe's *Meister* does not have "what might be called an interest. It cannot be swallowed in one gulp. One must sip it drop by drop like old Hungarian wine in order to enjoy the pleasure it is capable of imparting."[28] Odoevski forthrightly admits that when he first read *Wilhelm Meister* "greedily" the novel failed to hold his attention. "Had it not been a work of Goethe, perhaps I would never have taken it up again." But he returned to it, forcing himself to read it "a few pages a day. Only then did I establish a close rapport with all the personages of the novel. Wilhelm grew kindred to me, became my alter ego. All that was happening to him, his every word, now acquired for me not a bookish but, as it were, a familial interest."[29]

In this quality of the book Odoevski recognized its unique greatness, the genius of its creator. He knew few novelists who had been able to infuse their work with such vitality, to recreate life in all its complexity as Goethe had done in his *Meister*. The great majority of writers, according to Odoevski, "elaborate the plot but fail to develop the character of their heroes. Thus they debase a work of art into an anecdote which, no matter how interesting, is quickly forgotten, and, with repetition, grows intolerably stale."[30] Goethe has avoided this pitfall and has created in his *Wilhelm Meister* a work that will delight and instruct endless generations of perceptive readers.

Odoevski stands alone among the Liubomudry with his awareness of Goethe's stature as a scientific thinker. Though we do not know which of Goethe's scientific writings Odoevski had read, there is ample evidence of his lively interest in Goethe as the natural scientist. Odoevski is one of the very few Russians who, at the time, could appreciate the novelty of Goethe's approach to problems in the natural sciences and the importance of his findings. He was keenly aware of the stultifying, numbing influence upon man's creative spirit of rampant overspecialization. Goethe, together with a few kindred spirits such as the Russian scientist, linguist, and historian Lomonosov, was greeted by Odoevski as "a savior of mankind from threatening mental stagnation." These poet scientists represented to him the last best hope for real progress in a pseudo-civilization in which artists no longer recognized any productive interaction of their art with science, and scientists—in their turn—had grown utterly blind to the significant role of art—thoughts that curiously anticipated our present debates on the "two cultures."

Odoevski was especially scornful of England's scientists, who had permitted themselves to be lured into complete spiritual sterility by the mechanistic pseudo-scientism of Francis Bacon and the crass materialism of Jeremy Bentham. He accuses them of being "preoccupied with screws and wheels and behind the wheels—with gold!" Odoevski considers it "utterly hopeless to expect from them any creative, fertile thoughts." "Not a single English savant," he claimed, "has shown such creative vigour as have Goethe, Carus, and Oken."[31]

And wherein lies the secret of Goethe's productive genius? Odoevski's answer is unequivocal. It is Goethe's capacity to bring the intuitive powers of the artist into a fertile interaction with the powers of observation and analysis. Goethe's unfailing intuition and his artistic genius turned upon the secrets of nature enable him to "break with today's onesided, narrow, or, to use a polite term, specialized methodology" and to "initiate a new science with a method *all its own,* which will not be limited to the analysis of any one isolated aspect of nature but will embrace within its living organism nature's totality, a new science which, like nature itself, will be alive, homogeneous, variegated—and all this in sharp contrast to our present-day science which is lifeless, indefinite, and one-sided."[32]

No doubt we hear in these passages the voice of Odoevski the faithful follower of Schelling's nature philosophy with its emphasis on intuition rather than mechanical experiment and analytic ratiocination.   And yet, these statements contain overtones that would indicate a view more modern than was the Romantic. Odoevski seems to seize far more incisively the specifically Goethean approach to the discovery of nature's secrets than did other Russian followers of Schelling. Odoevski is unique in his awareness of Goethe's un-

romantic preoccupation with the concrete details of natural phenomena, of his inductive bent in painstaking study of them. Truly
surprising, how clearly Odoevski perceives Goethe's unique effort
to avoid confining mechanistic methods and to develop a "synoptic
view" (Zusammenschau) of nature. With Goethe he shares the
conviction that only to such an empathetic approach would nature
yield its secrets; with Goethe he rejects the "screws and wheels" as
ineffectual means to gain a true understanding of nature, not as a
heap of lifeless "disjecta membra," but as a complex living organism. Odoevski's views on Goethe as a natural scientist did not
crystallize fully until the closely knit circle of the Liubomudry had
been dissolved in the late 1820's. Thus, Odoevski's insights could
no longer make their impact on the members of the group. In fact,
these views seem to have had little effect on Odoevski's Russian
contemporaries and followers, though their faint echo can be detected in Aleksandr Herzen's rediscovery of Goethe's unique importance as a scientific thinker. They do foreshadow in a striking
manner the appreciation of Goethe as a natural scientist that was
to be voiced by some of the most perceptive modern Goethe
scholars.[33]

While Odoevski's preoccupation with Goethe the natural scientist attracted no Russian disciples, his glorification of Goethe as the
incomparable poet-philosopher was eagerly taken up by the Liubomudry. Perhaps its clearest echo and most significant development
is to be found in the writings of the critic and literary historian,
S. P. Shevyrëv.

3. Stepan Petrovich Shevyrëv (1806–1864)

Prince Odoevski had for one of his closest friends a brilliant
young Russian, Stepan Petrovich Shevyrëv. This gifted young man
from the provincial town of Saratov was quick to attain a leading
position in Moscow's intellectual circles, a co-editorship of the influential periodical, *Moscow Messenger* (1827–30), and, in 1834,
an adjunct professorship at Moscow University.

Shevyrëv began his intellectual career in the Liubomudry
group as a devout disciple of Schelling but soon grew critical of

Schelling's neglect of concrete, historical fact, of his emotional and vaguely generalizing approach, specifically in his appreciation of literature. Shevyrëv felt that such deep insights into the nature of art as were undoubtedly offered by Schelling should be supplemented by and fused with a proper regard for the historical facts, the empirical details of literature in its organic growth. In the concluding chapter of his *Theory of Poetry,* which he wrote as Ordinarius of Moscow University, Shevyrëv expressed the hope that in his "native land . . . the empirical study of art will gain ascendancy over the currently predominant philosophical school," and thus would lead to a sound and comprehensive theory of esthetics.[34]   In brief: Shevyrëv rapidly developed from a pure idealist in Schelling's tradition to one of the most articulate Russian champions of historicism in literary scholarship.

It is necessary to stress these characteristics of Shevyrëv's orientation, for it is this fusion of enthusiasm, imagination and idealism with a positivist's fact-conscious empiricism that explains his unique contribution to Russian scholarship on Goethe, which in thoroughness, perceptiveness, and scope was to remain unique in Russia for a long time to come.

Shevyrëv made his debut as Goethe's translator and interpreter in the Liubomudry's official organ, the *Moscow Messenger,* with a successful rendering into Russian of an excerpt from the "Helena" scene and with an interpretation of the *Phantasmagoria* which was destined to remain his most important and widely acclaimed contribution on Goethe.

Goethe's masterpiece appeared in the spring of 1827 under the title, "Helena, a Classic-Romantic *Phantasmagoria.* An interact to *Faust,*" and reached Moscow with little delay. Young Shevyrëv, scanning the book mart with an eager eye for literary novelties, at once laid hold of the work and could rejoice in a great literary coup for himself as well as for his periodical. While the *Moscow Telegraph,* the chief competitor of the *Messenger,* told in its pages of a mere rumor of the existence of a new work by Goethe, Shevyrëv gleefully announced for the *Messenger* not only an excerpt from the "rumored" work in Russian translation but also an essay on it which would set aright the many half-truths spread about Goethe's unique creation by the *Telegraph:* "In the next issue of the *Messenger*," Shevyrëv triumphantly wrote, "we shall present the contents of a fragment from the glorious *Phantasmagoria* of Goethe, and shall attempt to prove, into the teeth of the opinions held by that Frenchman from whose letter the editor of the *Telegraph* drew his information, that the *Phantasmagoria* is *not* a mere addition to Goethe's *Faust*, but rather an independent, unified, artistic whole; that these lofty visions of the great, incomparable soul [Goethe's] are not *strange*, not *dark*, but represent an allegory of pure, enchanting and altogether original form, that its plot does *not* stretch from the fall of Troy to the siege of Missolonghi, and, finally, that there is in it *no* Byron and *no* Greek mythology."[35] With this "announcement" in mind, the modern scholar approaches Shevyrëv's essay with some misgivings. Granted that it was natural for Shevyrëv to consider the *Phantasmagoria* as "independent" of *Faust*, since he knew nothing about *Faust*, Part II. Granted that Byron could not be recognized at once in the figure of Euphorion. But how could Shevyrëv deny the "existence of Greek mythology" in the work, or that it does, in fact, stretch from the fall of Troy to modern times?

Still, upon examination the essay proves a surprisingly perceptive and sensitive interpretation. As announced, it appeared in the "following" issue of the *Messenger*.[36] This number, which might justly be titled, "Shevyrëv on Goethe," opens with Shevyrëv's translation: "Fragment from the Interact to *Faust*;"[37] it has for its centerpiece his essay[38] and closes with a "Dialog," "The Journalist and the Evil Spirit," in which Shevyrëv is obviously influenced by the exchange between poet and director in Goethe's "Vorspiel auf dem Theater," as well as by the Pact scene and the Earth Spirit scene from *Faust*. Mephisto appears as "ruler of the epoch," as the "first capitalist" to offer to the journalist a contract: "You want fame?" he asks with a Mephistophelean smirk, "then sign. Here is the contract." Shevyrëv's journalist, quite unlike Goethe's Faust, resists the Tempter, remains faithful to the "wise Angel of the word"—to truth.[39]

Shevyrëv's translation is a remarkable achievement, considering that it is an altogether unprecedented attempt. His skill is especially impressive in the famous exchange between Faust and Helena in which Goethe weds, with such profound intent and incomparable effect, antique rhythm to modern rhyme. A rendering of Shevyrëv's translation into English could serve no purpose, since in such a rendering the subtleties of the all-important rhyme scheme would certainly be lost. It appears, therefore, most appropriate to furnish for our Russian readers Shevyrëv's original text of the famous dialogue between Helena and Faust:

FAUST:	Kol' mil tebe iazyk narodov nashikh,
	Chto skazhesh' ty o ikh sozvuchnykh pesniakh?
	Oni zvuchat do glubiny dushi.
	No skoro ty postignesh' tainu etu:
	Tebia nauchit ei liubvi beseda.
HELENA:	No kak uznat' prelestnoe isskustvo?
FAUST:	Legko, moi drug.—Lish' govori ot chustva.
	Kogda dusha vzvolnuetsia zhelaniem,
	Gliadish' i zhdësh', kto podarit—
HELENA:	lobzaniem?
FAUST:	Togda dushe vsë snitsia krasota,
	I tselyi mir izcheznet—
HELENA:	kak mechta!
FAUST:	Kto zh ukrotit pylaiushchuiu krov'?
	Kto serdtsu zhizni dast?
HELENA:	Moia liubov'.[40]

Shevyrëv's faithfulness to the subtle interplay of the rhymes in Goethe's original, the surprising ease and naturalness, a truly poetic inevitability with which this is accomplished bear impressive testimony to his talents.

The same cannot be said of his rendering of Goethe's thought. Shevyrëv distorts it into a Zhukovskian sentimental-Romantic context. Goethe's glorification of full existence in the moment without a backward glance or flight into the future becomes a Romantic yearning for liberation from life into a sublime world of beauty.

FAUST:	Nun schaut der Geist nicht
	Vorwärts, nicht zurück,
	Die Gegenwart allein—

HELENA: Ist unser Glück.*

becomes in Shevyrëv's rendering:

FAUST: Then the soul dreams of beauty
          All the time,
          And the whole world disappears—
HELENA: Like an apparition."

There are other flaws: an occasional loss in clarity and force of imagery; some vagueness of expression that, at times, results in outright distortion of Goethe's meaning. And yet, in its ability to convey much of the mood and theme of one of Goethe's most complex and demanding creations, this early rendering by Shevyrëv was not soon to be outdone.

The most significant contribution to the gradually developing appreciation by Russia of Goethe's work we find in Shevyrëv's essay. It becomes evident at once that he grasped Goethe's central intent to juxtapose the ancient and the medieval worlds and from their interaction to have modern Romantic art arise allegorized in Euphorion, the son of Helena and Faust. We may quarrel with details of Shevyrëv's interpretation, as, for instance: with his localization of the action "on the banks of the Euphrates River";[41] with his naïve explanation of Lynceus' failure to announce Helena's arrival: "He saw the mists, knew the castle's gates were closed, and could not imagine that out of the mists the goddess of beauty would emerge";[42] or, finally, with his insistent "proof" of the *Phantasmagoria's* independence of Faust on the grounds that Faust here is *not* a doctor of philosophy, that *no* mention is made of Faust's former torments or of the struggle of the "two souls" in his breast. "Faust's life is represented here full, enviable, a life of blissful love," completely at odds with the tormented existence of the hero in Goethe's *Faust*.[43] We note these and other instances of Shevyrëv's failure to grasp certain aspects of Goethe's "Helena" scene, and yet we cannot but be impressed with the essential aptness, even incisiveness, of this first Russian

---

* FAUST: Now the spirit does not look forward, nor backward,
            Only the here and now
  HELENA: Is our happiness.

interpretation of Goethe's profound work, considered by many at its appearance as an impenetrable enigma.

In the *Phantasmagoria,* Shevyrëv recognized an eminently successful allegory which magically rejuvenates the ossified Faust theme of the Chapbook (Spiess' *Faust*) by giving it a new and timely meaning: the spiritualization of sensuous beauty and the elevation of women from a chattel and a slave to the worshipfully adored ruler of the knight's possessions and person. "Helena, who is almost slain by the jealous and vengeful Menelaus in those ancient days when beauty was still a slave to man's sensual appetites, that same Helena becomes the object of pure and soulful adoration in the Middle Ages, a ruler, before whom the knights of the cold North, inflamed by love, surrender not only all their possessions . . . but even their very self and all the riches of their soul."[44] Shevyrëv credits Christianity with this transformation: "Beauty gained these rights only with the dawn of Christianity. The light of pure love, irradiating our religion, illumined all the feelings of man, and from that moment woman became the wondrous half of his transfigured soul."[45] In this part of his interpretation we hear the voice of the future Slavophile. However, Shevyrëv did not belabor this Orthodox point of view but returns to his central thesis, the sublimation of beauty, and with it of the arts, specifically poetry. "Together with the triumphant transfiguration of beauty there took place the transformation of that art which serves it, of poetry . . . . When the captivated knight embraced beauty not with a sensuous but with a spiritual love, then it was that love outwinged the narrow confines of this earth, . . . then it was that song no longer would proclaim this earth but the heavens with its harmonious consonance, with rhyme. As feeling answers feeling in the dialog of the lovers, so must one word make answer to the other."[46] Thus it was, according to Shevyrëv, that Goethe's genius solved for us "the riddle of the birth of Romantic poetry." "In his *Phantasmagoria* the poet-seer has uncovered for us many secrets of history and of poetry. Here he has solved the riddle of the birth of Romanticism and of resonant rhyme."[47]

This "birth of Romantic poetry" Shevyrëv recognized as the

central "message" of Goethe's "Helena" scene, not theoretically presented but set forth palpably in its total content and style. This insight is Shevrëv's most impressive achievement. He clearly recognized the essentially "Classical" style of the first part, in contrast to the "Romantic" style of the second, which he considered to begin with the scene at Faust's castle. Here he proves his uncommon sensitivity to the formal elements of composition. "The first part," he argued, Goethe carried out in "a consistently epic form of presentation." Here the protagonists do not "converse," they "narrate"; they do not express their thoughts and feelings the instant they arise under the momentary and immediate stress of present events but rather "relate and restate recollections and reflections as they were called up in an 'epic' past by bygone happenings." This Shevyrëv considered to be the reason for the "placid calm of this first half, for the complete absence in it of sudden, overwhelming emotions," for "the pervasive impression here is not of immediacy but of epic distance and of recurrence."

Shevyrëv developed his argument by contrasting the second part with the first. The second part of the *Phantasmagoria* was for him "the complete antithesis of the first, being composed in the Romantic taste." In this part Goethe introduced, as one of the central figures, Euphorion "that allegory of Romantic art of the musical poetry of our Christian era which sings its songs from the heart and measures their rhythms with its beat. And these songs are as multiform as the emotions of the human soul. In this poetry all is celestial, all is spiritual, except Euphorion's lyre and cape." According to our critic, "the action of this part is restless and rapid, as is its language. Every emotion expresses itself as present at the very moment of its inception, and unfolds as the words are uttered which well from the heart, from that fountainhead of all feelings. Here one is lost in the riotous multiformity of sensations, to which corresponds the multiformity of rhythms and meters. That is why Goethe has called this *Phantasmagoria* 'Classico-Romantic.' "[48]

Shevyrëv may have been overstating his case, yet he undeniably seized upon an essential characteristic of Goethe's work. In helping to define and develop the poetics of the Liubomudry, especially their view of "Romantic poetry," he adds a significant lineament to the Russian image of Goethe as the "poet-seer" who with all-but-mystic powers of divination and a poet's creative imagination has set forth in an inimitable work of art the pure essence of the Classical and the Romantic styles, of ancient and modern art.

Shevyrëv's essay greatly impressed a certain Nikolai Borchardt, a minor functionary in the Ministry of Culture, an avid reader of the *Moscow Messenger* and an enthusiastic admirer of Goethe. He wrote a brief evaluation of Shevyrëv's interpretation of the "Helena" scene, prefacing it with a few biographical data on its author, giving to this "fragment" the rather ambitious title: "Goethe's Würdigung in Rußland zur Würdigung von Rußland." In it he welcomed Shevyrëv's contribution as a sign that among "the sons of Russia there is awakening a striving toward the lofty and the spiritual." He realized that "the thoughts and the feelings expressed by the young poet [Shevyrëv] are not equal to the genius of the creator of 'Helena,'" yet they did, in his opinion, "bear eloquent witness to the type of appreciation of Goethe which now finds expression in the language spoken from the shores of the Baltic to the far-off peninsula of Kamchatka."[49]

Borchardt translated Shevyrëv's essay into German and sent it together with his "fragment" to Goethe on February 12, 1828. Goethe's diary carries the following entry on March 1.:

Letter from Moscow from Nicolaus Borchardt. . . . For lunch the Messrs. Riemer and Eckermann. Stayed after the meal, and the consignment [Sendung] from Moscow was discussed."[50]

Obviously, the "Sendung" had aroused Goethe's interest, all the more so since at this very time the leading French periodical *Le Globe*[51] and the *Foreign Review* of Edinburgh[52] had also published appreciations of his "Helena." Thomas Carlyle was the contributor to the *Review,* the article in *Le Globe* was signed by Jean Jacques Ampère. Reading these first reactions to his work by an international trio of critics, Goethe was struck by the fact that together they furnished a splendid illustration of the three possible attitudes in the appreciation of a product of art, or for that matter,

—of nature. In his journal über *Kunst und Altertum,* Goethe wrote:

> Here the Scot strives to penetrate the work; the Frenchman seeks to understand it; the Russian, to make it his own. And thus Messrs. Carlyle, Ampère and Shevyrëv have actually exemplified, each in his way and without collusion, the several categories of possible participation in a product of art or nature.* [53]

Goethe closes this note by stressing that these three "categories of participation" need not be mutually exclusive, that, in fact, they usually fuse and interact with one another.

Goethe's designation of Shevyrëv's method as predominantly "aneignend," "appropriative," is strikingly apt. Not only does it precisely characterize Shevyrëv's activity as Goethe's translator and interpreter, but, beyond that, it is equally applicable to the efforts of the entire group of the Liubomudry who did indeed strive to "appropriate," to make their very own the thought and artistry of the incomparable poet-philosopher of Weimar. The trio of international voices continued to occupy Goethe's thoughts, as numerous references in his diary, letters, and conversations clearly indicate.[54] On May 1, two months after the arrival of Borchardt's letter, Goethe sent his reply. Great must have been Borchardt's joy and pride upon receipt of Goethe's letter, which he hastened to submit to the *Moscow Messenger.* Pogodin, its editor, promptly published it "with the greatest of pleasure" in a two-column spread with the German original in the left and a generally faithful Russian translation in the right-hand column. [55] The letter is a carefully worded document running three full pages in the Weimar edition.[56] In it Goethe seems to have a twofold purpose: first, to encourage his Russian admirers in further pursuit of their literary studies, and, secondly, to urge them find their "proper place" in the world at large and in the "particular social circle" assigned to each, advice given, it would seem, with a lively appreciation of the

---

* Hier strebt nun der Schotte, das Werk zu durchdringen: der Franzose, es zu verstehen, der Russe, sich es anzueignen. Und so hätten die Herren Carlyle, Ampère und Schewireff ganz ohne Verabredung die sämtlichen Kategorien der möglichen Theilnahme an einem Kunst- oder Naturproduct vollständig durchgeführt.

conservative policy which Goethe's and Weimar's benefactor, Czar Nicholas I had introduced as his answer to the Decembrist uprising:

> Since you are called upon—so runs Goethe's advice—to participate in a most significant epoch at such a noteworthy turning point in history, you should set no limits to your studies, in order to return all the more surely to where a noble, pure and simple influence is most needed, in order that many an obstacle be removed and much of benefit be furthered. . . . Continue to strive calmly for self-cognition, come to feel your worth and dignity, but at the same time learn to know the assigned position which is yours in the world and quite especially in your well-defined [social] circle.*

With reference to Shevyrëv's essay, Goethe is full of praise, though perhaps somewhat vague. He confesses that, even though his earlier contacts with Russia had made him aware of its "high esthetic culture", he was "quite unprepared"

> to find flourishing in the distant East feelings toward me as tender as they are profound, feelings such as could hardly be found more winsome and more gracious in Western lands, where culture has been developing for long centuries.

> To find the problem, or rather the tangle of problems, which my "Helena" presents, resolved both with such incisive perceptiveness and with such heartfelt piety [so herzlich-fromm] could not but surprise me, even though I have grown accustomed to experience the fact that cultural growth in recent times cannot be measured by the measuring-standards of earlier days.[†]

---

* Da Sie an so merkwürdigem Wendepunkt, an bedeutendster Epoche theilzunehmen berufen sind, so setzen Sie Ihren Studien keine Gränzen, um desto sicherer dahin zurückzukehren, wo eine edle, reine, einfache Wirkung noth thut, damit manches Hindernis beseitigt und viel Gutes gefördert werde. . . . Fahren Sie fort, ruhig dahin zu wirken, daß der Mensch mit sich selbst bekannt werde, seinen eigenen Werth und Würde fühlen, aber zugleich auch die Stellung erkennen lerne, die ihm gegen die Welt überhaupt, besonders aber in seinem bestimmten Kreis gegeben ist.

† Ich war ganz unvorbereitet in Bezug auf mich jene so zarten als tiefen Gefühle in dem entfernten Osten aufblühen zu sehen, wie sie kaum holder und anmuthiger in den seit Jahrhunderten sich ausbildenden westlichen Ländern zu finden sein dürften.

Das Problem oder vielmehr den Knäul von Problemen, wie meine Helena sie vorlegt, so entschieden-einsichtig als herzlich-fromm gelöst zu wissen, mußte mich in Verwunderung setzen, ob ich gleich schon zu erfahren gewohnt bin, daß die Steigerungen der letzten Zeit nicht nach dem Maß der früheren berechnet werden können.

Surely, this is a handsome compliment by Goethe to the Russian critic, despite the note of smiling irony carried by the "herzlich-fromm" to the initiated ear.

Shevyrëv's stature as the leading Russian champion of Goethe was greatly enhanced by this accolade from the "German patriarch." Still, he did not rest on his newly won laurels. The very next number of the *Messenger* carried a lengthy review of Byron's *Manfred*,[57] in which Shevyrëv sets up two types of poets and of poetry which may be fairly defined as "Realistic-objective" and as "Romantic-subjective." According to Shevyrëv,

> the first type of poetry depicts life in all its elements: traits of character, actions, incidents, emotions, etc., down to their smallest details hardly discernible to the normal eye. The other uses plot merely as a framework within which to set forth a lofty thought or an intense feeling or some few rich minutes of life, minutes in which we live with all the powers of our soul. This type of poetry eschews details; its strokes are colossal, lofty, bold; its colors are sombre, nebulous; here objects lose their physical reality; all that lives and breathes appears as a mere specter, a phantom, a shadow, a cloud; here all is changeable, ephemeral, all except thought and feeling, which dominate everything else and infuse everything with soul, with harmony, lend the work of art whatever definiteness it has.[58]

Shevyrëv placed Byron into this second category, as one might have expected. Goethe he first assigned to the "objective" group, together with such "realists" as "our own Pushkin," Walter Scott, and James Fenimore Cooper, but hastened to correct this "excessively narrow" definition of Goethe's genius by emphasizing its all-embracing scope: "There are some poets who were capable of combining in their work these two types of creativity, and foremost among these is Goethe, who with his *Götz* and *Wilhelm Meister* belongs to the first, with his *Faust* to the second category."[59]

Shevyrëv concludes this essay with a startling bit of misinterpretation, springing in part at least from lack of information. He categorically denies any relationship in content or in form between Byron's *Manfred* and Goethe's *Faust*. "There is no use comparing Manfred with Faust. In them we have two antithetical creations, two harmful extremes. Manfred, having rejected all, insists on

living withdrawn unto himself; Faust, having surrendered himself into
the hands of the demon, wants to live exclusively in the external
world. They have but one thing in common: they both perish."[60]
We must remember that Shevyrëv knew nothing at this time of the
"Prolog in Heaven," nothing of the second part of *Faust* except, of
course, the "Helena" scene, which failed to furnish him clear evidence of Goethe's intention to save his ever-striving hero in the end.

Shevyrëv's next and final contribution to the *Messenger* on the
theme of Goethe was his review of *Götz von Berlichingen* in the
Russian translation by his friend M. Pogodin.[61] In it Shevyrëv fails
to match the perceptiveness and originality of his essay on "Helena,"
even though he is here on more solid ground than in his interpretation of *Faust* in the review on *Manfred*. In this review he depends heavily on Goethe's account in *Dichtung und Wahrheit* of the
inception and development of *Götz*. His point of view is that of
the literary historian rather than of the esthetician, which it had
been so predominantly in the "Helena" piece. Moreover, the voice
of the Eastern Orthodox Christian and incipient Slavophile, audible
in the earlier essay, has become far more distinct.

Shevyrëv opens his discussion with the contention that French
culture has suffered decline. "The brilliant era of French literature
has passed, its influence on other nations has dwindled." The reason
—a spirit of agnosticism and skepticism pervading French thought.
"Voltaire has lost face in Germany. . . . The young generation
of Germans has recognized his constant prevarications and has
exposed them; Voltaire's blasphemous efforts to uproot, along
with the abuse of faith, the sacred teachings themselves, has aroused
resentment in Germany, a country where philosophy and poetry
both draw their insight and inspiration from the Christian religion."
Nor could the French Encyclopedists satisfy the Germans' yearning
and search for truth. Moreover, Voltaire had "enfeebled French
tragedy, much as Euripides had the Greek, by degrading it to the
level of ordinary existence." Herder and Lessing had, in the mean-
time, introduced Shakespeare to Germany. "This giant," according
to Shevyrëv, "was destined to fructify German poetry, . . . to be
the mentor of Goethe and of Schiller." Under his influence "Goethe

was able to cast off altogether the shackles of the French school," under his influence "the seed of two great works, *Götz* and *Faust*, was planted in Goethe's mind. . . . He was struck by the inspired thought: to present in the person of Götz von Berlichingen an honest, upright man who strove in times of complete anarchy, motivated by love for his fellow man, to fill the void of lawlessness with a benevolent self-rule." Shevyrëv would have us see Goethe's Götz as a "loyal subject who voluntarily submits to the sacred voice of the supreme authority of his monarch, prepared to die rather than to betray his pledge of fealty." It is not difficult to recognize in this interpretation the point of view of Shevyrëv, the "loyal subject of his monarch," with a trend in his intellectual development leading him straight toward the Slavophiles' program of orthodoxy and nationalism" and away from Goethe and his work.[62]

At the time of his review of *Götz*, however, Shevyrëv was still full of appreciation and praise of Goethe's greatness. He acclaimed him as "the mighty genius whose destiny it was to stand at the head of a new era of poetry, to be the author of modern esthetics, the founder of a whole new culture. Shevyrëv credited Goethe with "a gigantic undertaking in his tragedy of *Götz*, worthy of a genius," with a "loftiness of concept" matched only by Schiller in his *Tell*. "Only a Goethe could draw on one canvas the huge contours of an entire epoch, of the [German] Middle Ages with all the social groupings of feudal society, not excepting its imperial head." Shevyrëv admired Goethe's boldness: "Who but Goethe would have dared to cast the supreme representative of the Empire [Maximilian] not in the foremost but in a hardly noticeable role of his tragedy?" He recognizes in the poet-dramatist a lofty idealism which "has enabled him to embody in his hero [Götz] all that was noblest in the age. Götz' death is the apotheosis of a free knighthood, dedicated to the protection of human rights. . . . With the last breath of the last knight, freedom takes flight from this earth."

It is characteristic of Shevyrëv's enlightened liberalism, which was still strong in this phase of his development, that he singles out the ideals of "human rights" and "freedom" for special emphasis and that he points out, as particularly effective scenes, those in which Goethe sharply attacked the clergy of the time, gave a sympathetic treatment of the rebellious peasants or offered a devastating portrayal of Weislingen as the typical sycophantic courtier: "How brilliantly has Goethe revealed in the briefest of scenes the boorishness, servility, venality, and pedantry of the servants of the church. . . . With what empathy he draws the misery of the poor peasants that drove some to despair and others to excesses of blind violence. . . . In Goethe's weak, effeminate, flighty windbag of a Weislingen we meet the very personification of life at court."

Dwelling as he does on the "organic unity" of Goethe's characters, Shevyrëv gives us the first specific instance in Russia of a perceptive appreciation of this facet of Goethe's genius. "Each 'persona' is a unified, integrated likeness of himself; you always see the selfsame Götz, the selfsame Adelheid, the selfsame Weislingen." Shevyrëv's phrasing may lack clarity and aptness. Nevertheless, he has unquestionably seized upon an essential characteristic of Goethe's "personae," the lifelike unity and consistency of their "Gestalt."

Seeing *Götz* as Goethe's supreme achievement, Shevyrëv acclaims the German poet's ability to go beyond Shakespeare, to outdo in his drama the British "giant" within his own domain—the theater. "Shakespeare had presented on his stage only the important figures of history; the lives of his tragedies, like in Hume's great historical writings, are exclusively those of kings [*sic*]. Goethe in his tragedy opens up entirely new vistas not only for art but for historiography as well. Does not Goethe challenge us in his creation [Götz] with the precept to recognize henceforth in history the all-embracing human drama that it is, to treat history henceforth as a living, inspired portrayal of human beings from all walks of life, in every conceivable environment, social condition and circumstance?" Shevyrëv rather spoiled his case when he addressed his readers in a blatantly didactic vein which was much favored in the pages of the *Messenger* as in other journals of the time, probably under the influence of the English moral weeklies; with uplifted finger he admonishes us "to open Goethe's *Götz* and learn from the poet the great lesson that history teaches us: the under-standing of the motives of man and of ourselves!"

Shevyrëv's brief and rather critical comments on the form of the drama come as quite an anticlimax. He finds the play "sketchy" and "ill-suited for the stage in the swift sequence of its scenes." He hastens, however, to warn us not to criticize the author, who had not written his drama for a contemporary theater. Shevyrëv would have us realize that, as a tragedy, Goethe's *Götz* is beyond criticism, "for it fulfills the central requirement of the genre: it shows man in his struggle against fate."

There is not a word in Shevyrëv's review on the merits of Pogodin's translation. Pogodin had attempted to reproduce in it the "realism" of Goethe's dialog by introducing Russian anachron-isms, provincialisms, and colloquialisms, peasant slang and jargon. Pogodin was unsuccessful, especially when one compares his effort with Pushkin's brilliant use of "realistic" dialog in *Boris Godunov*. Shevyrëv most likely withheld comment so as not to offend the in-fluential editor of the *Messenger* and his close personal friend.

Thus it was in the pages of the *Messenger* that Shevyrëv de-fined his view of Goethe. In his subsequent academic writings he added some salient features, some critical touches, but he did not change the basic contours of this image of Goethe. On the huge canvas of his *History of Literature* (1835) which includes the out-lines of Indian, Hebrew, Greek, and Roman literature, we catch hardly a glimpse of Goethe. Though the dramas of Racine and Shakespeare are compared at some length with their Greek proto-types, there is no mention of Goethe's *Iphigenie* in connection with Euripides' dramatic masterpiece. Only three times does Shevyrëv refer to Goethe's life and work in order to illustrate some rather peripheral theses in the book. Once he uses Goethe's "calm and happy life" in the "quiet of his family circle and his study" to prove that a poet need not lead a turbulent existence in order to write dramas—dubious theorizing at best, and a superficial oversimpli-fication of Goethe's life to boot.[63] Another time he quotes Goethe's statement in *Dichtung und Wahrheit* that "he [Goethe] had re-ceived his first artistic instruction in the workshop of the craftsman, in the throne room of the Emperors and in the imperial archives of his native city of Frankfurt."[64] This passage may have helped Shevyrëv to demonstrate his point that life itself offers the great artist his earliest and most important education, it may have helped him prove the importance of the influence of milieu upon an artist's work, but it certainly does nothing to enrich Shevyrëv's portrait of Goethe.

Of greater significance is his comparison of Goethe with Schiller, though even this is little more than an amplification of the Liubomudry's basic view of Goethe as the paragon of a perfect balance of poetic and philosophical gifts. While Schiller's poetry always depends for its value, according to Shevyrëv, on the "golden nugget of thought," "Goethe has freed his imagination to a far greater extent from one-sided domination by ideas." With this statement Shevyrëv is clearly in the best tradition of the interpretation of Goethe by the "Lovers of Wisdom." But what follows is a startling indication of a growing critical awareness of certain shortcomings in a central work of Goethe. Pointing to his *Faust,* Shevyrëv now detects "in it the stamp of an idea of a most abstract kind" and goes on to stress that "in his latest works, Goethe *has fallen into* the symbolical, the allegorical style and has therewith shown, more clearly than ever before, German poetry to be the fruit of science."[65] To be sure, Shevyrëv still credits Goethe with a Protean empathy: "He so freely, so easily transports his muse on the wings of imagination into the graceful forms of Classical poetry, into the musical sonnet, the Italian 'ottava rima.' And *yet,* here, too, we see that this freedom and ease are the product of *study and erudition.*"[66] The pejorative note of the "fallen into" and the "yet" in these passages is significant. Shevyrëv seems to imply, ever so cautiously, a loss of that fine balance between Goethe's imaginative and analytical faculties, a preponderance of the cerebral effort of "study and erudition" as threats to creative spontaneity and inspiration. This critical note becomes even more evident if we compare this passage with Shevyrëv's unreserved praise for Goethe's "symbolic and allegorical style" in his essay on "Helena," where he acclaimed Goethe's "Classico-Romantic *Phantasmagoria*" as "an allegory of pure, enchanting and altogether original form," "an eminently successful allegory" which "rejuvenates magically the ossified Faust-theme of the Chapbook."[67]

Shevyrëv's other academic *magnum opus*, his *Theory of Literature*,[68] pays far more attention to Goethe. In it a whole section is devoted to him. Shevyrëv begins his characterization by stressing Goethe's "objective" or "empirical" orientation in his theoretical and imaginative writing. "The author of *Götz* was the foremost representative in his age of this *objective* orientation in art." Again, as in his *History of Literature*, Shevyrëv compares Goethe with Schiller, in order by way of contrast to characterize Goethe's genius the more precisely: "Schiller had chosen the cerebral, the philosophical approach to art, Goethe the empirical. . . . Schiller had sought to arrive at form by way of concept, he moved from theory toward practice; Goethe laid hold of form directly through palpable experience and the observation of concrete phenomena."[69] Being wary of the ways of philosophers, Goethe early and eagerly followed Winckelmann and Lessing, who "had given to German esthetics an 'objective orientation.' " According to Shevyrëv, Goethe had embraced, as a central law of esthetics, "the basic principle of Lessing's *Laokoon,* the clear and consistent division of art into its various genres." Shevyrëv buttresses his view with quotations from Goethe's "Einleitung in die Propyläen"[70] and his review of Sulzer's *Die schönen Künste,*[71] and goes on to claim that "in all of Goethe's creations, the genres and forms of poetry return, as it were, to their pristine form, including their national idiosyncrasies." Thus it was, according to Shevyrëv, "that the 'objective' or 'empirical' orientation of Goethe's esthetics enabled him to create the richest variety of genres and styles in his work, to achieve an all-embracing eclecticism" or "esthetic universalism." "The poets of all the world, of all ages and nations participated in the education of Goethe, creating in his *oeuvre* a veritable pantheon of world literature, possible only in Germany, that land of artistic eclecticism." Shevyrëv proceeds with a listing of the world-wide influences on Goethe's works: Homer on the *Achilleis* and *Hermann und Dorothea,* the Greek tragedians on *Iphigenie* and especially on the first part of the

"Helena" scene (from *Faust,* Part II), Shakespeare on *Götz* and *Egmont,* Rousseau on *Werther* and *Dichtung und Wahrheit.* "French tragedy has left its impression on *Tasso* and the *Natürliche Tochter,* the middle-class drama on *Clavigo, Stella* and *Grosscophta,* the Arabian-Persian East on the *Divan,* the English family novel on *Wilhelm Meister* and the *Wahlverwandtschaften.*" Then, turning to *Faust,* Shevyrëv claims that it "combined the influence of Spanish and English drama together with a special infusion of the Germanic spirit in its content." We detect an echo of Shevyrëv's interpretation of "Helena" when he presents that *Interact to Faust* as "a synthesis of classical and modern poetry" and Helena as "a female Janus, composed of the ancient Greek and the modern European woman." Finally, in Goethe's lyrics, Shevyrëv hears "the strains of the lyre of all the nations: here resound Pindar's lofty ode, the rich rhythms of Petrarch's sonnet, the voices of Tibullus and Ovid in the *Römische Elegien.* In the *Divan* we are charmed by the Ghazal. Here the French 'romance,' the knightly 'ballad,' the German folksong join their voices. And in this grand chorus there sparkles and flashes, with its sharply cut and contoured form, the epigram of Greek provenience, and the ancient Germanic proverb makes us pause in thought on its profound wisdom. Here every genre is whole in its unmarred artistic purity. Truly, Goethe's work can serve us well as a text of universal poetry. Such was the fruit of Germany's 'critical eclecticism' [esthetic universalism] when —fully matured—it informed Goethe's creative genius." Aside from furnishing evidence of an extensive if not intensive acquaintance with Goethe's works, Shevyrëv traces here Goethe's "eclecticism" which we had met before—in Uvarov's definition[72]—as Goethe's "Protean" muse, to that "empirical criticism and eclecticism which had been introduced into German literature by Lessing and developed to a universal range by Herder." Here Shevyrëv placed in historical perspective and emphasized a facet of the Russian image of Goethe that was to be a prevalent and permanent one, namely, of Goethe the "foremost representative of *poetic universalism* in its *creative* [as against its *critical*] manifestation."[73]

Moreover, the Russian critic furnishes in his *Theory* the definitive statement of the Liubomudry's acclaim of Goethe as the leading exponent of "l'art pour l'art." He quotes from Goethe's "Der Sänger" the lines:

> Ich singe, wie der Vogel singt,
> Der in den Zweigen wohnet.*

and with them gives the champions of "pure art" their motto. Then he "translates these lines into the language of a contemporary philosopher [Schelling] as 'art has its goal in itself' " and continues his argument by pointing out that "Schelling had given this insight its theoretical formulation while Goethe had actually given it artistic form in the vast range of his creations. For Goethe, art represents a higher world than nature's with its own truth and its own goals," and again: "That which Schelling has established in theory, Goethe has carried out in his work as artist. The great German poet has fixed art's purpose solely in art itself, divorcing it from any and all extraneous aims."[74] Thus, Shevyrëv spelled out, with all possible emphasis, the central tenet of the esthetics of the Russian "Lovers of Wisdom." He buttressed it with liberal and relevant quotations from Goethe's essay, "Über die Wahrheit und Wahrscheinlichkeit der Kunstwerke,"[75] which he had early recognized as central in the dialog on "pure art," had translated and published it in the *Messenger*[76] as early as 1827, the year of his preoccupation with Goethe's "Helena" scene.

In the closing pages of the section on Goethe of his *Theory,* Shevyrëv rose to the defense of the German poet against one of Goethe's most vociferous critics, Wolfgang Menzel, whose *Deutsche Literatur* (1827) had caused a stir in Russian literary circles. He accused Menzel of moral bigotry which blinded him to Goethe's supreme achievement of having "raised art to the loftiest level of total independence from mundane reality, high above Germany's soil [the social and political milieu] into an ethereal world completely alien to the terrestrial." Goethe, according to Shevyrëv, may leave a materialist like Menzel mired in his bigotry, completely insensitive to the poet's true greatness, but "he does transport every

---

* I sing as the bird sings who dwells in the branches.

idealistic German into the realm of his longings, of his dreams, there to forget life's imperfections in contemplation of sublime beauty. Menzel is indignant that the all-powerful genius of Germany, this mighty ruler over the minds of men, did not fashion poetry into an instrument of political ideology, that in his name and under his aegis there did not come about an era of regenerated [socio-political] life, but that instead a new period of art arose, the *Kunstperiode*." Menzel may be indignant in his blindness, but he cannot tarnish Goethe's fame or gainsay his achievement. Thus defending Goethe against his detractor, Shevyrëv enthroned him as the poet sublime whose realm is not of this world, as the patron saint of the Liubomudry and all future Russian apostles of "l'art pour l'art."

Shevyrëv's admiration for Goethe was not to remain at this high pitch. As he rapidly moved from esthetic idealism of the Liubomudry to the position of the Slavophiles, he began to suspect Goethe of excessive "analytical intellectualism," especially in the works of his late period. We remember the note of criticism that had crept into his remarks in the *History of Literature* on the "allegorical and symbolic" style into which "Goethe had fallen" in his *Faust*. Now, in "A Russian View of the Contemporary Cultural Scene in Europe," published in the Slavophile journal, the *Muskovite*,[77] in 1841, Shevyrëv takes up this theme again, this time in sharp outspoken criticism: "The latest symbolical creations of Goethe exhibit an excessive preponderance of this [the philosophical] element: such a late creation is the second part of *Faust*. Here I observe how German poetry is turning to ashes and is about to ossify into a philosophical skeleton. That is the reason the Hegelians express such special sympathy with this second part of Goethe's *Faust:* in this decay of poetry they find the germ of their own beings. To use Goethe's simile: Faust and Helena have produced in Germany their own Euphorion: yet, this is not the lively, playful, winged and irrepressible Byron of Goethe's drama, but rather a dry-as-dust philosophical abstraction; the Euphorion of German poetry turned out to be Hegel's logic." But Hegel's logic had become the bête noire of the Slavophile Shevyrëv, who had rapidly developed into an implacable foe of enlightened thought and, specifically, of progressive dialectics in the Hegelian spirit. What a far cry indeed this evaluation of Goethe's "later work" was from Shevyrëv's enthusiastic reception of Goethe's "Helena" in 1827!

As Shevyrëv's orientation in esthetics and politics became ever more reactionary, his comments on Goethe grew fewer and finally ceased altogether. In his late publications one does not find any references to Goethe which add significantly to Shevyrëv's interpretation of the German poet. But by that time Shevyrëv had contributed his full share to Russia's appreciation and appropriation of Goethe's personality and work.

4. The Liubomudry in Weimar

In those early years of unqualified admiration for the poet-sage, Shevyrëv had made his all-but-obligatory pilgrimage to Weimar. Together with his young friend, Nikolai Matveevich Rozhalin (1805-34), he was introduced to Goethe by Countess Zinaida A. Volkonskaia, a gifted poetess in her own right, the celebrated "Muse of the Liubomudry." She had met Goethe for the first time on May 1, 1813, at Teplitz, where he had sought safety before the Russian troops threatening to overrun Weimar in their victorious pursuit of Napoleon's shattered army. Now, some fifteen years later, on May 12, 1829, the Countess stood again before the venerated "Patriarch of Weimar" and introduced to him her Russian friends. All three have left vivid descriptions of the meeting.

From Shevyrëv we have three accounts. The first one, in a letter to his friend A. P. Elagina, written under the immediate impact of the event, is surely the most realistic portrait of the aging poet. Shevyrëv was impressed with Goethe's "fiery eyes!" But, he continued, "they alone seem to be charged with life; as for him, he barely moves upon this earth. There he sat in his chair, his arms limp at his side, his fingers constantly contracting. Everything seems to oppress him, especially unfamiliar faces. It was as if he had no time to take in new impressions."[78] Shevyrëv's retrospective report, written eight years later, idealizes this first impression, obviously striving to make with it his contribution to the Romantic image of Goethe, the Olympian.[79] As he awaits the appearance of the poet, Shevyrëv can compare his feelings only "with those he had experienced upon first seeing the mighty Ocean, eternal Rome, Saint Peter's Cathedral, Mont Blanc." Soon "the majestic figure of Goethe slowly and calmly moved toward us. The most impressive feature in his appearance, as in the bust of Jupiter, was his high, deeply furrowed forehead. Under it, his dark eyes sparkled with the fire of youth. The regular Grecian profile still was firm and true: powerful shoulders and a marvelously erect torso supported that noble, ancient head." In sharp contrast to his first report, Shevyrëv now remembers Goethe sitting in his armchair, "in the posture of a Jupiter in repose, his hands upon his knees, his fingers moving like the talons of an eagle or the claws of a lion as he would now extend, now contract them." It is marvelous indeed how imagination at a distance in time and space can transform sober first impressions to create the mythical image of Jupiter-Goethe!

Still, compared with the description left us by the "Romantic muse," Countess Volkonskaia, even this glorification of Goethe seems restrained. In a most elaborate and, to say the least, daring simile, Volkonskaia compares the ever-active, infinitely creative, all-embracing genius of Goethe to a "ceaselessly creative, bustling, ancient, populous city, where Greek temples with their marble statues in their simple harmonious lines rise gloriously side by side with the gloomy, mysterious Gothic cathedrals, with their limpid spires, their gossamer crenulations, their gravestones of medieval knights." Obviously, the Countess is striving to "picture" for us with this elaborate metaphor the Classic-Romantic synthesis achieved by Goethe in his works. To give an impression of the heights to which Zinaida's adoring muse could soar in her worship of the master, we must quote her metaphor in full: "In this ancient city all is inspired, dignified, immortal; monuments, books, edifices, mausoleums speak to the ages of the glorious deeds of glorious men. In this beauteous city, all is activity: savants delve in the archives of all the ages; artists dream and create: poets, contemplating the universe, grow intoxicated with inspiration and in their transport begin to speak in tongues. In this populous city, emotions are all aflame; there is a chorus of sounds; the lyre can be heard, hymns, psalms, folksongs and passionate songs of love, they all fuse in harmony and rise like the scent of incense." We notice, of course, that Zinaida is dwelling here in her imaginative manner on the familiar theme of Goethe's "Protean," his "eclectic" or "universal" genius so highly esteemed by the Liubomudry. She ends her flight of imagination with a glance at "the heavenly constellations that sparkle and burn over this city like the inextinguishable stars of eternal fame above the glorious head of the ancient sage."[80]

After these flights of Romantic fancy, Rozhalin's recollections sound prosaic, almost cynical. This seems the more surprising because Rozhalin was among the most ardent worshipers of Goethe. Goethe was to him quite literally "the measure of all things"; he worshiped in him a poet endowed "with a genius co-extensive with nature itself, a genius that recognized itself in nature's limitless multifariousness and therefore could find for all his thoughts counterparts in natural phenomena, for all his feelings—living allegories."[81] Goethe's *Werther* was for him the "book of books" in which he found his own impressionable nature, his own transports and despair, his own yearning for love and friendship. Here one is clearly justified to speak of an "elective affinity." Thus, it is no mere chance that Rozhalin's translation of *Werther,* a labor of love and empathy, is to this day unexcelled in its faithfulness to the original. After judiciously comparing the extant renderings of *Werther,* Zhirmunski has this to say: "Rozhalin recreates, more successfully than any other translator of *Werther,* the emotional style of the sentimental-Romantic prose of the original, inspired, passionate, or melancholy. In comparison with the rationalistic simplification by Galchenko and Vinogradov and the realistic 'lowering' [of style] by Strugovchikov, Rozhalin's translation, despite its rather dated language, remains to this day the most adequate rendering as the product of an age which was still attuned to *Werther,* not only in its tastes but also in its ideology."[82] His affinity to

Werther was generally recognized and his friends amiably dubbed him "Werther"-Rozhalin. Perhaps it was precisely his exaggerated admiration for *Werther's* creator that made Rozhalin "freeze" at the prospect of meeting the worshiped master. We know that he actually begged Countess Volkonskaia to let him accompany her incognito as her personal servant. Or was it perchance the inescapable "letdown" after such high expectations that dictated the cold, almost ironical account of the longed-for meeting? Characteristicly it begins: "Volkonskaia and Shevyrëv have been at Goethe's," just as if he had not been one of the party. Then follows his ambivalent description of the poet: "There he stood, in the center of his living room, with an important ministerial mien. But when he saw our bunch [gur'bu] he took fright and it required all the tact of the Countess to put him at his ease. Fortunately, she had been forewarned by Chancellor Müller that Goethe could be very timid and uncomfortable in the presence of strangers. We stayed for more than an hour and I could see my fill of him, sitting as I did, right at his side. His features have etched themselves into my memory. . . . Goethe is very dignified and one is immediately aware of his being very irritable. His gaze is unbearable, it is positively unpleasant. This is probably due to the fact that his dark eyes are circled by some sort of strange, light-grey rings and appear birdlike." Surely, no romanticising here; but rather an amazingly realistic rendering of details sharply observed. Rozhalin, nevertheless, bestows an accolade on Goethe, not on Goethe the person before him, but rather on Goethe as idealized in a bust by Trippeli (Alexander Trippeli) which stood directly next to one of Byron. "One need but compare this head of Goethe with Byron's bust to recognize at once which of the two poets was the more glorious both in his person and in his genius"—Goethe, most certainly! The conversation disappointed Rozhalin. "Goethe spoke at length about Napoleon, whom he knew well and who, he told us, carried his *Werther* always with him. But, alas, the conversation did not touch on anything really important, on nothing at all in which Goethe could have revealed himself as a poet," and this, Rozhalin hastens to assure us, not because of Goethe's old age: "In fact, Goethe has preserved much of his youthful freshness and is in good health. He pampers and shelters himself and is being sheltered even more by others."[83] This description, like Shevyrëv's, was written immediately following the visit and sent in a letter to their mutual friend, A. P. Elagina.

Some months later, Rozhalin writes of the experience to his parents.[84] Whether it was a case of 'distance makes the heart grow fonder,' whether he had overcome the chilling effect of the actual meeting or whether he was adjusting his message to a different audience, Rozhalin's admiration and even love for Goethe speak as clearly in this letter as they were clearly absent in the former. He is "very happy" to have seen Goethe at long last. "My long-cherished dream has finally come true! I have made the personal acquaintance of the poet whom I consider to be the greatest of modern writers, of all the poets of the Christian era." The sketch that follows of the aging poet is done with a far friendlier pen: "Goethe has a most dignified bearing and yet is kind and affectionate. He is still unusually hale and active for his years. His face is beautiful. . . . He shows interest in all that touches on Russia, has read all Russian verse available in French, German, English, and Italian translations, was eager to know about translations into Russian from English and German literature. And yet, he *is* an infirm old man, has chosen his burial place next to the grave of his friend Schiller. I have seen the spot." Do we catch an elegiac note in these parting words of "Werther"-Rozhalin?

Through Chancellor Müller, Goethe invited him for another meeting, but, not unlike Grillparzer, a kindred spirit to Rozhalin in more than reticence and wrong-headed pride, Rozhalin declined and hastend to leave Weimar, never to return to that "little city, so quiet, so marvelously clean," which he "could not but compare with a quiet, withdrawn, and pensive person."

On August 25, Rozhalin arrived in Dresden, where he attended a memorable performance of *Faust,* given at the Hoftheater as part of the festivities in celebration of Goethe's eightieth birthday. Rozhalin was enthralled by it. He wrote to his friend Elagina: "We went to see Faust and saw—a miracle!" Nevertheless, Rozhalin did not lose his sharp, critical eye. He noted the shortcomings

of the performance, found the "first monologue ruined by the rant-
ing of the actor . . .," Gretchen lacking in charm and grace, and he
was "furious with the crazy Tieck [Ludwig Tieck] for having
poured together the scene of Valentin's murder with Gretchen's
prayer to the Virgin, and her pangs of conscience in the Cathedral,
thus spoiling everything." It is easy to sympathize with the Russian critic for the impression must have been grotesque indeed,
certainly not what Goethe intended. But these shortcomings were
more than offset for Rozhalin by the superb acting of one Pauli,
"who is truly worthy of his fame. . . . His talents are many; he is
equally great as devil, robber, hero, and all these accomplishments
he fused wonderfully in his Mephisto. He was 'the icy vessel for
hellish flames.' " Rozhalin had seen a number of dramas performed at the Hoftheater; none had impressed him as deeply.
"Faust on the stage has the effect of pure tragedy. The witches'
kitchen and the *Blocksberg* climb (!) were excellently done with
splendid scenery. The pity is that with the rapid tempo of performance one cannot grasp the meaning of these scenes, one fails
to catch the thought and thus is merely frightened by them."
Rozhalin wanted to see this *Faust* a second time, but discovered
to his dismay that the announced repeat performance had been
cancelled. Surprised and piqued, he writes to his friend in reactionary Russia: "As you probably know, the local royal family
is Catholic; they are almost the only Catholics of the entire
population. And would you believe it, the two young princes (both
25 years old) were deeply offended at Faust's words: 'Wer kann
sagen?' etc.', whereupon their 'little father' takes fright and clamps
down the lid on the performance. You cannot imagine the bigotry
and sanctimoniousness of this family!"[85]

Other developments on the German intellectual scene surprised
and saddened the perceptive Russian traveler. "There is strong
opposition here to the philosophical school," he reports to Elagina.
"Schelling has stopped publishing and has thus sealed its fate.
His followers have likewise fallen silent. Steffens writes only novels.
Hegel alone is active, but he is old, and insults and vilifications
rain down upon him. The enemies of philosophy have banded to-

gether under Goethe's flag and swear fealty to him alone. Their motto is: Goethe has perceived everything, solved everything, and has accomplished this—without philosophy!" We can understand the Liubomudry's disappointment with this hostile tension between the followers of the poet and the camp of philosophy when we remember that they acclaimed precisely the fine balance of these two elements in true genius. It must have been small consolation to Rozhalin to come upon some new works of Goethe: "A short while ago his *Wilhelm Meister* has appeared with some small changes in the *Wanderjahre* and, what is most important (because really new), the third part of his correspondence with Schiller."[86]

It is obvious that Rozhalin surveyed Germany's cultural scene with a trained and perceptive eye. All the greater is our loss in his untimely death as still another victim in the long line of Russia's supremely gifted thinkers and poets, cut down in their most active years by jealousy and hatred, by blind accident and sickness: Venevitinov, Pushkin, Lermontov, and Rozhalin!

After nearly five years of fruitful labors in Italy as a classical philologist, acclaimed by his contemporaries as Russia's future Winckelmann, Rozhalin felt himself succumbing to galloping consumption. He hastened home, longing for final rest in native soil. He died immediately upon arrival without a chance of setting down a record of his experiences in Europe. His belongings, sent after him by slower coach, were held at a way station that burned to the ground, and all his notes perished in the conflagration. We shall never know any of Rozhalin's thoughts and emotions as he followed, literally, in the footsteps of his admired predecessor Goethe on his own "Italian Journey." How often must he have conjured up the German poet's thoughts, discoveries, experiences, in order to compare them with his own! We shall never know and can but lament our loss together with his friend Pogodin who, "smitten by this cruel blow to the very soul," exclaimed in stunned disbelief at such senseless cruelty of fate: "My God! It's just as if the man had never walked this earth!"[87]

The last Liubomudry to visit Goethe in Weimar, just half a year before the poet's death, was Koshelëv. He was, as we recall,

a member of Venevitinov's inner circle. Still, his interests centered on philosophy rather than literature. Thus, his remarks on
Goethe in his voluminous *Notes* are rather disappointing and add
little of importance to the appreciation of the German poet. However, he has left us an account in his *Diary* of the festivities in
Weimar on Goethe's eighty-second birthday, and in his *Notes* a
record of his two visits with the octogenarian. The *Diary* entry,
since it has never been translated, will be given here in full, as a
rare eyewitness account of the celebration by a Russian traveler.[88]
Though Goethe had withdrawn to the idyllic retreat of Ilmenau,
"fearing," as Koshelëv reports, "the excessive emotional strain of
the festivities," he was nonetheless present not only in the hearts
and minds of the celebrants but, as it were, in effigy as well, for
the high point of the program was the unveiling of his bust, done by
the famous French sculptor, Pierre Jean David. Here are Koshelëv's
recollections of the event:

> At break of dawn the whole city [Weimar] had come alive
> with excitement: the gentlemen had donned their newest
> frock coats, the ladies their best finery. Shortly before
> eleven I went to the library, where I found the cream of
> society assembled (two hundred tickets had been sent out).
> At the stroke of eleven, music resounded, a cantata com-
> posed by Goethe's friend, Chancellor von Müller, inspired
> with deep feeling and noble thought, performed by the best
> artists of the city. The singers had their places in the choir
> on the third floor, so that the sounds seemed to be floating
> down from heaven, which greatly enhanced their effect. Fol-
> lowing the music, Chief Librarian [!] Riemer delivered a
> speech in which he dwelled on the theme of brotherhood
> among the nations, citing as a most striking example of such
> brotherly feelings the French sculptor David's readiness to
> leave Paris and to spend months in Weimar, without remuner-
> ation, moved solely by a desire to pass on to coming genera-
> tions the image of the greatest genius of our times by sculpt-
> ing his bust of Goethe, a task which had occupied him for
> many years. Under the strains of music, the curtain cover-
> ing David's bust, finally dropped to the general delight of
> the assembled multitude.

Koshelëv would not judge the degree of likeness but recognized in the bust a labor of love and genuine inspiration. "A pity," he observed, "that the hall was so very much too small for such a colossal sculpture. It had to stand much too low and received its light not from above but from the side," an observation which Goethe corroborated when he saw the work and its position.[89] "At two o'clock," our diarist continues,

> we again gathered for dinner in exclusive company. Toasts were drunk to Goethe, to the ladies, the final toast to international goodwill (Völkereintracht). Each toast was accompanied by speeches, songs, and recitation of poems. Müller on offering his toast to Goethe's health, made a most moving speech. Everyone listened at first with due respect, and soon with evident and genuine sympathy. Following his speech, Müller read a letter sent to Goethe by eighteen English, Scottish and Irish poets, who had joined under the chairmanship of Walter Scott to present Goethe with a valuable ring. In conclusion, Müller proposed to drink a final toast to Goethe from the cup sent by the Free City of Frankfurt to its most famous son. The dinner lasted until eight o'clock and was followed by a court ball at the Belvedere.[90]

Koshelëv had to wait until September 4 for Goethe's return. When he was received he experienced the same disappointment as had Rozhalin. Goethe insisted on presenting himself as the Privy Councilor of the Grandduchy of Weimar, solely interested in the affairs of the Russian court, and would not let Koshelëv catch even a glimpse of the revered poet. Koshelëv "departed more than disappointed."[91] Nevertheless, his diary notes give us a most detailed, vivid picture of Goethe as he met the Russian visitor that memorable morning. Koshelëv is obviously awed by Goethe's presence: "I cannot express what I felt as I gazed upon this greatest genius of our age." Yet he manages to catch every detail of his appearance and dress: "Goethe was dressed in a frock coat of light pea-green color, a scarf wrapped loosely about his neck, exactly as Stieler [Joseph Stieler] had painted him. Though Goethe is eighty-four [*sic*], he is still exceedingly active and sprightly, so that at first sight one could judge his age as between sixty-five and seventy: his face is extremely expressive, especially its upper part. He holds himself very erect, his eyes are full of life and fire. . . ."[92] Early next morning, September 5, Koshelëv was about to leave Weimar when an invitation reached him for a second meeting with Goethe the same evening. Unlike Rozhalin, Koshelëv accepted. This time he found Goethe in the company of his intimate friends,

> Chancellor Müller, the painter Meyer, and three or four other persons. There was not so much as a mention of the Grandduchess or of the Russian Czar. The conversation was exclusively on literary matters. Goethe complained that politics and realism were destroying belles lettres and art in general, that under present conditions art had become quite powerless to influence people. Since true artists cannot possibly compromise with prevailing taste, they must rise to the highest level, must reveal to the people an altogether new and different realm, must conquer them with the power of new ideas. Meyer, too, spoke with great wisdom. At quarter to eleven Chancellor Müller rose, a sign that it was time for us to take our leave.[93]

Next morning, Koshelëv left Weimar, never to return. Nor did he return in his *Diaries*, his *Notes* or his letters to the world of Goethe.

We have one final revealing record[94] by a Liubomudry of his emotions and thoughts on revisiting Weimar long after Goethe and its other famous men of letters had departed from the scene. It is once again from Shevyrëv, a report which he wrote upon his return to Weimar in 1837 only to find the city much changed. It oppressed him now with an atmosphere "as of a mausoleum of literary Germany, of a Pompei with its streets of graves." A painful feeling of uneasiness came over him as he entered Goethe's house, "ascended the familiar grand staircase, saw the plan of Rome still hanging on the same wall, the statues still standing in their accustomed places. . . . And yet," Shevyrëv exclaimed in sadness, "how lifeless everything, how changed! The very dust on the steps speaks to me of the master's absence." But, "mirabile dictu," in this house of the departed, a totally new realm of Goethe's world was suddenly opened up to him, one that had been unapproachable for all but a chosen few during the lifetime of the poet. It is his study, his bedroom that Shevyrëv was seeing for the first time. "I entered—before me was a small, square, rather low-ceilinged room with tiny windows—its furnishing of a simplicity that bordered on indigence." Shevyrëv had been awed by Goethe on his first visit, when the Privy Councilor received him and his friends in the splendor of his salon. But it was in the humble surroundings of Goethe's sanctum that the greatness of Goethe's inner world all but overwhelmed Shevyrëv precisely by its contrast to the modesty of the outer setting:

> Now, . . . in these two small, cramped, miserable rooms was revealed to me that rich, inner world in which he lived, intentionally surrounding himself with such an uninviting, ordinary exterior. Here I imagined how his noble, majestic figure moved slowly, calmly, from corner to corner, an eagle or a lion in his narrow cage. But what riches of soul, what a splendorous inner world must have been his, that he could lock himself deliberately into this tiny chamber, could renounce all the allurements of comfort, though every luxury was within his means to enjoy. Still, on second thought, Goethe never did have a study, or rather he had one only in so far as he needed a place to sit and to walk in; his real study was his mind, encompassing the entire world. Forty years of such a marvelously creative life in such a cramped and darkish room with but two tiny windows to the world outside! Here were conceived Tasso, Faust, Wilhelm Meister, Helena. . . . What an instructive sight has been revealed to us upon the death of this great one, with the opening to us of his private sanctum! This cage in which the mighty genius dwelt is proof of an iron will, this poverty, almost of a beggar, speaks of the miraculous riches of his soul. . . . Here is the secret of the German genius! Yes, Goethe's study is indeed the symbol not only of his life but of all Germany! Here we behold the essential form of the existence of that whole nation: external poverty—internal riches, a miserable mode of outer existence—a wondrous world of thought. To us Russians, used as we are to material pomp, Germany seems at once confined and insignificant. And, to be honest, I too am ready to smile at Germany's innocence of all the comforts of life. Yet, here in Goethe's study I fathomed that nation's secret; in and through this pitiable exterior, I

saw more clearly than I had ever before the hidden treasures of that nation's spiritual life.

Such was Shevyrëv's final tribute to Goethe. He could pay it in all sincerity both as a former "Lover of Wisdom" and in his new position as a sympathizer with the Slavophiles, for, in the praise of transcendent genius scornful of worldly power and comfort, the Liubomudry and the Slavophiles could join with unfeigned enthusiasm.

Our delineation of the Russian Romanticists' image of Goethe would not be complete without a discussion of Fëdor Ivanovich Tiutchev's attitude toward Goethe. We now turn to a consideration of that great Russian poet in his relationship to the personality and work of the great German.

5. Fëdor Ivanovich Tiutchev (1803–1873)

Tiutchev's genius was slow in gaining recognition. When his first poems appeared, interest in lyric poetry was rapidly ebbing in Russia, and verse was being forced into the background by the ascendancy of prose, especially of the novel. Not until the Symbolists initiated a lyrical renaissance at the end of the century was Tiutchev's voice heard and appreciated. Now he is being acclaimed by Russians as one of their great triumvirs of lyrical poetry: Pushkin, Lermontov, Tiutchev.

His poetry is unmistakably Romantic, though much of it was written well after the high tide of Russian Romanticism. In his philosophy and esthetics he stands close to the Liubomudry. Their mystical pantheism informs his best and most characteristic poems. He shared their view of genius as that magical combination of intuitive and analytical powers. With them he placed Goethe among the greatest creative spirits and proclaimed him the foremost poet-philosopher of his age.

Tiutchev, the son of an old aristocratic Russian family, enjoyed the education typical of those circles: early instruction by tutors at home, then the university, Moscow University in his case. The tutors and teachers who influenced Tiutchev most markedly in his formative years were the poet-critic S. E. Raich and Aleksei

Fedorovich Merzliakov. Raich was very close to the Liubomudry circle and an active and influential contributor to the *Moscow Messenger*. Merzliakov is known to us as Ordinarius at Moscow University, as the tutor of Lermontov and, in his younger days, as an intimate friend of Andrei Turgeniev and Vasili Zhukovski. He and Raich were to be Tiutchev's expert guides to German literature and especially to the world of Goethe and Schiller.

At nineteen years of age, Tiutchev entered the foreign service and, as a junior member of the Russian diplomatic mission, left for Germany in 1822 to spend some sixteen years, with brief interruptions, in his beloved city of Munich. He made the acquaintance of outstanding personalities in the city's cultural life. Prominent among these were Heinrich Heine, Friedrich Schelling and the architect Friedrich von Thiersch, a celebrity in the Munich of those days.[95] Heine, whose poetry Tiutchev was the first to translate into Russian, counted him "among [his] best Munich friends" and Schelling is reported to have said of him: "That is an extraordinary, a very well-informed person, with whom one always enjoys conversing." There can be no doubt that Tiutchev had mastered the German language to perfection, that he followed the development of German literary and cultural life with keen interest. He knew Goethe's works intimately in the German original and kept abreast of the newest publications. Already in 1833 he had "among his best works" a rendering of the first act of *Faust,* Part II. But, as he writes to his friend I. S. Gagarin, he inadvertently burned it. "On returning from Greece [1833] I decided one evening in the twilight hour to sort my papers and in the process destroyed a large part of my poetic work. Only a long time afterwards did I notice the loss. At first I was a bit put out, but soon consoled myself with the thought that, after all, the Alexandrian Library, too, had perished in a conflagration. Among these papers, by the way, was my Russian rendering of the first act of the second part of *Faust,* perhaps the best of all my poetic works."[96]

Together with Vasili Zhukovski, Afanasi Fet, Viacheslav Ivanov and Boris Pasternak, Tiutchev stands in the forefront of the greatest Russian poet translators of Goethe's works. There are altogether fifteen items from Goethe[97] among Tiutchev's numerous translations from leading classical and modern European writers. Goethe leads all the rest, not excluding Heine and Schiller, Tiutchev's other two favorite German poets.

Tiutchev began his translation work in 1826 with a rather free variation on Goethe's quatrain, "Sakuntala." Here he was still working very much in the manner of Zhukovski.[98] He expanded the original four lines into fourteen of regular iambic meter, prettified and sentimentalized the original, losing altogether the thrust of its compact lines, which in the German original culminate with such effect in the all-embracing name: Sakuntala. This was Tiutchev's apprentice piece. He was quick to perfect his own translation technique, which aims conscientiously at a faithful rendering of the German poems' content and, what is more significant, its form: rhythm, rhyme, and meter. The majority of Tiutchev's translations of Goethe are from the years 1827 to 1830,[99] the apogee of his preoccupation with Goethe's lyrics.

Tiutchev's selections from Goethe's *oeuvre* must have greatly pleased the Liubomudry as they read many of them in leading periodicals, the *Northern Lyre (Severnaia Lira), Galatea,* the *Moscow Observer (Moskovski Nabliudatel'),* and others.[100] In *Galatea* they could read Tiutchev's translation of Goethe's "Der Sänger" with its famous lines: "Ich singe wie der Vogel singt. . . ." These he had changed, significantly, to: "By God's will I sing as a little bird under His sky,"[101] a variant which must have been eminently acceptable not only to the Russian Romanticists but also to the most orthodox of Slavophiles. In the same journal they found "Geistesgruß" with its medieval setting, which Tiutchev rendered to perfection, though changing the "strong sinews" of Goethe's "Rittergeist" to "a fist of iron" with a witty nod to "Götz mit der eisernen Hand"; in the *Telescope* they came upon: "Nachtgedanken," so congenial to the Romantic muse with its projection of human emotions into nature, its empathetic personification of the stars, with its nocturnal mood, its sonorous diction which he emphasized by introducing terms like "Ory" (Horen) for "Stunden," "goremyki" for "unglückselige," terms derived from the Classical style of

Derzhavin and Lomonosov, which was to Tiutchev's taste despite his Romantic predilections. Here again he achieved a high degree of fidelity in reproducing the rhythm and even the specific complex meter of the original.

To this series of selections, made consistently from a Romantic point of view, the "Hegire" verses from Goethe's *West-östlicher Divan* make a most natural and effective addition. I would claim that in his Russian version Tiutchev more than equals the effectiveness of some of Goethe's key lines. Goethe's admonition to return from the crumbling modern world of power politics and intellectual aberrations to our patriarchal origins with their peace, simplicity, religious faith, and intuitive wisdom was so congenial to Tiutchev's basic philosophy that he could find the most convincing, heartfelt words to express it. His lines: "thought is narrow, faith is spacious [prostorna], words are strong and dignified when they are living revelation [otkrovenie]," serve to express his innermost conviction and render Goethe's verse:

> Glaube weit, eng der Gedanke.
> Wie das Wort so wichtig dort war,
> Weil es ein gesprochenes Wort war,*

if possible with even greater forthrightness, certainly in a more orthodox spirit.

As could be expected, we also find among Tiutchev's selections the "Harfner-Lieder" from the Liubomudry's favorite novel by Goethe, *Wilhelm Meister:* "Wer sich der Einsamkeit ergibt," "Es schleicht ein Liebender," and, of course, "Wer nie sein Brot mit Tränen aß." In his rendering of the first two, Tiutchev makes the bold attempt at imitation of Goethe's irregular meters which, while none too successful, represents a daring departure from the canon of regularity in rhyme, rhythm and meter which was still sacrosanct even at this relatively late date (1828-29) in the development of Russian prosody. His translation of "Wer nie sein Brot . . ." is a miniature *chef d'oeuvre* of faithfulness to thought, emotional pitch and all the formal details of the original, a veritable Russian mir-

---

* Faith is spacious, narrow the thought, as the word was so important there, because it was a spoken word.

ror image of the German poem. Here we seem to hear in the medium of the Russian language Goethe's own voice, clear and true, not the elegiac tones of a sentimental age which sounded in Zhukovski's earlier translation of these verses.

To the most famous lyric from *Wilhelm Meister,* Mignon's song, Tiutchev turned late in his career as translator, probably not before 1850, perhaps because this poem had been so frequently translated into Russian. As he pointed out to N. V. Shushkov: "The 'Romance' [!] from Goethe has been translated several times in our country, but since this poem is one of those that has become a veritable lyric proverb, it will always remain a touchstone for the connoisseur."[102] In the end, he could not resist the challenge and added his own version. One cannot say that he improved significantly on the others. His version is marked by several rearrangements of Goethe's lines, the most significant of which is the reversal of the sequence of strophes two and three of Goethe's poem. Evidently Tiutchev felt that Mignon's pilgrimage to the longed-for land of her dreams should logically proceed by way of the "Wolkensteg" to the "schimmernde Gemach" and culminate not in the Alpine wilderness but in the "glänzende Saal" with its "Marmorbilder" which in his rendering "stand silent and sad" (molcha i grustia)—an unexpected echo of Karamzin-Zhukovski sentimentalism. Like Zhukovski in his earlier translation, Tiutchev tampers with Goethe's meaningful triad of "Geliebter", "Beschützer", "Vater" by inexplicably turning "Beschützer" into "vlastitel'," i.e., into a "ruler" or a "master."

It would seem that in this case the faithful rendering of the content of Goethe's poem was not Tiutchev's main concern, that he saw his challenge in its form and in its elusively varying patterns of rhythm, meter, and rhyme. In rendering these, he unquestionably improved on his predecessors, even on Zhukovski.

Still later, probably in 1870, Tiutchev undertook, as his last translation from Goethe, a rendering of Klärchen's song from *Egmont*[103] "Freudvoll / und leidvoll. . . ." With this he proved once again his control of the formal elements of the original. He reproduced with greatest faithfulness the limpid rhythms of the song.

Yet, not even he could match Goethe's conciseness and direct simplicity in expressing the full range of feeling in the "Seele, die liebt."

Finally, we must turn to the six[104] excerpts from Goethe's *Faust*. In these selections Tiutchev remains faithful to the Liubomudry's predilections and again shows us a predominantly "Romantic" Goethe. In fact, two passages of his choice had already been translated by Venevinitov: The Faust dialog with Wagner "Vor dem Tor" at sundown,[105] and his monolog in "Wald und Höhle," the one extolled by the Russian Romantics as the most poignant expression of their view of Goethe as the all-embracing genius: "Erhabner Geist, du gabst mir, gabst mir alles."[106] The startling result of Tiutchev's effort is an impressive change in the basic tonality of the verses from Venevitinov's predominantly elegiac tone to one of grandiloquent pathos. It is remarkable how adequate his style proves to be in the difficult task of rendering the emotion-charged yet controlled language of the original.

The full sonority and high pathos of his verse Tiutchev develops in his impressive version of the Song of the three Archangels from the "Prolog in Heaven." His excerpts from Faust's dialog with the Earth spirit[107] and his suicide monolog in the Easter scene[108] express in their full force Faust's heaven-vaulting exaltation and his abysmal despair, while in Gretchen's "König in Thule" *(Zavetnyi Kubok)* he manages to convey a sense of the artless simplicity of this "folk" ballad—no mean achievement in a literary language scarcely emancipated from a highly formalistic convention. Only Pushkin might have done it better!

With these selections Tiutchev opened to Russian readers new vistas of Goethe's dramatic masterpiece. These and his translations of Goethe's greatest lyrics are assured of a permanent place in Russian literature as they were done with the inspired skill of a truly great poet-translator.[109]

Tiutchev's original lyrics are rich in echoes from Goethe's poems. Chulkov in his article on "Tiutchev and Goethe" tells that, in examining the Russian poet's manuscripts, he came upon a loose leaf on which Tiutchev had scribbled a strophe from

Goethe's "Rastlose Liebe":

> Alle [!] das Neigen
> Vom [!] Herzen zum [!] Herzen,
> Ach wie so eigen,
> Schaffet das Schmerzen.*[110]

Surely, other Goethean verses must have been ever present in Tiutchev's mind and would find again and again their echo in his own lyrics. Thus, in his poem "Shifting sands . . ."[111] we come upon the line, "Dark night, like a hundred-eyed beast, peered from every bush," an obvious echo of Goethe's "Wo Finsternis aus dem Gesträuche mit hundert schwarzen Augen sah," from his "Willkommen und Abschied."

In the poem "Plavanie,"[112] "Swimming"—a more precise but less Tiutchevian title would be "Boatride" or "On the Sea"—such lines as "From heaven the stars lit our way, / From below sparkled the wave" (S nebu zvëzdy nam svetili / Snizu iskrilas' volna), or "And the sea rocks them to sleep / With its gently streaming wave" (I baiukaet ikh more / Tikho struinoiu volnoi) call Goethe's lines to mind from his "Auf dem See," "Die Welle wieget unsren Kahn . . ." and "Auf der Welle blinken / tausend schwebende Sterne," despite Tiutchev's transformation of Goethe's well-known setting into the modern situation of a steamboat trip. In fact, this transformation serves to make us all the more keenly aware of his characteristic variation on Goethe's poem: he dwells on its images of "shining stars above," "their reflection in the waves below," "the waves' gentle rocking," calling up the "golden dreams of retrospection," but changes Goethe's vigorous affirmation of the present, his praise of nurturing nature into a sustained mood of passive surrender to reverie and slumber, and Goethe's invigorating hour of daybreak into the nocturnal setting of a moon- and starlit seascape.

Zhirmunski draws our attention to the Goethean echoes in Tiutchev's poem: "Peoples' tears, oh, peoples' tears . . ." (Slëzy, liudskie, o slëzy liudskie . . .),[113] which have the sad and haunting cadence of the repeated lines of "Wonne der Wehmut": "Trocknet

---

* All the affection from heart to heart, oh, how strangely it creates pains.

nicht, trocknet nicht, / Tränen der ewigen Liebe!"

Instances of this type of recall of images and rhythms of Goethe's lyrics could be multiplied at the risk of creating the erroneous impression of mechanical borrowing by the Russian poet. Nothing could be farther from the truth! Rather, these echoes arise from a deeply rooted affinity of the two writers. Central to this kinship is their common love, admiration, and longing for the Mediterranean lands, for Italy. "Standing on the icebound shores of the Neva River," Tiutchev yearns for the sunlit, sensuously beautiful, harmonious life of the Italian South.[114] It is not by accident that this poem, which gives such poignant expression to Tiutchev's *Italien-Sehnsucht,* closes with lines that are a distinct echo of the refrain of Mignon's song: "Dahin, dahin . . .," "Tuda, tuda na tëplyi iug" (Thereto, to the balmy south),[115]—a final line that seems to call for the closing words of the German poem for its completion: ". . . laß uns ziehn!"

But these same "Italian" poems also reveal the salient difference between the German and the Russian poet. For Goethe Italy was refuge, liberation, regeneration. For Tiutchev this promised land has become unattainable, its peace and harmony theatened, nay, shattered by our very entering it. The "locus classicus" for this characteristic variation on the Italian theme is the poem, "Italian Villa" (Italianskaia Villa),[116] a Tiutchevian counterpoint to Mignon's song. In Goethe's poem the "marble statues" in the "shimmering hall" look at Mignon in deep compassion: "Und Marmorbilder stehn und sehn mich an: Was hat man dir, du armes Kind, getan?" Mignon feels secure in the certainty of finding sympathetic understanding in the land of her dreams. When Tiutchev and his friend enter the "Italian Villa" with its enchanted garden, the idyllic bliss and the Elysian harmony are irretrievably shattered: "A hectic trembling ran along the branches of the cypress tree, the fountain suddenly fell silent" as "the angry life of modern man with its rebellious fever crossed the sacred threshold"[117] of Elysium. There is to be no salvation for the denizen of northern climes and modern times. He carries the destructive curse within his blood and with its evil spell turns cosmos into chaos.

Both the kinship of Tiutchev to the German poet and his distance from Goethe's more harmonious nature find once again their eloquent expression in the poem, "Two voices" *(Dva Golosa)*, inspired by Goethe's Freemasonry hymn, "Symbolum." The relation of the Russian poem to Goethe's has been repeatedly observed and analyzed.[118] Clearly, the majestic, mysterious, ritualistic sonority of its strophes is attuned to the German prototype. The central leitmotif of the Russian poem:

> "Above you the stars are silent on high
> Below you the graves are silent as well."[119]

is obviously patterned after the German poem's lines:

> ". . . Stille
> Ruhn oben die Sterne
> Und unten die Gräber."*

Yet, the message of the "Two Voices," both by Goethe and Tiutchev, is antithetical. To be sure, in both poems man's life is presented as a ceaseless struggle. But while Goethe has the voices of departed masters, "die Stimmen der Geister, die Stimmen der Meister," encourage "von drüben" man in his purposeful striving, sustaining his hopes: "Wir heißen euch hoffen!," Tiutchev replaces these "Voices from yonder" with the ominous silence of the Greek gods who look down "with a jealous eye" from their "carefree Olympian heights upon the struggling humans below."[120] This portrayal of the Olympians is strongly reminiscent of Goethe's in Iphigenia's "Parzenlied" which sings of the gods' carefree existence, "In ewigen Festen /An goldenen Tischen," holding limitless power in their immortal hands to wield it at their whim. This theme serves Tiutchev supremely well in stressing his message of stoic heroism which knows of but one "reward": ultimate release in death for the unflagging fighter from the hopelessly unequal struggle with an insuperable, hostile fate.[121] Goethe's Freemason hero fights a meaningful battle for mankind's progress, and he is sustained by the voices of those who had fought this good fight before him and who now are "weaving the crowns" ("Hier flechten

---

* Peacefully rest the stars above and the graves below.

sich Kronen") which await "the man of deeds": "Die sollen mit Fülle / Die Tätigen lohnen!" Tiutchev's hero, in his lonely struggle under the jealous eye of unfeeling gods, can also look forward to a "reward," the victory "wreath," "pobednyi venets" of the tenacious fighter, "conquered only by fate." But Goethe's "Symbolum" has lost its richness, its "Fülle." The meaningful life of man between the stars above and the graves below has become a lonely, embattled existence without a constructive purpose or goal—cosmos has been turned into chaos.

This pervasive pessimism, especially characteristic of Tiutchev in his later years, lends to many of his greatest poems an autumnal, a nocturnal somberness of tone and imagery that make it difficult to appreciate their underlying affinity to Goethe's generally sunlit lyrics, though Goethe too knew pain to be an inseparable element of the universe from the very moment of its creation: "Und er sprach das Wort: Es werde! / Da erklang ein schmerzlich Ach! / als das All mit Machtgebärde / in die Wirklichkeiten brach."

The profound affinity between these two poets sprang from a common mode of experiencing nature. Both poets approached it, essentially, as pantheists. Both recognized in nature not the well-tuned mechanism of the Deists but an organism imbued with divine spirit, animated with a soul. Goethe fathomed nature's secrets as the intuitive poet and probed them with the observant eye of the scientist. Tiutchev's experience was by intuition alone and carried far stronger mystical overtones. Nature to Tiutchev was a being, speaking its own mysterious tongue, audible to the poet who, by a magical rapport, is able to "penetrate to the dark roots of existence." In this power of the poet Vladimir Solovëv saw the "key" to his greatness. "Herein he is altogether original, . . . here is the key to his lyric genius . . ., here the source of the rich content [of his poems], their inimitable magic."[122] In poetic rapture Tiutchev once wrote: "All is in me and I am in all."[123] This *is* the "key," this *is* his magic!

This gift of empathy, of self-identification with the universe, was Goethe's too. Nature had given him leave "in ihre tiefe Brust / Wie in den Busen eines Freunds zu schauen," she taught him "meine Brüder / Im stillen Busch, in Luft und Wasser kennen."

But once again we are conscious of the basic difference between the two. Goethe looked into nature's breast, "wie in den Busen eines *Freundes,*" he recognized in its elements "seine *Brüder.*" Tiutchev delved to the "*dark* roots of existence." To Goethe nature reveals its harmony, its organic unity and structure which leads by way of evolution, of "Steigerung" and "Metamorphosis," from the proto-form to the more complex organisms and ultimately to man. Goethe experienced the universe as a cosmos which contains evil and imper-fection within its all-embracing harmony. The Russian is at heart a Manichean who sees the good powers of this universe locked in an unequal struggle with evil. In his dualistic deeply pessimistic view, the bright and ordered world is but an embattled island, washed by the waves of chaos, the human spirit but a perishable spark ever threatened by dark and ominous forces. The harmonious side of Goethe's personality and work held, for that very reason, great at-traction for Tiutchev as a refuge in a darkling world, as an assurance of a brighter, happier existence. Ivan Turgeniev even recognized in the Russian poet's affinity for Goethe the "core of his nature." "The very essence of his being—'le fin du fin'—that is his Western kinship to Goethe."[124]

It is to Goethe, the pantheist in rapport with all existence, the champion of evolution, to his positive, optimistic spirit, that Tiutchev pays homage in his famous eulogy, "On Goethe's death."[125] This poem proves that its author had grasped Goethe's innermost being and thought. In an eloquent metaphor he glori-fied Goethe as the "best leaf on the lofty tree of humanity, nurtured by its purest sap, unfolded by the sun's purest ray." That he chose this particular image proves Tiutchev's realization of the sig-nificance which the phenomenon of metamorphosis held for Goethe as a key to nature's deepest secrets discovered by the poet's intui-tion and the scientist's systematic observation. We may even recognize in the "sun's purest ray" an indication of his acquaint-ance with Goethe's thoughts in his *Farbenlehre.* The second strophe of the poem glorifies Goethe's empathetic consonance with nature and mankind. Fritz Strich has credited the Russian writer with a profound understanding of Goethe's "true and deepest being."

"Impressed with the basic idea of Goethe's nature-philosophy, he [Tiutchev] creates that grand image: Goethe is likened to a leaf, to that proto-phenomenon of the plant; he falls ripe and un-wilted, as a single human, as a leaf on the tree of humanity, as the proto-phenomenon of man from this tree of universal human life.

Nothing in the entire range of the European image of Goethe has approached so closely the true and deepest nature of Goethe as have these poems."*[126]

As a fitting climax to Tiutchev's appreciation of Goethe, this masterful encomium in Viacheslav Ivanov's German rendering will conclude our study of the Russian Romanticists' image of Goethe:

Am Baume der Menschheit prangst Du, gestaltet
Zum schönsten Blatt durch Erd- und Sonnenkraft.
Vom lichtesten, vom reinsten Strahl entfaltet,
Gesättigt mit des Baumes bestem Saft.
Einstimmig war dein Flüstern, lispelnd Zittern
Mit seiner Seele leisestem Getön;
Du rauschtest sibyllinisch mit Gewittern
Und spieltest mit dem Zephyrhauch der Höhn.
Kein Herbstwind war's, kein Sommerregenschauer,
Der Dich geraubt, Du übertrafst an Glanz
Das grüne Laub, an unverwelkter Dauer—
Und fielst von selbst, gleichwie aus einem Kranz.† [127]

---

* Von der naturphilosophischen Grundidee Goethes ergriffen findet er [Tiut-chev] das großartige Bild, wie Goethe, dem Blatt, diesem Urphänomen der Pflanze gleich, als einzelner Mensch, als Blatt am Baume der Menschheit, als Urphänomen des Menschen also, reif und unverwelkt von diesem Baum des allgemeinen Menschheitslebens fällt.

Nichts im ganzen Umkreis des europäischen Goethebildes ist dem wahren und tiefsten Wesen Goethes so nah gekommen, wie diese Gedichte es tun.

† You are resplendent on the tree of humanity, formed into the most beautiful leaf through the power of earth and sun. Unfolded by the most luminous, the purest ray, nourished with the tree's best sap. Consonant was your whispering, lisping trembling with the softest tone of its soul; you roared Sibyl like with the thunderstorms and played with the Zephyr-breath of the heights. It was not the autumn wind nor summer's rain that robbed you, you surpassed by your splendor the green foliage in unwilting permanence and fell of your own volition, as from a wreath.

It almost would seem presumptuous to attempt a brief summary of the Romanticists' extensive contribution to the Russian view of Goethe. At the very least, they have enriched Russian literature by their capable, often superb translations of Goethe's lyrics, of his *Werther,* as well as of significant portions from *Faust,* Part I. The second part remained to the Romanticists, as it was to Zhukovski, largely "terra incognita." Shevyrëv's translation and interpretation of the *Helena, Interact to Faust* was a unique achievement in this early period of Russian Goethe studies. All the more regrettable is the loss of Tiutchev's translation of Act One of *Faust,* Part II.

Expanding Zhukovski's range, the Liubomudry made the Russian reading public aware of the importance of Goethe's *Wilhelm Meister,* of the *Lehr-* as well as of the *Wanderjahre,* of his poetic autobiography *Dichtung und Wahrheit,* of the *West-östliche Divan,* even of the *"Römische Elegien,"* though the "classical" Goethe of *Tasso, Iphigenie,* and the *Natürliche Tochter* remained largely unexplored and untranslated, as did Goethe's works as a scientific thinker, despite repeated protestations by the Liubomudry of their high respect and regard for the "ruler in the realm of thought," with which, however, they generally meant "philosophical" rather than "scientific" thought, Odoevski being the one exception among them.

To the early image of Goethe as the sentimental author of *Werther,* to Zhukovski's Goethe as the sentimental lyricist and ballad-writer, they added their "Romantic" Goethe, the lofty Olympian enthroned in the ethereal realm of "l'art pour l'art," the poet-philosopher capable of unlocking the innermost secrets of the universe and of lending to his insights immortal artistic form. Granted that their view of Goethe was not without its distortions: they gave an altogether one-sided emphasis to Goethe's pantheistic view of nature, his powers of intuition, his lordly unconcern with the mundane and ephemeral, with the socio-political aspects of human existence, and underplayed the rational, analytical side of his nature, his common sense and circumspection as the practical and responsible Minister and Privy Councilor of the Grandduchy of Weimar. In fact, that "official" Goethe they resented, scorned. The Goethe of the parodistic, the satirical "storm and stress" productions remained unknown or alien to them, though his *Egmont* did receive their attention," his *Götz* was translated and its author acclaimed most effectively in Shevyrëv's review of *Götz*.

It is true that their Goethe seemed, at times, to step out from the pages of Schelling's *Naturphilosophie* rather than from those of his own novels, plays, and poems.[128] Nevertheless, the lineaments which the Romanticists added to the Russian image of Goethe were drawn perceptively, not only the contours of his inner life, but also his characteristic appearance, his habits and his gestures, down to the details of his dress. They left us most vivid impressions and recollections of the "Patriarch of Weimar" as they experienced him in his house "am Frauenplan": the chilling Privy Councilor, the altogether captivating poet and savant; the old man, frail and tired, and then again all spirit, verve, élan; his erect and dignified posture, a Jupiter with a regular Grecian profile and the fiery eyes of youth; "a lion or an eagle in the cramped cage" of his modest study, "the supreme ruler in the realm of thought," the "giant of Romantic poetry," the poet-seer of his age and all the ages.

Perhaps most significant of all, the Romantic poet-critics loosened the overwhelming grip of French culture upon Russian life and letters, replaced Ferney with Weimar, Racine and Corneille with Shakespeare, Schiller and Goethe, and brought into a fairer balance the importance to Russian literature of Byron and Goethe as exemplars and idols. There is no doubt that their contributions to Russia's appreciation and appropriation of Goethe had range and depth. Although repudiated by the politically oriented "Westerners," the Romantic view of Goethe continued to be of influence with the poets of "pure art" and grew in importance with the advent of the Symbolists at the end of the century.[129]

CHAPTER SIX

The Westerners

Stankevich—Belinski—Herzen

1. Nikolai V. Stankevich and his Circle

The Romantic image of Goethe, as developed by the "Lovers of Wisdom" in the early twenties, remained essentially unchanged and steadily gained in influence among Russian intellectuals throughout the twenties and thirties to reach its apogee at the end of the third decade, when Schelling's philosophy had been replaced by Hegel's in its overpowering influence on the Russian intellectuals. In the words of a contemporary observer of the cultural scene: "The cult of Goethe at the end of the thirties had become the hallmark of our Hegelians,"[1] or, as Herzen was to put it in his famous reminiscences, "A knowledge of Goethe, especially of the second part of his *Faust* (be it because of its inferior quality to the first or because of its greater difficulty), was considered to be as obligatory as proper dress."[2]

When, by 1825, the Liubomudry had ceased to be a closely knit group, their place was quickly taken by another exceptional set of young men, who "faithfully continued the tradition of Prince Odoevski's philosophical society [the Liubomudry] of the twenties."[3] The Circle counted among its members names that were soon to be famous: Nikolai V. Stankevich (1813–40), Mikhail Bakunin (1814–76), Timothy N. Granovski (1813–55), Vissarion Belinski (1811–48), Aleksandr I. Herzen (1812–70), and, more peripherally, Lermontov, Katkov, K. Aksakov and, at a somewhat later date, Ivan S. Turgeniev. These men were, if anything, even more ardent admirers of German culture than the Liubomudry had been. Germany was "the promised land" to them, the "Jerusalem of modern mankind."[4] When Granovski had reached "the goal of

169

his pilgrimage," Berlin, Stankevich wrote to him in undisguised envy: "So you are in Berlin! . . . I can imagine how your heart throbbed as you caught sight of that German city upon which each one of us has placed his most extravagant hopes."[5] To Mikhail Bakunin a stipend to Berlin, however modest, was a "matter of life and death." "I would subsist on bread and water, would live in a garret, would wear out my old coat, just to be able to study in Berlin."[6]

Like the Liubomudry, these young Germanophiles began as faithful disciples of Schelling. They were deeply convinced of Goethe's greatness as the incomparable poet-philosopher of the age. Their acknowledged leader was Nikolai Vladimirovich Stankevich, a figure strikingly reminiscent of the guiding spirit of the Liubomudry, Dmitri Venevitinov.[7] Like Venevitinov, Stankevich was loved and respected by his followers as a veritable father figure, despite his youth. Like Venevitinov, he exercised his great influence, not by an impressive array of published works,[8] but rather through personal contact and a far-flung correspondence which was to inspire Leo Nikolaevich Tolstoi to enthusiastic praise across the decades. "If you have not read the correspondence of Stankevich," he writes to his cousin, "for heaven's sake do so at once! Never have I been so impressed by any other book."[9]

Also like Venevitinov, Stankevich was a true "Lover of Wisdom," zealous in his search for truth, endowed with an uncommon flair for systematic philosophical inquiry. His was the rare gift of the true pedagog, "not to domineer but to inspire, not to rule but to guide and develop. Not being creative himself, his spirit lived in the thoughts and creations of those whom he educated."[10] He began, like Venevitinov, as a follower of Schelling, soon came under the influence of Kant and Fichte and ended as a confirmed Hegelian.[11] He was quite the equal of Venevitinov in his admiration of Goethe and in the effective championship of Goethe's fame in his Circle and beyond. Like Venevitinov, he died tragically young, at twenty-seven, plucked by tuberculosis from his philosophical and literary labors.

In his student days at Moscow University, Stankevich read

Goethe omnivorously, not in translation but in the original—a rare achievement even among the most devout Russian Germanophiles. He was particularly fond of Goethe's lyrics, knew many of them by heart and would quote from them "upon the slightest provocation, on all occasions, relevant or not."[12] Two of his translations, probably done in 1832, have been preserved. In his highly sentimentalized rendering of "An den Mond," young Stankevich was obviously under the influence of Zhukovski who—as will be remembered—had also attempted a Russian version of this early lyric by Goethe, in which the intimately personal and the universally symbolic elements are so intricately fused as to make this piece in its apparent simplicity one of the most difficult to translate. In the other effort, Stankevich strikes out independently with the ambitious choice of the "Gesang der Geister über den Wassern." While generally faithful to the thought of the original, Stankevich is guilty of one crucial distortion of meaning and imagery. Evidently for reasons of euphony, he substitutes in the opening lines for the German "Wasser" the Russian "volnam" (waves), thus corrupting Goethe's apt simile into the impossible unnatural image of "Waves" descending from and ascending to heaven: "The soul of man / Is like the *waves:* / From heaven it descends / It strives toward heaven . . ."[13] These two extant renderings form too limited a base for any judgment of Stankevich's ability as translator.[14]

When, in 1838, Stankevich finally reached Germany, his Jerusalem and his Mecca, and paid his visit to Weimar, Goethe had been dead for almost a decade and the other greats had long since departed. Stankevich found the "German Athens" as a city "unimpressive" but "hallowed by the memory of Goethe and Schiller."[15] He paid his respects to Goethe's daughter-in-law, Ottilie, and visited the graves of Schiller and Goethe, which he found, evidently to his surprise, "in the family tomb of the Dukes,"[16] as he hastens to inform his brother. This is the only record we have of his reaction to the poet's home and last resting place. Still, the visit obviously had a stirring effect on Stankevich. Under its impact he proposed to his friend Granovski to emulate Goethe and Schiller in their collaboration on the *Xenien* by publishing a similar almanac or journal and, elaborating on the plan, in a surge of enthusiasm, discovered the closest possible affinity in his friendship with Granovski to Schiller's friendship with Goethe. "We *are* Schiller and Goethe,"[17] he rapturously assured his friend. This lively sense of an affinity to Goethe and Schiller was productive not only of such euphoric flights of fancy but of valuable insights as well. In seeking to clarify for himself what he vividly felt to be a decisive contrast in the genius of the two German poets, he developed a characterization which was to echo and re-echo in the writings of the Circle. He attempted a summary statement of his conclusions on this complex problem in a letter to his friend Granovski. "In Schiller's head," Stankevich found a "rational reality; insistent questing after lofty ideals without any special respect for or attention to natural reality as a consequence of his [Schiller's] abstract-philosophical (not natural-philosophical) preoccupations; his task is thus both clearer and simpler [than Goethe's], one that can be accurately solved."[18] It is safe to infer that Stankevich recognized in Goethe, by contrasting implication, a genius paying "special respect and attention to natural reality," characterized by a "natural-philosophical" orientation in his thinking and artistic creation, occupied with a task of utmost complexity, incapable of being "solved accurately" even by a genius on the order of Goethe's.[19] This "definition" of the contrasting creative personalities is obviously indebted to Hegelian ideas and terminology, and possibly to Schiller's famous distinction of the "naïve" and the "reflective" ("sentimentalische") poets.[20] It was to reappear in the writings of Stankevich's friends and followers as the contraposition of the "objective" Goethe to the "subjective" Schiller and to form a basis for the changing valuation of these two authors by their Russian critics.

Stankevich's sustained interest in Goethe is evidenced by quotations from and references to Goethe's poems, his *Faust, Wilhelm Meister,* and *Italianische Reise,* liberally scattered throughout his correspondence. These references and quotations make it abundantly clear that Goethe was to Stankevich above all the wise guide on his way to a full experience of life and art, that unexcelled standard against which to measure his efforts at self-development and self-perfection. As Edmund Kostka aptly remarks, "Stankevich venerated Goethe and Schiller as sublime geniuses and preceptors of humanity, as models and leaders toward the lofty goal of moral self-education and universal happiness."[21] On his own "Italian journey," Stankevich literally followed in Goethe's footsteps. Contemplating the art treasures at Rome, he recalled the impression they had made on Goethe and compared it with his own reactions. On another occasion, he remembered Goethe's admonition not to let life slip by while we prepare ourselves, all too assiduously, for its experience: "Be sure to lay hold of a situation, of an impression—but do not linger too long, move on into God's wide world! How clearly did Goethe realize our dangerous tendency to lose ourselves in endless preparations for life, only to have life pass us by in the end. *He* felt and recognized this danger—but do *we?*"[22]

Much like Venevitinov, Stankevich liked to quote from Goethe to transmit in the great poet's words his own moods, experiences and impressions to his friends and correspondents. Thus he quoted to his friend Ianuari Neverov from Goethe's "An den Mond" with the express intention of sharing with him through the medium of these poignant lines the elegiac mood in which he himself was caught up at the time of the writing:

> Fließe, fließe, lieber Fluß
> Nimmer werd ich froh –
> So verrauschte Scherz und Kuß. . . .*

Breaking off abruptly at this point, Stankevich assured Neverov that "the rest of it does not apply to my condition: "Und die Treue so. . . .' No, I cannot complain of unfaithfulness!"[23] Again to Neverov he sends the closing lines of Goethe's "Willkommen und Abschied,"

> Doch welch ein Glück geliebt zu werden
> Und lieben, Götter, welch ein Glück!†

with the self-pitying complaint: "Alas, at this time I have no occa-

---

* Flow, flow, dear river. I shall never grow happy. Thus banter and kisses passed away.

† Yet what bliss to be loved, and to love, O gods, what bliss!

sion to repeat this exclamation."[24] And to Granovski he quotes, in a boisterously jocular vein, lines from Gretchen's famous spinning song, distorting Venevitinov's infelicitous translation into an outright parody of Goethe's original, to let his friend know in this way of his earthy yearnings for Bertha, the sweet charmer of his Berlin days: "How I wish I could see her / And grab her and hug her / And kiss her and kiss / And, dying, from her lips tear still another kiss." We can see Stankevich slyly smiling as he parenthetically disclaims authorship of this "translation": "(Venevitinov's, not mine!)"[25]

It is not often that Stankevich strikes this tone of levity in his letters. Far more frequent are the statements of his sincere striving to penetrate to the hidden central meaning of Goethe's message, to experience the full power of his artistry and to convey to his correspondent his experience in vivid language, frequently making use of metaphor and simile. These passages are highly revealing of Stankevich's approach to Goethe's work as a perceptive, imaginative interpreter who added his elaborations to the Romantic portrayal of the German poet. His range of acquaintance, especially with Goethe's lyrics, was significantly greater than that which was typical of the Liubomudry. Still, even the ballads of Goethe's Classical and late periods continued to be seen through Romantic eyes. Titles of poems abound, among them, of course, those of such standard pieces as "Der Sänger," "Erlkönig," "Der Fischer," "An den Mond" and many others. Yet it is the ballad, "Der Gott und die Bajadere," which attracted Stankevich time and again as that magical key to the very essence of Goethe's inimitable artistry. He even planned to write a drama on its theme, "to express therein my conception of love *in genere,* to represent the gradual purification and sublimation of the soul." He finally dropped the plan because he found it "barren dramaticly'," but chiefly because, as he wrote: "I could never hope to *express* Goethe's idea as clearly as I *understand* it."[26] This "idea" Stankevich found to be not merely "expressed" (vyskazana), but actually "embodied" (voploshchena) in the ballad: "When I read this ballad I do not meet in it with a single gnomic line, not with a single maxim. He who would take the last lines, 'Die Götter die [!]

heben verlorene Kinder mit feurigen Armen zum Himmel empor!'
for the idea of the entire poem would indeed be mistaken. This
passage is merely an intensification, which in no way diminishes
the Indian atmosphere pervading the entire poem. And yet, how
clear is the thought of the whole! The culpable soul is purified
by divine love! Here the idea is not merely *expressed,* it is *embodied!*"[27] In another interpretation of this ballad Stankevich
strove to lay hold of its meaning more precisely, to convey it in
vivid metaphorical language: "Kenner des Großen and Tiefen
[Goethe's epithet for Brahma] acts like a human being among
fellow humans. He does not cast lighting bolts as did the thun-
derer of old to destroy the fallen creature man, then to light the
flame of beautiful life; rather, he selects for his instruments of
transformation the mighty terrestrial forces of *love* and *suffering.*
Purified by them, life wings its way upward to the source of all
life!"[28] Another Goethe ballad which literally overwhelmed Stankevich as a "gigantic procreation of genius" is "Die Braut von
Korinth." "It is impossible not to kneel in adoration before Goethe
on having read this creation! The awesome union of love and
death, pale lips sucking the wine of blood, the expired breast
warmed by the flame of voluptuous passion, the strength of youth
drained in that one brief instant of consummate delight—this over-
whelms the soul, shocks every nerve, so that—the poem ended—
one experiences that strange quiet which reigns in nature after a
nocturnal thunderstorm, the clouds having passed to the other side
of the sky and the stars just beginning to shine from under its
receding shroud."[29] Obviously, here a thoroughly Romantic sensibility has experienced Goethe's "Classical" ballad, a sensibility
quite oblivious of the poem's pagan setting and controlled diction, one that revels in Vampirism and *Liebestod* and expresses its
sensuous experience of a work of art in the typical language of "Romantic fallacy."

It was to be expected that such a sensibility would be irresistibly
drawn to the enigmatic figure of Mignon, would worship her
"poetic being" as an embodiment of "love and longing unto
death." In fact, Stankevich did write a hymn to her that was "Ro-

mantic" in every one of its rapturous words. We must hear it to appreciate the fervor of empathy and with it, the informed attention to details of Goethe's plot and character delineation. It is obvious that Stankevich was deeply stirred by the being and fate of this unique creation of Goethe's genius, and intended not merely to express his profound experience but actually to embody it in his encomium to Mignon and her song:

> "How divine does this poem become," he exclaimed, "once we realize the circumstances surrounding that poetic being, Mignon! For her, reality had disappeared the instant he [Wilhelm], whom she had loved with all her fiery soul, had enjoyed before her very eyes the bliss of love in the embrace of another [Philine]; the world was hidden under a funereal shroud, but all the more vividly there awoke in her the vague recollections of her childhood! Italy with all its glories, made still more beautiful by her inflamed imagination (which grew more active as reality receded from her consciousness), became the goal of all the longings of the wondrous maid. For desire does not die as talent does. One desire hardly undone by hopelessness, the next arises on its ruins! But failing this, there must of necessity follow the total collapse of all one's mental powers or even death itself. This was Mignon's fate! On the one hand, faced with the impossibility of fusing her life with the life of the beloved, on the other, tortured by her longing for the land of her childhood, embellished (newly created) by her imagination, she pined away; all her being (from the scene of the performance of *Hamlet* onward) turned into pure "Sehnsucht," into a fervent yearning which increased in the same measure as her life's energies ebbed away. Finally, exhausted by the struggle, in the vestments of an angel, she confessed her deepest desire, her presentiments of her heavenly homeland, toward which all her thoughts were straining! And then—the end! And the splendid creation of nature returned to the womb of the mother, escaping from amidst the people who had proven themselves unworthy of her! And all that is expressed by: "Kennst du das Land . . .? Oh, how one wished one could hear these feelings, distilled in sound! Here is their proper sphere. The music to this poem would have to possess the power of transporting the soul, of enchanting it (I cannot express it otherwise). Failing this,

its composer would either be no genius or else incapable of understanding Mignon. This music must move me to grasp your hand and to exclaim: Dahin, dahin/ Möcht ich mit dir, o mein Geliebter, ziehn![30]

This sympathetic exploration of Mignon's pathological state, her return in death "to the womb of the mother [nature]," the interpretation of "Das Land" as Mignon's "heavenly homeland," the emotional tension of the entire passage with its excess of exclamation points—all these emphases, which are not necessarily distortions in an interpretation of such a figure and fate as Mignon's, place Stankevich's appreciation of Goethe's enigmatic creation into the Romantic tradition, next to E.T.A. Hoffmann's mystical, musical realm.

With such interpretations, with his basic conception of poetic creation as an unconscious or rather a supraconscious act, in which the poet does not express his ideas but rather embodies them in similes and metaphors of symbolic import and organic unity—with such an esthetic sense Stankevich could not but perpetuate and elaborate the Liubomudry's image of Goethe and pass it on, in turn, to his devout disciples.

We know, moreover, what this "Romantic" image of Goethe presupposes as well as produces by way of esthetic principles: First and foremost, an art that knows no ulterior goal and carries its purpose within it, a "pure art," "l'art pour l'art" that eschews all material motives, social, economic or political, or rather devines their deeper meaning, penetrates below surface appearances and reveals their essence, their symbolic significance. In this view of art, the artist is not a *faber* but a *creator,* not controlling but controlled by the creative forces, his moment of inspiration, a moment of "poetic somnambulism." He is a Proteus endowed with unlimited powers of empathy into the human condition of all ages and all lands. At the same time, he stands apart, removed from all time-bound concerns of man, unswayed, unaffected by ephemeral ideologies and, for this very reason, capable of an all-embracing and imperturbable "objectivity" which accepts reality in all its facets as "being" and therefore as "rational" and, carrying this Hegelian axiom[31] one typical step further, as being "God-ordained."

It was Mikhail Bakunin who most effectively developed Hegel's esthetics and his philosophy of law and religion into this esthetic gospel of the Stankevich Circle with its emphasis on the "harmony of the divine world" and the "blessedness of all reality," producing in the process a highly Romantic version of Hegel's "reconciliation with reality." Hegel's dictum, "What is real is rational and what is rational is real," was reinterpreted by Bakunin in a Christian Orthodox spirit until it came to stand as proof positive of the perfection of this world under the benevolent guidance of the Almighty. To the Beyer sisters Bakunin writes: "God's kingdom exists, it exists for him who has freed himself from his circumscribed individuality and whose will has become one with the divine will. . . . This kingdom is the true life and this true life is bliss."[32] In Bakunin's famous preface to Hegel's *Gymnasium* speeches[33] we read: "In life all is beautiful, all is blessed! The very suffering in it is necessary as the act of apperceiving spirit, as the transition from darkness to light." Bakunin carried this acceptance of life, in its cosmic as well as socio-political aspects, to such length that the dialectic nature of Hegel's famous dictum was totally lost and all criticism of reality became a sign of a finite mind out of harmony with the divine spirit, the fatal symptom of subjectivity or, using a Hegelian term, of "Schöngeistigkeit," of "fair-souledness," the life-estranged attitude "of a beautiful but impotent soul, steeped in the contemplation of the beautiful but at the same time barren qualities of an abstract ideal and uttering empty phrases."[34]

Such a "fair-souledness" Bakunin discovered and condemned in Schiller's personality and works. In sharp contrast to this "fair-souled" Schiller, Bakunin recognized Goethe as the very embodiment of an all-encompassing affirmation of "objective" reality. Goethe embraced all existence, encompassed all its contradictions and resolved them into harmony and beauty. Goethe truly achieved "reconciliation with reality" and in so doing became, together with Hegel, the supreme guarantor of the justness of Baku-

nin's world view. "Reconciliation with reality in every relationship
and every sphere of life is," according to Bakunin, "the great task
of our epoch; Hegel and Goethe are the leaders in this reconciliation."[35] Bakunin knows but one true "bliss," "the vital consciousness of being alive, of embracing all human emotions, joys and
griefs, delights and sufferings. . . . I do not wish another kind of
happiness. With Goethe's Faust I say: Und was der ganzen
Menschheit zugeteilt ist, / Möcht ich in meinem Innern selbst ge-
nießen."[36]

Stankevich's Schelling-inspired esthetics and Bakunin's Hegel-
inspired "affirmation of reality," which we have sketched here, were
to exert, in that order, a decisive influence on a young member of
the Circle, Vissarion Belinski, who was destined to rise by the
sheer energy of his mind, by his total dedication to the study of
literature and by a sharp and merciless pen to undisputed preeminence in Russian literary criticism during a crucial period in its
development. As we trace Belinski's view of Goethe, we shall
hear, time and again, the clear echo of the voices of Stankevich and
Bakunin, who guided him during the initial stages of his turbulent
development.

2. Vissarion Grigorievich Belinski (1811-1848).

In his study of Vissarion Belinski, Herbert Bowman makes us
vividly aware of this Russian critic as a "central figure of his
age."[37] Bowman finds "Belinski's representativeness" in "the faithfulness with which the dialectic of his career parallels the direction
of his time," in his "sensitivity to the prevailing winds of doctrine
in his day and quickness to take up into himself the currents of
intellectual and spiritual life that moved through his world,"[38] and
finally, in the fact that "the entire philosophic development of an
age, from the idealism of the thirties [the initial position of the
Stankevich Circle] to the socialism of the forties is worked out in
the struggle of his personal development."[39] Thus, it is indeed no
exaggeration when Zhirmunski characterizes "the history of Be-

linski's Goetheana as one of the most interesting and revealing phases in the development of Russian literary and sociological thought at its turning point from Romanticism to Realism."[40]

This authoritative evidence encourages us to center our attention on the writings of Vissarion Belinski, assured that in these writings we have before us the most comprehensive and vivid record of the Russian appreciation of Goethe, both in its positive as well as its negative phases, during two crucial decades in Russian cultural development, to be exact, in the second half of the thirties and in the forties, until Belinski's premature death in 1848.

The preeminence of Belinski in Russian literary criticism presents us with something of a paradox. Here is a man whose education, to put it mildly, lacked thoroughness, who never completed a provincial high school (in Chambar in the province of Penza, southeast of Moscow), who was expelled from Moscow University without a degree, who all his life struggled valiantly but vainly to master foreign languages and to the end was unable to read German without the help of a dictionary[41] or his German-speaking friends, yet who was able to become "the spokesman of his age"! Not that Belinski was not painfully aware of his shortcomings. To his friend Konstantin Aksakov he bitterly complained: "Oh, how much there was moving about in my head and is still moving of right fine plans and projects—and they all will come to naught because of my dreadful lack of languages, especially of German."[42] And to Botkin he confessed: "I do not know German, even though I talk about art and Goethe and Schiller. What a predicament!"[43] Yet this "predicament" was powerless to rob him of his supreme self-confidence which, assuredly, was an important factor in his startling achievements. A short year later he boasts to Botkin: "I *do understand* Goethe and Schiller better than all those who know them by heart even though I do not know German . . ."[44]

Relying in his studies of Goethe almost exclusively on Russian translations,[45] heavily indebted to his friends for guidance—Bakunin had introduced him to *Wilhelm Meister* and *Egmont,* Botkin to the *Wahlverwandtschaften*[46]—Belinski proved himself not only an eager and intelligent reader and listener but soon a productive student and interpreter of Goethe. In details he often erred, as when he dated Goethe's *Roman Elegies* as contemporaneous with his *Götz,* while placing the ode on "Prometheus" into the "more mature period of Goethe's life."[47] But in his judgments, evaluations and characterizations he was more often than not intuitively right, even though these judgments and characterizations were rarely the product of long and careful analysis.[48] His is not the coldly logical, systematic approach to literature. As has been well said, "into a major phase of Russian literature and cultural development he [Belinski] came not so much as its systematic analyst but rather as its evangelist."[49] Precisely as an "evangelist" Belinski was destined to give voice to the feelings and thoughts, the principles and values of the whole epoch, while delivering his fervently felt personal message.

Belinski's letters and critical writings are replete with references to Goethe's personality and works. Some of these are mere jottings, others are extensive and impassioned discussions and evaluations, such as, for instance, his defense of Goethe against the German critic, Wolfgang Menzel, an essay occupying a central place in Belinski's critical *oeuvre* at the very threshhold of his "breakthrough" to a "realistic" esthetic and a new-found social consciousness. Belinski's earliest appreciation of Goethe is essentially limited to adulatory generalities and clichés borrowed from the arsenal of epithets so well stocked by the Liubomudry and inherited by the Stankevich Circle.

In Belinski's first important essay, the "Literary Reveries"[50] of 1834, Goethe is apotheosized in the manner of the most devout of the Liubomudry as the "poet-philosopher of our time," the "all-embracing giant of poetry"[51] whose genius Belinski "worships with a holy faith."[52] "Only in some out-of-the-world Dagistan could one still seriously debate and put forth as a novel discovery the fact that Shakespeare, Goethe and Schiller are indeed truly great."[53] Together with these giants of the drama, "Goethe's fertile imagination has created that splendid and limitless world in which you live not with your own life's energy but, transported by their creative powers, far beyond your puny ego and drab life."[54] Young

Belinski was fond of quoting that famous fourth stanza of Baratynski's eulogy on the death of Goethe, which extols the German
poet's pantheistic union with all creation:

> Sein Atem war eins mit dem atmenden All
> Er verstand das Gemurmel der Quellen . . .*[55]

Belinski agrees wholeheartedly with Pushkin's glorification of
Goethe's *Faust* as "the *Iliad* of our times."[56] "Someone [Pushkin]
has said that the *Faust* of Goethe is the *Iliad* of our times. That is
an opinion with which one cannot but wholeheartedly agree."[57]
"Here you have our Homer, the prototype of *the poet of our
time!*"[58]

Goethe's lyrics Belinski placed among the "newest 'ideal poesy' which traces its origin to classical antiquity and derives from
that source its dignity, grandeur and its poetic, elevated diction
which contrasts so sharply with the commonplace, conversational
language and eschews all that is petty and mundane."[59] Goethe
not only reached back to classical antiquity as a source of his
poetry but he also embraced in his work the most modern trends
in literature. In the spirit of Hegelian dialectics Belinski argued
that Goethe had resolved in his "most modern art" the antithetical
extremes of Classicism and Romanticism in a higher synthesis:
"Deriving historically from the latter [Classicism], having in
herited the full depth and breadth of its limitless content and
having become enriched by the subsequent infusion of the Christian
spirit and by the acquisition of new knowledge, it [Goethe's art]
harmonized within itself the riches of its Romantic content with
the plasticity of Classical form." Thus, the "artistic value" of
Goethe's lyrics is "not accessible by means of a facile appreciation
of its ideational content only; rather it is to be found in the
splendid elegance, the grace and perfection of its form."[60]

Amidst these hosannas to Goethe, still very much in the tradition of the Liubomudry and the Stankevich Circle, it is striking to
hear already in Belinski's first essay ("The Literary Reveries")
his independent critical voice raised distinctly, even if softly and
briefly as yet. Although he "sacredly believed in Goethe's genius,"

---

*See footnote on p. 97.

he did have his doubts about "the Hellenism" of Goethe's *Iphigenie,* "I must confess, I have little confidence in the Hellenism of his *Iphigenie!"* Belinski expresses herewith a view which stands in the sharpest possible contrast to the Liubomudry's dogma of the Protean nature of the true poet, of his limitless power of empathy. He dared to argue that "the greater the genius of a poet, the more he is the son of his age and the citizen of his world and that from this it follows that all his attempts to express a national culture completely alien to him are bound to result in a more or less unsuccessful work bearing the marks of imitative falsification [poddelka]."[61] To be sure, in the context of the "Reveries" this is still an isolated statement, all the more startling by this very isolation. It adumbrates a theme which was to become central in Belinski's "Realistic" period as a criterion whereby to judge the stature of a poet.[62] Moreover, it serves as an illustration of Belinski's "unsystematic" mode of thinking and puts us on guard against a too-facile periodization of his thought into the "early" and "late," the "Romantic" and the "Realistic" periods. To be sure, a basic reorientation took place in the crucial year 1840, yet hints scattered through his earliest essays foreshadowed a distancing from the Schelling-Hegelian esthetics and, with it, from a blind worship of Goethe.

We will recall that among the prime motivations for the formation of the Liubomudry circle had been the abrupt break these young Russian intellectuals made with French rationalism, materialism and atheism and their ardent espousal of German idealism and transcendentalism in philosophy and literature. The Stankevich Circle perpetuated and developed this attitude, and Belinski gave it its most strident expression: "The French are a superficial people, they live a life of externality and ostentation. . . . To the French everything in the world is as clear-cut as $2 \times 2 = 4$. Theirs is a finite mentality, which is good enough in its place when it is a matter of understanding ordinary occurrences of everyday life but which turns to *violence against God* as soon as it enters the highest spheres of knowledge."[63] These "highest spheres" Belinski recognized as the true domain of the German mind: "To their [the

Germans'] spiritual insight are revealed the inner, the mysterious aspects of phenomena, that invisible, hidden spirit which instills them with life and with significant meaning. To the Germans every aspect of life is a magical hieroglyph, a sacred symbol, or, finally, an organic, living creation." To them "the realm of knowledge is the House of God which they enter with washed feet and a cleansed soul, with the trembling awe and love for the Source of all Being. Here lies the reason why, in science as in art, everything carries for the German the mark of religiosity and all life is for him a sacred and lofty mystery, which can be grasped only through revelation, its comprehension being bestowed upon the elect as a divine gift."[64]

For Belinski this German spirit found its richest expression in the personality and works of Goethe. "Goethe himself was the fullest expression of Germany. With his *Faust* . . . he has given us the symbol of the spirit of his native land in a form at once thoroughly his own and characteristic of his epoch."[65] Vindicating the supremacy of the German poetic genius, Goethe "has restored art to its former dignity which it had lost in the period of French Classicism."[66] His works were the poetic text to Germany's newest philosophy; "Goethe has penetrated by different and independent paths to the same ultimate truth that Hegel had reached in his philosophy."[67]

This "ultimate truth" reached independently by Hegel and Goethe was the new gospel of "objective reality" which Belinski embraced with characteristic fervor, sweeping aside his former idols Schelling and Schiller, disavowing with special vehemence "fair-souled" Schiller's "abstract ideal of the good and the beautiful."[68] Belinski had been introduced to this "new gospel" by his friends in the "Circle," by Katkov and especially by Bakunin. This is how Belinski records this important event of his "reconciliation with reality" in a letter to Stankevich:

> I arrive in Moscow [September 1837] from the Caucasus; Bakunin arrives; we live together. That summer he had been looking over Hegel's philosophy of religion and law. A new world opened up before us. "Might is right and right is might." No, I cannot describe to you with what emotion

I heard those words; it was a liberation. I understood the meaning of the downfall of empires, the legitimacy of conquerors; I understood that there is no crude material force nor conquest by sword and bayonet, nothing arbitrary, nothing accidental . . .

Before this, Katkov had conveyed to me as well as he was able, and I received as well as I could, certain conclusions from [Hegel's] *Aesthetics*. Good heavens, what a new, bright infinite world!

. . . The word Reality became for me the equivalent of the word God. In vain you advise me to look more often at the blue sky [metaphor for the Schillerian "ideal absolute"], the image of the eternal, so as not to fall into the cookhouse reality [read: "objective" reality]. My friend, blessed is he who can see in the image of the heavens a symbol of the eternal; [but] more blessed is he who can illumine the cookhouse by the idea of the eternal.[69]

Even more rhapsodic are Belinski's recollections of that liberating moment when he discovered "the healthy and normal poetry of Goethe" and "sent to the devil Schiller and his abstract idealism."[70] With the headlong passion typical of our "Vissarion the furious" (neistovyi Vissarion)[71] he cursed Schiller for his "subjective-moralistic" idealism, for his destructive idea of duty, his abstract heroism, for his "fairsouled" war on reality which had led Belinski "to despise society, the state, mankind itself, to shun nature and a natural existence, to renounce the very thought of marriage—and all that in the name of an abstract ideal of a society erected on thin air." Schiller's *Don Carlos*, "that apotheosis of abstract love for all mankind without substance," had plunged Belinski into an "abstract heroism" which led him "to hate everything (and with what a fanatical, what morbid hatred)." Under its spell, despite his "unnatural, overwrought elation," he had "the lively sense of being a complete zero." "What did that Schiller not do to me!" Belinski exclaimed in exasperation, "to what extremes did he not bring me!" And he asked Stankevich: "Do you remember how on reading that altogether ethereal love affair between Max and Thekla it became a settled matter with us that to enter into a relationship with a maiden would be a base and dishonorable act, for if she were a virgin it would be dastardly in the extreme to rob her of her virginity, and were she not, then to make her pregnant would be an equally dastardly act? . . . Do you see where that idealistic Schiller had led us?"[72]

And then came their liberation! As they spoke of Goethe, read his works, Belinski felt literally beside himself with the sense of a newly won freedom, of a new life in palpable reality. "It was then that we spoke of Goethe, and what became of me! What feelings seized me as I read 'Morgenklagen' and then 'Auf Kieseln im Bache.'[73] New world! New life! Off with the yoke of duty, to the devil with dessicated moralism and with idealistic ratiocinations! Man can live again—every one of life's moments is great, real, sacred."[74]

With the same elation Belinski received the Russian version of Goethe's "Römische Elegien," sent him by his friend, the translator Strugovchikov. Here again, more intensely even, he experienced that "concrete reality," that pulsating rhythm of life which liberated him from the chimera of Schillerian idealism "built on thin air." "I do not know how to thank him [Strugovchikov] for Goethe's 'Elegies,' " Belinski wrote to their mutual friend Panaev: "I simply gorged myself on them; as in the waves of the ocean of life I bathed in these hexameters."[75]

There is ample evidence that Belinski was very much alive to the importance the Mediterranean world and Greek antiquity had for Goethe: he obviously realized that without these experiences Goethe could not have written such poetry, would not have created such a "reality." "The Greeks understood, far better than we do, life and women," he wrote to Botkin, "Goethe's 'Roman Elegies" are the very best catechism of love, and it is for them that I admire Goethe more fervently than for anything else he has ever written."[76]

In an enthusiastic review of the Russian version of the "Elegies," Belinski singles out as their "basic element", "the love of first youth, the *Hellenic* love, the poetic love" and continues: "The young poet trod the classical soil of Rome; his soul unfolded freely beneath the azure skies of the South, in the shade of the olive and laurel trees, amid the monuments of classical art. There the people resemble graceful statues, there the women call to mind the lineaments of the Venus de Medici. A life of leisure, contemplation and voluptuous sweetness, imbued with a sense of the graceful, completely coincides with the ideal of the artist. Goethe plunged into this life with the self-abandon, the infatuation of which only a poet is capable. His days he dedicated to learning, his nights to love. . . . Like the verses of the ancients, Goethe's 'Elegies' capture the fleeting sensation, thought or event in the permanence of an image, beguiling by its grace, wit, and artlessness."[77] This basic theme was restated and developed in another essay on the "Elegies."[78] Here Belinski placed the work "among those of Goethe's creations which characterize most effectively his objective genius." The key word "objective" led Belinski into a comparison of Goethe's "objective," "classical" artistry with Schiller's "subjective," "eccentric" genius, much to the disadvantage of the latter. "In that period of life, when the devouring, eccentric activity of Schiller's subjective genius exhausted itself in the battle with the external world, Goethe's calm, contemplative, concentrated genius luxuriated in 'reality' under the happy skies of Italy, in the lap of beautiful nature, amid the monuments of ancient arts. He experienced fully a Grecian period of life and in the plastic, antique symbols of the sacred Hellenic muse gave to mankind his poetic rendering of this experience."

No doubt, Belinski was impressed with Goethe's self-immersion in the Mediterranean, Classical world. He admires his ability to transmit this experience in sublime artistic form. "How fitting a choice for these Elegies is their hexameter verse, breathing youth, tranquillity, naïveté and grace! How much plasticity is there in his verse; what a high-relief quality his images have! You actually forget that he is a German and nearly your contemporary, just as he all but forgot it, taking the Capitolean Hills for the Olympus and entering at the hand of Hebe the palace of Zeus."[79]

And yet, when we remember Belinski's outspoken criticism of Goethe's *Iphigenie*, his thoroughgoing enjoyment of such totally un-Grecian occasional pieces as Goethe's "Wechsel" or his "Mor-

genklagen," we may well wonder whether it was really the "Greek-
ness" of the "Elegies" that elicited Belinski's overflowing praise,
whether it was not rather their eminently successful realization of
an intense sensuous experience which captivated Belinski. Was it
not rather that "ocean of life" and of love in its verses which
swept him on its waves into a new freedom of sensual apperception
of reality, unburdened him of moral taboos, idealistic scruples, and
"abstract ratiocination"? A significant sentence in the letter to Botkin would seem to bear us out: "It seems to me that in this world
the only true wise one is the artist, and all the rest are insane."
Basicly, Belinski's admiration went out to the inspired poet, to
that "wise one," be it Shakespeare or Pushkin or Goethe, who
was able to embody with incomparable vitality and verisimilitude
"objective reality." This ability Belinski recognized as being independent of and far more basic than any particular "influence" playing upon the poet during any particular period of his creative career.
It is this mysterious power to give artistic form to "blessed reality,"
that Belinski experienced in the "Elegies." This is the unique
quality which places them among his favorite works of Goethe.
It is precisely this "blessed *reality*" which Belinski found lacking
in Goethe's *Iphigenie* and therefore turned away from that "Classical" masterpiece, which bore for him "the marks of imitative
falsification."

Here is the vantage point from which we can gain a clear
view of Belinski's basic esthetic criterion during this particular
phase in his development as a critic, a phase during which Hegel's
influence reigns supreme and which is, therefore, generally referred to as Belinski's "Hegelian" period of "reconciliation with
reality."[80] "Look at God's marvelous world," he exclaims in this
spirit of enthusiastic affirmation of life, "in it all is splendor, all is
supreme wisdom. . . . Everywhere there is beauty, everywhere
grandeur, everywhere harmony!"[81] Belinski considers art to be
great only by virtue of its complete fidelity to this "glorious
reality," as "a mirror of reality." The hallmark of the "foremost
genius of art" is his ability to embody in his works life in all its
multiformity and vitality, to give it a completely "objective" re-

presentation. Such a supreme genius creates, unaffected by any forces extraneous to the creative impulse, unconcerned with morals or conventions, unswayed by considerations of fame or gain or any external or internal impulses other than the compulsion to mirror in his artistic medium "objective reality." Or, employing Belinski's favorite metaphors, such an artist surveys all creation from his Olympian heights with the all-seeing "eye of the eagle," (orlinym vzorom). Such "foremost genius of art" Belinski recognizes in Homer, Shakespeare, Walter Scott, in Pushkin and in Goethe, but not in Byron and Schiller, these latter being "subjective," "one-sided" artists and their works not true but distorting mirrors of reality. Schiller, his one-time idol, is now demoted to "that strange half-artist and half-philosopher" who lacks "the objective, dispassionate eye which can be discerned in the works of Goethe, the Olympian."[82] Shakespeare is now enthroned as a paragon of the "objective" poet because he did not have 'ideals' in the generally accepted meaning of that word. He harbors no doubts, is not constrained by habits or tendencies [sklonnostei], he has no favorite ideas, or favorite types" and again: "For Shakespeare there does not exist good nor evil; for him there exists only life, which he calmly contemplates and comprehends [soznaët] in his creations, enthralled by nothing, giving preference to nothing."[83] Belinski applies this same esthetic criterion of excellence when he writes with reference to Goethe's *Faust:* "I am convinced that epic poetry, in order to be truly great, . . . must *mirror the life of a whole nation. It must be, moreover, an unconscious expression* of the creative spirit, *independent of conscious volition and personal predilections of the artist;* it must be original in the highest degree and as such must stand at the furthest remove from all imitation. Such a creation is the *Iliad,* is Goethe's *Faust.*" And he adds significantly: "Not of such highest quality are by contrast the *Aeneid, Jerusalem Delivered, Paradise Lost, the Messias,* for these are created not intuitively, indigeneously [samobytno] but in imitation of the *Iliad* [!]; as such they do not live their own life, but derive their existence from an alien source. For that reason, they do not encompass the full picture of the life of the people to which they belong, *nor do they mirror faithfully the spirit of the times* in which they were created." One may well quarrel with this sweeping devaluation of the greatest masterpieces of world literature. We must, however, accept it as a revealing statement of Belinski's esthetic views during this period and of his high esteem of Goethe as the supreme "objective genius" of modern art, as a brother in spirit of Homer and of Shakespeare.

And yet, when Belinski comes to apply this highest criterion to the whole range of Goethe's works that were known to him, he finds several of them falling short of greatness as products not of "objectivity" and "intuitive immediacy" but of didactic or sentimental "reflectionism" (refleksia). He condemns Part II of *Faust* as such a product because of an excess of allegory and symbolism, of that "dry rot of poetry." "This second part [of Faust]," he writes to his friend Panaev, "is not poetry but dry, dead, decayed symbolism and allegory."[85] This criticism shows Belinski freed of the influence of the Hegelians, who extolled *Faust* Part II precisely for its profound symbolism and allegory as the incomparable poetical text to their master's philosophy. With his typical frenzied single-mindedness, Belinski now takes to task even such favorite works of the Romantic admirers of Goethe as his *Wilhelm Meister,* the *Wahlverwandtschaften* and *Werther.* To Botkin's praises of the *Elective Affinities* he replies: "Be it as you wish. Still, after your acclaim of *Werther* and of *Wilhelm Meister,* I am full of suspicion for your present infatuation with the *Wahlverwandtschaften.* I am certain that it is the same sort of thing as *Wilhelm Meister:* one part wine to one part water; such works, while they do offer a great deal in their individual parts, as a whole they only increase the morbidity of spirit and reflectionism without leading us into the fullness of contemplation."[86]

In his essay, "Menzel, the Critic of Goethe," written at about the same time as these letters, Belinski refuses to acknowledge *Werther* as a successful work of art, brands it "a fragment," the product of a "tormented condition of his [Goethe's] spirit,"[87] lacking that all-important "objectivity and dispassionate tranquillity" which to him are at this time the sine qua non for the act of true poetic creation. Belinski glories in the fact that the "poisonous breath of reflectionism has not touched Pushkin and thus has not deprived humanity of this great artist." "What a completely *artistic nature,* our Pushkin! Surely, he would never have written that allegorico-symbolical Galimatias, known as the 'Second Part of *Faust';* he was not capable of writing the sort of products of reflectionism that are *Werther* and *Wilhelm Meister* . . . No, dear friends, go to the devil with your Germans! Here [in the works of Pushkin] we sense the spirit of a Shakespeare of our times."[88] He admits to Botkin that he is "enraptured with Goethe's *symbolic* [i.e. 'reflective'] poem 'Prometheus.'" Yet he insists that reflective poetry not be mentioned when the discussion turns to "true poetry," for he holds firm to the "axiomatic truth" that "only *intuited* images have absolute reality, never those *manufactured* ones, those *fabrications of a calculating human cleverness.*"[89]

Belinski is not at all disappointed at not being able to read the *Wahlverwandtschaften,* because, as he put it most incautiously: "Even though I have not read them, I know what kind of nothingness they are: unartistic, unpoetic, a belletristic work, granted, containing a few potential moments and artistic elements." And, pursuing this generalization based on second-hand information, he proceeds to place Goethe, "the author of novels" well below Walter Scott. He praises the English writer as "a true artist" while dismissing the "novelist Goethe" as a mere "belletrist, comparable in stature possibly to Victor Hugo but never, never to Scott!"[90] Even the oft-repeated, all-but-sacrosanct triad of the greatest "objective artists," Homer, Shakespeare, and Goethe, is shattered by Belinski in at least one pronouncement, with Pushkin dethroning Goethe: "At this time I have three gods of art, before whom I kneel almost daily, besides myself in a rage of exaltation. Homer, Shakespeare, Pushkin!" Here we have the "neistovyi Vissarion," the "furious Vissarion" in his most wildly rapturous mood.

It is significant that these extravagant and rashly unsubstantiated judgments are to be found exclusively in Belinski's letters. In his essays, Belinski remained faithful to his admiration of Goethe. In fact, in his defense of Goethe against Menzel, to which we now turn, we find the ultimate statement of his discipleship to Goethe, "ultimate" both in the sense of most explicit and comprehensive as well as in that of "final," this statement dating immediately prior to Belinski's sudden abandonment of the Hegelian position and his radical swing to his anti-Hegelian "*un*reconciliation with reality,"[91] which was to occur toward the end of the year 1840, only a few months after the appearance of his essay, "Menzel, the Critic of Goethe."[92]

Let it be stated here, by way of recapitulation and emphasis, that, in the years 1834 to the beginning of 1840 surveyed up to this point, Belinski's esthetics did not change as fundamentally as might appear. True, he rejected Schiller's "idealism built on thin air" and came to espouse the "healthy and normal poetry of Goethe" with its "concrete reality." Yet, throughout this period the basic esthetic canon of "pure" art remained binding on Belinski with its central thesis of "art for art's sake," the artist enthroned above the world of mere mortals with their ephemeral social, economic, and political concerns, divining and recording in his works the eternal verities of cosmic life. It is, we must remember, from this basic position that Belinski carries his attack against Menzel in defense of the inviolable greatness of Goethe, the man and the artist.

The famous-infamous *Die deutsche Literatur* of Wolfgang Menzel with its sharp attack on Goethe had been translated into Russian by V. Komorski and had appeared early in 1838 in a two-volume edition which attracted considerable attention in literary circles.[93] For Belinski it served as the leaven which brought his thoughts on Goethe and, generally, on the role of the artist and of art to a violently productive ferment. Menzel had launched a heavy-handed attack on Goethe. He had deposed him from the status of genius to that of a mere talent; he had accused him of lack of patriotism, of political indifferentism and servilism, had branded him a "political chameleon." As an artist, Goethe appeared in Menzel's book in the role of a conscienceless eclectic, ready to change his style and themes in conformity to the changing vogues at home and abroad. Mounting his heaviest attack, Menzel casti-

gated Goethe for his refined Epicureanism, his irresponsible fri-
volity, sensuality, blatant egoism and, generally, for a reprehensible
lack of morals. Goethe's work, claimed Menzel, stood before the
nation as a symptom of and as a contributing cause to Germany's
utter demoralization and catastrophic decline in its political, social
and cultural life.

On every score, Belinski felt challenged to counter Menzel's
attack, because in launching it Menzel had proceeded from a view
of art and the artist diametrically opposed to that still held at this
time by Belinski. Menzel, this "little-big man,"[94] as Belinski calls
him derisively, had blundered into a realm forever closed to the
likes of him, into the ethereal sphere of art. Belinski likens
Menzel to the spider in Krylov's fable that clung to the tailfeathers
of the mighty eagle—Goethe!— to be carried aloft to the snow-
capped heights of the Caucasus, there to suffer an ignominious
fate: "one puff of wind, and the pitiable creature found itself back
in the lowlands where it belonged, while the eagle on mighty
wings soared into his native spheres of the limitless ether." Menzel,
that "little-big man" with his "limited mind," in his attack on
Goethe, that "prototype of the modern poet" and on his works,
those exemplars of "pure art," had completely failed to grasp the
truth which Belinski held to be unassailable, namely, that art has
no purpose outside itself, that the artist knows no allegiance or
obligation save to his muse. Else how could Menzel have com-
mitted the inexcusable error of taking Goethe for "a factotum who
can be ordered to sing a song of praise now to the sacredness of
marriage, now to the joy of patriotic self-sacrifice, now to the
sacred obligation of paying one's debts in good faith."

This "little-big man," this myopic critic Menzel accused Goethe,
that "poet supreme," of silence during the world-stirring events of
the French Revolution, called it a grave failing, a capital crime.
In the first place, what basis in fact does Menzel have, asked Belinski, for his insinuation of political indifferentism on the part of
Goethe, what for his charge that Goethe let pass the great world
events without a comment? Had not Menzel himself acclaimed
Goethe's genius as "that fullest, truest reflection of this great epoch,"

as the "resonant harp" whose strings responded to every stirring of life roundabout? Here Belinski once again quoted his favorite stanza from Baratynski's eulogy on Goethe: "Sein Atem war eins mit dem atmenden All" to drive home his point that in a deeper sense Goethe was indeed in full rapport with his time and with all times. "To carry out time-bound tasks and to achieve time-bound goals we have the little-big people, the Arndts and the Körners. The truly great, the exemplars of mankind, have a different sense of time and different goals—the world and eternity." The truly great are always in harmony with the will of God, with the universal idea; that is the source of their strength and of their success in their labors. "Theirs is the instinct for truth and reality, what exists they accept as logical, necessary, and real, and that which is logical, necessary, and real they accept as existing." Hegel's voice could not have been more distinct had he himself been the speaker. "Therefore," Belinski wrote, continuing his Hegelian argument, "Goethe did not demand and did not desire the impossible but rather delighted in the necessary and the real." Thus, "for him the necessity of German partition was as firm a conviction as for Pushkin his faith that the Russian sea would never go dry, that instead the 'Slavic streams would all flow into the Russian sea.' "

And what of Menzel's charge of Goethe's servilism, his "Fürstendienertum"? Belinski brushed it aside as of no substance whatever, "for in the first place, to live at court or not to live there—that is a question of supreme indifference, for in both conditions a man can be equally great and philanthropic; and secondly, in attacking the *person* one should never confuse him with the *artist. . . .* Art has its own laws, on the basis of which its creations should be judged." On an earlier occasion Belinski had given an even more pointed answer. Speaking of the complete invulnerability of genius to material enticements, he had used Goethe as a striking example. "What did Goethe offer in payment to his mighty benefactors?" he had asked on that occasion and had answered, driving home his point: "A few distichs for gala occasions, some bad hexameters, but certainly not his *Werther,* or *Wilhelm Meister,* or his *Faust*."[95]

To Menzel's accusation of Goethe for his amoralism, Belinski makes his most elaborate reply. This reply is highly characteristic of Belinski's Hegel-oriented ethics, his absolute equation of ethics with esthetics. "Whatever is artistic," he argued, "is by that very token ethical; whatever is inartistic may perchance not be immoral but certainly is never ethical in the highest meaning of that term." From this point of view Goethe, this supreme artist, necessarily appeared to Belinski as the paragon not of conventional morality (Hegel's *Moralität*), to be sure, but of that higher ethics, of Hegel's *Sittlichkeit*. Menzel in his hopelessly conventional morality had been incapable of grasping this truth. Unjustifiably he demanded of Goethe that he present in his works not living characters but "walking allegories with labels on their foreheads inscribed with the mottos: moderation, orderliness, modesty, and so forth." Menzel expected a "moral ending" in all works of literature in which we would find the "do-gooder" properly rewarded and the "bad man" punished. He completely failed to comprehend that goodness is its own best reward and evil its own most severe punishment. And with these "myopic and warped" criteria Menzel had undertaken to fathom Goethe's genius, to comprehend the "higher morality" in Goethe's creations! A hopeless undertaking! Menzel was doomed to stand exposed in all the poverty of his mind and emotions "among those vampires who by their cold touch extinguish life, . . . in whose warped little minds genius and immorality would always remain synonymous." Small wonder that Goethe ever and again roused their most intense hatred. The reason was only too obvious to Belinski. Was not Goethe the "all-embracing genius," capable of empathy with all creation through the power of his poetic clairvoyance, and for that very reason unable to surrender to any one-sided sympathy, incapable of joining any exclusive doctrine, system, or party? Was he not as many-sided as nature itself, which he loved so passionately, understood so profoundly? And Belinski calls on his readers to observe how contradictory and consequently how "immoral" Nature is—"immoral" at least in the terminology of our bigots! She will say one thing in one place and maintain the very opposite at another. In truth, what an amoral being! And just such an "amoral being" Goethe was too, Goethe that truest mirror of nature, who—like nature—spoke with many different tongues in the many different phases of his creative career. Here Belinski delivers a rhapsodic evocation of Goethe's many-faceted development as an artist which is quite as short on logical and chronological accuracy as it is long on adulatory enthusiasm and rhetoric. It deserves to be quoted as the most revealing statement of Belinski's view at this time of Goethe's artistic achievement, as startling in its aberrations as in its intuitive insights:

> In the days of his stormy youth, steeped in the spirit of Classical antiquity, enthralled by the magnificence of life and nature of poetical Italy, Goethe wrote his "Roman Elegies," that wondrous glorification of ancient life and art, and at the same time he resurrected in his *Götz* the life of knightly Germany, deranged all Europe with his account of the *Sufferings of Werther* and created in his *Wilhelm Meister* the apotheosis of a man who in this wide world does nothing at all of usefulness but instead devotes himself exclusively to the fullest enjoyment of life and art, to love, to suffering and to thought. Later, in his more mature years, Goethe gave artistic expression in his "Prometheus" to the revolt of the enlightened mind against conditions and authorities accepted on faith alone, and, in his *Faust*, to the life of a subjective spirit in its striving toward reconciliation with rational reality through doubt, suffering, struggle, denial, collapse and resurrection. But alongside Faust he placed Margarete, that ideal of feminine love and devotion, that submissive and uncomplaining sacrificial victim of suffering, who accepted her death as her salvation, as expiation of her sin, in the Christian meaning of that word. . . . Indeed, to contain Goethe in any narrow classification is difficult and not only for a Menzel! That was the reason why Menzel became infuriated and called him [Goethe] an amoral indifferentist.

To denigrate Goethe, Menzel had juxtaposed Schiller to him as a paragon of morality. Menzel should have known better! Had he been a critic of real insight, he would have recognized that "Goethe was a genius of an incomparably higher order, a true poet never carried away by one-sided interests, always encompassing the totality of life, beholding everything from a sublime vantage point . . . In fact, Menzel should have realized that it had been Schiller's lifelong ambition to achieve Goethe's comprehensive *objective* view of life and that in the end Schiller had actually been able in some measure to realize that ambition." Belinski admits that Schiller's "early works, his *Räuber* and his *Kabale und Liebe* are noble outbursts of a flaming, inexhaustible love of mankind, and as such are 'moral.' Yet compared to 'absolute truth' they are decidedly 'immoral'!" And once again Belinski traces Schiller's shortcomings to the "subjective" nature of his genius. "With these works Schiller had sought to realize eternal verities, yet could express with them only his *subjective and therefore limited* orientation." Compared with these "artistic stillbirths and monstrosities," the artistic perfection and moral loftiness of Goethe's creations shine forth all the more splendidly.

Still, Goethe, too, had his "moments of weakness and abberation"! Such a "moment," for instance, was his *Werther.* Here Goethe had "forsaken his artist-self, had stepped forward as an ordinary mortal" to express "a momentary condition of his mortal self, an oppressive and tormenting condition." That is why, when reading *Werther,* "we feel tortured and depressed instead of being calmed and uplifted," why *Werther* "seems fragmentary, a cutting, screeching dissonance of spirit." This particular work, therefore, Belinski cannot call " 'moral' in the sublimest meaning of that word." "Yet can it be possible," he asks urgently, "that *one* such unsuccessful attempt could blot out the whole rich harvest of a creative lifetime?!" Had not Goethe given expression to this "tormenting condition of his spirit" precisely to set himself free from it by the very act of expressing it, to return forthwith to his healthy, normal, "objective" artist-self? Belinski answers this question in unqualified support of Goethe against all his detractors and even against Goethe's own fallible self. At the end of Belinski's most comprehensive statement on Goethe, the German poet remained enthroned for the Russian critic on his serene Olympus, the unchallenged ruler in the realm of art. But, alas, how brief was that reign to be!

Hardly had Belinski put this encomium of Goethe to paper when, in a letter to Botkin on December 30, 1840, we find him extolling Schiller and casting down his idol Goethe: "Let me confess to you," he wrote to his friend, "that I cannot now think of Schiller without growing breathless with enthusiasm, while toward Goethe I am beginning to feel something actually akin to hatred. And, by God, I would no longer raise a hand against Menzel, even though I still consider that fellow an idiot. Heavens! What leaps, what zigzags in my development! Frightening to think of it!

Yes, I now realize, at long last, my kinship to Schiller, I am bone of his bones, flesh of his flesh, and if there is anything that should and could interest me in life and in history, then it is he, Schiller, who has been created to be my God, my idol."[96]

What was the cause of this sudden drastic change in Belinski's point of view? Why the rising hatred toward Goethe the man and artist whom, a few weeks earlier, he had so vigorously defended? The answer is to be found in Belinski's basic reorientation of his view on life and art. It had come to Belinski with the suddenness and force of a revelation that his Hegelian reconciliation with reality was a tragic error, that instead of accepting the repulsive Russian reality in a spirit of tolerance and compliance, in a stance of inward-oriented and self-centered aloofness, it was the sacred duty of man and especially of an artist, a writer, to face reality, to recognize its shortcomings and in a spirit of a newly gained "sociality"[97] to join in the battle for progress and the liberation of mankind from oppressive reaction. Belinski was now prepared "to suffer and to die" for this conviction, being tormented by the thought of his "infamous reconciliation with unsavory reality." He had realized with sudden certainty that "criticism of reality is no less sacred a historical right than is acquiescence to reality, a right, nay a duty which man must exercise, must fulfill, lest human history should turn into a stinking stagnant pool."[98] Belinski had finally recognized Hegel's philosophy for what it really was, "a passing phase in the history of the human spirit;" he had realized at long last "that the absolute nature of Hegel's philosophy is a devilish lie, that it is better to die than to come to terms with it."

Belinski had deep personal reasons for being furious with Hegel. It had been Hegel's philosophy that had led him to "make peace with the abominable Russian reality."[99] With bitter irony Belinski inveighs against the Hegelian motto: " 'That which exists is reasonable.' " "Yes, indeed," he cries out, "yes, indeed, the executioner, too, *exists,* his existence is real; and yet, the fact of his existence is disgusting and not at all reasonable. No, from this moment forward the *liberal* and the *human* shall be one and indivisible for me; and the absolutist and the knut-wielder, they will be of one ilk." Now he accepts the idea of liberalism as a highly rational and Christian idea, "since it is liberalism's task to regain for the individual his inalienable rights and to reestablish his full dignity."[100]

Obviously, Belinski's "*un*reconciliation with reality" was as complete as it was sudden, carried out in the true spirit of "Vissarion the furious." From it there flowed with impassioned urgency the reactions to his former positions along his entire intellectual front—esthetic, social and political. France was rehabilitated as the home of those "energetic, noble people, who spill their blood for the sacred rights of humanity, that vanguard of humanity *au drapeau tricolore!*" In the language of Heine, whom he embraced as that "wonderful, splendid personality," Belinski defended "la belle France" against any and all unfavorable comparisons with Germany, some of the most vehement of which he himself had penned not so long ago. He was ready to admit that "there are many loudmouths and phrasemongers in France, but, for all that, in Germany there is a crowd of *Hofräte,* philistines, sausagemakers and other reptiles" (gofratov, filisterov, kolbasnikov i drugikh gadov).[101] These brave and idealistic people were ably led in their righteous cause by such newly discovered heroes of Belinski's as George Sand, that "inspired prophetess, that energetic advocate of the rights of women," and Béranger, "the French Schiller, apostle of reason, . . . prophet of political and intellectual freedom."[102]

On the other hand, the Germans and their literature are now condemned for the very traits which such a short time ago Belinski had so fervently espoused. "The German is born neither for the world of society (as is the Frenchman), nor as a citizen with a well-developed political sense. . . . The German's relationship to life and the world is purely intellectual. Here is the source of his ethical asceticism. Having grasped the underlying idea of a phenomenon, he remains indifferent to the fact that this phenomenon as it exists in reality falls far short of his ideal conception of it . . . Thus he easily manages to live at peace with any sort of actuality. For the German," Belinski concluded, "to know and to live are two completely separate functions." In sharp contrast to this German attitude, "the Frenchman considers science and art to be the means for social reform and the liberation of humanity from oppressive and humiliating chains."[103]

"The German strives and labors with only one goal in mind— to comprehend the truth. He writes for his fellow savants; he scorns the common people." Here Belinski found the source of the German's "turgid, awkward and often pedantic style." According to him, "the German manages to turn the most popular subject into a veritable Eleusian mystery, while the Frenchman will write for you a most lucid, even enthralling, learned treatise on the most obtruse and dry subject. The German contemplates reality, the Frenchman creates it. The German loves the science of man, the Frenchman loves man. . . . The German can lay hold of reality only as an object of contemplation." This explained for Belinski "the intellectual-contemplative, the subjective-idealistic, the rapturously ascetic, the abstract-scholarly character of the German's art and science."[104] "German literature," he wrote, "fails to depict society, excels in portraying isolated individuals whose entire biography consists in the flux of private emotions, in fantastic daydreams; these characters find their deepest delight in the self-satisfied contemplation of the profundity of their own personalities. Theirs is an empty, idle life of private sensations instead of an active striving toward the achievement of an ideal existence in reality."[105] This literature in its "ethical asceticism, in its indifference to the historical and social aspects of life," leads of necessity to a "supine reconciliation with reality, no matter what that reality might be."[106]

To this "ethical asceticism" Belinski traced the German's signal success in lyrical poetry and music but also his dismal failure in the other genres of literature.[107] Apodictically he pronounced "the novel and the drama to be closed realms to the Germans."[108]

Goethe, as the typical representative of this "ascetic" German literature, was severely taken to task for the very qualities that had formerly aroused Belinski's admiration: Olympian aloofness, ethical and political indifferentism, introversion.[109] To Bakunin's sisters Belinski denounced Goethe as "the very embodiment of egoism" which he finds "particularly dangerous when it is passed off for self-abnegation." He urged the ladies to examine closely the character of Egmont in Goethe's drama of that name as a mirror image of Goethe's personality. "Penetrate into the character of Egmont and you will recognize that he is playing with sacred emotions as with an object of lofty spiritual gratification, yet these sacred feelings are not part of him, are not inherent in his nature. 'How sweet is the habit of living,'[110] he exclaims, and in reply I would exclaim: 'Oh what a low creature you are, you Netherlandic hero!' For Egmont patriotism is nothing more than a tasty dish at the feast of life, not the sacred emotion that it should be. The dedicated and lofty soul of Schiller, tempered in the white heat of an ancient sense of citizenship, would never have been able to give birth to such a putrid ideal of a smirkingly self-satisfied personage, who toys with all that is sacred and great in life." Belinski then pointed out to the sisters an article in the journal *Patriotic Notes* on "Goethe and Countess Stolberg"[111] which had helped him to recognize Goethe for the egoist he really was, the prototype of his Egmont. "Here was Goethe, in love with a girl [Lili Schönemann] and loved by her in turn—and what does he do? He toys with this love! He dotes on the sensations roused by the affair, analyzes them, broods over them like the hen on its eggs, and all the while the human being that is the object of his love means nothing to him. . . . Here it is, that idealized, poeticized cold egoism of a self-centered life, fixed only on its own sensations, oblivious of those who roused these emotions, much like the usurer who dotes on his profit, not thinking of those who with their blood and tears brought him that profit." Belinski condemned this attitude as "the most dangerous form of egoism." "Such an egoist accepts the sacrifice of love and is blithely certain that he embodies the most lofty, ethereal and selfless love." Such a one claims to love "everything" and actually loves "nothing," for "everything is tantamount to nothing." And this "most dangerous form of egoism" was Goethe's. "It was in that very manner that Goethe loved 'everything,' from the angel in heaven to the infant on this earth, to the worm in the sea—and that is precisely why he failed in the end to love anything or anybody at all. Zhukovski had written of him: 'And he encompassed all in life / And would not be slave to anything . . .' and in writing this he was not aware that with this praise he condemned Goethe. . . . But God be with him, with this Goethe! He is a great man—I stand in awe before his genius, yet, nonetheless, I cannot but despise him. Not long ago I read his *Hermann and Dorothea*—what revolting trash!"[112]

In a letter to Bakunin, Belinski was more laconic but quite as drastic in his criticism of Goethe the man: "Surely," he wrote, "Goethe *is* great as an artist, but as a person he is *abominable!*" He followed this brutal rejection of Goethe the man with a veritable paean to Fichte and Schiller: "Now there have risen again before me in all their radiant greatness the colossal images of Fichte und Schiller, of these prophets of humanity, these heralds of God's kingdom on earth, these high priests of eternal love and truth, which they preach not merely by way of bookish ratiocinations, not in a posture of Brahmin contemplativeness, but by means of vital and reasoned *That*."[113] And to Botkin, Belinski wrote these lines of downright abuse of the once-admired "sage of Weimar": "What a swine Goethe is—as a person! Without will power, without strength, a 'beautiful soul,' a real Clavigo [Belinski's pet hate even in the days of his Goethe worship], worse than we are, we sinners. Well, to the devil with him!"[114] Need one comment on the prejudiced emotionality of this type of "criticism"?

In his essays, Belinski's voice was more muted, his criticism less direct. Yet the attitude was basically the same: He condemned

Goethe the man, paid the obligatory homage to his "genius," yet took exception to the content and style of most of his works, in part or *in toto*. To be sure, Goethe still seems to hold his place in the hallowed company of Byron and Schiller: "Byron, Schiller and Goethe—these are philosophers and critics in poetical form. Of them it is least justifiable to say that they are poets and nothing more." Yet to this concession to Goethe's greatness Belinski added at once a highly revealing caveat: Because of Goethe's "all-too-German nature and because of the ascetic [i.e. asocial] view of the world," he could not consider Goethe to be a true brother in spirit of these "prophets of progress and of the liberation of mankind." Instead Goethe represented for Belinski "the poet who *sings like a bird,* to himself only, even though he does print his songs for the people."[115]

Despite this rather cautious language, Belinski's rejection of Goethe is clear enough. We will remember that the Russian champions of "l'art pour l'art" had taken for their motto and battle cry Goethe's famous lines from his ballad "Der Sänger": "Ich singe wie der Vogel singt." We also recall that in his "objective" period Belinski had praised these "bird" poets and Goethe as their leader. However, after his sudden conversion to "sociality" the "bird" poets' song became loathsome to him. "Only a bird sings just because it feels like singing, without sympathizing with the sorrows and joys of its bird clan. . . . And how bitter a thought it is that among those people who at birth had been anointed with the sacred oil of inspiration, that among these there are—birds! These people are able to find all their happiness in their singing, they are above mankind and feel superior to their suffering brethren, who turn to them their pleading eyes filled with entreaty and expectation. But they plead in vain, for these bird poets live withdrawn into themselves, find their joys and consolations in their own breast and proudly call this poetized egoism a lofty existence high above lowly actuality." These "birds" "do not have a life's philosophy nor deeply felt convictions, nor a doctrine, nor any roots in their nation or their epoch! They write only for the purpose of writing as birds sing merely to be singing."

Belinski is convinced that these "bird" poets doom themselves to a fleeting existence and to complete ineffectualness. For he knows: "The spirit of our times is such that even the greatest creative force will impress us only for fleeting moments if it limits itself to the 'song of the bird,' if it builds its world out of touch with the historical and philosophical reality of contemporaneity, if it imagines that the earth is unworthy of it, that its proper place is in the clouds, that worldly sufferings and hopes are not to obtrude themselves on its mysterious visions and poetical contemplations." This, according to Belinski, will be the fate of Goethe, of this foremost "bird" poet whose life and work he now considers to be the product of "poeticized egoism," of a deep-rooted ethical and socio-political indifference.

Goethe would thus appear to be hopelessly isolated in his self-created aviary. And yet, for Belinski, the power of the *Zeitgeist* is so all-pervasive that even a "bird" recluse such as Goethe could not help but feel its breath. "But even he [Goethe] was forced to share in the spirit of his times: his *Werther* is the piercing cry of our epoch, his *Faust* poses all the ethical questions which arise in the breast of an introspective person of our time, his 'Prometheus' breathes with the breath of our era, many of his minor lyrical pieces are but expressions of philosophical ideas."[116] It should be noted that Belinski now acclaims the very works which a short while ago he had condemned. To be sure, even in his "objective" period he had admitted to being "enraptured with Goethe's symbolic poem 'Prometheus.'" But *Werther* had drawn severe criticism as a "subjective" work written by a "tortured" soul out of harmony with the cosmic spirit and *Faust* had been condemned for its excessive philosophical freight conveyed by means of symbol and allegory, those discredited media of artistic expression, that "dryrot of poetry." Now "reflective" and "subjective" poetry stand rehabilitated as the genuine voices of this epoch. "Our era is the era of the conscious, philosophical spirit, of contemplation, of reflection. Therefore reflection is the legitimate element of the literature of our time, and almost all the great poets of our day have made their full contribution to it: Byron with his *Manfred,*

Cain and with other of his works, Goethe especially with his *Faust;* all the works of Schiller are predominantly reflective, contemplative."[117]

In a letter to Botkin of December 11, 1840, written at the very time of his "conversion," Belinski expounded his acceptance of "reflective" poetry (here called "philosophical") as an integral part of "artistic" (i.e. "objective") literature. "There is," he wrote, "artistic literature (the highest: Homer, Shakespeare, Walter Scott, Cooper, Byron, Schiller, Goethe, Pushkin, Gogol); there is religious literature (Schiller, Jean Paul Richter, Hoffmann, Goethe himself); there is philosophical literature (*Faust,* 'Prometheus,' in part *Manfred,* and other works). It is impossible to draw hard and fast boundaries between these, because they do not remain in a relationship of indifference to each other but, like elements, enter into and modify one another." And he exclaimed with evident relief: "God be thanked, finally there has been found for each and every one of them a place [in his esthetics]!" Belinski had found the explanation for "such marvelous passages in *Faust* (that is, even in Part II) as for instance the scene of the 'Mothers' . . .—I cannot read this passage without a sense of holy trepidation."[118] A few weeks later, on January 22, 1841, Belinski reiterated his discovery of "reflective" poetry: "I have finally understood what a great thing *reflective* poetry really is. We are no Greeks: the Greek world exists for us as a *past* (even though greatest) moment in the development of mankind, but it can no longer offer us full satisfaction. Childhood—is a wonderful time, a time of fullness, and yet, he who has reached the age of thirty will be bored in the company of children, no matter how much he loves them."[119] From this newly won point of view, Belinski placed Goethe above Pushkin precisely for Goethe's "reflective" treatment of nature in contrast to Pushkin's "objective" depiction of it. "In this very fact is to be found Goethe's immeasurable superiority over Pushkin, because Goethe is all thought and does not simply depict nature but forces her to confide to him all her most sacred and intimate secrets. This is the source of Goethe's pantheistic contemplation of nature. . . . For Goethe, nature was a book filled with ideas; for

Pushkin it was—a living picture full of an ineffable but mute charm."[120] Comparing Goethe and Schiller in their attitudes toward Greek culture, Belinski came to the conclusion that Goethe "sought and expressed the more philosophical side of it and in doing so was true to himself" (i.e., to his "philosophical," his "reflective" bent).[121]

It is this spirit of reflectiveness, and the resultant richness of ideational content of his works, that raises Goethe above Heine, even though Heine had taken his place among the idols of this latest period in Belinski's development, this period of "critical realism." "Many poems of Heine are so excellent that one could take them for Goethe's, and yet Heine, despite this fact, is but a pigmy compared to the colossal Goethe. What then is the difference between them?" Belinski asked and answered categorically, "It is the *idea,* the *content.*"[122]

Belinski was equally explicit in his rehabilitation of "subjective" literature, which is most closely associated in his mind with the "reflective." In his famous essay on the works of Lermontov, one of the central pieces of this period, he wrote: "In our times the absence of the *inward-oriented, subjective* element is a *shortcoming* [in a literary work of art]. The objectivity of the ancients is not for us. He would not be a modern poet, not an artist of our day, who could not view history and life *subjectively,* in terms of and through his own idiosyncratic temperament."[123] It is his *subjectivity* which does not permit the poet "to remain a stranger to the world in a mood of apathetic indifference but forces him to let pass through his soul all the phenomena of the outside world, infusing them with its living breath."[124] Then, as if intent on taking with the left hand what he had given Goethe with the right, Belinski reminds us that "even Goethe had been criticized—and not without very good reason—for the absence from his work of the historical and social elements and for his placid satisfaction with existent reality. This was, in fact, the very reason why Schiller's works, being more *human* and *humane* though of *lesser artistic merit,* found a stronger echo among mankind than did Goethe's poetry."[125]

There had been a time when a *"subjective, fair-souled"* Schil-

ler had received short shrift at Belinski's hands. Now the subjective poet, personally involved in the trials and tribulations of
his fellow men, stands in Belinski's highest esteem. Now he takes
issue with Goethe's "l'art pour l'art" point of view. In a conversation with Eckermann, Goethe had posed the question: "What type
of reader would I like to have?" and had answered: "Such a one
who would forget me, himself and all the world, and would live
exclusively in my work."[126] Belinski's reaction to Goethe's words is
highly revealing of his hypersensitivity to any attempt to divorce
art from life and turn it upon itself. "The thought expressed by
Goethe places art as a goal in itself, thereby withdrawing it from
any contact with *life,* which is always *higher than art,* art being but
one of the countless aspects of life." Using Goethe's statement for his
point of departure, Belinski strays far afield in expounding his
views on the proper task of the critic. He grants that "Goethe's
statement does have a profound meaning if taken not as an absolute
but as a first necessary step in the critical process."[127] Unquestionably, the critic, to be successful, must fully enter into the spirit of a
poet, "forgetting everything else." "It is impossible to study Byron
without, for a time, becoming a Byron in one's soul, nor Goethe
without temporarily turning into a Goethe."[128] Belinski is certain
that "a poet can be studied and properly understood only on his
own terms: You cannot measure a Goethe with the measure of
Byron any more than you can measure Byron with Goethe's;
they were antithetical natures, and he who would condemn Goethe
because he did not live and write like Byron, or vice versa, would
be uttering the greatest possible nonsense. . . . The natures of
Goethe and Schiller were diametrically opposed, yet that very opposition was the cause for their friendship and the mutual respect
of these two great poets. Each of them held high those very traits
in the other which he could not find in himself. It can never be
the task of the critic to discover why Goethe failed to live and
write as Schiller did; it *is* his task to understand *why* Goethe
wrote and lived as Goethe did and not as someone else."[129]

Having delivered himself of these unobjectionable if rather
trite observations, so much more effectively expressed in Goethe's

motto: "Wer den Dichter will verstehen, / Muß in Dichters Lande gehen," Belinski took up his attack on the introverted "ascetic" critics and poets. "German criticism," he claimed, "in examining the creations of art, always centers its efforts on the work of art itself and on the spirit of the artist, thus becoming locked within the narrow limits of esthetics, escaping from them only in order to turn on rare occasions to an examination of the poet's personality without ever paying the slightest attention to history, to society, in brief, to life. And for that reason life has long since left behind those German poets who with their work aid and abet such critics."[130] On another occasion he explicitly named Goethe as a "poet of the past," outdistanced by the onward march of history. "It is painful to see how people who understand nothing in the business [literary criticism] give all to Goethe, taking all from Schiller. . . . If one must compare these poets at all, then, truly, it is far from established who of the two will be the mightier ruler in the kingdom of the future; in fact, there are many who—not without good reason— already sense that Goethe, a poet of the past, is dead in the present, a king dethroned."[131]

This harsh judgment of Goethe as a "poet passé" we find in a critical essay on Baratynski's poetry[132] and, specifically, on his fa- mous poem, "On Goethe's death," a long-time favorite of Belinski's. Now Belinski is ready to accept only its fourth stanza as a valid expression of Goethe's pantheistic rapport with nature: "Sein Atem war eins mit dem atmenden All."

For the rest, he now finds the poem to be a collection of vapid generalizations and uncritical flatteries which shed no light whatever on the characteristic figure of Goethe and could be ad- dressed with equal justification, or rather lack of it, to any other poet. For his special censure Belinski singles out those lines of the poem which credit Goethe with an all-embracing genius that "knew no limits save infinity itself," lines which can be traced in their es- sential thought back to the early encomiums of Goethe by Zhukovski and Andrei Turgeniev and which formed a central element in the Romantics' view of Goethe. Belinski takes Baratynski to task for having "claimed for Goethe far too much, leaving his claims completely unsubstantiated when he wrote: "Es flog sein Gedanke weit und breit / Seine Schranke war die Unendlichkeit." He cannot but admire the beauty of these lines but insists that they are chimerical. He would have us cast Romantic fairy tales aside and realize that "there simply never has been nor ever will be a genius all-comprehending and capable of accomplishing everything single-handedly. Even Goethe had his limitations. For him, too, there existed a whole sphere of life which, because of his German temperament, remained 'terra incognita' for him. That sphere of life was given its poetic expression by Schiller."[133] It is not difficult to recognize the "sphere of life" Belinski had in mind; it is the historical, socio-political sphere, closed to the "German temperament" unendowed with the "subjective" spirit of "sociality," insensitive to the sufferings and to the aspirations of his fellow men.

Belinski spoke of this same limitation in Goethe's genius metaphorically in a comparison of the German poet with Byron. He used here a personification favored by the poets of his time, the figure of the Demon. We remember that Pushkin, under the influence of Goethe's Mephisto, "that spirit of doubt and negation," had given the figure an altogether negative aspect in his poem, "Demon," personifying in him "that life-killing scepticism that corrodes the very best and most creative stirrings in our soul, the evil spirit of our age." We have seen how Lermontov, depending on Pushkin, Goethe and Byron in his treatment of the figure, had drawn a more positive portrait of the Demon in his epic poem of that title. His Demon, though a "restless, depraved and corrupted spirit," harbors in his soul memories of his former celestial being. In the "loveless and haughty heart" of this "fallen angel" there glows the spark of the fire of idealism that had been his, of striving for the lofty and the beautiful. His wooing of Tamara is not only the evil Tempter's lust for the seduction and destruction of an innocent soul but also the yearning for the sphere of purity and beauty in which Tamara dwells, which has been forever closed to this "mournful spirit, spirit of banishment," cast out of Paradise. Now, with Belinski the figure of the Demon comes to stand at the very opposite pole of Pushkin's "spirit of doubt and of negation."[134]

Belinski's Demon personifies all the positive aspects of the modern age: intellect, analysis, social and political activism, the spirit of progress and rebellion, of "sociality." Belinski's Demon grows into a figure positively awesome in its imposing grandeur; he serves humanity by inspiring the greatest minds in history. "He has inspired Socrates with the fierce sincerety of his ethical philosophy, has dictated to Aristophanes his comedies, . . . has helped Columbus in discovering America, he has invented powder and print, has guided Ulrich Hutten's pen in the angry satire of his *Epistolae obscurorum virorum.*"[135] Only the bravest could withstand the awesome aspect of this fiery spirit of ruthless criticism, of progress and rebellion. Goethe had not been one of this small circle of the select. "Goethe had *merely caught hold of his tail* in his Mephisto and had dared cast but a short sidewise glance into his face. It was the colossal Byron who had the courage to look this spirit unflinchingly into the eye, who proudly dared to vie with him in the power of his intellect and who, as his peer, clasped his hand in eternal friendship."[136]

Though from his newly acquired position of "critical realism" Belinski rejected the Romanticists' image of the omniscient, omnipotent, all-encompassing Goethe, he was more than ever impressed with Goethe's enormous intellectual powers, his energy and openness of mind, his extraordinary eagerness and ability to keep abreast of the swiftly moving intellectual current of the age. As a fervent convert from a Romantic to a Realistic esthetic, Belinski suspected the creation or the apperception of great art by an act of clairvoyant intuition. He had developed a healthy respect for sound training and systematic acquisition of knowledge as the high road to greatness both for the creative artist and for the critic of art. He was now convinced "that without profound and sustained scholarship, without the cultivation of an esthetic feeling in the spirit and by the method of science it is impossible to understand literature, that the immediate, intuitive feeling, without reasoning and perspicacity, results in nothing save personal prejudices in judging an author and his work." Belinski had nothing but disdain for the glib dilettante and would-be critic who "with us [in Russia] judges so lightly and with such a show of importance a Shakespeare whom he has not read even in translation, whom he had seen only on the Russian stage—or a Byron, or a Goethe, a Schiller, or even a Homer."[137] The great works of Goethe, "so rich in ideas" Belinski now recognized to be the products "not only of a great talent, but also of an erudition, of an intellectual development based on the unflagging pursuit of the swiftly rushing spiritual life of the contemporary world."[138] In sincere admiration he exclaimed: "How much did Goethe *know,* how profound was Schiller's erudition!"[139] He traced this depth and breadth of erudition to "the millennial historical development of world-wide scope which informs the creations of Shakespeare, Byron, Schiller and Goethe."[140]

Belinski had experienced the impact of such works upon himself in all their power, had recognized the source of this power. "When you read such creations . . . you feel that you are striving toward something definite, you delight in something substantial; you absorb in yourself a new strength, your very being experiences increase and growth. . . . Then you suffer with the suffering of our poet and partake of his bliss because in his suffering and in his bliss you recognize the suffering and the joy of all humanity, the soul of the epoch, the interests and preoccupations of the times. Your poet conquers you, he makes you experience everything in the very light in which *he* sees the world. Such an influence over the soul of the reader is wielded by the very great poets, by Byron, for instance, by Schiller and Goethe."[141] Thus Belinski actually credited Goethe with empathy into the joys and sufferings of his fellow men, with a feeling for "the soul of the epoch," with participation in the "interests and preoccupations of the times," in brief, with "sociality." He wrote this passage at the very time (1841) that he was launching his vitriolic attack against the "egoist" Goethe, one more proof of Belinski's bifocal view of Goethe: while "loathing" the man, he continued to admire the poet. To be sure, this admiration had become far more critical. Belinski was of the opinion—and was not afraid to state it—"that there are few poets in the world who have written so much that is truly great and immortal as did Goethe, and at the same time there is not a poet of world stature who has written such a heap of sundry ballast and trivia."[142] He urged a careful reexamination of Goethe's total work. Such an examination, he asserted, would show Goethe to have been guilty, on occasion, of the characteristic German national vices of cloying sentimentality, banality and fatuity. "In no other language" did Belinski find "such a wealth of lofty songs of love," and yet, "in that very language there has been written," so he claimed, "an unequaled number of effusions of the heart, cloyingly sentimental to the point of downright insipidness." And in making this claim he was not referring "to the products of petty talents or of the altogether ungifted." He pointed to Goethe's works. "What can there be more saccharine" he asks, "more banal than Goethe's *Stella,* his *Brother and Sister,* his *Hermann und Dorothea* —and yet, Goethe was a great genius!"[143]

Belinski considered Goethe "weak and sweetly sentimental in many of his dramas." "He [Goethe] likes to choose for the heroes of his dramas weak, insignificant, pampered and effeminate characters, such as Weislingen (in his *Götz*), Clavigo, Fernando (in his *Stella*), among others. In his Egmont he realized his ideal of the 'beautiful character,' but this ideal turned out to be nothing but the ideal of the 'beautiful egoist,' who cares not a rap for anything except his ego. This subjective, antihistorical orientation, reaching its extreme form, was bound to lead Goethe into writing such worthless, pathetically inept, sweetly sentimental dramas as are—I dare repeat it—'Brother and Sister,' 'Clavigo,' 'The Good Women,' 'The Pledge' [*Das Pfand*], 'Stella,' and so forth."[144]

Despite this low opinion of Goethe as a dramatist, Belinski was nevertheless ready to defend Goethe's a-historical treatment of Egmont, arguing that "the dramatist had never intended to depict in his tragedy the historical Egmont, that seventy-two-year-old head of a numerous family, but rather a young man, passionately yearning for life's raptures, who yet is ready to sacrifice these for the happiness of his nation." And he concluded his argument with a summary statement that sounds like an echo of Lessing's thoughts in the twenty-fourth piece of his *Hamburgische Dramaturgie:* "Every 'persona' in a tragedy belongs not to history but to the poet, even though it carries a historical name." To buttress his argument, Belinski quoted approvingly Goethe's "most apt" words on the problem: "For the poet there does not exist a single historical figure; he wants to give expression to his inner world, and for this purpose he honors some historical persons by attaching their names to his creations."[145]

Belinski's opinion of Goethe's Egmont as expressed here is certainly a far cry from the one he had written to Bakunin's sisters. There Egmont was dismissed as "a low creature, self-satisfied and self-centered, to whom patriotism was nothing more than a tasty dish at the feast of life." Now he is a youth thirsting for life's joys, yet ready for "self-sacrifice in the service of his nation"—still another striking example of Belinski's often inconsistent, self-contradictory, emotion-charged view of literature, which, being his mission, his very life, would never be to him an object of distant scrutiny or of detached evaluation.

Belinski seems to have been of a similarly divided mind on Goethe's *Wahlverwandtschaften*. In a letter to Botkin he damned the work and its author in no uncertain terms. "Recently I have performed a brilliant feat of patience—I have read 'Ottilie' [*Wahlverwandtschaften*]. Heavenly saints! I never thought Goethe, this German Olympian, could turn out to be such a hopeless Teuton in this famous novel of his. Granted that the basic thought is clever and true, but its artistic development—O mighty Allah why have you created the Germans? . . . I fall silent. . . ."[146] In an essay of the same year (1847), he again stressed the "German" quality of the work, but this time implies that this trait is a virtue rather than a failing of the work and the author. He doubted that Russians would ever be able to appreciate the novel. "There are simply too many features in this work that strike a Russian reader as hopelessly queer." "However," Belinski continued, "for the Germans such features are not at all strange, being aspects of German life *faithfully rendered*." Remembering that Belinski in his "realistic" period considered the indigenous quality of a work as the very hallmark of greatness, we can safely conclude that with this statement he did in fact acclaim the *Wahlverwandtschaften* as "an outstanding work of the great author."[147]

The two works which steadily gained in Belinski's esteem are Goethe's "Prometheus" and his *Faust*. The ode had been admired by the critic even in his "objective" period despite its "symbolical" nature. Now it acquired for him a special significance as Goethe's most radical utterance in behalf of man's liberation from the yoke of reactionary authority, just as the drama of Aeschylus had been in its time. Goethe's "Prometheus" is considered by Belinski to be "in some respects a poetical commentary on the 'Prometheus' of Aeschylus. It is the selfsame ancient thought but here expressed more clearly, more definitely, developed more fully. It has acquired in Goethe's poem a new power, a new significance as a result of world-wide historical development." Belinski felt that "the Promethei of our day can finally exult in their future triumph and no longer need fear the predatory bird [the eagle of Zeus]. People having been roused to [political] consciousness, the downfall of Zeus" seemed assured. "Sooner or later, his altars will be overturned and the knees of the mortals will be bent in worship of the God of truth, of love and of mercy."[148] Thus, Goethe's poem became for the "Realist" Belinski a rousing call to political action, proclaiming the approaching triumph of the progressive "Promethean" forces against Russian autocracy. He celebrated the poem as "one of the most colossal of his [Goethe's] creations," "preeminently a poem of our times."[149]

Faust was now acclaimed as a masterpiece of "reflective," of "progressive" poetry. Even its Part II, Belinski's former "bête noire," is now approved despite its often "dark and incomprehensible allegory." In a spirit of startlingly unprejudiced openmindedness, Belinski strove to do justice to both factions, to the "l'art pour l'art" critics as well as to the liberal or "left" Hegelians in their interpretations and evaluations of Goethe's *chef d'oeuvre*. He would not quarrel with those who insisted on seeing in *Faust* "an example of 'pure art,' subject only to its own, individual laws." However, for his part, without offence to the "honored champions of pure art," he would hold high "Faust as the faithful mirror of contemporary German life," as the poetic record "of the total philosophical movement in Germany from the end of the former century to the beginning of the present one." Therefore it no longer surprised or irritated Belinski that "in Part II, Goethe could fall into allegory which often grew dark and incomprehensible." The reason had become obvious to him. It was "the abstract nature of the profound ideas Goethe sought to express in his masterpiece."[150] This is Belinski's surprisingly circumspect way of taking Goethe's *Faust* out of the hands of the "pure art" proponents and claiming it for the growing clan of the "critical realists."

The conciliatory tone of this passage may be considered characteristic for the maturing critic. Not that "Vissarion the furious" had suddenly turned meek. Let us remember that his famous letter to Gogol, with its fervent plea for the progressive cause and its furious invective against the renegade poet, was written but a few months before the critic's death. No, Belinski never lost his strong convictions or his trenchant pen! It was rather that with increasing distance from the days of his violent "conversion," Belinski became less the evangelist of his newly won creed. He came to view literary phenomena in their historical setting, was able better to appreciate their relative values, to give to the great of world literature their due while yet maintaining his critical detachment. The majority of his later judgments on Goethe, which grow fewer with passing time, are informed with this new calm and circumspection. He realized full well that "Goethe did not belong to the clan of those cheap hucksters of ideas, sentiments and poetry." Yet he held to his judgment that Goethe, "because of his practical and historical indifference" could not "become the ruler of the hearts of modern men, despite all the breadth of his world-encompassing genius."[151] Or again, in a comparison of Goethe with Schiller, this newly gained sense of balance and fairness of judgment are clearly evident: "In his poetry Goethe steps before us as the contemplative thinker, the mighty master of the inward world of the human soul. In Schiller's poetry we will bow in love and awe before the advocate of mankind, the prophet of humanism, before the ardent admirer of all that is lofty and morally beautiful."[152] Belinski was obviously intent on measuring each poet with his own measure, aiming at precision in characterization and fairness in evaluation.

With the same circumspection he now strove to fix Goethe's position in the cultural and literary currents of his time, especially his relation to Romanticism. As late as March 1840, Belinski still had placed Goethe in the company of the "Romanticists," Schiller and E.T.A. Hoffmann, in the tradition of the Liubomudry and the Stankevich Circle: "Schiller, Goethe, Hoffmann: They represent the Holy Trinity—the profound, inward, many-sided German spirit."[153] Yet shortly thereafter, in 1841, he had developed his independent judgment, a far surer sense of value: "Hoffmann is a great talent, to be sure, yet he is a phenomenon of a far lower rank in comparison with Goethe and with Schiller. He expressed only one side of the German spirit, while they, each in his way, have plumbed its full depth and given expression to all its facets."[154] And in 1846, he took the Schlegel brothers to task for their "sorry courage" of placing Tieck on the same level with Goethe and Schiller.[155]

It is but natural that Belinski, the avowed "critical realist," would have developed a jaundiced view of Romanticism and would consider Goethe's involvement with the movement as an aberration by an otherwise reasonable and rational man. Moreover, with him the concept "Romanticism" applied to all works which treat medieval, legendary and mythological subjects in a nonrealistic manner. Thus, Goethe's *Werther,* his *Faust,* his ballads "Der Erlkönig" and "Der Fischer" are all taken for evidence of Goethe's participation in the movement. Yet he failed to mention Goethe's *Divan,* which would have served as a far more apt example of Goethe's Romantic "sins." Evidently he did not know the work. The following quotation presents an extreme statement of Belinski's view on Goethe as a Romanticist, lumping together as "Romantic" the most diverse works: "Goethe himself—a man of highest moral fortitude, the poet of thought and sound reason, has expressed in a medieval legend the sufferings of contemporary man *(Faust),* and in his *Werther* he appeared as a Romanticist again in the spirit of the Middle Ages [*sic*]. Many of his ballads (for instance 'Der Erlkönig,' 'Der Fischer' and others) are infused with the spirit of the Romanticism of that time."[156] Surely, this is a statement lacking not only in sound professional knowledge but even in common sense. On the other hand, his brief concluding summary of Goethe's relation to Romanticism, which avoided detailed reference to specific works, could pass for a sound enough judgment: "Goethe and Schiller were not fully the representatives of the Romantic movement," he wrote, "yet both made their contribution to it in no small measure, especially the latter."[157]

Belinski's final extant statement on Goethe the man and the poet is also his most comprehensive. It is in the nature of a summation of his long struggle in coming to terms with this "colossal genius" who both attracted and repelled him, repelled him chiefly with his egocentric personality, irresistibly attracted him by the force and scope of his poetic message. In Goethe Belinski would have us

> distinguish between the man and the artist. As an artist Goethe was great, but as a man he was most ordinary. Not art, but his personal character forced him forever to hobnob with the powerful of the earth, to live and to breathe by the graciousness of their smiles, just as, in turn, he would show the coldest inattentiveness toward everything that could disturb his Olympian—speaking poetically—and his egotistical —speaking prosaically—serenity. Yet, nonetheless, Goethe, as an artist, as a poet, was the true son of his native country, of his epoch, who fully expressed with his genius if not all then certainly a great number of the most essential facets of contemporary reality. This is proven by his revulsion from everything that is abstract, turpid, mystical, . . . and by his striving toward everything that is simple, clear, definite, thisworldly, earthly, real, affirmative, and by his fervent empathy with nature, which expressed itself not only in the pantheistic world view in his poetry, but equally in his great services to the natural sciences. How could one not but think in this context of his lively sympathy for the ancient world amid the general attraction for the barbarities of the Middle Ages, whence poetry carried nothing but vulgar ideas and ugly forms. And here is the reason why now, in our times, the skeptical and cold Goethe in his native Germany is attracting to himself new readers and admirers in the same measure as

the fiery, chivalrous and noble Schiller is losing them from day to day.[158]

It is surprising to note how perceptive Belinski's prognosis of the relative future popularity of the two greatest German poets proved to be—and not only in their native Germany, but in all of the Western world.

As the development of Belinski's attitude toward Goethe was complex, a brief summary statement would seem in order. The "leaps and zigzags" in his appreciation of Goethe, of which Belinski himself had complained at a moment of dissatisfaction with his turbulently changeable values and views, can be fairly reduced to three main periods. During the first, the "idealistic" period, he praised Goethe in the traditional manner of the Liubomudry and the Stankevich Circle as the supreme poet-philosopher, as the all-embracing, all-comprehending genius of Olympian grandeur and serenity, as the "Homer of our day", while all the time it was Schiller and Byron who were enshrined in the *sanctum* of young Belinski's heart as his true heroes and his worshiped idols.

In the second, the Hegelian or "objective" period, Schiller was cast out of Belinski's favor and Goethe enthroned as the incomparable "objective" genius who had accepted with an all-understanding spirit "being" in all its aspects, had achieved a perfect "reconciliation with reality." Thus Goethe's works could be the faithful mirrors of "concrete reality," of "blessed reality." Goethe's immense vitality, his forthrightness in depicting sensuous life, untrammeled by moral scruples (especially in his *Römische Elegien*), was rapturously greeted by Belinski as his liberation from the unnatural, enslaving bonds of Schillerian "abstract idealism built on thin air," from Schiller's "fair-souledness," and "noble heroism." But hardly had this point of view crystallized in the late thirties and the early months of 1840 when by December of that year another abrupt and drastic re-orientation in Belinski's whole world outlook took place, ushering in the third and final period of "critical realism."

With the force of revelation, Belinski suddenly realized that the Hegelian-inspired "reconciliation with reality" had been a dreadful mistake and that it was man's proper task and a poet's and critic's sacred duty to face reality critically, to uncover and to pillory its shortcomings, those unspeakable vices of Russia's past and present —and to lead mankind on its march toward a better future of freedom and human dignity. Now Schiller was reestablished in Belinski's favors as the human and humane champion of the downtrodden and the enslaved, as the prophet of the future triumph of liberty, while Goethe came to be viewed with a sharply critical eye. Goethe the *man* was condemned for his egoism, his social and political indifference, his subserviance to the Weimar court—a criticism expressed in much the same tone and manner as that of Menzel, against whom Belinski had so vigorously defended Goethe but a few months prior to his sudden "*un*reconciliation with reality." Goethe the *poet* is now criticized for the very "objectivity" which had been, but a few months before, Goethe's claim to greatness. He is now placed among the "l'art pour l'art" poets, the "bird" poets who sing for the sake of singing without regard for mankind's trials and tribulations, joys and sorrows. Their "songs" Belinski now consigns to quick oblivion. Being out of touch with the *Zeitgeist,* they would never capture the hearts of contemporary men or be of lasting influence in a progressive future. Belinski boldly announced that "Goethe is a poet of the past, is dead in the present; he is a king dethroned."

Goethe's works were then subjected to a critical examination which several of them failed to pass, not only the minor dramas but also some works of greater stature, such as *Clavigo* and *Hermann und Dorothea,* because of their lack of historical and sociopolitical content, or a rootedness in the life of the nation and the epoch, or for their bourgeois platitudinousness and saccharine sentimentality. Yet, many of the masterpieces came off surprisingly well. To be sure, Belinski was of divided mind on *Egmont,* the *Wahlverwandtschaften* and *Wilhelm Meister.* But *Faust* gained ever greater favor with him as the outstanding example of "reflective" poetry and as a faithful mirror of the intellectual and cultural life of Germany in the modern era. It is Goethe the lyric poet who received highest acclaim from the mature Belinski: "Goethe is great," he exclaimed in one of his last references to the German poet; "he is *unbearably* great in the major part of his lyric creations, in his *Faust*—this lyric poem in dramatic form—in his 'Prometheus,' in which he himself appears as the usurper of the heavenly fire, in his 'Braut von Korinth' and in a great number of preeminently lyric creations."[159]

As the fervor of Belinski the "convert", gradually cooled, the sharp attacks on Goethe, prevalent in the years 1841 through 1843, gave way to a more calm and circumspect appraisal of his merits and his faults. Thus, one might speak of a fourth period, a peaceful epilogue. The mature critic was able to view Goethe more objectively. He recognized him to be the product and the spokesman of his nation and his time: "Goethe, as an artist, as a poet, was the true son of his native country, of his epoch, and fully expressed with his genius if not all then certainly a significant number of the most essential facets of contemporary reality." High praise indeed from the "critical realist" Belinski.

By tracing in detail the various phases of Belinski's appreciation of Goethe I have contributed to a history of the attitude toward the German poet prevalent among the liberal, "Western" group of the Russian intelligentsia. Belinski was that group's most effective spokesman. In his writings he traced with the sharpest and most trenchant pen the group's development in the 30's and 40's, beyond their initial Schelling-oriented and conservative Hegelian positions toward a new social and political consciousness and, in esthetics, from their initial Romanticism toward the new gospel of "critical realism." Yet there was another member of the "Western" group who could vie with Belinski as a thinker and writer on the socio-political and literary trends of his times and whose approach to and appreciation of Goethe was sufficiently original and influential to warrant our special attention—Aleksandr Ivanovich Herzen.

3. Aleksandr Ivanovich Herzen (1812-1870)

Aleksandr Herzen was a precocious boy. In his autobiographical *Notes of a Certain Young Man,* he recalls that his childhood "came to an early end. I threw away my toys and turned to books. . . . The growing love for reading quickly taught me French and German."[1] His rich and eccentric father showed little interest in Herzen's formal education, which he turned over to French and German tutors.[2] Herzen quickly developed a lively dislike for his German teacher, who was a crashing bore and pedant, doing nothing for the young boy but drill him mercilessly in German grammar. Thus it was that Herzen's early contacts with German literature came not through tutorial guidance but rather by chance, perhaps on the promptings of his German mother, a woman of no great education but with an abiding love for literature, especially for her favorite author, Schiller.[3]

Herzen was at once completely captivated by Schiller's world "of the heroic and the great." Schiller was to him "a revelation which caused a revolution in my life."[4] The passing of years never dimmed this youthful enthusiasm for the German poet. As a man nearing his thirties, hard tried by imprisonment and exile, Herzen still "blessed" Schiller, to whom he owed "the most sacred minutes" of his youth. "How many tears did I not shed upon your poems! What altars did I raise to you in my heart! . . . And even now in times of sadness your lofty songs give me new strength of spirit."[5]

In sharp contrast to this instant infatuation with Schiller, Herzen's admiration of Goethe's genius was slow in developing. At first he was repelled by Goethe's apparent aloofness. He admitted that "for a long time" he considered "Goethe inferior to Schiller." He missed in "Goethe's breast . . . Schiller's humanly tender heart." He was actually afraid of him. "I was afraid of Goethe," he confessed, "he hurt me deeply with his disdain of me. At that time I was still quite unable to grasp Goethe's world-embracing sympathy." In retrospect, Herzen realized that as a youth he lacked the maturity necessary to comprehend the genius of Goethe, of Shakespeare. "To understand Goethe and Shakespeare . . . one had to have experienced life, the hard blows of fate, one had to have shared the sufferings of Faust, of Hamlet, of Othello. For a sympathetic understanding of Schiller, on the other hand, all that was required was a yearning for the sublime." This "yearning for the sublime" was the pervasive mood of young Herzen. Small wonder that he turned to Schiller. By way of a characteristic metaphor he recaptures for us his youthful feelings toward the two poets. "Let Goethe, so I thought, be the sea in the depths of which there lie hidden untold treasures: I love far more the German river Rhine, flowing past feudal castles . . ., that Rhine, the witness of the Thirty Years' War, that Rhine in whose waters are mirrored the cloud-shrouded peaks of the Alps. The trouble was that I quite forgot this river too flowed into the world-encircling ocean, inseparably fused with sky and earth. Only much later did mighty Goethe enthral me. At that early time I could not yet fathom him, even though I did have some sense of his oceanic wave, his depth, his breadth."[6]

The metaphors of "sea" and "river," applied to Goethe and Schiller, proved favorites with Herzen. We meet them already in an early letter (1833) in which he outlined to his friend Ogarëv his plans of study: "The very task I have set myself is to *study Goethe*. Schiller is the turbulent river; from afar you can hear the roar of its furiously rushing waters which sweep along in their whirlpool your little skiff the moment you set it afloat. Not so Goethe; he is deep as the sea; there is no definite current here; its majestic waves undulate calmly."[7]

To his intensive, systematic studies of Goethe, Herzen brought a respectable reading knowledge of German and an early acquaintance with a few of Goethe's lyrics and with his *Werther,* over which, he wrote in retrospect, he had "cried like a fool."[8] He made rapid progress and soon his first-hand knowledge of the author could vie with that of the Goethe enthusiast Nikolai Stankevich and surpassed by far that of his friend Belinski. Throughout Herzen's voluminous correspondence, his autobiographical, essayist, and fictional writings, quotations from Goethe abound, usually in the German original, often in his own translation or paraphrase.[9] It is not surprising to find numerous quotations from and references to such favorites among Goethe's writings as his *Faust, Wilhelm Meister, Werther* or "Prometheus." More unusual sources of Herzen's quotations are the *Italienische Reise, Eckermanns Gespräche mit*

Goethe, or the frequently quoted ballads, "Die Braut von Korinth" and "Der Gott und die Bajadere." Yet, these sources may well have been suggested to Herzen by Stankevich, who considered these particular works to be "keys" to an understanding of Goethe's personality and work. However, when we find lines quoted from such minor dramas as *Die Aufgeregten*[10] or *Der Bürgergeneral,* from the *Kampagne in Frankreich,* from Goethe's "Epigramme," his "Sprüche," and the "Maximen und Reflexionen," and even from his *Osteologie,* then we have proof indeed that Herzen struck out independently in his readings of Goethe.[11]

For the mature Herzen, the works of Goethe and Shakespeare came to equal "a whole university." He advised his son to read and reread these poets, for, as he put it, "reading them you will experience the epochs, but not as you would in scientific works, where you are given nothing but the final clear-cut results of research. In their pages you will be their fellow traveler, walking in step with these giants along the byways and highways of the ages."[12] And in another letter he drew his son's attention to Goethe's *Faust,* where he would find portrayed with extraordinary felicity the contrasting types of the pedant and the savant, "the pseudo-scholar *à la* Kachenovski-Wagner and the born thinker *à la* Ogarëv-Faust."[13] Moreover, we can add on the strength of a letter to Herzen's future wife N.A.Zakharina that this identification of his friend Ogarëv with Faust, Herzen would apply—except for a significant disclaimer—to himself as well. "You don't know," he wrote, "the suffering which questing thought can inflict. Oh, I, too, was in love with science, I, too, would have surrendered to Mephisto—had it not been for you!"[14] Faust was for Herzen the very personification of the questing spirit suffering the agonies brought on by unquenchable yearning for truth. He bade us

> look at Faust and his "famulus." For Faust "Wissenschaft is an existential problem, "to be or not to be": he can plunge to nether depths, despair, fall into error, lose himself in pleasures of all sorts, and yet, his nature pierces deeply through surface appearances, his very lies contain more truth than does the innocuous truth of a Wagner. That which is difficult for Faust is easy for Wagner. Wagner is

astonished at Faust's inability to comprehend the obvious. Wagner is not tortured by his conscience. On the contrary, it consoles and calms him, affords him succor in adversity. But this peace of his he has bought for small change, because he never did really know the agony of spirit. Where he saw unity, pacification, the resolution of problems—and could smile, there Faust perceived divisiveness, hate, the growing complexity of problems—and suffered.[15]

In this Faustian suffering Herzen felt himself a closer kin to Goethe's questing hero than to Goethe himself. For in the "realist Goethe" he saw a man who was "too much the philosopher" to be ever swept into the vortex of ultimate despair. "Goethe could find peace with himself and the world in abstract spheres. When 'the spirit of negation' appears as such a jester as Mephisto, then the dissonances are still capable of being resolved in a highest harmony, and in good time there will resound for all creation—'sie ist gerettet'. Not such a one was Byron's Lucifer in *Cain*,"[16] and, we may add, not such a one was Herzen in his outlook on this less-than-perfect world; his was, if not a tragic, then certainly a deeply troubled mood of unresolved and unresolvable dissonance with his times.

It was Herzen's lifelong habit to "read over and over again the works of the great 'maestri': Goethe, Shakespeare, Pushkin." He persisted in this habit "because by means of these repeated readings" he could "palpably observe and measure [his] improvements or retrogressions." He could "even determine the direction of [his] development."[17] Moreover, Herzen knew how to draw consolation and support in adversity from Goethe's wisdom. At a time of extreme crisis in his life, caused by his unfaithfulness to his wife, which brought her to the brink of death and him into the living hell of self-recriminations and self-hatred, Herzen quotes the words of Goethe's Tasso:

> Und wenn der Mensch in seiner Qual verstummt
> Gab mir ein Gott, zu sagen, wie ich leide.*

These lines Herzen interpreted to be Goethe's testimony to the therapeutic power of the word, a power he himself was ex-

---

* See footnote p. 41.

periencing in the act of setting down in his diary his confession of
the "accursed baseness of his character," of his "criminal immorality," of that base animal impulse that had driven him to deceive his
trusting, ailing wife with a pretty, buxom servant girl of the house-
hold. Goethe's words sustain Herzen in his grief as they seem to
corroborate and strengthen the sense of relief he himself drew from
the act of verbalizing his confession: "The word, once spoken,
draws the poison from the soul. The most terrible period of heart-
rending sorrow or of fear is the time when words still fail us, when
we have not as yet the strength to speak, when we are still too
terrified to articulate our trespass, to confess it even to ourselves.
The word, once uttered, is tantamount to a partial realization of
the sorrow, of the fear; it is the beginning of their concretization
outside of ourselves."[18] Herzen here strives to give voice to an experience which Goethe had so frequently and eloquently attested
to: verbalization as expiatory confession, "Dichtung" as Catharsis.

In an earlier period of deep depression, half-crushed by hated
toil in the Novgorod Chancellery, Herzen had also turned to Goethe
for aid. Under the overpowering pressure he confided to his diary
his utter despondency. "And then, as if terrified by my own words,
I instantaneously wrote down Goethe's 'Spruch':

> Gut verloren - *etwas* verloren!
> Ehre verloren - *viel* verloren!
> Mußt Ruhm gewinnen
> Da werden die Leute sich anders besinnen,
> Mut verloren - *alles* verloren
> Da wär es besser nicht geboren.*

This "instantaneous" jotting down of Goethe's "Spruch" is the
reflex action of a man in mortal danger, striving to save himself, it
is the act of exorcism of the life-destroying spirit of despondency.
To Herzen Goethe's words are "the greatest truth" from which he
draws a very personal lesson: "Therefore, should I ever be conscious of complete loss of spirit, I shall certainly fail—but," he adds
with evident relief, his flagging courage buoyed, "it seems I am still

---

* Possessions lost—*something* lost! Honor lost—*much* lost! You must gain
fame, then people will change their mind; courage lost—*everything* lost. In
that case it would be better never to have been born.

far from that."[19]

Many of his favorite theories Herzen buttressed and emphasized with quotations from Goethe. One such favorite thesis was
the superiority of a "young" and "virginal" Russia over the old, de-
cadent West, burdened with a long and oppressive tradition. With
evident delight he discovered in Goethe's "Zahme Xenien" the famous lines addressed to the United States,

"Den Vereinigten Staaten"

Dich stört nicht im Innern
Zu lebendiger Zeit
Unnützes Erinnern
Und vergeblicher Streit.* [20]

He considered these lines to be far more aptly applicable to Russia
than to the United States and used them at every turn to lend
Goethe's authority to his favorite theme.[21]

When Herzen quoted from Goethe's lyrics—and he did this
frequently—he usually sought to enhance with these quotations
the emotional impact of his thoughts. In doing so, he cared little
about the applicability of the central message of Goethe's poem to
his particular argument as long as the specific line or lines he
plucked from its context would strike home. Thus he opens his
"Epilogue" to the ill-fated Revolution of 1848 with lines from
Goethes' "Die Braut von Korinth":

Opfer fallen hier,
Weder Lamm noch Stier,
Aber Menschenopfer unerhört.†

Herzen seemed quite unconcerned whether the ballad as a whole in
its mood and message supports the theme of his "Epilogue." Or
again, he affixed to his autobiographical reminiscences "From the
Other Shore" as a rousing motto the lines from Goethe's "Prometheus":

Wähntest du etwa
Ich sollte das Leben hassen,

---

* You are not disturbed within, in active times, by unnecessary recollections
and by vain quarrels.

† Sacrifices are slaughtered here, not lamb nor steer, but unheard-of human
sacrifices.

In Wüsten fliehen,
Weil nicht alle Blütenträume reiften?*

or used as an epigraph to his tale, *The Second Encounter,* Goethe's
song of the Harfner from *Wilhelm Meister:* "Wer nie sein Brot mit
Tränen aß."[22] Such examples could be multiplied.[23] A less acceptable practice than this not-always-appropriate use of Goethe's lyrics
was Herzen's manner of citing Goethe as witness against himself,
thereby to "prove" with utmost effectiveness a shortcoming or failing of the poet. Thus, in commenting critically on Goethe's attitude
toward the Italian people, he quoted a line from the *Venezianische
Epigramme:* "Leben und Weben ist hier aber nicht Ordung und
Zucht,"[24] and proceeded to interpret these words as "proof" of
Goethe's lack of understanding, even his resentment of the Italian's
love of untrammeled self-expression, of their determined resistance
to bureaucratic regulations. This line demonstrates, so runs Herzen's
argument, "that Goethe, who understood so profoundly Italy's nature and art, had nothing for the Italian people save these few verses
of angry accusation, devoid of any note of hope or consolation."
They show "that Goethe had no ear for the heartbeat of the people,"
that he had no appreciation of the logic of history, of the fact that,
"if in the second half of the eighteenth century there had been in Italy
the kind of 'Ordnung und Zucht' they had in Weimar, there would
surely not have been the 'risorgimento' in the second half of the
nineteenth."[25] Thus runs Herzen's "proof" of Goethe's reactionary
stance, a "proof" based on one line extracted from the *Epigramme.*
Obviously, Herzen's method is less than fair to the poet. Nor is this
an isolated instance. We shall meet a far more extensive example
of this dubious practice in Herzen's portrayal of Goethe in his historical narrative, *The First Meeting.*

But let us first define briefly the philosophical and esthetic
background which determined Herzen's approach to Goethe. It is
characteristic of Herzen that in his philosophy in general and his
esthetics in particular he did not pass through the socalled "objective" period of Hegelian "reconciliation with reality" so typical of
the members of the Stankevich Circle, especially of Bakunin and

---

* "Did you think I should hate life and flee to the desert just because not all
the blossom dreams ripened?"

Belinski. Instead, he moved from his early idealism inspired by Schelling[26] and Schiller directly to the left-wing position of "critical realism." By 1834 he had gathered around him at Moscow University a group of fellow students who thought of themselves as spiritual descendents of the Decembrists, as inheritors and apostles of their revolutionary ideals. They were very much alive to the liberal stirrings in Germany, admired Heine,[27] and sympathized with Wolfgang Menzel's attack on Goethe, taking it uncritically for a daring denunciation of the "Olympian autocrat" from a liberal, democratic point of view. For their foremost models they took the French utopian socialists, Saint Simon, Proudhon, Fourier. Thus they broke completely with the world view of the Stankevich Circle, with its philosophy and esthetics. As Herzen was to write in his autobiography, *My Past and Thoughts:* "They [the members of the Stankevich Circle] did not like our almost exclusively political orientation; we did not like their almost exclusively speculative one. They called us 'frondeurs' and Frenchmen, we called them sentimentalists and Germans."[28]

It was this general orientation that pervasively determined Herzen's early critical view of Goethe. In fact, his was among the first Russian voices daring to challenge the inviolable image of Goethe as the semidivine genius, not subject to human error or flaw.[29] Still, even Herzen could not escape altogether the powerful influence of the Romantic image of Goethe as it had been developed by the Liubomudry and was continued and elaborated by the Stankevich group. But with Herzen this youthful period of uncritical, derivative admiration of Goethe was to be very short. It found its clear expression in but one essay, his first, on E.T.A. Hoffmann.[30] Here Goethe was apotheosized in unmistakably Romantic superlatives as "the Zeus in the realm of art," the "poet-Buonarroti," the "Napoleon of literature." More original is Herzen's preference of Goethe to Walter Scott, who was generally ranked equal if not superior to the German poet by Russian critical opinion of the time. "Do not search," he warned, "in the tepid prose of Walter Scott for a poetic unfolding of impressive characters, . . . of those wondrous creations of luminous imagination, for those 'schwankende Gestalten' which remain indelibly fixed in your memory, do not expect to find there a Faust, a Mignon, all those most memorable creations of Goethe!" Goethe's *Werther,* a work which the mature Herzen was to criticize so mercilessly, was acclaimed here as the "song of pristine love, lofty, impassioned, a song which begins with a tender adagio and ends as a frenzied shriek of death, a soul-shattering addio!" And next to this "song of love" Herzen places Goethe's "song of youth," his incomparable *Wilhelm Meister,* "in which everything breathes with the fresh breath of youth, all is seen through the prism of youth—these seemingly unrelated scenes which yet are all fused by a common life, a common poetry." Herzen was profoundly impressed with Goethe's power of character-delineation. "Behold those characters!", he exclaims. "That touchingly tragic figure of Mignon, longing for the land of the lemon and orange trees with its clear skies, its warm breath, Mignon, unsullied as a dove in her purity." And over against her, as a striking contrasting figure, "behold the voluptuously sensuous, fiery Philine, luxuriant in her beauty, . . . a young bacchante drunk with passion, detesting the light of day, living in the secretive shimmer of the evening lamp, all aglow in his [Wilhelm's] embraces." And finally, "completing this chorus of passions, behold the heart-rending figure, the majestic bas-relief of the blind old harpist, whose bread is bitter to him and whose tears flow in the silence of the night!"[31]

These effusions, in their excess of rhapsodic praise and rhetorical flourish, clearly indicate Herzen's youthful, inept imitation of the Goethe cult typical of the Liubomudry. Soon he was to be free of this influence. Barely a year after his Hoffmann essay, he was working on the *First Meeting,*[32] a groping effort at the type of biographical fiction, of *Dichtung und Wahrheit,* for which he was soon to be famous. It is in this early piece that Herzen dared to point an accusing finger at Goethe, dared to censure the "Zeus in the realm of art" for his Olympian aloofness, his egotism, for his myopic view of history, for his philistinism, his servility, his "Fürstendienertum." To be sure, he did not speak out in his own person against the "Olympian." He used an indirect method of attack, placing his invective in the mouths of fictional characters. In his narrative piece,[33] a "German traveler" has two meetings with Goethe, the first one during the ill-fated campaign in France, the second in Weimar after the campaign's collapse. It is through his eyes that we see Goethe as Herzen would have us see him: it is by way of his comments and of those of some other personae of the tale that he drives home his criticism of Goethe. Moreover, Herzen makes ample use here of the questionable device we have met with before, of casting Goethe in the role of witness to his own short-comings. His deception is all the more effective since his narrative has the appearance of historical truth, being based in part on Goethe's account of the allied invasion of France in the year 1792.[34] In this "historical setting" Herzen had Goethe appear in situations and involved him in conversations all of which are designed to emphasize various negative facets of his personality. Thus, Goethe's "Fürstendienertum" is adumbrated by a cleverly edited version of Goethe's description of his chance meeting during the campaign with the King of Prussia.[35] The very fact that Goethe makes mention of this episode is turned by Herzen into "proof" of his fawning admir-ation of the high and the mighty. To underscore this reprehens-ible trait, Herzen added to Goethe's version the apocryphal sen-tence: "This incident shall for a long time remain fixed in my memory."[36] As another "proof," this time of Goethe's facetious attitude in the face of the most dire events, Herzen quotes Goethe's description of how the poet sought to buoy the flagging spirits of his companions with a merry tale of light-hearted courage during Louis the Holy's crusade against the infidels.[37]

It would be easy to list endlessly Herzen's "quotations" from Goethe's *Kampagne in Frankreich*. To compound the dubiousness of this method of characterization, Herzen placed into Goethe's mouth extended statements which are invented from first to last. In an imaginary "conversation" he had Goethe express his surprise at how the French revolutionaries, "this band of insane dreamers, could have grasped such power, despite the disgust roused by them in the whole French nation." Herzen's Goethe then proceeds to lament the ruinous effect of the upheaval on "la belle France." Goethe had hoped to visit a resplendent France, "to see the throne under the lilies of which had flourished those mighty geniuses, that superb literature!" He certainly had not expected to witness "this second coming of the barbarians who destroyed all that had once been great." Herzen's Goethe curses "the whole world of politics, which had always been totally alien" to him, and yearns "for those other spheres," the realm of art, in which he knew himself "to be the ruler." We search in vain for anything remotely akin to this "conversation" in Goethe's *Kampagne in Frankreich.* It is adroitly invented by Herzen to cast a glaring light on Goethe's hostility toward the French Revolution, his generally antisocial and anti-political attitude.

These passages of Goethe's fictional self-characterization Herzen underscored with comments on Goethe by the personae of his "historical" tale. Thus the German Traveler expresses his amazement at Goethe's ability to concentrate on purely private interests, especially on his *Farbenlehre,* "in the momentous year 1792, amid an army suffering defeat, under the impact of colossal events," the significance of which, to the consternation and dismay of the Traveler, "Goethe completely fails to grasp." Goethe's *Dichtung und Wahrheit* the Traveler characterizes as a "monument to the poet's narcissistic introspection" and accuses Goethe of "neglecting the biography of mankind while being totally absorbed with his own." "Yes, yes," he exclaims, "read this precious commentary on his works, that grandiose confession of egoism, and you will discover therein the whole of Goethe: there you will see his ego as it swallows up all of existence!" One cannot but smile at the unconscious self-criticism inherent in this distorted evaluation of Goethe's autobiography by Herzen, that inveterate autobiographer who stands no less centrally in his life's work than does Goethe in his, and whose "chef d'oeuvre," *My Past and Thoughts,* is admittedly indebted to Goethe's *Dichtung und Wahrheit.*[38]

In his portrayal of Goethe, Herzen emphasized still another character trait, Goethe's eclecticism. In his interpretation, this oft-dwelled-upon facet of Goethe's personality reappears as the poet's insincerity, his penchant for dissimulation and mystification, traits which Herzen detests. "I hate dissimulation and mystification, be it in Goethe or Victor Hugo," exclaims Herzen through his mouth-piece, the Traveler, and follows with the pointed question: "Or is it possible that you like him as court poet, as the manufacturer on order of odes celebrating the coming and going of the high and the mighty, of 'Prologues' and 'Masques'? . . . There is just no sincerity in Goethe, in a great part of his works! He *parades* before the foot-lights on the stage of a theater instead of moving on the stage of life in the light of the sun." To convince the reader of this trait of "in-sincerity and dissimulation" in Goethe, Herzen had his Traveler re-count two anecdotes, both of which have, characteristically, a basis in fact but are in most of their details pure fiction. "When Lavater met Goethe for the first time," so runs the Traveler's anecdote, "he could not restrain himself from exclaiming: 'I would not have thought you to have such features!' Now Lavater, this great physiognomist, rarely erred." The point was, explains the Traveler, "that Lavater in reading Goethe's works had believed every line to be from Goethe's very soul and on the basis of this impression had con-structed in his mind certain lineaments and features of Goethe's face which he could not discover upon meeting him." The rea-son: Goethe had dissimulated, had not been his own self in his writings. Specifying Lavater's experience of Goethe's insincerity, the Traveler-Herzen commits a blatant anachronism. He presents Goethe as the author of the *West-östliche Divan* at the "first meet-ing" with Lavater: "There was actually nothing at all in Goethe of an Eastern nature," claims the Traveler, "and yet Goethe proceeded to force his prodigious talents to the unnatural task of writing the *West-östliche Divan*," thus misleading and "mystifying" poor La-vater. Surely, no comment is needed on the biographical accuracy of this portion of Herzen's tale and his "portrayal" of Goethe.

The second anecdote of the Traveler pursues a similar aim by the device of contrast. Goethe is here compared—to his distinct disadvantage—with Schiller, the unassuming, sincere idealist. Again Herzen employs his favorite anecdotal form, a "mélange" of truth and fiction. He shows us Goethe attending a "resplendent social gathering, surrounded by his admirers, collecting compliments from all sides, regaling the company with his improvisations, all the while placing enormous importance on each and every one of his words and gestures." But, in a corner by himself, silent and inconspicuous sat "someone steeped in thought. For a long time this someone observed Goethe intently with his blue eyes in which it was clearly writ that this man was not of this earth, that his soul was sorrowing after that world which was the creation of his holy vision, his pristine inspiration. This someone loved Goethe for his *Werther* and his *Berlichingen;* he had come especially to see him, to gain his friendship. This someone finally rose and said: "No, he and I, we shall never be close!' " "And do you know," Herzen pointedly asks, "who that someone was?" and furnishes the startling dénouement: "None other than—Schiller!"

Having delivered this "coup de grâce," Herzen keeps both his narrative and his invective against Goethe moving by introducing a "speculative philosopher," who objects vigorously to this presentation of the relationship of the two poets. He points to the historical fact that "Goethe and Schiller became inseparable friends, they loved one another." But the Traveler silences all opposition with the dogmatic assertion: "Goethe overhelmed with his genius and his authority the shy and humble Schiller, but never could these two men find each other in sincere friendship!"

Herzen continued to use the effective device of contrast by conjuring up the figure of an "old Prussian Colonel." This is a man of "frightening sincerity," who has always shared the sufferings of his soldiers, who is a stout champion of the people's cause and is endowed with an unerring instinct for the true shape and meaning of events. Challenged by Goethe's aristocratic bearing, he characterizes himself as a "simple man" who "never felt himself to be a ruler or a genius." He had always remembered the proverb he learned in his boyhood: Homo sum et nihil humanum a me alienum puto." While Goethe with a most supercilious air makes light of the army's plight, assuring his listeners of their safe return when they would tell of their adventures "in good company, 'devant des dames," this "simple man of frightening sincerity" predicts a tragic end to the campaign and gives heartfelt expression to his "shame" at such an ignominious defeat of his army. He would "sooner die on the battlefield than bear the shame of such a campaign"—sound views and noble sentiments of which, by implication, Goethe was quite incapable. Herzen's intentions were obvious enough. By setting up in his "Old Colonel" a paragon of simple, democratic virtues and sound instincts, he underscored once again Goethe's shortcomings; his egocentricity, aristocratic aloofness and utter blindness to the gravity of the historical events in which he was participating.

Having survived the disastrous defeat of the allies, the Traveler has a second opportunity to observe Goethe at close range, this time in the Weimar Theater during a performance of Goethe's political farce, *Der Bürgergeneral*. In this scene Herzen shows us Goethe in the sorry role of an author who had produced a resounding failure, and now is forced to attend, "angry and resentful," the fiasco of his "little joke." The Traveler, observing Goethe in the ducal loge, "could not help but be extremely sorry for the great poet who had entranced the world with his creations and now had to suffer the fate of a journalist who had completely missed the right tone for his subject and the occasion." For once, Herzen had little need to force facts. Goethe himself frankly attests to the debacle. In his *Kampagne in Frankreich* we find his laconic report of this ill-conceived and ill-timed affair. "The piece [*Der Bürgergeneral*] produced the most repulsive effect even among friends and well-wishers. They stubbornly insisted, in an attempt to save me and themselves, that I had not been the author, that capriciously I had merely lent my name and made a few strokes of the pen on an inferior product."[39]

Does this instance of corroboration by historical fact of Herzen's narrative prove the justness of his portrayal of Goethe? A comparison of his fictional version of Goethe's participation in the campaign with the poet's record of the events tends to bear out quite the opposite. Drawing upon this very source, Herzen could have given us, with far greater justice, a positive portrayal of Goethe than his negative picture. For Goethe's vividly realistic eyewitness report of the illfated venture and of his role in it contains rich evidence against his alleged egoism, his antisocial and reactionary stance and in support of his wholehearted, active, ever-observant participation in the events and dangers of the campaign,[40] his intense awareness of the suffering of the people, his profound sympathy with the unfortunates[41] and his circumspect efforts to alleviate their plight. Finally, there is in his account impressive proof of his profound insight into the far-reaching import of the momentous events: "Here and now begins a new epoch of world history,"[42] he had predicted as he witnessed the fierce but futile allied bombardment of the French positions at Valmy. Such prophecy does not spring from indifference to world events; it is the product of a mind fully involved with history in the making. Goethe attested explicitly to this fact. He considered it a most fortunate coincidence that he had been able to finish his drama, *Torquato Tasso,* just at the time when the French Revolution, its causes and its effects, began to absorb all his attention. "Fortunately my *Tasso* could still be completed; from that time on, however, world events totally occupied my mind."[43] Evidence such as this did not support Herzen's critical view of Goethe and was therefore suppressed in his "historical" narrative.

The grand debate sparked by the Traveler's account of his encounter with Goethe at the Weimar Theater, so effectively closing Herzen's tale, has for its central purpose the further development of this negative view of the German poet. The chief protagonists in this debate are the Traveler and the "speculative philosopher," who turns out to be a faithful exponent of the Romantic esthetics of the Liubomudry and the Stankevich Circle. He challenges the Traveler's demand that a poet of Goethe's stature should also exhibit a lively sense of politics. "Why should a Goethe step forward on the political stage," he asks, "being a king in the other realm, in the realm of poetry and art? Is it possible that you, a German, could not imagine an artist, a poet who would not be, at the same time, a politician?" These challenging questions have a familiar ring for us. They are those Belinski had posed in his attack on Menzel, the critic of Goethe.[44] The Traveler's reply is highly revealing of Herzen's "realistic" concept of genius. "It is not politics that I demand of genius," he answers. "I demand of him that he show sympathy with all that is great; he must not, he cannot remain indifferent to the lot of mankind, unaffected by great events in the past or the present. Nor is omniscience given even to genius!" And turning on the philosopher, the Traveler accuses him of being "a dreamer" who still sees in Goethe "that lightning-wielding Zeus, pronouncing world-shaking truths and lofty prophecies." "I for my part," continues Herzen, speaking through his Traveler, "I for my part have never effaced myself before the high and the mighty in genuflection and adulation. I have always looked upon them without rose-colored glasses and have discovered, in the majority of cases, that they 'sont ce que nous sommes,' that they too have their seamy side. You, poets at heart that you are, would not admit to that seamy side in your idols—and yet without flaw individuality is incomplete, is doomed to lifelessness." Thus Herzen consigns the Romantic theory of flawless genius to the realm of myth and proposes instead his new ambivalent view of Goethe as an artist of astounding creative powers but with a "seamy side" to his fallible human nature. He is "prepared to bend his knee before the creator of *Faust,* and at the same time to snub the Privy Councilor von Goethe." Even Goethe's appearance elicits that ambivalent reaction from the Traveler. Goethe is characterized by him as the "Weimar diplomat with the head of Zeus." He is impressed with "the force of [Goethe's] character manifested in the regular lineaments of his face, by that high forehead and his noble bearing." "Yet," he assures us, "one look and you will realize that this man of dignity and grand repose is no friend of yours, so oppressive, so downright tyrannizing is Goethe's presence; that glance of his does not stretch out a hand to you in friendship, it enslaves you, forgives you in condescending fashion your nothingness. . . . To be sure, Goethe's manners were those of a man of the world and yet the imprint of Germanism was unmistakable on his entire being which *we* [Russians] would call 'steif.' Wherever Goethe passed, people would bow and scrape and he would accept these signs of respect as proper tribute to his greatness; he would accept them with that certain delicacy of manner which raised *him* still higher while plunging *you* lower still."

And the Traveler sums up his attitude toward Goethe with laconic finality: "I was impressed with the genius of the man, but love him I can not!"

Herzen's ambivalent view of Goethe must be clearly differentiated from that of the Liubomudry and the Stankevich Circle. They, too, rejected the Privy Councilor Goethe. But *they* rejected him because his official role involved the "pure poet" in the trivialities of mundane existence, subjected him to the daily demands of *mere* administrative, socio-political concerns. Herzen, in contrast, rejects Goethe the man and in part the artist as well, precisely because, in his view, neither the Privy Councilor nor the poet had become *sufficiently involved* in this mundane existence, in the social and political life of the people. Herzen was determined to put an end to the Romantic adulation of the "pure poet" and of "pure art," to replace it with a hard-headed appraisal of Goethe's great gifts but also of his considerable shortcomings: his egoism, his narcissism, his insincerity, his socio-political indifference, his lack of what Belinski had called a "sense of sociality."

That Herzen's determination to point up Goethe's shortcomings was not a passing phase with him is amply proven by passages liberally scattered throughout the voluminous output of his long writing career. In his recollections, *From the Other Shore,* published in 1850, we read the following elaboration of the theme of Goethe's egocentricity: "Goethe alienates himself from reality, he is complacently satisfied with his greatness and in this extreme complacent self-satisfaction he is unique. Fichte and Schiller, Rousseau and Byron, were they of that type? And all those people who suffered agonies striving to raise the masses to their level, were they like Goethe?" Herzen left no doubt where his sympathy and admiration lay: "For me, the sufferings of these people, their inescapable, burning torments driving some to their death, some to the executioner's block, others again to the insane asylum, these sufferings are for me of far greater value than is Goethe's grand repose."[45] In 1851 Herzen still spoke of Goethe's servility, his "Fürstendienertum,"[46] and as late as 1865, in his biographical sketch of Mazzini, he returns to his attack on

Goethe for "his colossal egoism, . . . his placid inaction, his coldly scientific inquisitiveness in matters of human concern,"[47] that is, his lack of genuine empathy with the human condition. Finally, in one of his latest essays, in the "Appel à la Pudeur," Herzen once more asserts that Goethe "did not know how to conduct himself with dignity" in his dealings with titled nobility.[48]

Herzen was indeed insistent and, it must be admitted, successful in propagating this critical evaluation of Goethe. As we have seen, it was taken up by Belinski. It passed down the long line of left-wing critics, Pisarev, Dobrolubov, Chernyshevski, finally to Engels, whose authority, in turn, was to make it part of the official canon of the Soviet interpretation of Goethe. Yet, for all its ideological fertility, this was not Herzen's most viable and valuable contribution to the Russian image of Goethe. With this critical view of the German writer, he had merely replaced one "preconceived theory" with another. This new image of Goethe was as much the product of a prejudicial reading of the German poet as was the Romantic concept of the "Olympian Goethe," the idol without flaw. Far more substantial, capable of withstanding close scholarly scrutiny, was Herzen's discovery of Goethe as "one of the greatest representatives of Realistic art."[49] As his Soviet biographer Elsberg has justly stressed, "Herzen valued in Goethe, specifically and above all, that unique combination of a limitlessly many-sided and many-colored realistic representation of life with the perceptive and purposeful comprehension of its deeper meaning."[50] This felicitous understanding of Goethe's creative temperament was not given to Herzen the propagandist, a prominent facet of his character of which Herzen himself was keenly aware.[51] Rather, it was the achievement of Herzen the devoted, systematic student of Goethe. In fact, the view of Goethe as "the supreme realist" comes to stand again and again in outright contradiction, down to specific formulations, to Herzen's critical characterization of Goethe as the intraverted, asocial, even antisocial egoist out of touch with life. It is almost as if two men, not one, were viewing the figure of Goethe; Herzen the "propagandist" with his ideological anti-Goethe stance and Herzen the observant, objective student of a great artist and thinker. It is curious that this contradiction in his attitude toward Goethe never seems to have disconcerted him, or, at any rate, not to an extent sufficient to have caused the revision of either of these clearly contradictory views.

In developing his interpretation of Goethe as the realistic artist, Herzen credits the poet with "sympathy for life,"[52] with the very trait, that is, which the ideologist Herzen had denied the "aloof" and "intraverted" poet. Coming from a reading of Hegel, full of admiration for the philosopher, he was ready to admit that he knew of no one who so completely understood life and could so aptly express all that he understood—*save Goethe.*[53] Under the impression of Feuerbach's work on Leibniz, he was moved to exclaim: "Only eternally slumbering Germany has such colossal sudden awakenings as were Leibniz, Lessing, Goethe! What gigantic activity, what many-sidedness!"[54] And he named Goethe together with the "other great realist" Napoleon as "the foremost representatives of our preeminently realistic epoch."[55] Surely, being placed in such company does not make of Goethe the "pure artist," the asocial, apolitical egoist. Instead, Goethe is here acclaimed as peer of the foremost representatives of enlightened thought, of social and political activism.

As one of the characteristics of the "true" artist, that is, of the "realist," Herzen now emphasizes Goethe's deep rootedness in his nation's culture, his rapport with his people, his mission as the voice of his people's subconscious.

> The poet and artist, in those of his works which are truly his own, is always national [naroden]. No matter what he sets out to create, whatever the thoughts he wants to express, the goals he wants to achieve in his creations he will always express with them, intentionally or not, some elements of his nation's character, and will express them more profoundly, more clearly than they would be expressed by the nation's history. Even when he tries to divorce himself from all that is national, the true artist will not lose those chief traits by which we can recognize of *whose blood he is.* Goethe is a German, be it in his *Iphigenie,* be it in his *Divan.* Poets are, in the Romans' expression, 'prophets.' Yet, they do not prophesy that which does not exist or that which might occur

by chance; they articulate that which—though not yet evident—is present in the subconscious of the people, slumbers in its depths.[56]

Already in his first essay on E. T. A. Hoffmann (1834), Herzen had been "afraid" to group Goethe with the Romanticists. "It is a frightening thought," he wrote on that early occasion, "to include Goethe in this trend [the Romantic]: Goethe was far too great to have had any 'trend' whatever, much too lofty to have taken part in these homeopathic upheavals."[57] In a somewhat later essay, "Dilettantes—Romanticists" (1835), Herzen pointed to Goethe as to the German poet who, like Schiller, was able to encompass in his works both the Classical and the Romantic spirit, embracing them in his contemporaneousness. "In these two giants the antithetical movements were fused by the fire of genius in a vision of wondrous fullness."[58] Yet, at this early stage Herzen was far from acclaiming "realism" in art. He was then still reading Goethe's *Werther,* for instance, with typically Romantic eyes as the "pristine, lofty, fiery song of love, opening with the softest adagio and closing with the most heart-rending addio."[59] Now he rejects the "monopoly of love along with all other monopolies." "Love is but one aspect of human life," he argues. "Man does not live in order merely to be in love. . . . What a pitiful, lost existence, the life of a Werther, to point to a famous case! How much there is in him of insanity and of egoism."[60] To be sure, Werther possessed that certain magnetism of persons obsessed with an overpowering passion. Yet, he embodies for Herzen "not the lifegiving fire but rather the flame that destroys and consumes life." Herzen pities this monomaniac existence; he admits that he had once "cried bitter tears over the last letter of Werther, over the touching details of his tragic end." But now he sees clearly "what a vacuous youngster [pustoi malyi] this Werther really was!" He would have us compare him with Schiller's Karl Moor or Max Piccolomini or Tell and, "so as not to offend Goethe," with one of Goethe's characters too, for instance "with the architect in the *Wahlverwandtschaften.*" Then we would see at once the point Herzen is trying to make, namely, that "into the lives of those heroes, too, there entered the passion of love, yet with them it did not swallow up all other interests. By their passion they did not cut themselves off from the universal concerns, from politics, art, and the sciences. On the contrary, they infused these spheres with the passion of their love and, in turn, brought all the breadth and grandeur of these other worlds into their passion. That is why," Herzen concludes, "their loves, whether happy or tragic, never degenerated into insanity."[61]

The mature Herzen valued most highly the products of Goethe's "realistic genius," his "Prometheus," the "Gretchen" tragedy in *Faust,* his *Wahlverwandtschaften.* He acclaimed the ode of "Prometheus" as that "loud and energetic protest against oppression in all its forms and in all the ages," that selfsame protest which Aeschylus had voiced in his dramatic masterpiece. "What an embodiment of resounding, energetic protest that chained Titan, disdainful of Zeus, cursing him!"[62]

Herzen applauded Goethe for his courage in introducing to German readers the figure of the unwed mother: "Honor and fame to our teacher, the old realist Goethe; he had the boldness to place a pregnant woman alongside the pristine virgins of Romanticism and was not afraid to sculpt with his mighty verses the changed forms of a *mother-to-be,* comparing them with the supple limbs of the future woman."[63] Herzen read Gretchen's tragedy as the imperishable document of Goethe's "profound sympathy with the young mother who has to hide the fruit of her love as a stigma of her shame," as Goethe's bold step on the road toward the emancipation of women and the "rehabilitation of the flesh." Unaware of the historical locus of the Gretchen tragedy in German "storm and stress," or else caring little for historical accuracy, Herzen claimed that with this work Goethe was helping to realize the dreams of that better world which had so profoundly impressed Herzen in the writings of the French Utopian Socialists, of George Sand, of Heine and of the Young Germans, the *Jungdeutsche.*[64]

Herzen stepped forward in the role of a forceful champion of Goethe as a progressive, liberal thinker in the debate on the *Wahlverwandtschaften* which was then being carried on in Russian literary circles. Together with Belinski, he attacked the reading of the work by the German literary historian and critic, Heinrich Theodor Rötscher, as an apologia for and an apotheosis of the institution of marriage, "that bedrock of all ethical order."[65] Countering Rötscher, he proclaims the *Wahlverwandtschaften* to be an unequivocal defense by Goethe of those elemental "Naturgewalten" which would not be tethered in their vital force by any of the outworn moral codes of church and state. In a letter to Ogarëv he was eager to convince his friend, who read the work in Rötscher's spirit, of the justness of his, Herzen's, interpretation. He insists that "Goethe did *not* intend to write a moralist parable, rather he sought in this work for a solution of the deeply troubling problem posed by the conflict between the formalism of marriage and the irrepressible forces of the elective affinities." Herzen is certain that "marriage did *not* win out with Goethe—Rötscher notwithstanding. . . . On the contrary, Goethe was presenting the tragic contradiction arising from the terrible collision of the unsublimated passions with the hollow formalities of the social organization—tragic contradictions resolvable only in death."[66] For him the deepest tragedy in the fates of the protagonists of this "drama" lies in the fact that "they all are in the right," that there is here no question of moral guilt.[67]

Herzen repeated his interpretation no less emphaticly in a letter to N. H. Ketsher: "It seems Ogarëv looks at the *Wahlv* . . . [*Elective Affinities*] from Rötscher's point of view," he wrote. "Now Rötscher's view may be well and fine, but it certainly is not Goethe's. No, do penetrate to the depths of this tragic collision, into this baleful clash of forms, of these 'Naturgewalten,' of the spirit in chains, passions resolved only in secret death. A great poem!"[68] Clearly, Herzen read Goethe's novel with the eyes of a disciple of Saint Simon, George Sand and Heine, who had taken their gospel of the "emancipation of the flesh" very much to heart. Yet there is, at the same time, in his interpretation still another influence at work which is, if anything, of even greater importance, namely, the influence of the scientific thought of the time that had caught his attention at an early age and never lost its fascination for him. An American student of the Russian writer, M. Malia, aptly observes that Herzen read in Goethe's work, to some extent even read into it, "a naturalistic, almost physiological view of the sensual attraction. . . ."[69] We have interesting corroborative evidence of his early tendency to view Goethe's message in such "naturalistic, almost physiological terms." In her reminiscences Herzen's cousin, T. P. Passek, told of a debate in the family circle on the *Wahlverwandtschaften* and recorded verbatim the part Herzen took in it. She quotes him as stating with the disarming aplomb of youth that "the meaning of the term [elective affinity] was perfectly clear." He felt certain that a "*chemical kinship* is the source and origin of sympathy and antipathy between people."[70] That is, he takes it for granted that the elective affinities have their source in the physical realm, are conditioned by physical processes.

This ability to discern and appreciate in Goethe's belletristic and scientific work the "naturalistic, physiological view" of man and of nature makes Herzen a pioneer in the Russian interpretation of Goethe. It was the trained vision developed in a lifelong, devoted study of the exact and natural sciences that enabled him to lay hold of and to transmit to his Russian contemporaries a first impression, however rudimentary, of Goethe's achievements in the vast scope of his minerological, geological, morphological, and osteological research. Herzen did this more knowledgeably than had Vladimir F. Odoevski, far more perceptively and selflessly than S. S. Uvarov, the President of the Russian Academy of Sciences, that "intimate friend" of the "sage of Weimar."[71] Here we find Herzen's chief contribution to the elaboration of the Russian image of Goethe. Unfortunately, it was to remain an isolated, if a very important, episode in the Russian Goetheana of the nineteenth century.

The first explicit evidence of Herzen's preoccupation with Goethe's scientific work we find in his *Diary* under the dateline, November 9, 1844. "I have read Goethe's works on the natural sciences. What a giant! It is quite impossible to keep up with *what* he has accomplished or to grasp completely *how* he has been able to achieve so much." He recognized in Goethe's scientific work the spirit of the poet. "The poet has not been lost in the natural scientist! His science is that same poetry of life, of reality, is endowed with the selfsame pantheistic spirit, has the same depth."[72] Though this passage is the first *explicit* testimony of Herzen's interest in Goethe's scientific work, we have earlier *implicit* evidence of his preoccupation with Goethe the evolutionist and leading exponent of "speculative empiricism." In an essay written in 1830 with the significant title: "On Indivisibility in the Plant Kingdom,"[73] he posited the theory that "almost all plants—in the aspect in which they present themselves—are not simple and indivisible but rather are a collective of their parts [*sic*]." According to him, "many writers have enlarged on this theory, especially Goethe. However," he continued, "in my opinion this theory in its full scope belongs to Darwin, who opens his *Phitologia* with a discussion of the indivisibility (individualitas) of buds."[74] This reference would seem to indicate that Herzen's acquaintance with Goethe's work on plant metamorphosis—however cursory and second-hand—dates back at least to the year 1830.[75] In another essay: "Dilettantism in Science," written in 1842, fully two years before the diary entry, he quoted in support of his central argument the lines from Goethe's poem "Epirrhema": "Nichts ist drinnen, nichts ist draußen; / Denn was innen, das ist außen."[76] These lines neatly define his own position in his attack against the Romantic "dreamer-dilettantes" and the "materialistic empiricists," both of whom he proscribes as "enemies of science and progress." Adopting a central tenet of Goethe's *Naturphilosophie* for his text: "Natur hat weder Kern noch Schale / Alles ist sie mit einem Male,"[77] Herzen rejected the Romanticist's philosophy of nature as a quixotic quest after the "inner essence of being." These Don Quixotes, according to him, engage in the futile effort of "liberating the *inwardness* [vnutrenee] of life, they demand a kind of objectivized existence of this *inwardness*." They should know "that *inwardness* has no existence save in *outwardness* [vneshnee]." And then Herzen quotes the lines from "Epirrhema" which seem to have suggested the very wording of his argument, his insistent use of the terms "inwardness" and "outwardness," these literal Russian equivalents of Goethe's "drinnen," "draußen," "innen," "aussen."

Herzen then turns on the "materialist-empiricists" whom he accuses of "forcing the living organism upon the Procrustean bed of their anatomical laboratories." They "cause thought to freeze and congeal, hoping to analyze it all the more easily in that stagnant state." It is not difficult to recognize in the Russian's essay Goethean ideas, even some echoes of Goethe's typical phraseology.[78] "These skeptical and pedantic researchers," Herzen continues, "want to divide the poles [of spirit and matter]," forgetting "the profound truth that, without this polarity [!] there can be no attraction. As soon as they insert their scalpels into the living organism, they sever the vital spiritual-physical nexus, leaving in their hands nothing but lifeless abstracts—the blood congealed, the breathing stopped! For only in the continuous movement from pole to pole, in the interaction of spirit and matter, only in this eternal flux into which all being is ineluctably drawn, only there truth resides: this is its very rhythm of breathing, its 'systol' and its 'diastol' [!]. . . . Truth is a living truth . . . only so long as it remains an organic whole; tear it into parts and what remains is a dead abstraction with the stench of a corpse."[79]

> Wer will was Lebendigs erkennen und beschreiben,
> Sucht erst den Geist heraus zu treiben,
> Dann hat er die Teile in seiner Hand,
> Fehlt, leider! nur das geistige Band.* [80]

No, Herzen has not, in fact, quoted these lines. Yet they could well have introduced his essay as a most fitting motto.

Herzen's intensive, systematic studies of Goethe's scientific work were carried on chiefly in the year of the diary entry, 1844, in preparation of his famous *Letters on the Study of Nature (1844–45)*.[81] In these *Letters* Herzen gives the most complete expression to his view of Goethe the natural scientist, as the foremost "speculative empiricist," who was able to combine in his work the spirit of the idealistic tradition with the empiricism of the predominantly materialistic modern age. He is of the opinion that none of the other great minds born into the idealistic tradition, into the "Egyp-

---

* He, who would recognize and describe something living, strives first to drive out the spirit, then he does have the parts in his hand, but unfortunately the spiritual tie is lost.

translation of the essay "On Nature" (1780) which he ascribed to Goethe in accordance with the practice at the time. In fact, he saw in its passionate "storm and stress" language "the supreme example of the profound rapport which the artist Goethe enjoyed with life: the throb of sympathy with life pulses through every line, every word breathes his love for life, his intoxication with it." Moreover, Herzen had chosen, as a motto for the *Letters*[88] the lines from Goethe's ballad, "Der Gott und die Bajadere":

> Doch der Götter-Jüngling hebet
> Aus den Flammen sich empor,
> Und in seinen Armen schwebet
> Die Geliebte mit hervor.*

because, as he explained, these lines give poetic expression to the central theme of his *Letters*, which strive to establish as incontrovertible truth the indivisibility of spirit [Götter Jüngling] and matter [Geliebte], and challenge modern science to achieve finally a viable synthesis of the speculative and the empirical approach lest it stagnate. "Of course, I know very well," he wrote in his seventh letter, "I know very well that there doesn't appear a pamphlet which does not proclaim the conflict of idealism with empiricism to be a thing of the past. . . . Yet, what halfhearted voices these are, feeble and fruitless. Is that all we could expect as a result of those fertile, mighty ideas which the great Goethe had put forward? All leading minds of our age have come to realize the absolute necessity of the integration of empiricism with speculative philosophy, but, alas, beyond that theoretical realization of this ultimate need they have not progressed." Yet it was only too evident to Herzen that "the reintegration of these two sides is perhaps the most important mission of progressive science." Goethe's poem with its metaphorical language Herzen recognized as a rousing call to the realization of this mission. In contrast to the original Indian myth where the God [spirit] chastised and slighted the Bajadere [nature], in Goethe's ballad the divine youth, rising from the flames of the pyre, carries her aloft in his arms to eternal life,

---

* Yet the divine youth rises from the flames and together with his beloved in his arms soars upward.

proclaiming, in Herzen's interpretation of the poem's symbolism, the profound truth that "there is room also in eternal thought for that which is temporal."[89]   Herzen conceived his *Letters* in the spirit and under the aegis of Goethe, the poet-scientist.

Herzen considers Goethe's supreme scientific achievement to be his theory of *metamorphosis;* here, according to him, Goethe was truly a pioneer. "The point is," so runs Herzen's argument,

> that neither the study of the outward forms in isolation nor even the study of comparative anatomy can provide us with a full understanding of the nature of an organism. The "great Goethe" ["veliki Gete," a standing epithet with Herzen for Goethe the natural scientist] was the first to introduce the element of dynamic movement into comparative anatomy; it was he who first demonstrated the possibility of tracing the very process of change in the structure of an organism from its inception through the various stages of its gradual development. His discovery of the laws governing the changes of the parts of the seed into the stamen, the stem, the buds and the leaf and, in turn, the leaf's transformation into all the parts of the flower—led directly to the theory of the genetic development of the parts of the animal organism.

Once again Herzen stresses Goethe's extensive studies of osteology and speaks of one of his most momentous contributions in that field: "Goethe himself devoted much effort to osteology; preoccupied with this subject, while walking in a freshly dug-over cemetery he came by chance upon a skull lying next to its vertebrae; examining these, he was suddenly struck by the thought which subsequently received full citizenship in the science of osteology—the thought that the skull was but a special development of several vertebrae."[90]

While emphasizing Goethe's pioneering achievements and enthusiastically praising his singularly original approach, Goethe's ability "to ask the right questions and elicit the right answers," Herzen was at the same time conscious of the limits even of Goethe's power of insight. "Even Goethe's genetic theory remained what it basically was—pure morphology; reasoning along lines, so to speak, of the geometric development of structural forms, Goethe failed to consider their content, the very materials that constitute those

forms and change along with their change and their development."[91]
And in a significant diary entry, Herzen, the eager student of the
budding science of chemistry, made his criticism of Goethe still
more explicit: "The natural sciences," he wrote, "have had up to
now an extremely unstable basis, because they dealt exclusively with
morphology, slighting those elements that change *within* the forms.
Even Goethe's giant genius did not grasp the importance of the
chemical processes [khimizma] and his 'Metamorphosis of the
Plants' is mere morphology."[92]

Such then was Herzen's view of Goethe, novel in many of its
aspects, perceptive of many essential features of Goethe, the man,
the poet, the scientist. His approach to Goethe—as we have
shown—was not a case of love at first sight; rather it was characterized by an early critical bias against the man and even the poet,
an ideological bias against the aloof aristocrat Goethe, the "Weimar diplomat with the head of Zeus," a bias which never quite
disappeared but gradually became ambivalently paired with a growing appreciation of the incomparable "realistic artist" and mighty
pioneer in the natural sciences. But, above all, Herzen came to
realize that in Goethe the German spirit had found its culmination,
nay, that it transcended itself in the genius of this poet-thinker.
In *From the Other Shore*, he gave to this realization perhaps its most
memorable expression. "Look at Goethe," he wrote,

> he represents the intensified, concentrated, purified, *sub-
> limated* essence of Germany; he sprang from its soil, he
> could not have existed without the entire history of his people,
> but he had so far outdistanced his compatriots into that
> sphere to which he ascended, that they no longer could under-
> stand him clearly and that he, in turn, finally understood
> them only with difficulty; in him became concentrated all
> that stirred the soul of the Protestant world and it grew
> and flourished there so mightily that he soared over the con-
> temporary world like the spirit over the waters. Below him
> —chaos, incomprehension, scholasticism; in him—light of
> consciousness and the calm of cognition that had far out-
> stripped his contemporaries.[93]

No higher tribute could have been paid to Goethe by the "realist" Herzen, determined to be done with idolatry of the ineffable poet, determined to see him clearly as he was, with his greatness but also his faults, his sublimity as well as his "seamy side." May it stand here as the final stroke in the Westerners' portrait of Goethe.

That portrait—as we have seen—was not without its clashing incongruities and contradictions; it was an ambivalent statement of the achievements and shortcomings of the artist and the man. While shattering the Romantic myth of Goethe's infallibility as the god-like creator, the Westerners brought to their Russian contemporaries, at the same time, a deeper appreciation of the true greatness of the German poet as a "realistic" artist as well as of Goethe's remarkably fertile contributions to the natural sciences, thus both correcting and enlarging the Russian image of Goethe.

NOTES

Introduction

1. *Schiller in Russian Literature* (Philadelphia, 1965).

2. *The Russian Hoffmannists* (The Hague, 1963).

3. *Dostoevski the Adapter; a Study in Dostoevski's use of the Tales of Hoffmann* (Chapel Hill, 1954).

4. Cf. Bibliography: Introduction, section: Pushkin and Goethe.

5. Cf. particularly *Germanoslavica*, vols. I and II (1932-33). The 1949 anniversary produced relatively few substantial contributions.

6. "Goethes Beziehungen zu russischen Schriftstellern," *Essays und Studien zur Literaturgeschichte* (Braunschweig, 1889), pp. 231–237.

7. "Goethe bei den Slawen," *Jahrbücher für Kultur und Geschichte der Slawen*, N.F., VIII, Heft 1 (1932), pp. 37–57.

8. "Goethe in Rußland," *Osteuropa*, VIII (1933).

9. "Goethe in Rußland," *Zeitschrift für slawische Philologie*, IX (1932), 335–57; X (1933), 310–34.

10. Cf. Bibliography: Introduction, section: Western Scholarship.

11. "Russkie Pisateli u Gete v Veimare, *Literaturnoe Nasledstvo*, vols. IV-VI (1932), pp. 81–504. This issue of the *Nasledstvo* is one of the richest sources of information on our topic. A highly compressed summary of its contents was carried in *Germanoslavica*, vol. II (1933). Another important source is the Russian periodical *Zvenia*, II (1933).

12. *Gete v Russkoi Literature* (Leningrad, 1937).

13. *Op. cit.*, IX, 335–36. "In dem Verhältnis zu Goethe spiegelt sich die ganze geistige Entwicklung Rußlands,—in ihren Hauptzügen wenigstens."

14. *Op. cit.*, p. 5.

15. J. Thomas Shaw, *The Transliteration of Modern Russian for English-Language Publications* (Madison, Wis., 1967), p. 5.

16. "Salvation by Death," *The London Times Literary Supplement*, Feb. 23, 1967, p. 149.

I: Early Russian Reaction

1. *Zapiski* (Leningrad, 1928), I, 327 ff. For a brief mention of Figel, see R. Jagodich, "Goethe und seine russischen Zeitgenossen," *Germanoslavica*, II (1933), 370.

2. The title of the first edition was *Klavigo, tragedia v piati deistviakh gospodina Gete, perevedina s Nemetskogo* (Petersburg, 1780); the title of the 2nd edition was *Klavigo, tragedia gospodina Gete. Perevedina s Nemetskogo. Vtoroe ispravlennoe izdanie* (Petersburg, 1780). The translation was well received, for the second edition appeared in the year of its publication.

3. In the preface of the first edition. Cf. also Durylin, "Russkie Pisateli u Gete v Vaimare," *Literaturnoe Nasledstvo,* IV-VI (1932). R. Ziemann (transl.), *Russische Schriftsteller bei Goethe* (Berlin, 1957).

4. Durylin, *op. cit.,* p. 94.

5. Cf. Zhirmunski, *Gete v Russkoi Literature* (Leningrad, 1937), p. 47. The two renderings were to be followed by a great number of others. In fact, every important period of Russian literature had its own characteristic version of *Werther.* Thus the "sentimental" period (at the turn of the eighteenth century) produced the unfinished rendering of Andrei Turgeniev and Vasili Zhukovski, the "Romantic" period had its typical version in N. M. Rozhalin's (1829), the "forties" in A. N. Strugovshchikov's, which, to be sure, appeared belatedly in 1865; in the nineties we find two leading efforts, O. N. Khmelëva and A. R. Eiges (both 1892); O. B. Mandelstam's version seems to have remained so far (1962) the accepted if not "official" Soviet rendering.

"*Werther* in Russia" is a theme which has received little attention in Western scholarship. A. Bem's "Der russische Antiwertherismus," *Germanoslavica,* II (1932-33), pp. 357–359, gives a partial view of the problem. S.A. Atkins, in his excellent study, *The Testament of Werther in Poetry and Drama* (Cambridge, Mass., 1949), offers some bibliographical items but does not attempt a descriptive, analytical, or evaluative treatment of this problem. The great number of Russian imitations of Goethe's *Werther* are enumerated and briefly characterized by V. V. Sipovski in *Ocherki iz Istorii Russkogo Romana* (St. Petersburg, 1910), I, 375 ff.

6. Cf. Aleksei Veselovski, *Zapadnoe vliianie v novoi russkoi literature* (Moscow, 1910), esp. pp. 9, 110-12 *et passim.* Also A. N. Pypin, *Die geistige Bewegung in Rußland in der ersten Hälfte des 19. Jahrhunderts* (Berlin, 1894), *passim.* Also Gorlin, *op. cit.,* IX, 338: "Der Einfluß Goethes wird durch die Einwirkung der Franzosen gleichsam neutralisiert."

7. A. N. Radishchev, *Puteshestvie iz Peterburga v Moskvu* (St. Petersburg, 1905), p. 225.

8. This account of Karamzin's visit to Weimar is based on his "Pis'ma Russkogo Puteshestvennika," *Sochineniia Karamzina* (St. Petersburg, 1848), II, 138-54. All quotations are from these pages.

9. *Ibid.,* p. 304.

10. Karamzin, *Sobranye sochineniia,* 3rd ed. (Moscow, 1920), I, 103; "Poslanie k zhenshchinam: Zloschchastnyi Werter ne zakon: Tam grob ego; glaza rukoiu zakryvaiu."

11. K. N. Batiushkov, *Sochineniia* (St. Petersburg, 1887), pp. 477–78 (Letter of Oct. 30, 1813).

12. *Ibid.,* pp. 424-25.

13. Original in the Goethe-Schiller Archiv, Weimar. Quoted by Durylin, *op. cit.,* pp. 265–66. Italics mine. The Russian original of the italicized portion is: "Nezhnyi drug chustvitel'nych serdets" and "v sladkom voskhishchen'i."

14. *Sochinenia Nikolaia Grecha* (St. Petersburg, 1855), "Poezdka vo Frantsiiu, Germaniiu i Shvetsariiu 1817 g. Pis'ma k A. E. Izmailovu," II, 484-91. All quotations are from this source.

15. Great favorite at the Russian court. See our discussion of his attitude toward Goethe, pp. 24–30.

16. Maximilian Klinger (1752–1831) was one of the foremost representatives of the "storm and stress" school and a friend of Goethe.

17. "Otryvki iz zapisnoi knizhki puteshestvennika," *Sovremennik,* V (1837), pp. 304–05.

18. Cf. Aleksei Veselovski, *V. A. Zhukovski: Poezia chuvstva i serdechnago voobrazheniia* (St. Petersburg, 1904), p. 58.

19. See p. 10 above.

20. *Arkhiv brat'ev Turgenievykh* (Akademia Nauk, St. Petersburg, 1911–24), second fascicle, p. 44.

21. Veselovski, *op. cit.,* p. 58.

22. *Loc. cit.*

23. Original in the collection of A. F. Onegin in the Institute of Russian Literature of the Academy of Sciences SSSR. Reproduced by Durylin, *op. cit.,* pp. 290–91.

> Svobodnym geniem natury vdokhnovennyi,
> On v plamennykh chertakh eë izobrazhal;
> I v chustve serdtsa lish' zakony pocherpal,
> Zakonam nikakim drugim ne pokorennyi.

24. *Arkhiv brat'ev Turgenievykh,* p. 82.

25. *Ibid.,* pp. 81–82.

26. *Arkhiv brat'ev Turgenievykh,* p. 263 (letter of Sept. 18).

27. Aleksander Turgeniev's *Diary,* No. 4, sheets 3–4.

28. "Sovremennye Letopisi. Inostrannaia perepiska: Pis'ma iz Dres-

dena." *Moskovski Telegraf,* IV, No. 4 (February 1827), pp. 341–50.

29. A. I. Turgeniev, "Otryvki iz zapisnoi knizhki puteshestvennika," *Sovremennik* (1837), V, 294 f.

30. Given March 22, 1833, in the Imperial St. Petersburg Academy of Sciences on its 100th anniversary. Delivered in French as "Notice sur Goethe," it was immediately translated into Russian by I. Davydov under the title "O Gete"; it soon appeared in German translation in the *Literarische Blätter der Börsen-Halle,* No. 829 (July 3, 1833).

31. Georg Schmid, "Goethe und Uvarov und ihr Briefwechsel," *Russische Revue. Vierteljahrschrift,* vol. XVIII, Heft 2 (St. Petersburg, 1888), pp. 131-82.

32. Letter of December 27, 1810, in the Goethe-Schiller Archiv in Weimar. Reproduced in facsimile in *Literaturnoe Nasledstvo,* IV-VI (1932), 193.

33. Schmid, *op. cit.,* p. 152.

34. Quoted by Zhirmunski, *op. cit.,* p. 290.

35. *Arkhiv brat'ev Turgenievykh,* II, 412 (Letter of Feb. 16, 1810).

36. Otto Harnack, in "Goethes Beziehungen zu russischen Schriftstellern," *Zeitschrift für vergleichende Literaturgeschichte und Renaissance-Literatur,* vol. V (Berlin, 1890), p. 269, makes the excessive claim that "Uvarov was the *first* Russian to have studied Goethe." That "first" properly belongs to the young members of the Friendly Literary Society. Cf. p. 18.

37. Cf. Schmid, *op. cit., passim.*

38. S. Uvarov, *Nonnos von Panopolis, Ein Beitrag zur Geschichte der griechischen Poesie* (St. Petersburg, 1817).

39. S. Ouvaroff, *Etudes de Philologie et de Critique* (St. Petersburg, 1843), pp. 163-64.

40. See *Weimarer Ausgabe,* Bd. XLII, p. 127. Hereafter cited as *W. A.*

41. "Narodnost'" has approximately the meaning of German "Volk."

42. This and the following quotations are from: *O Gete. V torzhestvennom sobranii Imperatorskoi S-Peterburgskoi Akademii Nauk chitano Presidentom Akademii 22 Marta 1833 g.* (Moscow, 1833), p. 15 f.

43. *Gete v Russkoi Literature* (Leningrad, 1937), pp. 292 f.

44. *Loc. cit.*

45. Just prior to this time the Russian Romantic poets elaborated a similar view of Goethe as the "universal genius," a view which must have been known to Turgeniev and may also have influenced him.

46. *Loc. cit.*

47. *Ostapevski Arkhiv Kniazei Viazemskikh* (St. Petersburg, 1899), III, 30. (Letter is dated 1840).

48. V. Belinski, *Sobranye sochineniia v trëkh tomakh* (Moscow, 1948), II, 151.

II: Vasili A. Zhukovski: Goethe's Translator and Interpreter

1. Contributions to our topic include Matthew Volm's study, *W. A. Zhukowskii als Übersetzer* (Ann Arbor, 1945). This is a detailed evaluation and analysis of Zhukovski's translations of Goethe. Unfortunately, however, Volm has chosen to make of his work a polemic against M. Gorlin's views expressed in that author's "Goethe in Russia," *Zeitschrift für slawische Philologie*, IX (1932), 335–57 and X, 310–34. It cannot be said that this approach resulted in an acceptable contribution. Moreover, Volm's work, like Gorlin's, lacks biographical materials. Other sources: M. Ehrhard, *V. A. Joukovski* (Paris, 1938); *Literaturnoe Nasledstvo*, IV-VI (1932); V. Zhirmunski, *Gete v Russkoi Literature* (Leningrad, 1937). P. A. Viskovatov, "Ob Otnosheniakh Zhukovskogo i Gete," *Literaturnyi Vestnik* (Moscow, 1902), pp. 125–140.

2. See, e.g., Aleksei Veselovski, *V. A. Zhukovski: Poezia chustva i serdechnago voobrazheniia* (St. Petersburg, 1904), *passim*.

3. V. Belinski, *Polnoe sobranie sochinenii*, ed. S. A. Vengerov (St. Petersburg, 1901), IV, 5; VII, 469.

4. *Sobranie sochinenii i pisem'* (Moscow, 1934), II, 175.

5. *Gete v Russkoi Literature*, p. 97–98.

6. See chap. I, p. 18; also Veselovski, *op. cit.*, p. 22ff.

7. Ivan Kireievski (1806–56), the outstanding Slavophile literary critic, who would naturally stress Zhukovski's originality, still has to point out that his poetry "was reared on German songs [pesniakh Germanii] and transmitted to us that idealism which represents the distinguishing mark of German life, literature, and philosophy." Cf. *Polnoe sobranie sochinenii* (Moscow, 1911), II, 18.

8. Veselovski, *op. cit.*, p. 328, f.

9. V. A. Zhukovski, *Sochineniia v dvukh tomakh*, ed. A. D. Alferov (Moscow, 1902), I, 517: Zhukovski's letter (1817?) to his friend D. V. Dashkov.

10. I. A. Bychkov, *Neizdannye pis'ma Zhukovskogo k A. P. Zontag* (St. Petersburg, 1912), pp. 5–6.

11. *Dnevniki V. A. Zhukovskogo* (St. Petersburg, 1903), pp. 100, 108. Following quotations, unless otherwise indicated, are from the *Diaries*.

12. *Briefwechsel Sulpiz Boisserée* (Stuttgart, 1862), II, 321–22.

13. I. F. Struve (1763–1828), Russian chargé d'affaires at Weimar and frequent visitor of Goethe.

14. The inscription at the threshold, such as Goethe had seen in Roman houses, e.g., at Pompeii.

15. A copy of the Aldobrandini frieze in the Vatican was made by Johann Heinrich Meyer and presented to Goethe in 1797.

16. "Pis'ma V. A. Zhukovskago k Vel. Kn. Aleksandre Fedorovne iz Pervogo Ego Zagranichnogo Puteshestvia v 1821 G." *Russkaia Starina,* CX (1902), II, 357.

17. Zweite unveränderte Auflage (Leipzig: Verlag Duncker und Humbolt, 1874), pp. 133–34. (The German original was not available to me; I quote here on the basis of a Russian translation of the original by Durylin, *op. cit.,* pp. 331–32).

18. To S. Boisserée (Jena, Nov. 1, 1821). Cf. *W. A.,* Abt IV, Bd. 35, pp. 174–75.

19. To V. A. Joukoffsky (Weimar, Nov. 16, 1821). Cf. *W. A.,* Abt. IV, Bd. 35, pp. 172–73.

20. Zhukovski's letter seems not to have been preserved among Goethe's papers. A rough draft, however, did survive, was first published in the *Russki Archiv* (1870), pp. 1817–20, and is now in the possession of the Institute of Russian Literature in Leningrad. Cf. *Literaturnoe Nasledstvo,* IV-VI (1932), 333.

21. Zhukovski's attempt to render the German "Zwischenspiel" (dated Sept. 1, 1827). *Diaries,* p. 202.

22. A. I. Turgeniev, who also met the lady at the time, characterizes her as "clever, kind, learned; she taught the daughters of the Grandduchess Maria Pavlovna, knew Goethe quite well . . ." Cf. *Arkhiv bratiev Turgenievykh,* VI, 247.

23. *Goethes Unterhaltungen mit dem Kanzler Müller* (Hgg. von C. A. Burckhardt) (Stuttgart, 1870), p. 119. Henceforth cited as *Müller.*

24. *Gerhardt von Reutern; Ein Lebensbild, dargestellt von seinen Kindern* (St. Petersburg, 1894), pp. 51–52.

25. *W. A.,* Abt. III, Bd. 11, p. 106.

26. *Müller,* pp. 119–20.

27. Original in the Goethe-Schiller Archiv in Weimar. Cf. *Literaturnoe Nasledstvo,* IV–VI, p. 349.

28. *W. A.,* Abt. IV, Bd. 43, p. 94. Goethe's letter to J. H. Meyer, Meyer, Weimar, Sept. 30, 1827.

29. *Literaturnoe Nasledstvo,* IV-VI (1932), 347.

30. *Müller,* p. 120.

31. The Russian version has "chudesno-pyshnyi," "wondrously rich, luxuriant."

32. *Müller,* p. 121.

33. Ehrhard, *op. cit.,* p. 297.

34. A very cordial letter of Chancellor von Müller to Zhukovski, dated October 14, 1837, shows that his memory at Weimar survived the intervening years. Cf. "Briefe des Kanzlers Friedrich Müller an Wassily Andrejewitsch Zhukovsky" (Hgg. von Adelheid von Schorn), *Deutsche Rundschau,* XI (1904), 284.

35. *Polnoe sobranie v odnom tome,* ed. P. B. Smirnovski (2nd ed., Moscow, 1905), p. 61. Henceforth cited as *Polnoe sobranie.*

36. Cf. Veselovski, *Zhukovski,* pp. 355ff.

37. *Ibid.,* pp. 358–59.

38. *Polnoe sobranie,* sect. "Prose," pp. 156–57.

39. *Sochineniia Zhukovskogo,* ed. Efreimov (Moscow, 1878), V, 341.

40. "Moia Boginia" (Podrazhenie Gëte) in *Polnoe sobranie,* p. 23.

41. Kăkúiŭ bĕzsmértnŭiŭ / Vĕnchát' prĕdpŏchtítĕl'no / Prĕd vsémĭ bŏgínĭamĭ / Ŏlímpă nădzvézdnăgŏ, etc.

42. "Motylёk," *Polnoe sobranie,* p. 49. Goethe's dragonfly, that sharp, sudden, glittering symbol, has yielded here to the conventional butterfly. Cf. Charles Passage, "The Influence of Goethe, Schiller, and E. T. A. Hoffmann in Russia, 1800–40." Unpublished dissertation, Harvard University, 1942, p. 56.

43. A prose rendering of the relevant passage: "Alas, once the wings are touched with heavy fingers, all delicate colors are rubbed out. The butterfly does still exist, but beauty has all vanished. 'That is how joy deceives us–' I said with a deep sigh. 'It gleams as long as you don't touch it; a touch and all the gleam is gone.' "

44. *Für Wenige-Dlia Nemnogikh* (Moscow, 1818). The original purpose of this work was to serve as a text providing Zhukovski's royal pupil, Aleksandra Fёdorovna (Russian name of Charlotte of Prussia, daughter of Queen Louise) with Russian materials placed opposite well-known German texts, thus facilitating her study of Russian.

45. Cf. "Rybak" and "Zhaloba Pastukha," *Polnoe sobranie,* pp. 224, 253.

46. "Lesnoi Czar," *Polnoe sobranie,* p. 224.

47. Zhukovski translated this poem twice and imitated it in his own ballads, "Svetlana" and "Liudmila." Cf. *Polnoe sobranie,* p. 241, for the translation; "Svetlana," p. 203; "Liudmila," p. 197.

48. "Uteshenie v Slezakh," *Polnoe sobranie,* p. 51.

49. "Iz Gete," *ibid.,* p. 49.

50. "Mina," *ibid.,* p. 53.

51. "K Mesiatsu," *ibid.,* p. 51.

52. "Novaia Liubov'," *ibid.,* p. 53.

53. "Opiat' ty zdes ', moi blagodarnyi geni," *ibid.,* p. 261.

54. *Ibid.,* p. 62.

55. Walter Silz, "Goethe: 'Der Wanderer'," *Stoffe, Formen, Strukturen; H. H. Borchardt zum 75. Geburtstag* (Munich, 1962), p. 139.

56. "Obety," "Pamiatniki," "Mysli," *Polnoe sobranie,* pp. 66, 74.

57. "Orël i Golubka," *ibid.,* p. 160.

58. Cf. Gorlin, *op. cit.,* IX, 345.

III: Aleksander Pushkin and Michael Lermontov

1. *Sobranye sochineniia v chetyrëkh tomakh,* Adademia Nauk (Moscow, 1958), has 25 items of "plans, sketches, topics" and 16 of autobiographical jottings. Cf. IV, 503–632. Henceforth cited as *Sob. Soch.*

2. *Ibid.,* I, 491.

3. A. Pushkin, *Sochineniia,* in the series: *Russkie Klassiki* (New York, n.d.), pp. 305–06. Henceforth referred to as *Soch.*

The Russian critic V. Belinski, writing on the "scene" shortly upon its publication, stresses the originality of Pushkin's creation: "This work . . . was certainly no translation from the dramatic poem of Goethe, no variation of a theme." *Polnoe sobranie sochinenii* (St. Petersburg, 1901), III, 615.

4. The extreme positions in the debate are represented by V. A. Rozov in *Pushkin i Gete* (Kiev, 1908), who argues rather loosely that Pushkin turned to Goethe not only for inspiration but also for a great number of specific themes, and by A. Veselovski ("A. S. Pushkin i evropeiskaia poesia," *Zhizn',* V (1899), who flatly states: "The German lyrical element [and he singles out Goethe] was utterly alien to Pushkin

even in his early school days and failed to find favor with him after conscious contact with it in his mature years" (p. 15). More recent scholarship tends to side with Veselovski. See, e.g., M. Gorlin, "Goethe in Rußland," *Zeitschrift für slawische Philologie*, IX and X (1932–33), *passim;* V. Zhirmunski, *Gete v Russkoi Literature*, pp. 133–34; M. Karpovich, *Centennial Essays for Pushkin* (Cambridge, 1937), pp. 185–86. Fritz Strich, in *Goethe und die Weltliteratur* (Bern, 1946), pp. 340f., echoes Otto Harnack's "Goethes Beziehungen zu russischen Schriftstellern," *Essays und Studien zur Literaturgeschichte* (Braunschweig, 1889), and overestimates Goethe's influence on Pushkin. Also G. Glebov, "Pushkin i Gete," *Zvenia*, II (1933), 41–67.

5. Cf. chap, I, pp. 8–9.

6. *Zapiski* (Leningrad, 1928), I, 327–28.

7. Introduction to Luther's edition of Pushkin's *Werke* (Leipzig, n. d.), I, 9. Also see A. Veselovski, *op. cit.,* p. 175.

8. *Soch.,* p. 217.

9. Wilma Pohl, *Russische Faust-Übersetzungen, Veröffentlichungen des slawisch-baltischen Seminars der westfälischen Wilhelms-Universität Münster* (Meisenheim am Glan, 1962), No. 5, pp. 16ff.

10. See B. L. Modzalevski, *Biblioteka Pushkina* (St. Petersburg, 1910), *passim.* For a typical example of uncritical borrowing in Russian periodicals from the French source, see *Sorevnovatel'*, p. 23 (Moscow, 1823). Here an anonymous Russian critic writing on "Romantic Literature" admits frankly his total indebtedness to Mme de Staël. Her interpretation of the "artistic elements in German literature is of such perfection as to leave nothing to be desired and is thus the best possible." Therefore he "merely translates her words into his own tongue" (p. 227). On this problem see I. I. Zamotin, *Romanticism dvadtsatykh godov XIX-ogo stoletiia v russkoi literature* (Moscow, n. d.), I, 90ff.

11. See chap. V.

12. A. Veselovski, *V. A. Zhukovski* (St. Petersburg, 1904), I, p. 11.

13. *Moskovskii Vestnik*, XI (1828), p. 105.

14. Harnack, *op. cit.,* p. 326.

15. The "legend" launched by Harnack that Goethe had sent a pen (eine Schreibfeder) to Pushkin as a tangible token of his affection and esteem has been recently subjected to searching criticism by Maximilian von Propper in "Goethe und Puschkin – Wahrheit und Legende", *Goethe* (1950), XII, 218–59. Also A. L. Weinberg, "Pero Gete u Pushkina," *Zvenia*, II (1933), 67f.

16. Especially in A. S. Pushkin, *Polnoe sobranie sochinenii* (Moscow, 1935f). Henceforth cited as *Pol. sob.*

17. "Goethe bei den Slawen," *Jahrbuch für Kultur und Geschichte der Slawen*, "Neue Folge" (1932), VIII, 49f.

18. *Pol. sob.*, V, 105.

19. *Ibid.*, VI, 345.

20. *Sochineniia Pushkina*, ed. Akademia Nauk (Leningrad, n. d.), IX, bk. I, 210. Henceforth cited as *Soch. Pushkina.*

21. *Ibid.*, bk. II, p. 27.

22. *Pol. sob.*, VI, 22.

23. *Pis'ma Pushkina*, ed. Modzalevski (Moscow, n. d.), I, 74. On Pushkin's "exile" in its connection with this passage see also Strich, *op. cit.*, p. 340.

24. *Pol. sob.*, IX, 68.

25. Pushkin, *Sochineniia* (St. Petersburg, 1915), VI, 3.

26. *Soch. Pushkina*, IX, bk. II, p. 929.

27. P. N. Berkov, "Werther in Puschkins *Eugen Onegin*," *Germanoslavica*, II (1933), 72ff.

28. *Soch.*, p. 166. (*Evgeni Onegin*, bk. VIII, part 47) Following quotations are from this source.

29. TATIANA: "I have been married to another. To him I shall remain forever faithful."
    LOTTE: "Warum denn mich, Werther? just mich, das Eigentum eines anderen?"

30. A. Bem, "Faust v tvorchestve Pushkina" *Slavia*, XIII (1934), 378ff.

31. *Soch.*, p. 431. Pushkin characterizes Hermann as follows: "He has the profile of Napoleon and the soul of Mephisto." *Pis'ma Pushkina*, V. 521.

32. *Soch.*, p. 432. Following quotations are from this source.

33. *Soch.*, p. 89.

34. Glebov draws heavily on the fragmentary poem, "Faust in Hell" (*Soch. Pushkina*, IV, 194 and notes on pp. 276–80), on the "program" for "scenes from the age of knighthood" (*ibid.*, VII, 339), and on a plan for a drama "Pope Joan" (*ibid.*, VII, 256) to show the subtle influence of and covert parallels to Goethe's *Faust*. These fragments are too slight to furnish support for Glebov's thesis. Cf. Glebov, *op. cit.*, esp. pp. 45–54. Also cf. Zhirmunski, *op. cit.*, pp. 137–39.

35. *Pol. sob.*, IX, 56f.

36. P. V. Annenkov, *A. S. Pushkin v Aleksandrovskoi epokhe* (Moscow, 1874), p. 153.

37. The *Scene* first appeared in the *Moskovski Vestnik,* IX (1826), under its original title: "A New Scene between Faust and Mephisto." For a summary of all the Russian reviews and often very far-fetched interpretations, see J. Legras, "Pouchkine et Goethe, la 'Scène tirée de Faust,' " *Revue de Littérature Comparée,* XVIII (1937), 117–28. Legras comes to the obvious conclusion that Pushkin, despite his lack of knowledge of German, must have had a general knowledge of Goethe's *Faust.*

38. Here Pushkin may have been influenced by the *Fragment* (1790), where "Wald und Höhle" followed the "Brunnen" scene and thus came *after* rather than *before* Gretchen's ravishment.

39. A. Bem, *op. cit., passim,* tends to exaggerate Pushkin's dependence on the "Wald und Höhle" scene and neglects to give due stress to the salient differences. These had been early recognized by Belinski: "This work is the development and amplification of the thought which Pushkin had previously expressed in his small poem 'The Demon.' " *Polnoe sobranie sochinenii* (St. Petersburg, 1900), III, 615. Belinski did not seem to be aware of the interconnections between the Demon and Goethe's Mephisto which we have pointed out above.

40. *Soch.,* p. 305: "mne skuchno, bes."

41. Cf. V. Sechkarëv, "Über die Langeweile bei Puschkin," *Solange Dichter leben* (Krefeld, 1949), p. 144: ". . . es [the Scene] ist der gelungene Versuch die Langeweile als metaphysisches Problem in größter Kürze und Deutlichkeit zu behandeln." Cf. also Gorlin, *op. cit.,* X, 310: 'Dieser Faust hat . . . überhaupt nichts Faustisches: sein Grundgefühl ist nicht die ewige Unrast, die schöpferische Unruhe, sondern die Langeweile."

42. As has been convincingly demonstrated by John G. Frank, "Pushkin and Goethe," *Slavonic and East European Review,* XXVI (1947), p. 148f.

43. Sechkarëv, *loc. cit.*

44. Martin Heidegger, *Was ist Metaphysik?* (Bonn, 1931), p. 14.

45. R. Guardini, *Vom Sinn der Schwermut* (Zürich, 1949), pp. 26f. Cf. also Walter Rehm, *Gontscharow und Jacobsen oder Langeweile und Schwermut* (Göttingen, 1963).

46. *Soch.,* p. 306.

47. *Goethes sämtliche Werke, Jubiläums Ausgabe,* XIV, 255. Henceforth cited as *Jubiläums Ausgabe.*

48. Cf. A. Veselovski, *Zapadnoe vliianie v novoi russkoi literature*. (Moscow, 1910), p. 183 and n. 2. Veselovski categorically denies any influence by Goethe's *Götz* on Pushkin's *Boris Godunov*.

49. *Soch.*, pp. 221f. Cf. *Henry IV*, Part II, Act IV, Scene 4.

50. Especially in the scenes: "Devich'e pole," p. 197; "Korchma na litovskoi granitse," pp. 201f.; "Kreml', Dom Borisa," p. 224.

51. Pushkin seems to have relied for his knowledge of Goethe's play chiefly on Mme de Staël's discussion of it in *De l'Allemagne* and on French translations; the first, by A. Stapfer, had appeared in Paris early in 1825. The first Russian translation, by Pogodin, was published in 1828, three years after Pushkin had completed his *Godunov*.

52. Glebov, *op. cit.*, pp. 53–54.

53. Zhirmunski, *op. cit.*, p. 438.

54. For Schiller's preeminence as an early influence on Lermontov, see Edmund Kostkas' article on "Lermontov's debt to Schiller," *Revue de Littérature Comparée*, XXXVII, 1, 68–88; also his *Schiller in Russian Literature*, (Philadelphia, 1965), chap. II.

55. B. M. Eichenbaum, *Lermontov. Opyt istoriko-literaturnoi otsenki* (Leningrad, 1924), p. 33. Brodski, the Soviet biographer of Lermontov, has this to say of his appreciation of literature: "The role of the book, of reading, was an immense one in the life of Lermontov." *M. Y. Lermontov* (Moscow, 1945), I, 171. Henceforth cited as Brodski. Another useful source: S. Shuvalov, "Vliianiia na tvorchestvo Lermontova russkoi i evropeiskoi poezii." *Venok M. Y. Lermontovu –iubileinyi sbornik* (Moscow and Petrograd, 1914).

56. The voyage, as planned by the father, would have taken place in 1830, almost two years before Goethe's death.

57. Brodski, I, 16.

58. *Sob. soch.*, IV, 527–28.

59. Brodski, p. 34.

60. Brodski, p. 52.

61. Brodski, p. 68.

62. See chap. I, p. 18.

63. Brodski, p. 74. Belinski, however, recalled that Merzliakov was known to extol the beauties of such a "Classical" poet as Sumarokov while "poking fun at Shakespeare, Schiller and Goethe as exemplars of bad taste in esthetics." Belinski, *Sob. soch. v trëkh tomakh* (Moscow, 1948), III, 503.

64. See chap. V, pp. 125–131.

65. Brodski, p. 110.

66. Brodski, p. 129.

67. V. A. Mannilov, *M. Y. Lermontov* (Moscow, 1958), p. 9.

68. See E. Kostka, "Schiller's Influence on the Early Dramas of Lermontov," *P. Q.* XXXII (Oct. 1953), 396–410.

69. Brodski, p. 147.

70. A. I. Gertsen, *Sobranie sochinenii v 30 tomakh,* Ak. Nauk (Moscow, 1956), VII, 225.

71. *Sob. soch.,* IV, 529.

72. *Sob. soch.,* I, 49.

73. *Sob. soch.,* II, 481.

74. *Jubiläums Ausgabe,* I, 44.

75. *Sob. soch.,* II, 488–99: "Ditia moë/ Ostansia zdes' so mnoi:/ V vode privol'noe zhit'ë/ I kholod i pokoi./ Ia sozovu moikh sestër/ my *pliaskoi krugovoi*/ Razveselim tumannyi vzor/ I dukh ustalyi tvoi/ . . . O milyi moi! Ne utaiu,/ Chto ia tebia liubliu,/ liubliuu kak vol'nuiu struiu/ liubliu kak zhizn' moiu . . ." (italics mine). For additional examples of "borrowing" see E. Rosenkranz, *Lermontov und Goethe. Der russische Gedanke* (Bonn, 1929).

76. *Sob. soch.,* I, 491.

77. *Sob. soch.,* I, 195. Also cf. "Moë zaveshchanie," *Sob. soch.,* IV, 528f.

78. For convenient comparison, see *Deutsche Dichtung in russischer Übertragung,* ed. M. Hellmann (Weimar, 1948), p. 260; also *Jubiläums Ausgabe,* XVI, 143: "Ich habe deinen Vater in einem Zettelchen gebeten, meine Leiche zu schützen. . . ." Cf. also I. Eiges, "Perevod M. Y. Lermontova iz 'Vertera Gete,' " *Zvenia,* II (1933), 72–74. For the translation see *Pol. sob.,* I, 209–10. The translation comprises 15 lines of free versification of part of Werther's last letter.

79. "Wanderers Nachtlied: Ein Gleiches," *Jubiläums Ausgabe,* I, 64.

80. We find ourselves in disagreement here with Zhirmunski who, in his surprisingly brief reference to Lermontov's appreciation of Goethe, calls this translation by Lermontov "significantly distanced, . . . especially in its general emotional coloration," from Goethe's original. Zhirmunski, *op. cit.,* p. 439.

81. Brodski, 153.

82. "Zhurnalist, chitatel' i pisatel'," *Sob. soch.,* I, 475f.

83. *Sob. soch.,* II, 404.

84. Another such instance is the appearance of Faust and Mephisto in

the poem of political satire, "The Feast of Asmodeus" (Pir Asmodeia),
Sob. soch., I, 282.

85. *Sob. soch.,* IV, 61. All subsequent quotations are from this source.

86. See pp. 67–68.

87. Brodski, p. 297.

88. *Sob. soch.,* II, 523.

89. *Sob. soch.,* II, 548.

90. *Sob. soch.,* II, 528.

91. *Sob. soch.,* II, 507.

92. *Sob. soch.,* IV, 405.

93. *Sob. soch.,* IV, 365.

94. *Sob. soch.,* IV, 367f.

95. *Sob. soch.,* IV, 370.

96. *Sob. soch.,* IV, 377.

97. *Sob. soch.,* IV, 387.

98. *Sob. soch.,* IV, 404.

99. Cf. Gretchen's words: "Der Mensch . . . ist mir in tiefster Seele
verhaßt . . . Hab ich vor dem Menschen ein heimlich Grauen/ Und
halt ihn für einen Schelm dazu."

100. *Sob. soch.,* IV, 399. Cf. especially the Maksim Maksimich episode.
pp. 325ff.

101. *Sob. soch.,* IV, 365.

102. *Sob. soch.,* IV, 469.

103. *Sob. soch.,* IV, 437.

104. *Sob. soch.,* IV, 364.

105. *Sob. soch.,* IV, 438.

106. *Sob. soch.,* IV, 411.

107. *Sob. soch.,* IV, 442. In another self-analytical passage Pechorin
speaks of the "two halves of his soul." *Ibid.,* IV, 405.

108. Cf. for example, Zhirmunski, *op. cit.,* 438f.

109. Kostka, *Schiller in Russian Literature,* p. 80.

IV: The Pushkin Pleiade and the Decembrists

1. P. A. Viazemski, *Polnoe sobranie sochinenii* (Moscow, N. D.), XI,
83 and 218.

2. The poem bears the German title, "Kennst du das Land," and

utilizes this line as a refrain. Cf. Viazemski, *Pol sobr. soch.,* IV, 201–02.

3. V. A. Rozov, *Pushkin i Gete* (Kiev, 1908), p. 51.

4. A. Delvig, *Polnoe sobranie sochinenii,* ed. B. V. Tomashevski (Moscow, 1934).

5. *Sochineniia Pushkina,* Ak. Nauk, IX, 136, "Delvig."

6. *Iazykovski Arkhiv, vypusk I* "Pis'ma N. M. Iazykova k rodnym za Derpski period ego zhizni, 1822–29," (Moscow, 1913), p. 153.

7. *Ibid.,* 158.

8. D. S. Mirsky, *A History of Russian Literature* (New York, 1949), p. 122.

9. *Ibid.,* 104.

10. I am quoting from the German translation of Baratynski's poem by the Russian symbolist Viacheslav Ivanov, *Corona,* IV (1933–34), p. 697. For the Russian original cf. Baratynski, E., *Stikhotvorenie,* ed. I. Medvedeva (Moscow, 1945), pp. 93–94.

11. Cf. chap. II.

12. Gorlin, "Goethe in Rußland," *Zeitschrift für slawische Philologie,* IX (1932), 356–57.

13. Cf. chap. V.

14. A helpful source, especially on Küchelbecker, is the volume *Dekabristy i ikh vremia: Materialy i soobshcheniia,* ed. M. P. Alekseev and B. S. Meilakh, Ak. Nauk (Moscow and Leningrad, 1951).

15. Not to be confused with Prince Vladimir Odoevski (1803–69) whose views on Goethe will be discussed in Chap. V, pp. 119–124.

16. Durylin, "Russkie pisateli u Gete v Veimare," *Literaturnoe Nasledstvo.,* IV–VI, 394: "All sympathy, all love of this generation was lavished upon Byron—for Goethe there remained only a cold politeness."

17. M. I. Semevski, "Aleksander Bestuzhev v Irkutske. Neizdannye pis'ma ego k rodnym." *Russki Vestnik,* V (1870), 245–46 (letter of Dec. 14, 1828): "Pour moi, je plonge dans le germanisme et par pure vanité je vous prie de dire a Jakouskine que dans l'espace d'un mois de lecture je suis même capable de lire Schiller et Goethe sans l'aide de personne. . . . Maintenent je ne m'étonne plus que le fièvre de Schwärmerei gagnes les esprits faibles; dans les deux auteurs elle est investie d'une grace naive et entreinante."

18. *Ibid.*

19. *Ibid.* (Letter of Jan. 18, 1829).

20. *Ibid.,* p. 254 (Letter of March 25, 1829).

21. It took place in 1824 and was recorded by Bestuzhev in 1829. It was published in *Otechestvennye Zapiski,* October 1860, under the title, "Znakomstvo A. A. Bestuzheva s Griboedom," pp. 633–40.

22. N. K. Piksanov, *Griboedov* (Moscow, 1935), p. 264f.

23. A. S. Griboedov, *Sobranye sochineniia,* ed. N. K. Piksanov (Leningrad, 1930f), I, 11–12.

24. Cf. *Vtoroe polnoe sobranie A. Marlinskogo* (4th ed., St. Petersburg, 1847), III, pt. XI, 196–97.

25. "Coup d'oeil sur l'état actuel de la litérature russe," *Conservateur Imperial* (1817), No. 77. I am quoting from the Russian translation which appeared in the *Vestnik Evropy,* XVII-XVIII (1817), 154–57.

26. Letter of Dec. 21, 1845, reproduced in N. Dubrovin, "Zhukovski i ego otnosheniia k dekabristam," *Russkaia Starina,* CX (1902)', 94.

27. Cf. *Literaturnoe Nasledstvo,* IV-VI, pp. 663–66.

28. *W. A.,* Abt. III, Bd. VII, p. 251.

29. Cf. *Literaturnoe Nasledstvo,* IV-VI (1932), 382. Also compare *Russkaia Starina,* XIII (1875), 341–42.

30. Fëdor Petrovich Tolstoi (1783–1873), engraver, sculptor. Goethe's references to Tolstoi are in *W. A.,* Abt. III, Bd. VI, pp. 155 and 252. A brief essay on Tolstoi by Meier with Goethe's collaboration is in *Kunst und Altertum,* Bd. II, Heft I, pp. 177–81; another in Heft II, pp. 187–90.

31. *Mnemozina,* pt. I (1824), p. 89 (letter of Nov. 10, 1820). Also P. Kirchner and R. Ziemann (ed.), *Fahrten nach Weimar. Slawische Gäste bei Goethe. Beiträge zur deutschen Klassik* (Weimar, 1789), p. 21. Another meeting is recorded by Goethe under date of Nov. 23: "Der junge Küchelbecker. Mittag zu vieren . . ." (*W. A.,* Abt. III, Bd. VII, p. 251). We have no record by Küchelbecker of this meeting.

32. *Fahrten nach Weimar,* p. 21.

33. *Ibid.,* pp. 22–23.

34. Cf. *W. A.,* Abt. III, Bd. 7, p. 252.

35. *W. A.,* Abt. I, Bd. 34, p. 185.

36. *Literaturnoe Nasledstvo,* IV-VI (1932), 660–61

37. *Moskovskii Telegraf,* XI (1826), sect. 2, 3–5.

38. In the Russian periodical *Mnemozina,* part II (1824), 29–41, in the article "O napravlenie nashei poezii, osobenno liricheskoi, v poslednee desiatiletie," esp. pp. 33, 35, 41.

39. "Razgovor s Bulgarinym," *Mnemozina,* pt. III (1824), 157–77.

40. *Mnemozina*, pt. III (1824), 171–72.

41. *Mnemozina*, pt. IV (1824), 173.

42. *Mnemozina*, pt. V (1824), 190.

43. *Dnevnik V. K. Kiukhel'bekera. Materialy k istorii russkoi litera-turnoi i obshchestvennoi zhizni 10 – 40 godov XIX veka* (Leningrad, 1929), p. 199 (July 7, 1934). Henceforth cited as *Dnevnik.*

44. *Dnevnik*, p. 69 (Aug. 9, 1833).

45. *Dnevnik*, p. 50 (April 25, 1832).

46. *Dnevnik*, p. 188, "Several volumes of Goethe."

47. *Dnevnik*, p. 218 (Oct. 31, 1834).

48. *Dnevnik*, p. 199 (June 30, 1834). For a brief discussion of the influences on Izhorski see Zhirmunski, *Gete v Russkoi Literature,* pp. 157–58.

49. *Dnevnik*, p. 210 (Sept. 9, 1834).

50. *Dnevnik*, pp. 210–11 (Sept. 10, 1834).

51. *Dnevnik*, p. 195.

52. 1st ed., 1828; 2nd ed., in 4 vols., 1836.

53. V. K. Küchelbecker to N. G. Glinka on Sept. 13, 1839. No. 26 in *Dekabristy i ikh vremia; materialy i soobshcheniia,* ed. M. P. Alekseeva and B. S. Mailakha, Ak. Nauk (Moscow and Leningrad, 1951), pp. 78–79.

54. *Loc. cit.* (italics his).

55. *Loc. cit.*

56. *Loc. cit.*

57. *Dnevnik*, p. 252.

58. *Dnevnik*, p. 275 (March 5, 1841). Belinski's article is discussed in chap. VI, pp. 192–198.

V: The Russian Romanticists

1. As quoted by N. L. Brodski in *Evgeni Onegin, Roman A. S. Pushkina* (Moscow, 1950), p. 81.

2. *Zapiski A. I. Koshelëva (1812–1833 Gody)* (Berlin, 1884), p. 6f.

3. N. V. Riasanovski, *Russia and the West in the Teaching of the Slavophiles* (Cambridge, Mass, 1952), esp. pp. 18–20; P. N. Sakulin *Iz Istorii Russkago Idealisma* (Moscow, 1913), *passim.*

4. Sakulin, *op. cit.,* I, 139.

5. D. S. Mirsky, *A History of Russian Literature* (New York, 1949), p. 107.

6. In the journal *Galatea,* VII (1829), 40–41. As reported by N. L. Brodski in *M. Y. Lermontov* (Moscow, 1945), I, 184f.

7. D. V. Venevitinov, *Polnoe sobranie sochinenii* (Moscow, 1934), p. 100.

8. *Ibid.,* pp. 134–57: "Zemnaia uchast' khudozhnika"; "Apofeoza khudozhnika." Cf. *Jubiläums Ausgabe,* VII, 144–60.

9. *Jubiläums Ausgabe,* VII, 144.

10. Venevitinov, *Polnoe sobranie sochinenii,* p. 143. A comparison with Venevitinov's poem "Poet and Friend, an Elegy" (pp. 120–22) shows striking similarities in theme, general tone and rhythm with the translation.

11. The "Monolog Fausta v peshchere" was first published in *Moskovski Vestnik,* vol I (1827). All the others appeared for the first time in the *Collected Works* published in 1829. Now in Venevitinov's *Polnoe sobranie sochinenii,* pp. 143–76. Cf. *Jubiläums Ausgabe,*XIII,44–47(lines 1064–141) and 140–141 (lines 3217–50).

12. *Jubiläums Ausgabe,* XIII, 146–47 (lines 3374–413). Venevitinov, *Pol. sob. soch.,* pp. 160–62 (Pesn' Margarity).

13. Venevitinov, *op. cit.,* p. 161.

14. *Ibid.,* pp. 163–76. Cf. *Jubiläums Ausgabe,* XI, 245–59.

15. Venevitinov, *op. cit.,* p. 233.

16. P. N. Sakulin, *Iz istorii russkago idealizma. Kniaz V. F. Odoevski. Myslitel' – pisatel'* (Moscow, 1913), pt. 1, p. 503. Sakulin is our chief source. He quotes extensively from Odoevski's papers which have not been published. Henceforth cited as Sakulin.

17. Sakulin, pt. 2, p. 367.

18. Sakulin, pt. 1, p. 498.

19. Sakulin, pt. 2, p. 367. Schelling, Carus, and Herder are the other "elect."

20. *Loc. cit.* Cf. also Gorlin, "Goethe in Rußland," *Zeitschrift für slawische Philologie,* IX (1932), 352. Odoevski shows "eine größere Nähe zu Goethe . . . Das Interesse für die philosophische Seite des Goetheschen Schaffens erstickt bei ihm nicht das Verständnis für die Vielseitigkeit seiner Persönlichkeit . . ."

21. "4338—god. Peterburgskiia pis'ma. Ot Ippolita Tsungieva, studenta Glavnoi Pekingskoi shkoly, k Linginu, studentu toi-zhe shkoly." Only a fragment of the work has been published (In Utrenaia Zaria

[Moscow, 1840], pp. 307–52). I draw upon Sakulin's detailed summary and his extensive quotations from the unpublished portions. Cf. Sakulin, pt. 2, pp. 178–202.

22. Sakulin, pt. 2, p. 184.

23. *Russkie Nochi.* Cf. *Sochineniia Kniazia V. F. Odoevskago* (St. Petersburg, 1844), pt. 1, p. 156. Henceforth cited as *Sochineniia Kniazia.*

24. Cf. Sakulin, pt. 2, p. 231. "The central figure is Faust; it is precisely to him that the author has transferred all his own rights (prava!) and ideas, including his 'Russian skepticism.'" And on p. 239: "Evidently we are justified in characterizing Faust's philosophy with the same term that applies to the author's own world views, philosophico-mystical idealism."

25. Sakulin, pt. 2, p. 226.

26. *Sochineniia Kniazia,* p. 163.

27. *Sochineniia Kniazia,* p. 606.

28. Sakulin, pt. 2, p. 366.

29. *Loc. cit.*

30. *Ibid.*

31. Sakulin, pt. 1, p. 581.

32. Sakulin, pt. 1, p. 489 (Italics by Odoevski).

33. For example, R. Magnus, *Goethe as a Scientist* (New York, 1949); or Andreas Wachsmuth, "Goethes naturwissenschaftliches Denken im Spiegel seiner Dichtung seit 1790," *Sinn und Form,* XII, 20–42, among many others.

34. S. P. Shevyrëv, *Teoria poezii v istoricheskom razvitii u drevnikh i novykh narodov* (Moscow, 1836), p. 372.

35. *Moskovski Vestnik,* V (1827), No. 20, 476.

36. *Ibid.,* VI (1827), No. 22.

37. *Ibid.,* VI, 3–8.

38. *Ibid.,* VI, 79–93.

39. *Ibid.,* VI, 505, "Zhurnalist i zloi dukh."

40. *Ibid.,* VI, 6.

41. *Ibid.,* VI, 82.

42. *Ibid.,* VI, 83.

43. *Ibid.,* VI, 87f.

44. *Ibid.,* VI, 90f.

45. *Loc. cit.*

46. *Ibid.,* VI, 92.

47. *Ibid.,* VI, 91.

48. *Ibid.,* VI, 93.

49. *Moskovski Vesnik,* pt. IX (1827), pp. 326f.

50. *W. A.* Abt. III, Bd. 11, p. 186.

51. Vol. VI (1828), no. 34, pp. 309f.

52. No. II (1828), pp. 430f.

53. *Über Kunst und Altertum* (1828), VI, pt. 2, p. 424. Also in *W. A.* (1903), Abt. II, Bd. 42, pt. 2, p. 357.

54. See especially: *W. A.* Abt III, Bd. 11, pp. 191-93 (diary entries of March 12, 14, 15); *W. A.,* Abt. IV, Bd. 44, p. 101 (letter to Zelter); *ibid.,* p. 358 (letter to Carlyle).

55. *Moskovski Vestnik,* IX (1828), No. 11, 326–33).

56. *W. A.* (1909), Abt. IV, Bd. 44, p. 78–81.

57. *Moskovski Vestnik,* X (1828), 56–69.

58. *Ibid.,* X, p. 57.

59. *Ibid.,* X, p. 58.

60. *Ibid.,* X, pp. 62f.

61. *Moskovski Vestnik,* XII (1828), pp. 109–28. All following quotations in our discussion of Shevyrëv's interpretation of *Götz* are from these pages.

62. For a balanced discussion of Shevyrëv's relation to the Slavophiles, cf. Nicholas V. Riasonovsky, "Pogodin and Shevyrëv in Russian Intellectual History." *Harvard Slavic Studies,* IV (1952), 149–67.

63. *Istoria poezii* (St. Petersburg, 1887), I, 59, 62.

64. *Loc. cit.*

65. *Op. cit.,* p. 47.

66. *Loc. cit.* (Italics mine).

67. See above, p. 129.

68. *Teoria poezii v istoricheskom razvitii u drevnikh i novykh narodov* (Moscow, 1836), pp. 285–92. All subsequent quotations are from these pages unless otherwise indicated. Henceforth cited as *Teoria.*

69. *Teoria,* pp. 277f.

70. *Jubiläums Ausgabe,* XXXIII, 102–24. Shevyrëv's quotation is on p. 116, beginning with: "Eines der vorzüglichsten Kennzeichen des Verfalls" to "als wenn ein Rundes hervorbringen will."

71. *Ibid.,* pp. 13–19. Shevyrëv's quotation could not be located in this review.

72. See above, chap. I, p. 29.

73. *Teoria,* p. 276. The term "eclecticism" Shevyrëv had adopted from Menzel's *Literatur* but without Menzel's pejorative implications.

74. *Teoria,* p. 233.

75. *Jubiläums Ausgabe,* XXXIII, 84–91.

76. *Moskovski Vestnik,* pt. II (1827).

77. *Moskvitianin,* pt. I (1841), pp. 275 ff.

78. *Russki Arkhiv,* No. 1 (1879), pp. 138f.

79. "Dorozhnye eskizy po puti iz Frankfurta v Berlin," *Otechestvennye zapiski,* III (1839), 101ff.

80. A. Z. Volkonskaia, "Otryvki iz putevykh zapisok," *Severnye Tsvety na 1830 god,* pp. 216ff. For some reason this is not in *Fahrten nach Weimar. Slawische Gäste bei Goethe, Beiträge zur Deutschen Klassik* (Weimar, 1958). This contribution is heavily indebted to Durylin, *op. cit.,* and to Hans Wohl's article on this subject in *Goethe: Vierteljahrschrift der Goethe Gesellschaft, Neue Folge,* Bd. 3 (1937), pp. 183–200: "Weisheitsfreunde bei Goethe und im Goethehaus." Also R. Jagodich, "Goethe und seine russischen Zeitgenossen," *Germanoslavica,* I (1932), Heft 3, 347–81; II (1933), Heft 1, 1–14.

81. *Vestnik Evropy,* No. 17 (Sept. 1825), p. 28.

82. *Gete v Russkoi Literature,* p. 178, Cf. N. M. Rozhalin, *Stradaniia Molodogo Vertera. Perevod s Nemetskogo R.* (Moscow, 1828–29).

83. "Pis'ma N. M. Rozhalina k A. P. Elaginoi," *Russki Arkhiv,* No. 47 (1909), bk. 2, pp. 584ff.

84. June 4, 1829. First published in *Moskovski Vestnik,* pt. II (1830), p. 300. Cf. also *Russki Arkhiv,* no. 47 (1909), bk. 2, pp. 565f.

85. *Russki Arkhiv,* No. 47 (1909), bk. 2, p. 578.

86. *Ibid.,* p. 582.

87. N. Barsukov, *Zhizn' i trudy M. P. Pogodina* (St. Petersburg. 1889), IV, 249.

88. Cf. *Literaturnoe Naledstvo,* IV-VI (1932), 490. *Fahrten nach Weimar* does not have it; nor does Hans Wohl, *op. cit.*

89. Durylin, *op. cit.,* p. 491.

90. *Ibid.,* p. 490.

91. *Zapiski A. I. Koshelëva (1812–1883 gody)* (Berlin, 1884), p. 37.

92. Durylin, *op. cit.,* p. 492.

93. *Zapiski A. I. Koshelëva,* p. 37.

94. "Doroznye eskizy . . .," *Otechestvennye Zapiski,* III (1839), 122–24.

95. G. Chulkov, "Stichotvereniia prislannye iz Germanii," *Zvenia,* II (1933), 265.

96. *Russki Arkhiv,* No. V (1879), pp. 123f. (letter of Aug. 7, 1836).

97. Not counting the translation of "Wechsel" (Auf Kieseln im Bache . . .), which is now being credited to K. Aksakov. Cf. Zhirmunski, *Gete v Russkoi Literature,* p. 211.

98. This manner is best exemplified in Zhukovski's rendering of Goethe's "Meine Göttin." See our analysis in Chap. II, pp. 48–49.

99. The complete collection of his translations is available in F. I. Tiutchev, *Polnoe sobranie stikhotvorenii, redaktsia i kommentarii Georgia Chulkova* (Moscow and Leningrad, 1934). The first volume contains all items, except for Mignon's song and Klärchen's song from *Egmont,* which are in vol. II, pp. 54 and 235, respectively.

100. The first translation to appear in a Russian journal was "Sakuntala" in the *Northern Lyre* (1827). The *Galatea* brought a fragment from *Faust,* the dialog between Faust and Wagner in "Vor dem Tor" at sunset, in 1830; the same periodical published "Geistesgruß" and "Der Sänger," also in 1830. Two songs of the "Harfner" from *Wilhelm Meister* appeared in the *Orphan (Sirotka)* in 1831; finally, in 1832, the *Telescope* published "Nachtgedanken." The remaining nine translations appeared much later in posthumous editions.

101. "po bozh'ei vole ia poiu, kak ptichka v podnebes'e."

102. Quoted by Zhirmunski, *op. cit.,* p. 212.

103. *Egmont,* Act III, Scene 2.

104. Not counting the lost version of Act I of *Faust,* Part II.

105. From "Doch laß uns dieser Stunde schönes Glück" to the end of the dialog.

106. From "Erhabner Geist" to "Und lindern der Betrachtung strenge Lust."

107. From "Wer ruft mir" to "Du gleichst dem Geist, den du begreifst, nicht mir." There is here an intriguing textual problem. In the second edition of Tiutchev's collected works of 1900 the line: "Du gleichst dem Geist" is placed before the line "In Lebensfluten, im Tatensturm" and is mistranslated as: Thus, Faust, I am a spirit like you, I am your equal." (Tak Faust, ia dukh, kak ty, tvoi ravnyi ia," p. 413). The Akademia Nauk edition (1934), on the other hand, has the correct line-sequence and the correct translation: "Only that being which you can comprehend do you resemble—not me!" (Lish estestvom toboi postizhimym podoben ty – ne mne! [I, 149]). The authenticity of these contrasting versions can only be established by a comparison with the

274 The Russian Image of Goethe

manuscript (or manuscripts?) not available to me. It is hard to believe, however, that a translator of Tiutchev's skill would be found guilty of such a blatant misinterpretation as the version in the edition of 1900.

108. From: "Was sucht ihr mächtig und gelind" to "Die Träne quillt, die Erde hat mich wieder."

109. Tiutchev's translations are conveniently juxtaposed to the German originals in *Deutsche Dichtung in russischer Übersetzung,* ed. M. Hellmann (Weimar, 1948), pp. 293–314.

110. *Zvenia,* II (1933), 262.

111. Cf. *Sochineniia Tiutcheva* (2nd ed., St. Petersburg, 1900). We shall identify the poems by their numbers in this edition. "Pesok sypuchii po koleni," no. 44: "Noch' khmuraia, kak zver' stooki,/Gliadit iz kazhdogo kusta."

112. *Soch.,* no. 101.

113. *Soch.,* no 112. Cf. Zhirmunski, *op. cit.,* p. 207.

114. *Soch.,* no. 91: "Gliadel ia, stoia nad Nevoi."

115. *Soch.,* no. 91.

116. *Soch.,* no. 78.

117. "Vdrug vsë smutilos': sudorozhnyi trepet/Po vetviam kiparisnym probezhal:/ Fontan zamolk . . . chto eto, drug? Il' zlaia zhizn' nedarom/ . . . Ta zlaia zhizn', s eië miatezhnym zharom,/ Cherez porog zavetnyi pereshla?"

118. N. V. Aleksandrovskaia, "Dva Golosa," *Posev Almanak* (Odessa, 1921), pp. 95–99; Zhirmunski, *op. cit.,* pp. 207–08; K. V. Pigarëv, "Tiutchev, perevodchik Gete," *Urania* (1928), pp. 85–113.

119. "Nad vami svetila molchat v vyshine,/ Pod vami mogily, molchat i one."

120. "Pust' v gornom Olimpe blazhenstvuiut bogi!/ . . . . . ./ Puskai Olimpiitsy zavislivym okom/ Gliadiat na bor'bu nepreklonnykh serdets. . . ."

121. "Kto, ratuia, pal, pobezhdennyi lish' rokom,/ Tot vyrval iz ruk ikh pobednyi venets."

122. *Poezia F. I. Tiutcheva, sobr. soch.,* VI, 471.

123. *Soch.,* no. 11, "Sumraki": "Vsë vo mne – i ia vo vsëm. . . ."

124. As quoted by Chulkov, *op. cit.,* p. 261.

125. *Soch.,* no. 51, "Na smert' Gete."

126. Strich, *Goethe und die Weltliteratur,* p. 343. With "diese Gedichte" Strich refers to Tiutchev's and Baratynski's poems on the

death of Goethe. Cf. chap. IV, pp. 95–97 for our discussion of Baratynski's eulogy of Goethe. Cf. also E. Haertel, ed. "Russische Dichtung auf den Tod Goethes," *Goethe-Jahrbuch,* Bd. 31.

127. Viacheslav Ivanov, "Zwei russische Gedichte auf den Tod Goethes," *Corona,* IV (1933–34), 697.

128. Cf. Gorlin, *op. cit.,* IX, 351: "Die Moskauer Idealisten sehen Goethe nicht unmittelbar, sondern durch das Medium der Schellingschen Philosophie hindurch . . ."

129. Cf. also Josef Matl, "Goethe bei den Slawen," *Jahrbücher für Kultur und Geschichte der Slawen,* N. F., VIII, Heft 1 (1932), p. 41. Matl places the high points of Russian enthusiasm for Goethe in the twenties and thirties of the century and again with the Russian Neo-Romanticists and Symbolists at the beginning of the twentieth Century.

VI: The Westerners

Section 1 and 2; Stankevich and Belinski

1. A. Kornilov, *Molodye gody Bakunina* (Moscow, 1916), p. 347.

2. *Byloe i Dumy* (Moscow and Leningrad, 1931), I, 329.

3. Herbert E. Bowman, *Vissarion Belinski. A Study of the Origins of Social Criticism in Russia* (Cambridge, Mass., 1954), p. 40.

4. *Pis'ma Belinskogo* (Moscow, 1914), I, 96.

5. N. V. Stankevich, *Perepiska,* ed. A. Stankevich (Moscow, 1914), p. 446 (letter of April 14, 1836). Henceforth cited as *Perepiska.*

6. *Sobranie sochinenii i pisem* (Moscow and Leningrad, 1934), II, 246–47 (letter of May 13, 1839, to Stankevich).

7. See chap. V, pp. 116–119.

8. We have from his pen a mediocre drama, *Skopin-Shuiski,* an equally unsuccessful novel and some thirty poems, none of them distinguished.

9. *Tolstovski Muzei* (St. Petersburg, 1911), I, 114.

10. A. Veselovski, *Zapadnoe vlianie v novoi Russkoi Literature* (Moscow, 1916), p. 216.

11. Cf. D. I. Chizhevski, *Gegel v Rossii* (Paris, 1939), p. 75: "He [Stankevich] began under the influence of Schelling and Schiller, went through a phase of Kant and Fichte and finally turned to Hegel."

12. I. Sergievski, "Gete v Russkoi Kritike," *Literaturnoe Nasledstvo,* IV-VI (1932), 729.

13. Dusha cheloveka/ Volnam podobna/ S neba niskhodit,/ Stremitsia k nebu. . . .

14. N. V. Stankevich, *Stikhotvoreniia, tragedia, proza* (Moscow, 1890), pp. 27 and 36.

15. *Perepiska,* p. 568.

16. *Perepiska,* pp. 176f.

17. *Perepiska,* p. 468.

18. *Perepiska,* p. 473.

19. It is interesting to observe how this view is significantly substantiated by Schiller himself: "Weil mein Gedankenkreis kleiner ist, so durchlaufe ich ihn eben darum schneller und öfter und kann eben darum meine kleine Barschaft besser nutzen . . .," *Briefe,* ed. R. Buchwald, (Leipzig, n. d.) pp. 355–56 (letter of April 12, 1794).

20. Stankevich's "rational reality" would seem to be a translation of Hegel's "vernünftige Wirklichkeit." Stankevich's acquaintance with Schiller's "Über naive und sentimentalische Dichtung," could not be established on autobiographical evidence.

21. Kostka, E., *Schiller in Russian Literature* (Philadelphia, 1965), p. 28.

22. N. V. Stankevich, *Perepiska ego i biographia,* ed. P. V. Anenkov (Moscow, 1875), p. 332 (italics his).

23. *Ibid.,* p. 226.

24. *Ibid.,* p. 234.

25. *Ibid.,* p. 459. For our discussion of Venevitinov's rendering see chap. V, p. 118. For Venevitinov's "embrace" ("obniat' ") Stankevich substitutes "grab" (skhvatit'), for his "hold" (derzhat'), "Hug" (prizhat').

26. *Ibid.,* pp. 218 and 226 (letters of May 18 and June 2, 1833 to Neverov; italics his).

27. *Ibid.,* p. 236 (italics mine). Here Schelling's influence on Stankevich is evident, especially of Schelling's concept of the creative act being an unconscious one not of analysis or mere articulation but of imagination, of image-making in the sense of "Verbildlichung."

28. *Ibid.,* pp. 249–50 (letter to Neverov of Sept. 1833; italics his).

29. *Loc. cit.* Cf. also Gorlin, "Goethe in Russia," *Zeitschrift für slawische Philologie,* X, 317: "Man sieht: für den jungen Westler geht die Plastik der Ballade völlig verloren; sie wird zu einem orgiastischen

Musikstück, einem Seitenstück zu den dämonischen Erzählungen Hoffmanns."

30. *Op. cit.,* pp. 229–30 (letter of June 11, 1833).

31. The oft-quoted dictum of the conservative Hegel: "Was vernünftig ist, ist wirklich und was wirklich ist, ist vernünftig." Cf. his "Vorrede zur Rechtsphilosophie."

32. M. Bakunin, *Sobranie sochinenii i pisem,* ed. Steklov (Moscow, 1934), II, 22.

33. *Ibid.,* 166–78.

34. *Ibid.,* II, 171.

35. *Loc. cit.*

36. *Ibid.,* II, 253 (letter to his sister Barbara, June 1839).

37. Belinski had been repeatedly acknowledged in that role by his contemporaries, by I. Turgeniev, N. Chernyshevski and others. See Herbert E. Bowman, *Vissarion Belinski, A Study of the Origins of Social Criticism in Russia* (Cambridge, Mass., 1954), p. 12. Henceforth cited as Bowman.

38. Bowman, pp. 31–32.

39. Bowman, p. 12.

40. *Gete v Russkoi Literature,* pp. 252–253.

41. To Botkin he writes (Aug. 12, 1838): "In a manner I have deciphered a chapter of *Wilhelm Meister*. What a wondrous delight— I am beginning to enjoy searching out the words in a dictionary and with this help and my own deductions, I am groping my way toward their secret meanings." *Venok Belinskomu,* ed. Piksakova (Moscow, 1924), p. 52.

42. *Pis'ma Belinskogo* (Moscow, 1914), I, 102. Henceforth cited as *Pis'ma.*

43. *Pis'ma,* II, 130 (a letter with the late date of June 13, 1840).

44. *Pis'ma,* II, 244 (June 27, 1841; italics his).

45. Huber's *Faust;* Strugovchikov's "Römische Elegien," *Faust* and "Prometheus"; K. Aksakov's renderings of Goethe's lyrics. Of the German originals Belinski had in his library only *Wilhelm Meisters Lehrjahre* (*Sämtliche Werke,* Bd. V, 1814 ed.). Cf. "Bibliotheka Belinskogo," *Literaturnoe Nasledstvo,* LV, 431–572, esp. 555.

46. Zhirmunski, *Gete v Russkoi Literature,* p. 255; cf. also Lebedev-Polianski, *V. Belinski* (Moscow, 145), p. 54, and Bowman, p. 41.

47. *Sobranie sochinenii v trëkh tomakh,* ed. F. M. Golovenchenko (Moscow, 1948), II, 448. Henceforth cited as *Sob. soch.*

48. Kostka recognized this "strong point" of the Russian critic when he said of him: Belinski did sense with amazing quickness and certainty—on a narrow basis of factual content—the 'greatness,' the 'genius' of a writer." *Schiller in Russian Literature*, p. 114, n. 88.

49. Bowman, p. 14.

50. "Literaturnye Mechtaniia" (1834), *Sob. soch.*, I, 7–89.

51. *Ibid.*, p. 10.

52. *Ibid.*, p. 79.

53. *Ibid.*, p. 53.

54. *Ibid.*, p. 66.

55. Cf. chap. IV, pp. 95–97.

56. Cf. chap. III, p. 64.

57. *Literaturnye Mechtaniia, p.* 76.

58. *Ibid.*, p. 87 (italics his).

59. "O russkoi povesti i povestiakh g. Gogolia," (1835), *Sob. soch.*, I, 109–10.

60. *Sob. soch.*, I, 461–62.

61. *Sob. soch.*, I, 79.

62. Cf. e.g., the essay, "Ivan Andreevich Krylov," *Sob. soch.*, II, 705–31, or again, "Mysli i zametki o Russkoi Literature," *Sob. soch.*, III, 33–60, where we read: "The life of his nation furnishes the poet with the content of his work. It follows, therefore, that the worth, the depth, the significance of that content depend directly and immediately not on the poet himself, not on his talent, but on the historical significance of the life of his nation" (p. 44).

63. "Sochineniia Fonvisina i Iuri Miloslavski," *Polnoe sobranie sochinenii,* ed. Vengerov (St. Petersburg, 1917), IV, 5ff (italics his). Henceforth cited as *Pol. sobr. soch.*

64. *Loc. cit.*

65. "Opyt Drozdova," (1838). *Sob. soch.*, I, 288.

66. *Sob. soch.*, I, 107.

67. "Gamlet, Drama Shakespeara" (1838). *Pol. sobr. soch.*, III, 225.

68. Our chief documents of this event are two letters to Stankevich written August 19, 1839, and October 2, 1839, respectively; they record conversations which took place in 1837.

69. *Pis'ma*, I, 347 (letter of Oct. 2, 1839).

70. *Pis'ma*, I, 317.

71. Belinski was aware of this characteristic trait. In a letter to Bot-

kin he writes: "I break with an old idea with difficulty and pain. I reject it to the limit, and pass over into the new with all the fanaticism of a proselyte" (letter of Sept. 8, 1841, in Bowman's translation). Cf. Bowman, p. 46.

72. In the letter of Oct. 2, 1839, Belinski returns to his criticism of Schiller's portrayal of women: "His Thekla, this tenth, improved and corrected edition of Schiller's women, had furnished me with the ideal of womanhood, beside which there existed for me no other woman. Now your Bertha [Stankevich's girl friend of the Berlin days] stands for me 100,000 times higher, because she is a living, actual person, and not an abstract idea." *Pis'ma,* I, 347.

73. "Lezhu ia v potoke na kamniakh." The Russian translation of Goethe's lyrics by K. Aksakov and Strugovchikov had just appeared.

74. *Pis'ma,* I, 345–50.

75. *Pis'ma,* I, 314–15 (letter of Febr. 25, 1839).

76. *Pis'ma,* II, 185 (letter of Dec. 11, 1840).

77. *Pol. sobr. soch.,* VI, 241–72, esp. 256ff.

78. As quoted by Zhirmunski, *op. cit.,* pp. 269–70.

79. *Pol. sobr. soch.,* VI, 257.

80. For a good general discussion of this phase see Bowman, pp. 91–106, *et passim.*

81. "Gamlet, Drama Shakespeara" (1838), *Pol. sob. soch.,* III, 223.

82. *Pol. sob. soch.,* II, 193–94.

83. *Pol. sob. soch.,* III, 192–93.

84. *Sob. soch.,* I, 288 (italics mine).

85. *Pis'ma,* I, 333 (letter of Aug. 19, 1839).

86. *Pis'ma,* II, 68 (letter of March 1, 1840). Belinski's "refleksia" and "sozertsanie" are derived from Hegel's "Verstand" and "Vernunft," respectively.

87. *Sob. soch.,* I, 449.

88. *Pis'ma,* I, 341 (letters to N. V. Stankevich of Sept. 28 and Oct. 8, 1839).

89. *Pis'ma,* II, 68 (letter of March 1, 1840, italics mine).

90. *Pis'ma,* II, 125 (letter to Botkin of May 16, 1840).

91. Cf. Bowman, pp. 120–39, *et passim.*

92. *Sob. soch.,* I, 418–52. The essay appeared in March 1840.

93. 1st ed., Stuttgart, 1828; 2nd enlarged ed., Stuttgart, 1836. The Russian version was translated from the second edition with significant

omissions, e.g., the chapter on religion as well as the entire last (IV) part of the work. Its title: *Nemetskaia Slovestnost' iz Knigi Volfganga Mentselia,* pt. I-II (Moscow, 1837).

94. All quotations, unless otherwise noted, are from the essay "Menzel, critic of Goethe" (1840), *Sob. soch.,* I, 418–52.

95. "O kritike i literaturnykh mneniakh Moskovskogo Nabliudatelia" (1836), *Sob. soch.,* I, 258–59.

96. *Pis'ma,* II, 196.

97. This idea of "sociality" was suggested to Belinski primarily by the French utopian socialists whom he studied intensely at this time, together with the writings of Ludwig Feuerbach. "And so I find myself now caught up in a new extreme—it is the idea of *sociality* which has become for me the idea of all ideas, the essence of being, the question of all questions, the Alpha and Omega of faith and knowledge. All flows from it, for it and to it. . . . For me it [sociality] has swallowed up history and religion and philosophy." *Pis'ma,* II, 262 (italics his). The views of his newly won friend, Aleksander Herzen, were another strong influence.

98. *Pis'ma,* II, 185–87 (letter to Botkin, Dec. 11, 1840).

99. *Pis'ma,* II, 212 (letter to Botkin, March 1, 1841).

100. *Loc. cit.* (italics his).

101. *Loc. cit.* (italics mine).

102. *Pis'ma,* II, 249–50 (letter to Botkin, June 28, 1841).

103. *"Sochineniia Derzhavina"* (1843), *Sob. soch.,* II, 513.

104. "Obshchee znachenie slova literatura" (1843), *Sob. soch.,* II, 84–117. See esp. 107–08.

105. "Obiasnenie na obiasnenie po povodu poemy Gogolia 'Mërtvye Dushi' " (1843), *Sob. soch.,* II, 436.

106. *"Sochineniia Derzhavina"* (1843), *Sob. soch.,* II, 513.

107. *Ibid.,* p. 514.

108. *Loc. cit.*

109. In an essay on Gogol, Belinski explicitly ascribes to Goethe an "ascetic and antisocial spirit." *Sob. soch,* II, 338.

110. "Kak sladostna privychka k zhizni," an inexact quote of the lines "Süßes Leben! schöne freundliche Gewohnheit des Daseins und Wirkens." Act V, last scene.

111. Actually a review of *Goethes Briefe an die Gräfin Augusta Stolberg* (Stuttgart, n.d.), in *Otechestvennye Zapiski* of the year 1843. Vol. XXVI, part 2, pp. 43–68.

112. *Pis'ma,* II, 350 (letter of March 8, 1843).

113. *Pis'ma,* II, 232 (letter of April 6, 1841).

114. *Pis'ma,* II, 282 (March 1842).

115. "Rech' o kritike A. V. Nikitenko" (1843; italics mine), *Sob. soch.,* II, 354.

116. *Ibid.,* 357.

117. "Stikhotvorenia Lermontova," *Sob. soch.,* II, 670. Again we notice how closely related Belinski's terms, "reflective" and "contemplative," are to Schiller's "sentimentalisch."

118. *Pis'ma,* II, 193. Belinski returns to the "Mother" scene in his essay "Ideia Iskusstva." Here he uses Goethe's text in an attempt to clarify his concept of the "ideas," the "origin and being" of which he is seeking to define. *Sob. soch.,* II, 67–83. Belinski's interpretation contributes nothing of value to his view of Goethe.

119. *Pis'ma,* II, 210 (italics his).

120. "Sochineniia A. Pushkina," *Sob. soch.,* III, 417.

121. *Sob. soch.,* III, 278.

122. "Obiasnenie na obiasnenie . . .," *Sob. soch.,* II, 337 (italics his).

123. "Stikhotvorenia Lermontova," *Sob. soch.,* II, 670 (italics mine).

124. "Neskol'ko slov o poeme Gogolia: Pokhozhdenia Chichikova ili Mërtvye Dushi," *Sob. soch.,* II, 289 and 300.

125. *Sob. soch.,* II, 670 (italics his).

126. "Sochineniia A. Pushkina," *Sob. soch.,* III, 371–72.

127. *Ibid.,* p. 372 (italics his).

128. *Ibid.,* p. 376.

129. *Loc. cit.* (italics his).

130. *Ibid.,* p. 372.

131. *Sob. soch.,* II, 437–38.

132. "Retsenzia na stichotvoreniia Baratynskogo," *Sob. soch.,* II, 413–43.

133. *Sob. soch.,* pp. 437–38.

134. For Belinski's low opinion of Pushkin's "Demon" cf. "Sochineniia A. Pushkina," *Sob. soch.,* III, 615–16.

135. "Retsenzia na stikhotvorenia Baratynskogo," *Sob. soch.,* II, 434–35.

136. *Loc. cit.* (italics his).

137. *Sob. soch.,* II, 190.

138. "Obiasnenie na obiasnenie . . .," *Sob. soch.,* II, 338.

139. *Sob. soch.,* II, 161 (italics his).

140. *Sob. soch.,* II, 172.

141. *Sob. soch.,* II, 155 (italics his).

142. "Sochineniia Gete" (1842), *Otechestvennye Zapiski,* XXI, 16. Belinski's authorship of this essay, at one time disputed, has been definitely established by Zhirmunski. Cf. *Gete v Russkoi Literature,* p. 651, n. 92.

143. "Sochineniia Derzhavina" (1843), *Sob. soch.,* II, 516.

144. "Sochineniia Gete," *Otechestvennye Zapiski,* XXI, 16–17.

145. *Sob. soch.,* II, 57. It has not been possible to ascertain Belinski's acquaintance with Lessing's famous passage. Cf. *Lessings Werke,* ed. J. Petersen (Berlin and Leipzig, n.d.), V, 115. From "Die Tragödie ist keine dialogisierte Geschichte" to ". . . als aus dem Gegenteil ein Verbrechen mache!"

146. *Pis'ma,* III, 325.

147. *Sob. soch.,* III, 796–97.

148. "Drevnie Rossiskie Stikhotvoreniia," *Pol. sobr. soch.,* VI, 344.

149. *Ibid.,* p. 345.

150. "Vzgliad na Russkuiu Literaturu 1847 goda" (1848), *Sob. soch.,* III, 796–97. In his famous study of the "Works of Aleksander Pushkin" Belinski had already stressed the indigenous content of *Faust,* placing it alongside Homer's *Iliad* as an "expression of the spirit of the nation and the epoch." Cf. *Sob. soch.,* III, 471.

151. *Sob. soch.,* III, 412.

152. *Sob. soch.,* III, 384.

153. *Pis'ma,* II, 95 (letter to Botkin, March 19, 1840).

154. "Obshchaia idea narodnoi poezii" (1841), *Pol. sobr. soch.,* VI, 340.

155. *Sob. soch.,* III, 160.

156. *Sob. soch.,* III, 237.

157. *Sob. soch.,* III, 159.

158. "Sochineniia Gete," pt. 2, *Otechestvennye Zapiski* (Section: Bibliograph. Kronika), XXII, 34.

159. *Otechestvennye Zapiski* (1842), XXI, 16.

Section 3: Herzen

1. A. I. Gertsen, *Polnoe sobranie sochinenii i pisem,* ed. M. K. Lemke, 22 vols. (St. Petersburg and Leningrad, 1915–1925). Henceforth cited as Lemke.

2. Ia. Elsberg, *Gertzen. Zhizn' i tvorchestvo* (Moscow, 1956), p. 11.

3. Herzen's biographer Bogucharski claims to know that "she [Herzen's mother] read with her son the works of the famous writer Schiller in the German original," but adduces no evidence. Cf. *Aleksander Ivanovich Gertsen* (St. Petersburg, 1912), p. 15.

4. Lemke, II, 399–40.

5. Lemke, II, 400.

6. *Loc. cit.*

7. Lemke, I, 113 (letter of July 5, 1833; italics his). Cf. also Lemke, I, 404 (letter of April 3, 1837, to P. A. Zakharina).

8. Lemke, XII, 41.

9. For a perceptive explanation of Herzen's penchant for "quotations, paraphrases, literary and other reminiscences," see H. Gai, *Roman i povest' A. I. Gertsena 30–40kh Godov* (Kiev, 1959), p. 11f.

10. Herzen uses for an ironic motto of his first fictional effort, *Pervaia Vstrecha*, Luise's opening lines: "Was die französische Revolution Gutes oder Böses stiftet, kann ich nicht beurteilen; sowiel weiß ich, daß sie mir diesen Winter einige Paar Strümpfe mehr einbringt." Lemke, I, 286.

11. For a listing of Herzen's quotations from Goethe cf. L. Krestova, "Portret Gete pod perom Gertsena," *Zvenia*, II (1933), 75–96.

12. Lemke, X, 45 (letter of June 22, 1859).

13. Lemke, X, 209 (letter of Febr. 7, 1860). Cf. also letter to E. A. and N. A. Turgeniev of Oct. 17, 1848, Lemke, V, 251.

14. Lemke, I, 102 (letter of Febr. 26, 1838).

15. "Buddizm v nauke," Lemke, III, 225.

16. Lemke, XIII, 387–88.

17. Lemke, II, 401.

18. Lemke, III, 450 (diary notation of March 1845).

19. Lemke, III, 20, and XIII, 83. Both times Herzen omits the second and third lines of Goethe's "Spruch": "mußt rasch dich besinnen/ Und neues gewinnen." The last two lines of the "Spruch" Herzen also quotes in a letter to E. Th. Korsch dated June 4, 1857, and again in his essay "Revolutsia v Rossii." Cf. Lemke, VIII, 514, and IX, 4, respectively (Italics his). Cf. *Jubiläums Ausgabe,* IV, 112.

20. Cf. "Zahme Xenien, VI". Cf. *Jubiläums Ausgabe,* IV, 127.

21. Lemke, III, 302, 406; V, 120, 251; VI, 197; XIX, 114; XX, 79.

22. Lemke, V, 484; V, 530; I, 230, *Vtoraia Vstrecha.*

23. Cf., for instance, Lemke, II, 381, where Herzen opens a chapter of his "Zapiski odnogo molodogo cheloveka" with lines from Goethe's

"Zueignung" ("Ihr naht euch wieder schwankende Gestalten . . ."), a thoroughly apt epigraph. Another aptly chosen epigraph is Tasso's line, "Der Mensch ist nicht geboren frei zu sein," introducing Herzen's essay, "S togo berega" (Lemke, V, 450), or again the lines from Goethe's *Faust:* "Ich schau in diesen reinen Zügen . . .," with which Herzen opens the essay on the "Solar System of Copernicus" (Lemke, I, 91). Other examples abound.

24. Fourth "Venezianisches Epigramm." For a related passage in the *Italian Journey,* cf. "Verona, den 16. September, 1786."

25. Lemke, VI, 31–32 (italics his).

26. M. Malia argues the case of a long-lasting influence by Schelling. Cf. his *Alexander Herzen and the Birth of Russian Socialism* (Cambridge, Mass., 1961), esp. chap. V.

27. Lemke, I, 141: "Now Heine strikes out with his acid pen right and left against the old generation."

28. Lemke, XIII, 11. Cf. also Lemke, XIII, 576, where Herzen calls the members "dilettantes of revolutionary ideas."

29. Zhirmunski mentions Polevoi as an early critic of Goethe (*Gete v Russkoi Literature,* pp. 295f), and Krestova adds Nadezhdin to the brief list (*Zvenia,* II, pp. 87f). In chap. IV we set forth Bestuzhev's and Küchelbecker's critiques. Chronology makes a direct influence of these voices on Herzen highly unlikely, as they are all but simultaneous with his own strictures.

30. Written in 1834, published in the *Telescope* in 1836.

31. Lemke, I, 145–46.

32. *Pervai vstrecha,* Lemke, I, 286–300. This piece was begun in 1834 and completed during the Viatka exile, 1835–39. Its original title was "Germanskii puteshestvennik."

33. A revised version of this story is included in a second installment of the "Zapiski odnogo molodogo cheloveka." Lemke, II, 437–67. In our analysis we draw on both versions. The following quotations are from these sources unless otherwise indicated.

34. This quasi-historical fiction was to become Herzen's favorite narrative form. To N. Z. Zakharina he writes: "Let the impressions to which I am subject find their expression in separate tales where all is fiction and yet the basis of which is historical truth," Lemke, I, 271.

35. Cf. *Kampagne in Frankreich,* under the dates 28. and 29. Aug., 1792.

36. For easy comparison with Goethe's text, a verbatim translation of

Herzen's Russian text follows:

> I [Goethe] was driving in the duke's coach as always; suddenly there approached on horseback some kind of officer wrapped in his coat against the rain. Seeing the Weimar coat of arms on the carriage and the ducal livery, the officer came close to the coach and—imagine our mutual surprise when I recognized in the officer His Highness, the King of Prussia, and His Highness found instead of the duke—me! This incident shall for a long time remain fixed in my memory.

37. *Kampagne in Frankreich,* under the dates 27. and 29. Sept., 1792. Following is Herzen's heavily edited version of Goethe's account for ready comparison; Goethe is speaking:

> Our present life, full of privations, will serve us as a pleasant memory—there is in it its own poetry. Do you know, how the favorite of Louis the Holy used to console himself in captivity?: "Nous en parlerons devant les dames."

38. Lemke, VII, 157.

39. *Kampagne in Frankreich,* "Weimar vom Dezember 1792 bis zum April 1793."

40. One example must suffice (under 19. Sept., 1792):

> Ich war nun vollkommen in die Region gelangt, wo die Kugeln herüberspielten. . . . Es war als wäre man an einem sehr heißen Orte und zugleich von der Hitze völlig durchdrungen. . . . Hieraus erhellet nun, in welchem Sinne man diesen Zustand ein Fieber nennen könne. Bemerkenswert bleibt es indessen, daß jenes gräßlich Bängliche nur durch die Ohren zu uns gebracht wird; denn der Kanonendonner, das Heulen, Pfeifen, Schmettern der Kugeln durch die Luft ist doch eigentlich Ursache an diesen Empfindungen.

41. One example (under the dates 28. and 29. Aug., 1792):

> Als sich aber dieses Verfahren dahin auflöste, daß man die Herden unter Regimenter und Kompagnien verteilte, den Besitzern hingegen ganz höflich auf Ludwig den XVI gestellte Papiere überreichte, indessen ihre wolligen Zöglinge von den ungeduldigen, fleischlustigen Soldaten vor ihren Füßen ermordet wurden; so gesteh' ich wohl, es ist mir nicht leicht eine grausamere Szene und ein tieferer männlicher Schmerz in allen seinen Abstufungen jemals vor Augen und *zur Seele gekommen.* Die griechische Tragödie allein hat so einfach Ergreifendes (italics mine).

42. Den 19. September, 1792.

43. *Kampagne in Frankreich,* Weimar vom Dezember 1792 bis zum April 1793.

44. See pp. 192–198 above.

45. Lemke, V, 465–66.

46. Lemke, VI, 355.

47. Lemke, XV, 254.

48. Lemke, IX, 439.

49. Ia. Elsberg, *op. cit.,* p. 125.

50. *Loc. cit.*

51. Comparing himself with Ogarëv, Herzen writes to his friend: "Your way of life is more contemplative, mine more of the propagandist." Lemke, I, 117. Elsberg speaks repeatedly of Herzen's "natural bent for propaganda, free speech and the battle of ideas." *Ibid.,* p. 24, *et passim.*

52. Lemke, IV, 109.

53. Lemke, III, 329 (*Dnevnik,* May 30, 1844; italics mine).

54. Lemke, III, 344 (*Dnevnik,* Aug. 8, 1844).

55. Lemke, III, 191.

56. Lemke, XIII, 29.

57. Lemke, I, 141.

58. Lemke, III, 179–80.

59. Lemke, I, 145.

60. Cf. also the following entree in his diary (Lemke, III, 41):
    Is it possible that loving comprises all of man's mission, and does love alone make up the *Grundton* of his whole existence? There would seem to be a time for everything. . . . Man should not surrender totally to just one individual feeling, for his salvation lies in the realm of ideas, of social interests; the spirit of man soars between these two realms. If he neglects his heart, he would indeed be a monster, but the reverse is equally true.

61. Lemke, III, 261–62. Cf. also Lemke, III, 41, where Herzen emphasizes this thought with an insistence which can only spring from his deeply personal experience in his marital life.

62. Lemke, III, 26.

63. Lemke, XII, 476–77.

64. *Loc. cit.*

65. H. Th. Rötscher, *Abhandlungen zur Philosophie der Kunst* (Berlin, 1837–42). Vol I, "Das Verhältnis der Philosophie, der Kunst und der Kritik zum einzelnen Kunstwerk." Cf. esp. pp. 38–42. Herzen's reading of Rötscher is one-sided. While presenting Goethe's work as an "apotheosis of marriage," Rötscher nontheless insists on reading it as a "Totalität" in which both the "Grundpfeiler aller sittlichen Ordnung [i.e., die Ehe]" as well as the "Naturgewalten" receive their "poetic [i.e., balanced]" representation. See Rötscher's central thesis:

> In einem Gemälde, welches grade eine Apotheose der Ehe, als Grundpfeiler aller sittlichen Ordnung enthüllt, haben auch diejenigen ihre volle Bedeutung [i.e., the Count and the Baroness], und es ist nur die Schuld des Beschauers, wenn er nicht auch diese andere Seite mit Aufmerksamkeit betrachtet, welche mit der Ersteren [i.e., "den Naturgewalten"] die Totalität abgiebt" (p. 41).

66. Lemke, II, 417 (letter of Febr. 26, 1841).

67. Lemke, III, 41.

68. Lemke, II, 423.

69. Malia, *op. cit.*, p. 259.

70. "Iz dal'nykh let," *Vospominania T. P. Passek* (1878), as quoted by Zhirmunski, *op. cit.*, p. 333.

71. See chap. IV (Odoevski) and chap. I (Uvarov).

72. Lemke, III, 359 (italics his).

73. Lemke, I, 56ff. "O nedelimom v rastitel'nom tsarstve."

74. *Loc. cit.* Herzen here refers to Erasmus Darwin's *Phytologia*, vol. I (London, 1800).

75. Lemke, III, 163ff. The following quotations, unless otherwise indicated, are from this source, esp. from pp. 172–73.

76. In the cycle, *Gott und Welt*. Cf. *Jubiläums Ausgabe*, II, 249.

77. From Goethe's poems, "Allerdings: dem Physiker" and "Ultimatum," both in the cycle *Gott und Welt*. Herzen may also have found these lines in Goethe's *Morphologie:* "Freundlicher Zuruf." How persistent the influence of this Goethean thought was on Herzen is indicated by the appearance of these lines in his very first narrative piece, *The First Meeting,* as well as in some of his latest essays (Lemke, II, 455).

78. Compare also another essay of the same year, "Diletanty i tsekh uchënykh," with its mixture of Hegelian and Goethean terminology. Herzen speaks here of the Hegelian thesis-antithesis as of a "polarity [!] which is one of the aspects of human development, a sort of pulse-

beat with the difference, that with every beat of the pulse humanity takes a step forward" (Lemke, III, 193).

79. Compare also Herzen's second "Letter on the Study of Nature" (Lemke, IV, 34).

80. *Faust I*, Mephisto-Student scene. Cf. *Jubiläums Ausgabe,* XIII, 77.

81. Lemke IV, 22ff. The following quotations are from this essay unless otherwise indicated.

82. This passage is reminiscent of Baratynski's hymn to Goethe, the Romanticist "exaggerations" that both Herzen and Belinski criticized.

83. Herzen had a surprisingly low opinion of the Goethe-Schiller *Briefwechsel* which he forced himself to read "despite overwhelming boredom" with its "philistine and Gellertian [Ch. F. Gellert] contents and tone." Lemke, III, 305–06.

84. Lemke, III, 359 (italics his).

85. Lemke, IV, 20–21. Goethe's account of the incident runs as follows:

> Umrisse wurden gemacht, die das Behauptete klar vor Augen bringen sollten, jene kurze Abhandlung dazu geschrieben, ins Lateinische übersetzt und Campen mitgeteilt, und zwar Format und Schrift so anständig, daß sie der treffliche Mann mit einiger Verwunderung aufnahm, Arbeit und Bemühung lobt, sich freundlich erwies, aber nach wie vor versicherte, der Mensch habe kein *os intermaxillare.* ("Zur Morphologie" III. Teil: Über den Zwischenkieferknochen." *W. A.,* Abt. II, Bd. 8, p. 119.)

86. A passage in his essay collection, "From the Other Shore," indicates Herzen's familiarity with Goethe's observations on the skull-formation of the "fossilized steer." Lemke, V, 405.

87. Lemke, IV, 22–23.

88. Lemke, IV, 1.

89. Lemke, IV, 44.

90. Lemke, IV, 384.

91. Lemke, IV, 384.

92. Lemke, III, 444 (Jan. 17, 1845; italics mine),

93. Lemke, V, 465–66.

BIBLIOGRAPHY

This bibliography includes mainly works that are cited in the text. For easy reference, items are listed under the chapters in which they occur and are grouped as primary and secondary sources. Within each group, the items are arranged alphabetically by authors. In the "Introduction" which contains no primary sources, the titles are grouped into contributions by Western scholarship, contributions by Soviet scholarship, and contributions on the theme of "Pushkin-Goethe."

INTRODUCTION

1. Contributions by Western Scholarship:

Atkins, S. S., *The Testament of Werther in Poetry and Drama* (Cambridge, Mass., 1949).

Bergmann, Alfred, *Das Welt-Echo des Goethe-Jahres* (Weimar, 1932).

Bianquis, G. *Goethe et ses visiteurs russes à Weimar* (Paris, 1964).

Bittner, Konrad, *Die Faustsage im russischen Schrifttum. Prager deutsche Studien* (Richenberg i/Breisgau, 1925).

Frank S. "Goethe in Rußland, *Germanoslavica*, II (1933), Heft 1, pp. 55-60.

Gorlin, M., "Goethe in Rußland," *Zeitschrift für slawische Philologie*, IX (1932), 335-57; X (1933), 319-34.

Harnack, Otto, "Goethes Beziehungen zu russischen Schriftstellern," *Essays und Studien zur Literaturgeschichte* (Braunschweig, 1889), pp. 231-237.

Jagodich, Rudolf, "Goethe und seine russischen Zeitgenossen," *Germanoslavica*, I (1932), Heft 3, pp. 347-81; II (1933), Heft 1, pp. 1-14.

——, "Goethes Würdigung in Rußland," *Goethe-Almanach* (Wien, 1948), pp. 339-345.

Jashchenko, A. L., *"Faust* Gete: Rannie otkliki v Rossii," *Uchënye zapiski Gor'kovskogo Universiteta, no.* 65 (1964), 189-204.

——, *"Faust,* Gete i russki chitatel' XIX – nachala XX veka," *op. cit.,* no. 67, 202-18.

Jurjew, L., "Russische Schriftsteller und revolutionäre Demokraten über Goethe," *Neue Welt,* IV (1949), pp. 142-145.

Kaiser, B., "Das Goethebild der russischen Literatur," *Neue Welt,* IV (1949), pp. 133-141.

Kostka, E., "At the Roots of Russian Westernism: N. V. Stankevich and his Circle," *Etudes Slaves et Est-Européennes,* VI (1965), 158-76.

———, *Schiller in Russian Literature* (Philadelphia, 1965).

Luther, A., "Goethe in Rußland," *Osteuropa*, VIII (1933), pp. 315–319.

Masaryk, Th., *The Spirit of Russia* (London, 1919).

Matl, Josef, "Goethe bei den Slawen," *Jahrbücher für Kultur und Geschichte der Slawen*, N. F., VIII, Heft 1 (1932), pp. 37–57.

Pogodin, A., "Goethe in Rußland," *Germanoslavica*, vol. I (1932), Heft 3, pp. 333–47.

Purin, C. M., "Goethe und Rußland,' *Monatshefte*, XXX (1938), pp. 110–19.

Raab, H., "Deutsch-russische Literatur: Beziehungen in der Zeit von der Aufklärung bis zur Romantik," *Wissenschaftliche Zeitschrift der Ernst Moritz Arndt-Universität Greifswald* (1955-56), 91-99; also in *NDL*, V, 91–104.

Strich, Fritz, *Goethe und die Weltliteratur* (Bern, 1946).

Wellek, Réne, "Social and Aesthetic Values in Russian Ninteenth-Century Literary Criticism," *Continuity and Change in Russian and Soviet Thought*, E. J. Simmons, ed. (Cambridge, Mass., 1955), pp. 381–97.

Wexler, Alexandra, "Goethe in Rußland," *The Goethe Year 1749–1949* (London, 1952), pp. 228–33.

Wukadinovich, S., "Goethe und die slawische Welt," *Jahrbücher der Goethe-Gesellschaft*, XVIII (1932), 57-70.

Zabel, E., "Goethe in Rußland," *Jahrbücher der Goethe-Gesellschaft* VIII (1921), pp. 27–48.

2. *Contributions on the Theme: Pushkin - Goethe.*

Berkov, P. N., "Werther in Puschkins Eugen Onegin," *Germanoslavica*, II (1933), Heft 1, pp. 72-76.

Frank, J. G., "Pushkin and Goethe," *Slavonic and East European Review*, XXVI (1947), pp. 146–151.

Legras, J., "Pouchkine et Goethe, la 'scene tirée de Faust,'" *Revue de Littérature Comparée*, XVIII (1937), pp. 117–128.

Leschnitzer, F., "Puschkin, Goethe und ihre Völker," *Die Weltbühne*, VII (1952), no. 6, pp. 180–185.

Luther, A., *Pushkin und Goethe, Solange Dichter leben* (Krefeld, 1949).

Propper, Maximilian von, "Goethe und Puschkin—Wahrheit und Legende," *Goethe*, XII (1950), pp. 218–59.

3. *Contributions by Soviet Scholarship:*

Durylin, S., "Russkie pisateli u Gete v Veimare," *Literaturnoe Nasledstvo*, IV-VI (1932), 81–504.

Sergievski, I., "Gete v Russkoi Kritike," *Literaturnoe Nasledstvo*, IV-VI (1932), 723–58.

Zhirmunski, V., "Gete v Russkoi Poezii," *Literaturnoe Nasledstvo*, IV–VI (1932), 506–650.

————, *Gete v Russkoi Literature* (Leningrad, 1937).

Chapter I

Primary Sources:

Batiushkov, K. N., *Sochineniia* (St. Petersburg, 1887).

Belinski, V., *Sobrannye sochineniia v trëkh tomakh* (Moscow, 1948).

Figel, F. F., *Zapiski* (Leningrad, 1928).

Grech, N. I., *Sochinenii Nikolaia Grecha* (St. Petersburg, 1855).

Karamzin, N. M., "Pis'ma russkogo puteshestvennika," *Sochineniia Karamzina* (St. Petersburg, 1905).

————, *Sobrannye sochineniia* (Moscow, 1920).

Kozodavlev, O. P., *Klavigo, tragedia v piati deistviakh gospodina Gete, perevedina s nemetskogo* (St. Petersburg, 1780).

————, *Klavigo, tragedia gospodina Gete. Perevedina s nemetskogo. Vtoroe ispravlennoe izdanie* (St. Petersburg, 1780).

Ouvaroff, S., *Etudes de Philologie et de Critique* (St. Petersburg, 1843).

Radishchev, A. N., *Puteshestvie iz Peterburga v Moskvu* (St. Petersburg, 1905).

Turgeniev, Aleksander, *Arkhiv brat'ev Turgenievykh* (Akademia Nauk, St. Petersburg, Leningrad, 1911–24).

————, "Otryvki iz zapisnoi knizhki puteshestvennika," *Sovremennik,* V, (1837), pp. 304–5.

————, "Sovremennye letopisi," *Moskovski Telegraph,* IV, no. 4 (1827), pp. 341–50.

Uvarov, S., *Nonnos von Panopolis. Ein Beitrag zur Geschichte der griechischen Poesie* (St. Petersburg, 1817).

————, *O Gete. V torzhestvennom sobranii Imperatorskoi St. Peterburgskoi Akademii Nauk chitano presidentom Akademii 22. Marta, 1833 g.* (Moscow, 1833).

Viazemski, P. A., *Ostapevskii Arkhiv Kniazei Viazemskikh* (St. Petersburg, 1899).

Secondary Sources:

Atkins, S.A., *The Testament of Werther in Poetry and Drama.* (Cambridge, Mass., 1949).

Bem, A., "Der russische Antiwertherismus,' *Germanoslavica,* II (1933), Heft 2, 357–59.

Berkov, P., "K istorii pervonachal'nogo znakomstva russkoga chitatelia s Gete." *Gete, 1832–1932* (Leningrad, 1932).

Kovalevski, M., "Bor'ba nemetskogo vliianiia s Frantsuzskim v kontse XVIII i v pervoi polovine XIX stoletiia." *Vestnik Evropy,* October 1915.

Novikov, N. I., *Dramaticheski Slovar'* (Moscow, 1787).

Pypin, A. N., *Die geistige Bewegung in Rußland in der ersten*

Hälfte des 19. Jahrhunderts (Berlin, 1894).

Schmid, Georg, "Goethe und Uvarov und ihr Briefwechsel," *Russische Revue*, XVIII, Heft 2 (1888), pp. 131–82.

Sidovski, V. V., *Ocherki iz Istorii Russkogo Romana* (St. Petersburg, 1910).

Veselovski, A., *V. A. Zhukovski: Poezia chustva i serdechnogo voobrazheniia* (St. Petersburg, 1904).

——, *Zapadnoe vliianie v novoi Russkoi Literature*, 5th ed. (Moscow, 1916).

Chapter II

Primary Sources:

Bakunin, M., *Sobranie sochinenii i pisem'* (Moscow, 1934).

Belinski, V., *Polnoe sobranie sochinenii*, ed. S. A. Vengerov (St. Petersburg, 1901).

Boisserée, Sulpiz, *Briefwechsel Sulpiz Boisséree* (Stuttgart, 1862).

Goethe, Johann, Wolfgang von, *Goethes Unterhaltungen mit dem Kanzler Müller*, ed. C. A. Burckhardt (Stuttgart, 1870).

——, *Weimarer Ausgabe*, Abt. III, Bd. 11; Abt. IV, Bde. 35, 43.

Kireievski, Ivan, *Polnoe sobranie sochinenii* (Moscow, 1934).

Zhukovski, V. A. *Dnevniki V. A. Zhukovskogo* (St. Petersburg, 1903).

——, *Polnoe sobranie v odnom tome*, ed. P. B. Smirnovski (2nd. ed., Moscow, 1905).

——, *Sochineniia Zhukovskogo*, ed. Efreimov (Moscow, 1878).

——, *Sochineniia v dvukh tomakh*, ed. Alferov (Moscow, 1902).

——, *Für Wenige—Dlia nemnogikh* (Moscow, 1818).

Secondary Sources:

Bychkov, I. A., *Neizdannye pis'ma Zhukovskogo k A. P. Zontag* (St. Petersburg, 1912).

Ehrhard, M., *Joukovski et le pre-romantisme Russe* (Paris, 1938).

Passage, Charles, "The Influence of Goethe, Schiller and E.T.A. Hoffmann in Russia, 1800–40," unpublished dissertation, Harvard University, 1942.

Reutern, Gerhardt von, *Gerhardt von Reutern; ein Lebensbild, dargestellt von seinen Kindern* (St. Petersburg, 1894).

Silz, Walter, "Goethe: 'Der Wanderer.' *Stoffe, Formen, Strukturen. H. H. Borchardt zum 75. Geburtstag* (Munich, 1962).

Viskovatov, P. A., "Ob otnosheniakh Zhukovskogo i Gete," *Literaturnyi Vestnik* (Moscow, 1902), pp. 125–40.

Volm, Matthew, *W. A. Zhukowski als Übersetzer* (Ann Arbor, 1945).

Zamotin, J. J., *Romantizm dvadtsatych godov XIX stol. v Russkoi Literature* (Warsaw, 1913).

Chapter III

Primary Sources:

Belinski, V., *Sobranie sochinenii v trëkh tomakh* (Moscow, 1948).

————, *Polnoe sobranie sochinenii* (St. Petersburg, 1900).

Gertsen, A. I., *Sobranie sochinenii v 30 tomakh* (Akademia Nauk, Moscow, 1956).

Goethe, Johann Wolfgang von, *Sämtliche Werke, Jubiläums Ausgabe* (Stuttgart und Berlin, 1902ff.)

Lermontov, M., *Sobrannye sochineniia v chetyrëkh tomakh* (Akademia Moscow, 1958).

Pushkin, A. S., *Pis'ma Pushkina* (Moscow, n.d.).

————, *Polnoe sobranie sochinenii* (St. Petersburg 1900).

————, *Sochineniia: Russkie Klassiki* (New York, n.d.).

————, *Sochineniia* (St. Petersburg, 1915).

————, *Sochineniia Pushkina* (Akademia Nauk, Leningrad, n.d.)

Tiutchev, F. I., *Sochineniia F. I. Tiutcheva* (St. Petersburg, 1900).

Secondary Sources:

Annenkov, P. V., *A. S. Pushkin v Aleksandrovskoi epokhe* (Moscow, 1874).

Bem, A., "*Faust* v tvorchestve Pushkina," *Slavia*, XIII, (1935), 378ff.

Brodski, N. L., *M. Y. Lermontov* (Moscow, 1945).

Eichenbaum, B. M., *Lermontov. Opyt istoriko-literaturnoi otsenki* (Leningrad, 1924).

Eiges, I., "Perevod M. Y. Lermontova iz 'Vertera Gete'," *Zvenia*, II (1933), 72–74.

Glebov, G., "Pushkin i Gete," *Zvenia*, II (1933), 41–67.

Guardini, Romano, *Vom Sinn der Schwermut* (Zürich, 1949).

Heideger, Martin, *Was ist Metaphysik?* (Bonn, 1931).

Hellmann, M., ed., *Deutsche Dichtung in russischer Übertragung* (Weimar, 1948).

Karpovich, M., *Centennial Essays for Pushkin* (Cambridge, 1937).

Kostka, E., "Schillers Influence on the Early Dramas of Lermontov," *P. Q.*, XXXII (1953), 396–410.

————, "Lermontov's Debt to Schiller," *Revue de Littérature Comparée*, XXXVII, 68–88.

Legras, J., "Poushkine et Goethe, la 'scene tirée de Faust' ", *Revue de Littérature Comparée*, XVIII (1937), 117–128.

Mannilov, V. A., *M. Y. Lermontov* (Moscow, 1958).

Modzalevski, B. L., *Bibliotheka Pushkina* (St. Petersburg, 1910).

Pohl, Wilma, *Russische Faust-Übersetzungen, Veröffentlichungen des slawisch-baltischen Seminars der westfälischen Wilhelms-Universität Münster* (Meisenheim am Glan, 1962).

Rehm, Walter, *Gontscharow und Jakobsen oder Langeweile und Schwermut* (Göttingen, 1963).

Rosenkranz, E., *Lermontov und Goethe. Der russische Gedanke.* (Bonn, 1929).

Rozov, V. A., *Pushkin i Gete* (Kiev, 1908).

Sechkarëv, V. "Über die Langeweile bei Pushkin," *Solange Dichter leben* (Krefeld, 1949).

Shuvalov, S., *Venok M. Y. Lermontovu. Iubileinyi Sbornik* (Moscow and St. Petersburg, 1914).

Weinberg, A. L., "Pero Gete u Pushkina," *Zvenia,* II (1933), 67–71.

Zamotin, I. I., *M. Y. Lermontov* (Warsaw, 1914).

Chapter IV

Primary Sources:

Baratynski, E., *Stikhotvoreniia,* ed. I. Medved (Moscow, 1945).

Bestuzhev, A. A., *Vtoroe polnoe sobranie A. Marlinskogo,* (4th ed., St. Petersburg, 1847).

Delvig, A., *Polnoe sobranie sochinenii,* ed. B. V. Tomachevski (Moscow, 1934).

Griboedov, A. S., *Sobrannye sochineniia,* ed. N. K. Piksanov (Liningrad, 1930f.).

Iazykov, N. M., "Pis'ma N. M. Iazykova k rodnym za Derpski period ego zhizni, 1822-29," *Iazykovski Arkhiv,* I. (Moscow, 1913).

Küchelbecker, Wilhelm, "Coup d'oeil sur l'état actuel de la littérature russe," *Conservateur Imperial,* no. 77 (1817).

————, *Dnevnik V. K. Kiukhl'bekera. Materialy k istorii russkoi literaturnoi i obshchestvennoi zhizni 10–40 godov XIX veka* (Leningrad, 1929).

————, "O napravlenie nashei poezii, osobenno liricheskoi, v poslednee desiatiletie," *Mnemozina,* pt. II (1824), 29–41.

————, "Razgovor s Bulgarinym," *Mnemozina,* pt. III (1824), 157–77.

Semerski, M. I., ed., "Aleksander Bestuzhev v Irkutske. Neizdannye pis'ma ego k rodnym," *Russki Vestnik,* V (1870) pp. 245–76.

Viazemski, P. A., *Polnoe sobranie sochinenii* (Moscow, n.d.).

Secondary Sources:

Alekseev, M. P. and Meilakh, B. S. (eds.), *Dekabristy i ikh vremia: materialy i soobshcheniia* (Moscow and Leningrad, 1951).

Dubrovin, N., "Zhukovski i Ego Otnosheniia k Dekabristam," *Russkaia Starina,* CX (1902), 94 ff.

Kirchner, P. and Zieman, R. eds., *Fahrten nach Weimar, Slawische Gäste bei Goethe. Beiträge zur deutschen Klassik* (Weimar, 1958).

Mirsky, D. S., *A History of Russian Literature* (New York, 1949).

Piksanov, N. K., *Griboedov* (Moscow, 1935).

Chapter V

Primary Sources:

Koshelëv, A. I., *Zapiski A. I. Koshelëva (1812–83 gody)* (Berlin, 1884).

Odoevski, V. F., *Sochineniia Kniaza V. F. Odoevskago* (St. Petersburg, 1844).

————, "4338-god. Peterburgskia pis'ma. Ot Ippolita Tsungieva, studenta Glavnoi Pekingskoi Shkoly, k Linginu, studentu toi-zhe shkoly," *Utrenaia Zaria* (Moscow, 1840), pp. 307–52.

Rozhalin, A. P., "Pis'ma N. M. Rozhalina k A. P. Elaginoi," *Russki Arkhiv,* No. 47 (1909), bk. 2, pp. 584ff.

————, *Stradania Molodogo Vertera. Perevod s Nemetskogo R.* (Moscow, 1828–29).

Shevyrëv, S. P., "Dorozhnye eskizy po puti iz Frankfurta v Berlin," *Otechestvennye Zapiski,* III (1839), 101ff.

————, *Istoria poezii* (St. Petersburg, 1887).

————, *Moskovski Vestnik,* VI (1827), No. 22. (This number contains Shevyrëv's translation and interpretation of Goethe's "Interact to *Faust*," i.e. the "Helena" act of *Faust,* Part II.)

————, *Teoria poezii v istoricheskom razvitii u drevnikh i novykh narodov* (Moscow, 1836).

————, "Vzgliady russkogo na sovremennoe obrazovanie Evropy," *Moskvitianin,* pt. 1 (1841), pp. 275ff.

Tiutchev, F. I., *Polnoe sobranie stikhotvorenii. Redaktsia i kommentarii Georga Chulkova* (Moscow and Leningrad, 1934).

————, *Sochineniia Tiutcheva,* 2nd ed. (St. Petersburg, 1900).

Venevitinov, D. V., *Polnoe sobranie sochinenii* (Moscow, 1934).

Volkonskaia, A. Z. "Ostryvki iz putevykh zapisok," *Severnye Tsvety na 1830 god,* pp. 216ff.

Secondary Sources:

Aleksandrovskaia, N. V., "Dva Golosa," *Posev Almanak* (Odessa, 1921), pp. 95–99.

Alekseev, M. P., "Nochmals über Tiutschev und Goethe." *Germano-slavica*, Jahrg. II, 1932–33.

Barzukov, N., *Zhizn' i trudy M. P. Pogodina* (St. Petersburg, 1889).

Brodski, N. L., *Evgeni Onegin, roman A. S. Pushkina* (Moscow, 1950).

Chulkov, E., "Stikhotvoreniia prislannye iz Germanii," *Zvenia*, II (1933), 255–67.

Haertel, E., "Russische Dichtung auf den Tod Goethes," *Goethe-Jahrbuch*, Bd. 31.

Ivanov, Viacheslav, "Zwei russische Gedichte auf den Tod Goethes," *Corona*, IV (1933–34), 697f.

Jagodich, R., "Goethe und seine russischen Zeitgenossen," *Germano-slavica*, I (1932), Heft 3, 347–81; II (1933), Heft 2, 1–14.

Lednicki, Waclaw, "Goethe and the Russian and Polish Romantics," *Comparative Literature*, IV (1951), 23–43.

Magnus, R., *Goethe as a Scientist* (New York, 1949).

Pigarëv, K. V., "Tiutchev, perevodchik Gete," *Urania* (1928), pp. 85–113.

Riasanovski, N. V., "Pogodin and Shevyrëv in Russian Intellectual History," *Harvard Slavic Studies*, IV, 149–67.

————, *Russia and the West in the Teaching of the Slavophiles* (Cambridge, Mass., 1952).

Sakulin, P. N., *Iz istorii Russkago Idealisma, Kniaz V. F. Odoevski, myslitel'—pisatel'* (Moscow, 1913).

Solovëv, Vladimir, "Poezia F. I. Tiutcheva," *Sobr. Soch.* VI (St. Petersburg, n.d.), pp. 463–80.

Wachsmuth, Andreas, "Goethes naturwissenschaftliches Denken im Spiegel seiner Dichtung seit 1790," *Sinn und Form*, XII, 20-42.

Wohl, Hans, "Weisheitsfreunde bei Goethe und im Goethehaus," *Goethe. Vierteljahrschrift der Goethe Gesellschaft*, N. F., Bd. 3 (1937), pp. 183–200.

Yarmerstedt, V. K., "Mirosozertsanie Kruzhka Stankevicha i poeziia Koltsova," *Voprosy Filosofii i Psikhologii* (Moscow, 1894), pp. 162–81.

Chapter VI

Primary Sources:

Bakunin, M., *Sobranie sochinenii i pisem'* (Moscow and Leningrad, 1934).

Belinski, V., *Pis'ma Belinskogo* (Moscow, 1914).

————, *Polnoe sobranie sochinenii*, ed. Vengerov (St. Petersburg, 1917).

————, *Sobranie sochinenii v trëkh tomakh*, ed. F. M. Goloven-chenko (Moscow, 1948).

Darwin, Erasmus, *Phytologia* (London, 1800).

Gertsen, A. I., *Polnoe sobranie sochinenii i pisem*, ed. M. K. Lemke (St. Petersburg/Leningrad, 1915–25).

Herzen, A. I. *Byloe i dumy* (Moscow and Leningrad, 1931).

Lessing, G. E., *Lessings Werke*, ed. J. Petersen (Berlin and Leipzig, n.d.).

Menzel, Wolfgang, *Nemetskaia slovestnost' iz knigi Volfganga Ment-selia*, pt. I-II (Moscow, 1837).

Stankevich, N. V. *Perepiska ego i biographia*, ed. P. V. Anenkov (Moscow, 1875).

————, *Perepiska*, ed. A. Stankevich (Moscow, 1914).

————, *Stikhotvoreniia, tragedia, prosa* (Moscow, 1890).

Tolstoi, L. N., *Tolstovski Muzei* (St. Petersburg, 1911).

Secondary Sources:

Bogucharski, L., *Aleksander Ivanovich Gertsen* (St. Petersburg, 1912).

Bowman, E. H., *Vissarion Belinski. A Study of the Origins of Social Criticism in Russia* (Cambridge, Mass., 1954).

Chizhevski, D. I., *Gegel v Rossii* (Paris, 1939).

Elsberg, I., *Gertsen, Zhizn' i tvorchestvo* (Moscow, 1956).

Gai, H., *Roman i povest' A. I. Gertsena 30–40kh godov* (Kiev, 1959).

Kornilov, A., *Molodye gody Bakunina* (Moscow, 1916).

Krestova, L., "Portret Gete pod perom Gertsena," *Zvenia*, II (1933), 75–96.

Malia, M., *Alexander Herzen and the Birth of Russian Socialism* (Cambridge, Mass., 1961).

Piper, L., Mirovozrenie Gertsena (Moscow and Leningrad, 1935).

Polianski, S., *V. Belinski* (Moscow, 1945).

Pypin, A. N., *Belinski* (St. Petersburg, 1908).

Rötscher, H. Th., *Abhandlungen zur Philosophie der Kunst* (Berlin, 1837–42).

Sechkarëv, V., *Schellings Einfluß in der russischen Literatur der 20-er und 30-er Jahre des XIX Jahrhunderts* (Leipzig, 1939).

Struve, P., "S. P. Shevyrëv i zapadnye vnusheniia i istochniki teorii —aforizma o 'gnilom' ili 'gniiushchem' zapade." *Zapiski Russkogo* (Belgrad, 1940).

Tschizewskij, D., ed., *Hegel bei den Slawen* (Darmstadt, 1961).

INDEX

A. Index of Names

(Bold face numbers indicate a running account of the person's view of Goethe.)

Nonnos of Panopolis, 26
Novikov, N. I., 10

Odoevski, Aleksander I., 98, 114
Odoevski, Vladimir F., ix, 115, 116,
    119-124, 167, 169, 243, 266,
    269, 270
Ogarëv, Nicholas P., 222, 242, 286
Oken, Lorenz, 115, 123
Onegin, A. F., 254
Ossian, 49
Ovid, 141

Panaev, K., 186, 190
Passage, Charles, 3, 258
Passek, T. P., 243, 287
Pasternak, Boris, 156
Petersen, J., 282
Petrarch, Francesco, 141
Phidias, 21
Pigarëv, K. V., 274
Piksanov, N. K., 267
Pindar, 141
Pisarëv, D. I., 238
Plato, 120
Pogodin, M. P., 63, 115, 132, 135,
    138, 150, 263, 271, 272
Pohl, Wilma, 260
Polevoi, N. A., 107, 119, 284
Propper, Maximilian von, 260
Proudhon, Pierre Joseph, 228
Pushkin, Aleksander S., ix, 3, 44,
    45, 46, 60-74, 78, 90, 92,
    93ff., 97, 110, 117f., 134, 138,
    150, 155, 160, 188, 189, 191,
    194, 205f., 209, 224, 259,
    261, 262, 263, 268, 281, 282
Pushkin, Pleiade, 93-97
Pushkin, Sergei, 62
Pypin, A. N., 253

Racine, Jean Baptiste, 62, 138, 168
Radishchev, A. N., 11, 16, 31, 253
Radziwill, Anton Heinrich, 33, 43
Raevski, N., 65
Raich, S. E., 76, 116, 155, 156
Raphael, 108
Rehm, Walter, 262
Retzsch, Friedrich, 46
Reutern, Gerhardt von, 36, 257
Riasanovski, N. V., 268, 271

Richardson, Samuel, 11, 31
Riemer, Friedrich Wilhelm, 131, 151
Römer, Christine Ossipova, 75
Rosenkranz, E., 264
Rötscher, Heinrich Theodor, 242, 287
Rosseau, Jean Jacques, 11, 14, 31,
    56, 78, 83, 112, 141, 237
Rozhalin, N. M., 115, 144, 146-150,
    152, 153, 253, 272
Rozov, V. A., 259, 266
Ryleev, K. F., 98

Saint-Helaire, Geoffroy, Etienne, 247
Saint-Simon, Claude Henri de, 228,
    242
Sakulin, P. N., 121, 268, 270
Sand, George, 199, 241, 242
Sappho, 29
Sartre, Jean-Paul, 70
Schelling, Friedrich, 115, 118, 120,
    123, 124f., 142, 149, 156,
    168, 169, 170, 179, 183, 184,
    220, 228, 246, 269, 275,
    276, 284
Schiller, Friedrich, 3, 15f., 18ff., 21,
    25, 32f., 38, 42ff., 61f., 65f.,
    74, 76ff., 92, 94, 98, 102,
    105, 107f., 113, 135f., 139f.,
    148, 150, 156f., 168, 171ff.,
    178, 180f., 184ff., 189, 192,
    196, 198f., 201, 202f., 205f.,
    208f., 211, 215f., 221f., 228,
    233, 240, 246, 263, 275,
    276, 279, 281, 283, 288
Schlegel, August Wilhelm, 44, 48,
    62, 216
Schlegel, Friedrich, 216
Schlözer, A. L. von, 21
Schmid, Georg, 255
Schönemann, Lili, 201
Schopenhauer, Arthur, 70
Schweizer, Christian Wilhelm, 36
Scott, Sir Walter, 65, 73, 134, 152,
    189, 191, 205, 228
Sechkarëv, V., 262
Semevski, M. I., 266
Sergievski, I., 276
Shakespeare, William, 9, 22, 38, 46,
    48, 64, 65, 72f., 75, 94, 99, 106,
    113, 120, 135, 137, 138, 141,
    168, 181, 188, 189, 190, 191,
    205, 221, 224, 263, 278, 279

B. Index of Goethe's Works